Work and Wellbeing in the Nordic Countries

The Nordic countries have the world's best working life. Unlike in many other countries, global competition has not created inequality, uncertainty, long working hours, standardization and restrictive managerial control. The main reason for this lies in the way interests are expressed and conflicts are resolved. Both employees and employers are well organized and both recognize the interests of the other. Working life develops in a constant interaction between conflict and compromise.

This book examines working conditions in Norway, Denmark, Sweden and Finland. It explores how these good working conditions are created and maintained. The chapters explain:

- How work organization is formed
- How education, training and work place learning give access to the labour market
- How work is managed in the public sector
- How precarious work unfolds in the Nordic countries.

Work and Wellbeing in the Nordic Countries is addressed to all those who have an interest in the quality of working life. It will be of particular use to all students, academics and policy makers working in the fields of social policy, wellbeing, management studies, employment relations, work sociology and work psychology.

Helge Hvid is a professor at Roskilde University of Working Life Studies, Denmark. He has a PhD in Sociology from Copenhagen University. He has published extensively in working life issues such as psychosocial working environment, work organization, IT and work, rhythms of work and sustainable work.

Eivind Falkum is research professor at the University OsloMet. He holds a Dr. Philos grade within Political Science at the University of Oslo, with his thesis on power and opposition in the Norwegian working life. He has broad experience from organization and management studies in several empirical fields at different institutes of assignment research.

Work and Wellbeing in the Nordic Countries

Critical Perspectives on the World's Best Working Lives

Edited by Helge Hvid and
Eivind Falkum

Routledge
Taylor & Francis Group
LONDON AND NEW YORK

First published 2019
by Routledge
2 Park Square, Milton Park, Abingdon, Oxon OX14 4RN

and by Routledge
52 Vanderbilt Avenue, New York, NY 10017

First issued in paperback 2020

Routledge is an imprint of the Taylor & Francis Group, an informa business

British Library Cataloguing-in-Publication Data
A catalogue record for this book is available from the British Library

Library of Congress Cataloging-in-Publication Data
A catalog record has been requested for this book

ISBN 13: 978-0-367-66384-1 (pbk)
ISBN 13: 978-0-8153-8723-7 (hbk)

Typeset in Bembo
by Swales & Willis Ltd, Exeter, Devon, UK

Contents

Work and Wellbeing in the Nordic Countries

Critical Perspectives on the World's Best Working Lives

1st Edition

Edited by Helge Hvid and Eivind Falkum

AUTHORS:

Robert Salomon is Senior Researcher at Work Research Institute, OsloMet, Norway.

Arild Henrik Steen is Researcher at Work Research Institute, OsloMet, Norway.

Anders Underthun is Researcher at Work Research Institute, OsloMet, Norway.

Bitten Nordrik is Researcher at Work Research Institute, OsloMet, Norway.

Heidi Enehaug is Senior Researcher at Work Research Institute, OsloMet, Norway.

Christin Thea Wathne is Research Director at Work Research Institute, OsloMet, Norway.

Ida Drange is Research Professor at Work Research Institute, OsloMet, Norway.

Mari Holm Ingelsrud is Senior Researcher at Work Research Institute, OsloMet, Norway.

Per Bonde Hansen is Senior Researcher at Work Research Institute, OsloMet, Norway.

Pål Klethagen is Researcher at Work Research Institute, OsloMet, Norway.

Eivind Falkum is Research Professor at Work Research Institute, OsloMet, Norway.

Angelika Schafft is Senior Researcher at Work Research Institute, OsloMet, Norway.

Øystein Spjelkavik is Senior Researcher at Work Research Institute, OsloMet, Norway.

Kjetil Frøyland is Senior Researcher at Work Research Institute, OsloMet, Norway.

Jan Erik Karlsen is Professor Emeritus at The University of Stavanger, Norway.

Helge Søndergaard Hvid is Professor Emeritus at Roskilde University, Denmark.

Annette Kamp is Associate Professor at Roskilde University, Denmark.

Klaus Tranetoft Nielsen is Senior Associate Professor at Roskilde University, Denmark.

Janne Gleerup is Associate Professor at Roskilde University, Denmark.

Peter Hagedorn-Rasmussen is Associate Professor at Roskilde University, Denmark.

Søren Salling Weber is a PhD Fellow at Roskilde University, Denmark.

Niels Warring is Associate Professor Henrik at Roskilde University, Denmark.

Lambrecht Lund is Associate Professor at Roskilde University, Denmark.

Christian Helms Jørgensen is Professor (MSO) at Roskilde University, Denmark.

Agnete Meldgaard Hansen is Associate Professor at Roskilde University, Denmark.

Anders Jakobsen is a PhD Fellow at Roskilde University, Denmark.

Introduction

Helge Hvid and Eivind Falkum

> *Whether you look at unemployment, employment, income, equality, social security, or the quality of the working environment, the Nordic countries – especially Norway and Denmark – are at the top of the international rankings. This means that many other countries are examining the Nordic model and considering whether it is the best way to achieve their goals with labour market policy.*
>
> (Mark Pearson, Deputy Director of Employment, Labour and Social Affairs at OECD. FTF-aktuelt, 22–01-2017)

This statement rests on an analysis of data from the OECD Job Quality Framework,[1] which enables comparative studies of job quality across countries. Of all the countries surveyed, Denmark and Norway performed best across the parameters studied: employment, work-related health, wages, job security, and inclusion in the labour market. The relatively favourable working conditions in Norway and Denmark have not prevented those countries from maintaining their position among the richest in the world.

Those who primarily benefit from the good working conditions in the Nordics are the employees. For people between the ages of 20 and 65, work is a major part of the time they are awake, and work is an important factor in creating income, security and meaning in life. Therefore, we can expect high-quality working conditions to contribute to happiness. Actually, according to the 2016 *World Happiness Report*, Denmark was number one in the happiness index. In 2017, Norway topped the index, followed by Denmark. In 2018, Finland was number one in the happiness index, followed by Norway and Denmark. In the *Global Happiness Policy Report 2018*, the impact of working conditions on happiness was examined (Helliwell, 2018), showing a strong relation between working conditions and happiness.

In this book, we will examine how these relatively good working conditions are created and maintained. We will examine:

- How work organization is formed (Part II)
- How education and training give access to the labour market and keep employees in employment (Part III)

- How work is managed in the public sector (Part IV)
- How precarious work unfolds in the Nordics (Part V).

The Nordic approach

The Nordics are known for the creation of societies that combine two widely different visions: the socialist vision of equality in influence, income and development, and the liberal vision of a dynamic society based on individual freedom and free competition.

The liberal tradition in the Nordic countries leads to open economies with extensive trade with the outside world. International comparisons assess the business climate in the Nordic countries positively.[2] Flexibility in the labour market is high. Denmark is one of the OECD countries where it is easiest for employers to dismiss employees. The public sector in the Nordic countries is large, but the Nordic countries (especially Sweden) are leading in the privatization of public services.

The socialist tradition is reflected in the fact that economic equality, especially equality in wage income, is relatively high in the Nordic countries. Employment is high. The relatively large welfare states offer collective solutions in areas such as education, childcare, elderly care and pensions. Social mobility is high. Democracies have been developed with considerable popular participation, based on collective organization. There are a large number of associations pursuing certain interests. This is highly relevant in working life, where employees and management are generally organized in trade unions and employers' associations, respectively.

Interest for the 'Nordic model' has been quite considerable over the years, but the focus of this interest has varied.

The Economist published a special report on the Nordic countries (*The Economist*, 2013). Here the main interest was the liberal perspectives of the Nordic tradition: high-quality welfare states, governed by internal competition, and business and labour policies that meet corporate needs.

Others, generally with reference to Esping-Andersen (1990), have been interested in the social policy profile that characterizes the Nordic welfare states. Here, the universal character of welfare states is noted: the welfare state provides individuals with universal rights.

Finally, we have those who study the Nordic labour markets with their high levels of collective organization among both employees and employers (Andersen et al., 2014).

However, whether one studies business conditions, the welfare state or the labour market in Iceland, Norway, Denmark, Sweden and Finland, a closer look reveals major differences in institution building and legislation in the five countries. In Norway and to some extent in Sweden, the labour market is regulated by a combination of labour laws and labour agreements. In Denmark and to a degree in Finland, the labour market is almost exclusively regulated through agreements between employers' associations and unions. In Norway and Sweden, employees have relatively high individual employment security. In Denmark, employment security is very low. In Sweden, workers are organized in relation to the industry where they belong. In Denmark, boundaries between unions follow trade boundaries. The systems for unemployment benefit and the pension systems are quite different in the Nordic countries. . . and we could continue.

When we consider institutional structures, it is difficult to identify a 'Nordic model' which systematically differs from other countries. There are major differences between the institutions in the Nordic countries, and there are not many institutions in the Nordics that do not exist in any other non-Nordic country.

It is therefore more fruitful to refer to the Nordic approach than the Nordic model. In this book, we explore the Nordic approach to working life. We investigate how the Nordic approach influences working life and how experiences in working life help to maintain the Nordic approach.

In our view, the essence of the Nordic approach is an extensive organization of opposing interests. This is particularly true in the labour market, but it also applies to society in general. There is a profound acceptance that there are opposing interests in the labour market around which it is legitimate to organize. Employers see the unions as legitimate opponents, and the unions perceive employers and their organizations as a legitimate adversary. Both sides accept that their interests are different. They accept the need for both parties to give and take to reach a compromise between the opposing interests. Thus, the labour market is not regulated by 'social partners', as it is often expressed in the EU context, but by 'social parties' or by 'labour market parties'.

This approach has created communities that are highly market-oriented and, at the same time, have relatively high levels of solidarity and equality. It is largely the relationships in working life that have created these social characteristics.

Why Norway and Denmark?

Within the Nordic countries, Norway and Denmark are at opposite poles on certain parameters. Market principles are more influential in Denmark than in Norway. The labour market is largely regulated by both laws and agreements in Norway, while it is almost exclusively regulated through agreements in Denmark. Despite these differences, there is a striking similarity in the degree of equality and security in the labour market and in employee assessments of job quality. The explanation lies in the Nordic approach: the collective organization and the negotiated compromise.

Our intention is not to make a comparative study between the Nordic countries, nor between Norway and Denmark. We wish to present how the Nordic approach works by showing how defined aspects of working life unfold in Norway and Denmark. In most cases we present experiences from both Norway and Denmark. In some cases the emphasis is on Norwegian approaches because they are the most interesting. In other cases, we present Danish approaches.

Of course, we could have included experiences from the three other Nordic countries (and we do, but only to a limited extent). However, it is difficult to understand specific experiences without a certain understanding of the context. If we had included all the Nordic countries, the presentation of contexts would have been very comprehensive.

Critique as fuel for the Nordic approach

However, the authors of this book do not focus solely on the relatively good working conditions in Norway and Denmark. As researchers, they are all engaged in critical examinations of working life in the Nordic countries. This research does not produce an overall rosy picture of working conditions in Norway and Denmark, but rather presents a number of problematic issues:

- Work organization marked by standardization and individualized control
- Heavy workload
- Employees' limited influence in their workplace
- Gender segregation
- Working environment that creates sickness absenteeism, increasingly related to mental health problems
- Wage differentials
- Difficulties in entering the labour market
- Marginalization in the labour market
- New public management, instrumentalizing human relations
- Insecure employment relationships and conditions; precarious work is also an issue in the Nordics.

So, what is the right approach for understanding working conditions in the Nordic countries? Should we praise these working conditions, or should we criticize them? We suggest that we do both. Research on working life in the Nordic countries has historically nurtured widespread criticism of working conditions, which, historically, has proved to make a difference. The criticisms are widely picked up on by trade unions, professional associations, management researchers, employers' organizations and public authorities. Such criticism, and the conflicts it causes, is probably the main reason why working conditions are better in Norway and Denmark than in most other countries. Criticism matters.

Working life in the Nordics is generally following global trends: global competition creates heavy workloads. Digitalization has a strong influence on working life. International concepts for organizing work are also influencing working life in the Nordics. The principles of new public management govern the public sector. New groups in the labour market are experiencing precarious work. Work-related stress is also an issue in the Nordics. Criticism from our colleagues outside the Nordic region also tends to be relevant for those of us studying working conditions in the Nordics. However, comparisons often make it clear that technology and globalized competition do not determine working conditions. Those involved can influence the quality of working life, with the right approach and with the right institutional setting.

We cannot take for granted the position of Norway and Denmark as the countries with the best working conditions. Working conditions and the institutions that support these are constantly exposed to erosion, attacks and undermining influences. In order to maintain the relatively good conditions, work, work organization and institutions must constantly change.

Working conditions in Norway and Denmark are rooted in the history of the two countries and cannot simply be copied by other countries. However, we hope that insight into these two countries can provide inspiration for the organization of policies and the creation of institutions that promote high-quality working life.

Content of the book

In Part I we provide an overview. What are the characteristics of working life in the Nordic region? What is typical of relations between employers and employees? How are these relationships maintained and developed in the tension between institutions in the labour market, developments in technologies and markets, and changes in people's attitudes? In this Part, we present what we consider the core of the Nordic legacy, and it is argued that this core has made it possible to create a working life which, in most parameters, is better than in comparable countries. Similarly, the history of Nordic working life is briefly presented.

In Part II, organization and management are in focus. Democratization has been a very important theme in the development of working life in the Nordic countries, which has had a profound influence on working life, even though democratization is no longer on the agenda. We present efforts to democratize work as well as the state of democracy at work today. We explore how international production concepts are integrated into Nordic working life. The working environment, in terms of legislation and practice, is presented. Finally, we examine how working life is influenced by requirements for flexibility in time and space.

Part III is about education and learning as an inclusion mechanism in the labour market. The Nordic countries have a relatively high employment rate, although minimum wages are comparatively high. This is possible because the level of competencies is relatively high and because it is possible to learn and develop competencies when demands in the labour market change. In this section, education is presented as an entrance into the labour market for young people, and we discuss how this is influenced by the social parties. Further education is investigated as promoting or constraining mobility. Finally, there is a discussion on how to bring into the labour market people who, for different reasons, are marginalized with regard to employment.

In Part IV, new public management in the Nordics is explored. In the last 25 years, public employment in the Nordic region has been heavily influenced by the principles of new public management. However, these principles have had a distinctive design, character and consequence in the Nordic countries, in line with the Nordic approach.

Part V examines precarious work in the Nordic context. This phenomenon is first examined in general terms. Then it is shown how highly educated people are working under precarious conditions. We investigate how the introduction of temporary workers in the Nordics influences working conditions more generally. Finally, there is an examination of how platform economics is handled in a Nordic context.

Notes

1 Data are presented at www.oecd.org/statistics/job-quality.htm.
2 Denmark, Norway and Sweden are all in the top ten in the ranking made by the World Bank on 'Doing Business'. See www.doingbusiness.org/rankings.

References

Andersen, S. K., Dølvik, J. E. & Ibsen, C. L. (2014) *Nordic Labour Market Models in Open Markets*, Brussels: ETUI.

Esping-Andersen, G. (1990) *Three Worlds of Welfare Capitalism*, New York: John Wiley & Sons.

FTF-aktuelt (2017) *OECD: Nordiske arbejdsmarkeder sikrer de bedste jobs*, Copenhagen: FTF-aktuelt 22-01-2017.

Helliwell, J. F. (2018) Global Happiness Policy Synthesis 2018, In: *Global Happiness Policy Report 2018*, UN: World Happiness Council.

The Economist (2013) Special Report. The Nordic Countries. February 2013.

Part I

An overview

Introduction

Helge Hvid and Eivind Falkum

In this Part we will briefly present where we are (Chapter 1), and then we will explain how we came to be where we are (Chapter 2).

Chapter 1: Nordic working life, shaped through conflicts and compromises. By Helge Hvid, Eivind Falkum and Arild Henrik Steen.

In this chapter, there are references to some of the many comparative analyses that state that the Nordic countries, including Norway and Denmark, are rather special in terms of working conditions. You will also find explanations for this: the strong organization of collective interests, the general recognition and acceptance of opposing interests, and the building of an institutional network where interests can meet and compromises made, in individual work groups, and at company, sector, regional and national level. Further, we discuss other explanations: the culture, with its high degree of trust (but perhaps it was the interest-based institutions that created and still maintain the high degree of trust?), the welfare state (but are the Nordic welfare states so unique?) and the economy (which is quite successful, but without specific advantages).

Chapter 2: The peculiar history of Nordic working life. By Eivind Falkum, Helge Hvid and Per Bonde Hansen.

The main argument here is that conflict has been the driving force in the history of Nordic working life. The Nordic labour market systems were created through serious conflicts in the labour market. The social-democratic society was formed out of the conflicts, in which employees' interest in wages, employment and democracy at work were reconciled with employers' interests in free market conditions and earnings. During the 1980s, however, the social-democratic project weakened, and neo-liberal understandings began to penetrate society. It turned out that the Nordic approach was by no means a bulwark against neo-liberalism. On the contrary, a Nordic-influenced neo-liberalism developed, which, on the one hand, has provided far more space for the market, but on the other, has managed to maintain a certain degree of equality, safety and quality in working life.

Both chapters present the Nordic experiences as unique. However, it is also underlined that the Nordics are not alternatives to the global trends in work, organization and labour market. They represent a variant of the global trends. Employers and employees in the Nordic countries are facing the same challenges as in other developed countries. However, the approach to dealing with these challenges is somewhat different.

Chapter 1

Nordic working life, shaped through conflicts and compromises

Helge Hvid, Eivind Falkum and Arild Henrik Steen

The core of the Nordic model

In 1961, the Norwegian sociologist Sverre Lysgaard wrote the book *The Worker Collectivity. A Study of the Sociology of the Subordinates* (Lysgaard, 2001 [1961]), which made a significant contribution to the basic understandings that underlie the Nordic welfare societies. The book is a standard textbook in Norway and is also read widely in Denmark and Sweden, where most people can read Norwegian. It has never been translated, like much good Nordic working life research. The book presents an understanding of industrial workplace relations, which generally form the basis for the Nordic model.

Based on studies at a Norwegian paper mill, Lysgaard develops a theory of the relationship between workers and employers, not based on class theory but on system theory. Employers and management work in a technical/economic system, where efficiency and profit are paramount. This leads to unilateral, insatiable, relentless demands on the employees. Employers who do not follow the imperative of the system will be unable to continue for long as employers. The workers, on the other hand, form a human system. This system is not unilateral but highly diverse throughout life. The human system is limited (there are limits to how far it can fulfil the demands of employers) and is thus in conflict with the insatiability of the technical/economic system. Finally, the human system seeks security, which contrasts with the relentlessness of the technical/economic system.

At the factory Lysgaard studied, the workers could only ensure the maintenance of the human system by standing together. They formed a third system, the 'workers' collective', which was a buffer between the technical/economic system and the human system. The workers' collective created a certain balance between the two systems. The workers' collective accepted the imperatives of the technical/economic system, but defended wages, limited work performance and defended security.

The fascinating thing about the relationship between the technical/economic system and the human system is that the relationship is at the same time characterized by conflict and mutual dependency. The company wants as much from the workers as possible. However, the company and society as a whole are dependent on the workers' defence of their working conditions through the workers' collective. Without workers defending their working conditions, there would soon be no available workers for the companies. The workers rely on their shared strength to create decent working conditions. At the same time, however, they depend on the jobs the company creates, and therefore they are also dependent on the rational profit-seeking management of the company. We thus have a contradiction between two subsystems that depend on each other. This contradiction finds a solution through the workers' collective.

This basic understanding is the core of the Nordic model. The two sides of the labour market recognize each other's existence and eligibility. One party does not seek to wipe out the other party. However, at the same time, both parties are also aware that they are in conflict with the other party. Their eligibility is therefore dependent on their ability to produce results at the negotiating table or occasionally in open conflict.

A group of researchers (Karlsson et al., 2015; Axelsson et al., 2016) returned to Lysgaard's paper mill in 2010 and replicated Lysgaard's analysis. The factory had completely changed. In the 1950s, the work was physically hard, dirty and dangerous. In 2010, the paper mill was an automated process industry, and the workers monitored the processes, maintained the technical system and managed the workflow. These fundamental changes in the work, however, had not weakened the workers' collective. The workers still protected their wages, limited their performance and defended employment security through their collective. The biggest difference that had occurred in the 50 years was related to the technical/economic system. It was now quite clear that the technical/economic system was not one system but two systems. An economic system, represented by daily management, was still unilateral, insatiable and relentless. The technical system, however, was represented by technicians and workers who were oriented towards technical possibilities and limitations and quality. The workers' collective was now largely influenced by the technical system. It not only defended wages, workload and working hours but also the technical system. It thus defended quality standards and opposed overload of the technical system.

The development we saw at the paper mill can be largely transferred to the labour market as a whole. The physically hard and dirty factory work has declined, and a major part of the work has become knowledge-oriented. There are those who argue that earlier conflicts have been abolished (Nordström & Ridderstråle, 1999). Knowledge has become the main means of production. Knowledge is not owned by the employer but by the knowledge worker him/herself, and workers themselves can therefore decide how and how much they want to work.

However, it seems that present knowledge work is also in conflict with the economic system. Knowledge workers are not exempted from high demands, long working hours, stress and uncertain employment conditions

(Sørensen & Holman 2014). On the contrary, according to the Norwegian Work Life Barometer,[1] knowledge workers report long working hours, high workload and many and conflicting requirements (see Chapter 15). Knowledge workers are deeply involved in the maintenance and development of the technical system. At the same time, the daily lives of knowledge workers are highly influenced by the strength of their opposition to an economic system. Many knowledge workers have acknowledged that and build something that corresponds to Lysgaard's workers' collective, combining trade unions, professional communities and communities of practice.

Knowledge workers are highly organized in trade unions, elect union representatives at work and seek to protect themselves from the unsustainable demands of the economic system. However, knowledge workers not only defend their interests as employees, they also defend formal and informal professional quality standards. Similarly, the workers in the paper mill not only defended their interests as employees but also defended maintenance of the technical system and the quality of the product. The workers' collective defended both the human system and the technical system.

The content of the work, and the quality and social benefits of its products, have thus also become a key aspect of the relationship between employers and workers. This is not new, but it has become more pronounced. We see professional groups protesting and acting against a deterioration in the quality of their work. We see industry workers expressing their reluctance towards the quality of products delivered to customers. In other cases, conflicts regarding quality are less prominent, as when employers and workers work together to create employee-driven innovation (Høyrup & Møller, 2012). However, it is worth emphasizing that relations between employers and workers in terms of quality and social benefits of products are not separate from the more traditional conflict of interests of the labour market. Indeed, they are linked to it. Several studies conclude that worker involvement in work organization and work quality is best in companies where trade union representatives are most involved in the management (Falkum et al., 2017).

Hence, the fundamental narrative that formed the basis for the Nordic model is still present. The fundamental narrative lives in the vast majority of workplaces. The basic narrative is maintained by some of the strongest institutions in society: unions, employers' associations and the state.

In the Nordic countries, a kind of democracy and welfare state has been developed, which, more than in most other countries, relies on wage labour and the defence of conflicting interests. This is also reflected in the difference between EU and Nordic terminology. In the EU, people talk about 'social partners': there are different partners in a joint project, creating jobs and wealth. In the Nordic countries, people talk about the social parties, i.e. different parties representing different interests in the labour market. EU rhetoric relates to consensus, while Nordic rhetoric relates to compromise between differences (Kettunen, 2012).

Researchers at Fafo, a research centre affiliated to LO, the confederation of Norwegian unions, argue that the Nordic model is a political construction consisting of a balance of power and 'a constructive conflict partnership' (Dølvik et al., 2015). This concept also underlines the existence and acceptance of different, conflicting interests.

Organization of the labour market

The most significant aspect of the labour market in the Nordic countries is that conflict between employers and workers is recognized and institutionalized in a way that makes conflicts solvable and productive, both for the lives of workers and the economy. The foundation for this is, of course, labour market organizations that can act with great legitimacy and powerful resources. One of the things that provides legitimacy and power is members. The Nordic labour market organizations, both trade unions and employers' associations, have relatively large numbers of members.

Union density is around 70% in the Nordic countries, except for Norway, where it is about 50%. In all large European countries union density is significantly lower: less than 30% in the UK, less than 20% in Germany and less than 10% in France (ETUI, 2017). Union density peaked in the mid-1990s, both in the Nordic countries and in Western Europe, and has declined since then, but quite slowly in the Nordic countries.[2]

With regard to employers, the level of organization is also high but has been slightly declining over the last ten years in Denmark, where about 52% of private sector employees work in companies that are members of an employers' association (Navrbjerg & Ibsen, 2017). In the public sector, employers are organized 100%. In Norway the level of organization among employers is stable at about 68% (Nergaard, 2016).[3]

Another expression of the legitimacy and power of the labour market organizations is found in the proportion of employees covered by collective agreements that determine wages and working conditions. In Denmark, about 75% of the private sector employees are covered by collective agreements, and in the public sector 100% are covered (Navrbjerg & Ibsen, 2017). Similar figures for Norway are 57% in the private sector and 100% in the public sector (Nergaard, 2016).

Union density is gradually decreasing, while the organization rate among employers is more stable. However, this does not necessarily mean that the power of labour market organizations is diminishing. The power of organizations depends largely on the institutional framework for the exercise of power and the opportunities and resources of the parties to take advantage of the institutions.

It is characteristic of the Nordic countries that the relationship between the social parties takes place in many partially connected arenas. Many actors are involved, and many resources can be mobilized. It is thus typical of the Nordic countries that conflicts and cooperation between the social parties take place at all levels of society (Madsen et al., 2001; Kjellberg, 2009):

- At workplaces, where unions are represented through shop stewards. Out of the barely 1.5 million members of the collective labour unions in Denmark (Statistics Denmark, 2018), there are approximately 50,000 representatives of the employees (Sørensen, 2010), who are representatives of trade unions at workplace level. Some 85% of employees in Denmark have access to an employee representative (ETUI, 2017, p. 58).
- At the municipal and regional level, where the parties, together with the authorities, are involved in the development of education and employment policies.
- At industry level, agreements of working conditions are negotiated in the professions and trades.
- At the state level, where the social parties are involved in the development of social and business policies.
- And last but not least, at the national level where the social parties make collective agreements on wages and working conditions covering the whole labour market and negotiate the conditions for macroeconomics with the state.

At all these levels, the parties negotiate and/or are engaged in consultations. Sometimes an agreement cannot be reached and conflicts break out. However, most often the negotiations result in a compromise. The implementation of the compromises largely takes place because the parties have multilevel representation. For local union representatives, it is an obligation to secure local implementation of agreements and laws, decided far from where the representative works.

In principle, the state is not an actor in the national wage bargaining process. It is the responsibility of the social parties to reach agreements. Sometimes the government intervenes in order to make it easier for the parties to find solutions.

In most issues, conflicts at the national level are negotiated and regulated in a triangle of employers' associations, trade unions and the state. The involvement of the government and state administration in regulation of the conflicts between the social parties varies considerably with the issue. With regard to organization of work and participation, the state has a very limited role to play. In terms of wages and (to some extent) working hours, it is the social parties who act, locally and centrally. However, the state may take a mediating role if the parties cannot reach agreement. In Norway, working conditions are more regulated by legislation than in Denmark, where working conditions are largely regulated through agreements. Common to the two countries, however, is the social parties' strong involvement in the creation of new laws related to the labour market. Often there is high responsiveness to the social parties regarding general labour market policy, unemployment benefits and working environment. Stein Rokkan (1966) described this particular form of democracy in the Nordic countries, based on both parliamentarianism and what he called corporate pluralism.

Corporate pluralism is not only related to the labour market and labour market institutions. The Nordic countries also have a civil society that is highly organized, compared to other countries. In the Nordic countries, daily life is strongly influenced by associations and clubs related to one's local community, hobbies or special needs (e.g. associations for specific patient groups). It is reasonable to assume a relationship between the well-organized labour market and the well-organized civil society. Associations related to working life are a school for civil society associations and vice versa (Pateman, 1970).

In the following, we will draw an overall picture of how conflict and compromise in the various institutions of the labour market have shaped working conditions. We will look at two issues here:

- *Quality of daily work.* People active in the labour market spend a significant part of their waking hours at work. Therefore, the nature and quality of daily work is, of course, decisive for quality of life and health.
- *Salary and employment security.* Work is the most important source of income. Therefore, wage levels are important quality parameters for the quality of work. However, equally important is employment security. Employment security gives confidence about future income.

Both issues are mainly regulated through institutionalized negotiations, conflicts and agreements between workers and employers.

In the following sections, we will briefly describe the differences in the quality of daily work and the quality of pay and employment between Norway/Denmark and other developed countries.

The quality of daily work

The quality of working life is relatively good in Norway and Denmark. The weekly working hours prescribed by the law or agreements are on a par with most European countries. Actual weekly working hours are, however, lower than the European average. Annual working hours differ even more from the European average. Overall satisfaction with work is relatively high. Learning and development opportunities in work are relatively good, as is the working environment (Eurofound, 2012; ETUI, 2017).

We will now briefly describe how these relationships interact with the institutionalized class conflict in the two countries.

Working hours

Working hours are regulated partly through legislation and partly through agreements between the social parties. Here, too, legislation plays a more important role in Norway than in Denmark. Regular working hours, i.e. the number of hours worked per week, are defined in agreements between the parties. In Norway, the figure is 37.5 hours and in Denmark, 37 hours. Denmark and Norway are the two countries where a full-time employee works the fewest hours (EUROSTAT[4]). The length of holidays, which is set at six weeks in Denmark and five weeks in Norway, is also agreed between the parties. The same applies to maternity leave, study leave, etc. Large numbers of employees work either more or fewer hours than the norm, but agreements are in place regarding the terms of part-time work or overtime. Especially in Denmark, state involvement in these areas is very limited.[5]

The rules regulating working hours have been laid down in agreements between the social parties, and union representatives are an important factor in overseeing compliance with the agreements. The annual number of working hours is relatively low and has not risen in recent years (Bonke, 2016). However, that does not mean that issues related to working hours are uncomplicated and without conflict. On the contrary, there are often conflicts related to time flexibility, including the boundaries between work and leisure, and workplace and home. Digitalization makes it possible for many to do (part of) their work anywhere at any time. That could increase disputes on working time in the future. This is further elaborated in Chapter 7.

Work satisfaction

Eurofound (2017) finds that Norway and Denmark score quite high in job satisfaction compared with other European countries.[6] It is however questionable whether the job satisfaction indicator is an adequate measure of job quality. High job satisfaction may well be due to low expectations, not necessarily high job quality. However, it seems unlikely that expectations for job quality are lower in Norway and Denmark than in other countries. It is more reasonable to assume that the extensive regulation of workplace conflicts regarding work organization and content has made a difference.

As already mentioned, 85% of employees have access to workers' representatives, who may raise criticism of the employer. This may take place in a direct dialogue between the representative and the employer, or it may be in the works council, which, according to agreements, is obligatory for all workplaces with a certain number of employees. The main obligation of the works council is to find solutions to issues related to work organization and technology. The works council aims to search for solutions that satisfy both working conditions and productivity.

This local cooperation between employer and employees is supported by the parties at the central level. Shop stewards and working environment representatives are trained. The unions and employers' associations have created a cooperation board where one party at the workplace can file a complaint against a counterparty if it fails to comply with the provisions of the cooperation agreement. In addition, there are a number of sector-specific schemes to support the work of the cooperation boards. In Denmark, for example, the parties in the manufacturing industry have a consultancy scheme that helps companies to create good cooperation. In some areas, there have been collective agreements for a better psychosocial working environment, which also is related to good cooperation. The tripartite agreement in Norway on a more inclusive working life is another example. The parties at the national level have agreed to reduce sick leave and increase labour market participation among elderly and vulnerable groups. This agreement gives union representatives an argument for local improvements in working environment and working conditions in order to reach the targets in the inclusive working life agreement.

Further, the opportunities for individual employees to express their views seem to be better in Norway and Denmark than in the rest of Europe. Some 73% of Norwegian employees and 72% of Danish employees indicate that their organization holds regular meetings in which employees can express their views about what is happening in the organization (Eurofound, 2017). Only in Sweden is this opportunity for direct involvement at the same level. In the EU as a whole, 55% of employees have the option.

Autonomy and opportunities for learning and development

Here too, Norway and Denmark are in the European elite. To the question 'Does your work involve learning new things?', 89% of employees answered yes in both Norway and Denmark. For the EU as a whole, the figure was 72%. To the question 'Are you able to apply your own ideas in your work?', 10% of Norwegian and 8% of Danish employees replied 'rarely'. For the EU as a whole, 22% indicated that they could rarely apply their own ideas in their work (Eurofound, 2017).

There seems to be a greater degree of autonomy in work in Norway and Denmark than in the rest of Europe. Autonomy at work is considered to be a positive factor for health, productivity and employability (Karasek, 1989; Dhondt et al., 2017). The reason why Norway and Denmark score so highly on autonomy is probably that the sociotechnical tradition has been strong in Norway and Denmark (see Chapter 3), as it has also been in Sweden, Finland, Holland and Belgium.

In Norway and Denmark, the social parties have, since the late 1960s, been involved in establishing a framework for job development and autonomy. This is particularly true of Norway where comprehensive initiatives have been implemented (Gustavsen, 2007). Also, in Denmark, there have been many different initiatives to support the development of autonomy and learning (Hvid, 2001). In both countries (and in Sweden and Finland), autonomy and opportunities for learning and development have been promoted by a wide range of programmes launched by the social parties and by strong representation from employee representatives in companies. Studies have confirmed that in companies where employee representatives have a strong position, autonomy in daily work is comparably high (Falkum et al., 2017).

Working environment

Working environment conditions are better in Norway and Denmark than in most comparable countries (Aagestad et al., 2017) (see also Chapter 6). The main reason is not that working environment acts in the Nordic countries are more restrictive than in other countries. However, in one aspect, Norway is an exception. In Norway, demands for democratization of work have been included in the Working Environment Act (see Chapter 6). The Working Environment Act was not created in isolation from initiatives, demands and political pressure from the trade unions. However, it is hardly due to the nature of the working environment acts that the working environment is better in Norway and Denmark than in most other countries. Instead, it is because employees are organized at company level. Thus, the state authorities are not alone in overseeing compliance with the law. The regulation of conflicts between the parties at the workplace level, supported by sectoral institutions, has had a major impact on the quality of the working environment.

Wages and employment

The Nordic countries, as is well known, have quite large and generous welfare systems. However, the influence of the welfare state on the labour market is limited, especially in Denmark. Wages are determined unilaterally by the social parties. There is not, as in most highly developed economies, a statutory minimum wage. Similarly, working hours, length of holidays and employment security are also determined through negotiations between the social parties. The most important role of the state is to help the parties to reach a compromise through arbitration institutions and legislation on labour disputes, etc. In addition, the government in many cases helps to generalize agreements made by the parties.

With regard to education policy, employment policy and business policy, the state has a more independent role, but the social parties are deeply involved both in shaping policies and in their implementation.

Wage formation and equality

Equality in income is relatively high in Norway and Denmark. Norway and Denmark have a low Gini coefficient compared to other OECD countries.[7] One important reason is that the trade unions have succeeded in creating and maintaining a degree of solidarity in the coordinated, collective agreements on wages at the national level. This institutionalized wage formation has led to a relatively narrow pay gap. Another reason is that it has been possible to establish and finance a system of further education that has increased wages for many employees on low pay.

The gap between high and low wages is smaller in Norway and Denmark than in other countries. Unskilled workers have a higher salary than in many other countries, whereas highly skilled labour is cheaper than in other countries. Thus, it is more advantageous to start a form of production that mainly uses highly skilled labour than one dominated by labour-intensive, low-skilled labour. Further, relatively high wages for low-skilled labour have encouraged automation of work processes in order to reduce labour costs and have contributed to the relative success of Nordic industrial production in the global market. The Nordic experience seems to confirm the Calmfors–Driffill hypothesis that postulates a relationship between union density, coordinated wage formation and low unemployment caused by high productivity (Calmfors, 1993).

In most highly developed welfare societies, the development of the wage structure is characterized by polarization. An increasing proportion of the employees are in the highly paid segment, and an increasing proportion in the low-paid segment. The middle segment is shrinking. In the Scandinavian countries, the development of the wage structure is different. There is an increase in the high-wage segment and a decline in the low-paid segment. The proportion of employees in the segment in the middle is largely unchanged (Fernández-Macías, 2012).

The wage formation and bargaining systems in Denmark and Norway differ. Coordination is more explicit in Norway. However, both countries have some form of coordination and a practice where exporting industries are given a decisive influence in setting the maximum wage increases.

Employment security

When it comes to security, Denmark is an interesting and controversial case. Here employment protection as stipulated in laws and collective agreements is very weak, especially for blue-collar workers, in comparison with other European countries (Eurofound, 2009; Madsen, 2010). Denmark has therefore become known for its flexicurity model, with low employment protection, high social support for unemployment and an active labour market policy that contributes to high labour mobility through education, supported employment and support for unemployed people finding work.

In Norway, collective employment protection is weak. This makes it easier to reduce staffing or close affiliations than in most other developed countries. Individual employment protection, on the other hand, is quite strong and in line with other Western countries. Together with the compressed wage structure and the high level of competence, this provides a better capacity for adaptation than in many other countries.

The flexicurity model in Denmark and the low collective employment protection in Norway have to some extent been undermined by changes in labour market policy towards 'more stick and less carrot'. Despite the fact that law- and contract-based employment protection is far greater in Norway than in Denmark, employees indicate a high level of employment security in both countries (Eurofound, 2017).[8] A relatively large proportion of the population is certain that they can remain in employment. In both countries, employment security is considerably higher than in the rest of Europe. This paradox can be explained in several ways:

- The unemployment rate has been relatively low in Norway and Denmark for the past 20 years, which means that most people can soon find alternative employment quickly if they lose their job. Employment security is not only about protection against dismissals but is also very much about the chances of finding a new, decent job.
- In countries with strong statutory employment security, a relatively large group of employees cannot access the protection because they work more or less permanently in vulnerable temporary or short-term jobs. Employers prefer to have large numbers of staff in such jobs to make it easier to fire them.
- Lifelong learning and continuing training within and outside companies enables many employees to find alternative work (see Chapter 9).

Gender segregation in the labour market

The early women's movement focused on creating gender equality by improving women's living conditions and by limiting women's major commitments to the family. In this connection, women were to have access to contraception and abortion, education, public childcare and public elderly care. Household technology was meant to minimize women's domestic obligations.

The Nordic countries have been at the forefront of equal opportunities for women. Women have had free access to abortion for 45 years. Women now have a better educational background than men. Public services relieve women to some extent of traditional female tasks. All families have access to reasonable public childcare. The public sector takes care of elderly people in their own homes or, if necessary, in nursing homes. Cooking and laundry have become much less labour-intensive. Women and men in the Nordic countries have generous maternity/paternity leave, relative to other OECD countries. The policy of equal opportunities has had a great impact on women's labour market participation. The employment rate for women is almost at the same level as for men, and the Nordic countries score the highest among EU countries in the European Gender Equality Index (FIGE, 2013).[9]

However, the Nordic countries clearly show that these improvements in women's living conditions are not sufficient to create equality in the labour market in terms of wages, job quality and career opportunities. Gender segregation in the Nordic labour markets is still very prominent and has not become significantly more balanced.

It is still the case that most people work in jobs where either one or the other gender dominates (Emerek & Holt, 2008; Bloksgaard, 2011). Gender segregation and female part-time work is widespread (Drange & Egeland, 2016). Women are in administration, retail and care work. Men are in crafts, technology and management. The public sector is heavily dominated by female employees. Women are weakly represented in management positions, especially in the private sector, and there is almost no development in this area (Larsen et al., 2016). 'Female jobs' are generally lower paid than 'male jobs', and the degree of freedom in 'female jobs' is generally lower than in 'male jobs'.

Gender equality is apparently not achieved merely by creating equal conditions for the two sexes. Gender equality work must also include efforts to change the way employees and managers are 'doing gender': the everyday articulation of gender issues, expectations for the two sexes and the patterns of behaviour that characterize the two sexes. It could be a major task for the social parties to change the way 'gender is done' at work, but until now this has only been addressed to a limited extent.

The welfare state and the labour market parties

Often the welfare state is attributed the central role in providing the better working conditions and the lower inequality we find in the Nordic countries. However, we would argue that the labour market parties and the institutions they have created have played a greater role in making a difference in terms of equality, employment and working conditions.

The welfare state means a great deal in most people's lives, not only in the Nordics but in all OECD countries. The welfare states in Norway and Denmark do not seem to be unusually large. It is quite difficult to make comparisons on this point, but some estimates show that the magnitude of the Nordic welfare states in the overall economy is not extraordinary compared to other OECD countries. One indicator of the welfare state is the tax burden: the greater the share of the total economy being collected by the state in terms of taxes, the larger is the welfare state. Juul (2016) has made an assessment of the tax burden in the OECD countries, which includes reservations for a number of differences in national tax systems.[10] According to this estimate, Denmark has the 7th highest tax burden and Norway the 13th. Taxation thus does not seem to be extraordinarily high in Norway and Denmark, or in the other Nordic countries.[11]

According to Esping-Andersen's (1990) classical typology of welfare states, the Nordic welfare states show a high degree of decommodification. He argues that the welfare state, especially in the Nordic countries, has created a position for citizens that makes them relatively independent of demands from the market (decommodification). This applies particularly to the labour market. The Nordic welfare states have given their citizens universal rights to income, independent of the labour market. This universalist principle is in contrast to other welfare states, where citizens earn the right to social benefits through long seniority at the same company, or where the welfare system mainly provides social benefits to families and children.

However, there is a good reason to question Esping Andersen's thesis that decommodification is particularly advanced in the Nordic countries. Recent studies have shown that decommodification, calculated as Esping-Andersen did in 1990, is no longer a particular feature of the Nordic countries (Scruggs & Allan, 2006).

In addition, the term decommodification may not be a very good label for the Nordic welfare states (Kettunen, 2012). It may be more appropriate to describe the welfare states of the Nordic countries with the label 'fair commodification'. The Nordic welfare states have not reduced the impact of the labour market on the economy and on people's lives; however, the welfare states, alongside the social parties, have balanced some of the inadequacies of the labour market. The demand for labour in the market fluctuates. People selling their labour in the market are depending on a steady demand, since they need money every month. Therefore, labour productivity can be better maintained if there is a social system that ensures income security. However, if there is a demand in the labour market, the unemployed have to meet the demand. Social policy has thus not reduced the dependence and involvement of citizens in the labour market. On the contrary, social policy has supported and pushed the individual citizen to labour market participation, and social policy has made it possible and necessary for the individual to live a long life in the labour market.

In all the Nordic countries, social policy has had a strong orientation towards the labour market: citizens on social benefits should return to work as soon as possible. This *Arbeidslinjen*, which can be translated as 'workfare', has dominated social policy was adopted to social policies in Norway since 1935 by legal acts. It has been reinforced since the 1990 in both countries. To support labour supply, it has also been appropriate to regulate companies' use of labour. Companies tend to create working conditions that are harmful for the labour market: a company may be interested in high utilization of labour, but if this abolishes the workability of labour, it is a market imperfection. This imperfection can be countered by regulation, giving employees a say in work organization and the working environment and by state regulation of the working environment. In competence building, companies also tend to act inappropriately from a labour market perspective. Companies are often in favour of narrow competence building that only meets the demands of the individual company. However, if the labour market is to function optimally, it must be characterized by high mobility and flexibility, where labour is moving to the jobs with the highest productivity and value creation. The demand for mobility makes it appropriate to create training and competence building that go beyond the immediate needs of the individual company (see Chapters 10 and 11).

Precisely because of the strong relationship between the social parties and the state's interaction with them, the Nordic welfare states have not reduced the importance of market forces in the labour market. On the contrary, the welfare states have optimized the labour markets and supported the labour market to be an essential part of people's everyday lives.

Universal social rights, which according to Esping-Andersen (1990) characterize the social-democratic welfare states in the Nordic region, also encourage labour market participation. A social policy linked to family and children, which we find in most European countries, tends to restrict women's labour market participation. A social policy largely based on insurance paid by companies, which we also see in many European countries, also tends to reduce labour mobility. Universal rights lead to a high level of labour market participation and high labour mobility, and thus contribute to an optimal labour market.

However, there is another area where welfare states have contributed to decommodification. Welfare states have moderated the income differentials that the market creates by taxing the highest incomes heavily and paying social benefits to those with the lowest incomes. This redistribution mechanism applies in all OECD countries; it may still be stronger in Norway and Denmark than in the other OECD countries, in spite of being weakened in recent years (Juul et al., 2016). However, the social parties in the labour market have maintained relative equality in wage formation, which has led to lower income inequality in the Nordic countries (Barth & Moene, 2012).

To summarize: it is not primarily the welfare state that has created the specific characteristics of the Nordic countries. The Nordic welfare states are similar in size to those of many other developed economies. The welfare states in the Nordic countries achieve some social redistribution of wealth through progressive taxation and social benefits, just as other welfare states do. The interaction between the welfare state, the labour market and the social parties, on the other hand, have created a dynamic that has resulted in less inequality, greater participation in the labour market and more involvement than we see elsewhere.

The state has an important role to play in order to maintain and develop the institutional arrangements for wage formation, conflict mediation and the legal framework regulating and organizing the labour market.

Culture as an explanation

The culture of the Nordics is characterized by trust and high social capital (Svendsen & Svendsen, 2016). The argument here is that the high degree of trust is conducive to cooperation in the labour market and in the economy as a whole, both within companies and between companies. Trust and social capital support innovation. In addition, trust and social capital encourage responsibility and the individual's willingness to perform. The high degree of trust also makes it easier for the parties to reach compromises.

However, here the famous question arises again: which came first, the chicken or the egg? Were the institutions where the parties can meet, negotiate and find a solution, created because of the trust typical of the Nordic culture? Or is it the reverse, namely that the institutions where conflicts can be solved have created trust in the labour market and also in civil society?

The relatively high level of trust between the social parties has not always existed, which is also mentioned in the presentation of the history of Nordic labour market relations in Chapter 2. In this context, it is worth noting that the Nordic countries primarily have an institutional similarity rather than a historical similarity. All five Nordic countries are characterized by high levels of trust and social capital, even though their histories differ, especially in the case of Finland. In the 20th century, Finland had a civil war, a strong reliance on Russia and the Soviet Union, and a very late industrialization. Its relationship with the other Nordic countries helped establish institutions in Finland that were similar to those developed in the other countries. Today, Finland has the same level of trust and social capital as the other Nordics.

Whether culture creates institutions or institutions create culture is a difficult question. However, without institutions that can preserve and further develop trust and social capital, those cultural features would probably disappear. The established institutions in the labour market are an important foundation for the particular Nordic cultural features.

The economy: a prerequisite for or a consequence of the labour market?

From the perspective of the so-called 'supply economics', the labour market in the Nordic countries is inappropriate. Wages are high, especially for those called low-productivity employees, and working hours are short. Management decisions in companies are hampered by the fact that some decisions have to be discussed with employee representatives, and sometimes management has to follow employee wishes and demands. The Nordic labour market is like a heavy bumblebee. It should not be possible for the bee to fly, but it does. It tumbles around, zig-zags, but stays on its wings, and with quite considerable success. Norway has the second highest gross domestic product (GDP) per inhabitant in Europe, just behind Luxembourg. Denmark is ranked number 8, above Sweden and Germany (EUROSTAT).[12]

But surely the real source of the economic success of Norway and Denmark is the oil fields in the North Sea? Both countries have access to large oil reserves. But in fact, in Denmark, the oil industry forms only a minor part of the overall economy.

In Norway, however, the oil industry represents a much larger part of the economy. Oil revenues account for 14% of GDP and 40% of total exports, according to Norwegian Petroleum.[13] Yet Norwegian oil has not been alone in making the difference. Even before the Norwegian oil adventure started in the

1970s, Norway was a prosperous country. Although the Norwegian oil industry has contributed to raising the cost of living in Norway, there is still a large private sector that is able to compete in global markets. The oil industry has also led to technological innovation. The oil resources are located in deep seas far from land and are being extracted using advanced subsea robot technology.

The Nordic countries are all economies highly dependent on their competitiveness in the global markets. Exporting industries comprise a substantial part of GDP. However, production structure differs. We have already commented on Norway's dependency on oil. In addition, Norway also exports goods based on natural resources like hydro-power and fish.

Denmark is well known for its agricultural sector. In spite of a limited geographical area and a cold climate, Denmark is a major European provider of dairy and meat products. The manufacturing industries (pharmaceutical products and environment-enhancing products), together with other industries and services, however, account for the main volume of Danish exports. The Swedish and Finnish economies are also export-oriented but rely more on traditional manufacturing industries (e.g. metal, cars and paper). There are few similarities in what the Nordic countries produce and export. They are exposed to different global markets and different competitors. What they have in common is their reliance on global markets. This reliance has forced the Nordic governments, employers and trade unions to adapt rapidly to changes in the 'terms of trade'.

The Finnish researcher, Juha Vartiainen, stated that the Nordic countries have learnt to 'live with the market' (Vartiainen, 2014). He points out that the dependency on global markets is a key factor in understanding the development of institutional arrangements in the Nordic welfare states and in the labour markets.

The question thus arises: how does the strongly regulated Nordic labour market enhance or restrict economic development? The high minimum wage, set by collective agreements, is not only an economic constraint but also an economic advantage (Hoeller et al., 2012). In the 1950s, 1960s and 1970s, the two Swedish economists, Meidner and Rehn, strongly advocated the positive effects of the solidarity wage policy on the economy. The argument was that the solidarity wage policy would make low-productivity jobs unprofitable, and they would thus disappear. This is however not necessarily a problem. On the contrary, it makes it possible to move labour from low-productivity areas to high-productivity areas, if workers are helped with mobility-enhancing measures such as education, housing and support to move to where high-productivity jobs are located. This understanding of the potentials of the solidarity wage policy is found among present-day economists, such as the two Norwegian economists Barth and Moene (2012). They find that the OECD countries where wage differences are smallest and where the starting wage for young people is high are also the countries with the highest general and youth employment rates. Solidarity wages do not seem to harm employment; on the contrary.

Strong employee representation can make quick managerial decisions difficult. That is, however, not necessarily only a barrier to economic development. It might equally well be an economic strength. Peter Nielsen et al. (2012) have shown, by combining register data and questionnaire data, that Danish companies where employee representation is strong are also the companies with the greatest innovative capacity. In recent years, there has also been a considerable interest in employee-driven innovation, where employees' direct involvement in their own work combined with strong employee representation in companies create renewal and innovation (Høyrup & Møller, 2012).

The Nordic region: part of the global community

The Nordic countries are deeply involved in the global economy. Their economies are small and highly export-oriented. There is hardly any doubt that globalization of the economy has been a major advantage for the Nordic economies, because it has enabled the export of expensive speciality goods and raw materials, and the import of cheap standard goods. However, globalization also imposes a competitive pressure on all sectors of society, not least the labour market. Increased labour migration within the EU/EEA has put pressure on the wages of low-skilled blue-collar workers.

Industry and food production are highly exposed to global competition. However, private services are also increasingly exposed to global competition. The public sector is subject to a high efficiency requirement to ensure that it is not a burden on the economy. Here, benchmarks of cost and quality in other welfare societies make for partial global competition. The requirement of efficiency seems to be indispensable in all sectors of the economy.

Globalization means free movement of capital, and foreign investments are at a high level in the Nordic countries. Hedge funds and other financial institutions investing in Nordic business often have a fairly short-term horizon for their investments. This is challenging cooperation among the parties on the development of working conditions, which will usually have a long-term perspective.

With globalization, ideas and concepts flow more easily across borders. This means that management concepts, developed under other social, cultural and political conditions (often in the United States), cross national borders and are implemented in Nordic companies. However, these concepts can be difficult to reconcile with the working life traditions of the Nordic region.

Finally, globalization is expressed by the fact that labour travels across borders. In the Nordic countries, there has been quite significant immigration from the former communist countries of Eastern Europe, where there is no tradition of independent trade union organization and where dialogue-oriented management has not been practised that much.

All of this means that the development of working conditions in the Nordic countries largely follows developments in other comparable countries:

- Working conditions become more flexible and individualized
- Union density is declining
- Demands for efficiency are growing
- Work is standardized
- Inequality between the sexes is maintained
- Immigration puts pressure on working conditions in parts of the labour market
- Inequality grows (primarily due to capital income and property prices).

The so-called Nordic model is under pressure, but this is nothing new. It has been the case since the late 1960s, when the economies to a great extent were opened up to the world market. One might say that the model has shown its strength by dealing with new issues and challenges and finding new solutions.

Notes

1 The Work Life Barometer is an annual survey among employees executed by WRI for the Norwegian trade union confederation YS.
2 The decline in organizational density is primarily occurring in the private sector and in the low-paid areas. One reason may be that many low-paid workers are in temporary jobs and therefore have little incentive to be organized.
3 See also http://arbeidslivet.no/PageFiles/9979/Orggrad-arbgivere.png.
4 See http://ec.europa.eu/eurostat/web/products-eurostat-news/-/DDN-20180125-1?inheritRedirect=true.
5 In relation to the Working Environment Act, the state has laid down rules regulating the minimum time for rest periods.
6 In Norway 44% and in Denmark 47% of a representative sample of employees stated that they were 'very satisfied with working conditions' in their main paid job. No other European country scores as highly on this question. The average for the EU is 26%. The proportion answering that they were 'not very satisfied with their working conditions' was 5% in Norway and 8% in Denmark. This is at the same level as in European countries with relatively low unemployment.
7 www.oecd.org/social/inequality.htm#income.
8 Some 10% of Norwegians and 11% of Danes agree with the statement 'I might lose my job in the next six months'. Thus, employment security seems to be at the same level in Norway and Denmark, and at significantly better levels than in Europe as a whole. Regarding the statement 'If I were to lose or quit my current job, it would be easy for me to find a job with a similar salary', 53% in Denmark and 54% in Norway agree, and only 13% and 12% disagree. In no other countries in Europe are expectations for a positive job shift as great as in Denmark and Norway.
9 The index contains the following parameters: work (employment rate, degree of freedom in work, etc.), money (income and risk of poverty), knowledge (education), power (political and economic influence), time (time spent on domestic obligations), health and violence.
10 For example, Juul's estimation takes into account the fact that in some countries people who receive social benefits have to pay taxes. In these countries social benefits appear to be higher, but are not so high when the taxes have been paid. However, the national accounts show that social spending is high and the tax burden is extensive, which can be quite a false conclusion.

11 For Norway one should take into consideration that oil revenues finance almost 20% of total public expenditure.
12 https://ec.europa.eu/eurostat/statistics-explained/index.php?title=File:GDP_at_current_market_prices,_2007_and_2015-2017_FP18.png.
13 www.norskpetroleum.no/en/economy/governments-revenues/.

References

Aagestad, C., Bjerkan, A. M. & Gravset, H. M. (2017) *Arbeidsmiljøet i Norge og EU: En sammenlikning. Basert på data fra European Working Conditions Survey [The Working Environment in Norway and the EU: A Comparison. Based on Data from the European Working Conditions Survey]*, Oslo: STAMI-Report.

Axelsson, J., Karlsson, J. C. H. & Skorstad, E. J. (2016) Arbeiderkollektivet i dag: replikasjon og teoretisk utvikling [The Labour Collective Today: Replication and Theoretical Development], *Tidsskrift for samfunnsforskning*, No 2/2016. https://doi.org/10.18261/issn.1504-291x-2016-02-01.

Barth, E. & Moene, K. O. (2012) Employment as a Price or a Prize of Equality: A Descriptive Analysis, *Nordic Journal of Working Life Studies*, Vol 2 No 2. https://doi.org/10.19154/njwls.v2i2.2355.

Bloksgaard, L. (2011) Masculinities, Femininities and Work: The Horizontal Gender Segregation in the Danish Labour Market, *Nordic Journal of Working Life Studies*, Vol 1 No 2. http://dx.doi.org/10.19154/njwls.v1i2.2342.

Bonke, J. (2016) *Arbejdstid og familien: Arbejdstidsønsker/arbejdstid og skat/børn og skilsmisse/pensionering og samvær [Working Hours and Family: Working Wishes / Working Hours and Taxes / Children and Divorce / Retirement and Attendance]*, Syddansk Universitetsforlag og Rockwool Fondens Forskningsenhed.

Calmfors, L. (1993) Centralisation of Wage Bargaining and Macroeconomic Performance: A Survey, *OECD Economic Studies*, No 21, Winter 1993. https://doi.org/10.1787/521405217277.

Dhondt, S., Vermeerbergen, L. & Hootegren, G. (2017) Evidence of Workplace Innovation from Organisational and Economic Studies, In: Oeij, P. R. A., Diana, R. & Pot, F. D. (eds) *Workplace Innovation: Theory, Research and Practice*, Springer Verlag. https://doi.org/10.1007/978-3-319-56333-6_6.

Dølvik, J. E., Fløtten, T., Hippe, J. M. & Jordfald, B. (2015) *The Nordic Model Towards 2030. A New Chapter?* NordMod2030, Final report, Oslo Fafo-report 2015:07.

Drange, I. & Egeland, C. (2016) Å ta ansvar: deltidsvalgets ideologiske dimensjon. Begrunnelser for deltidsvalg i Norge [To Take Responsibility: Ideological Dimension of Part-Time Elections. Grounds for Part-Time Elections in Norway], In: Halrynjo, S. & Teigen, M. (eds) *Ulik likestilling i arbeidslivet*, Oslo: Gyldendal Akademisk, 122–141.

Emerek, R. & Holt, H. (2008) Det kønsopdelte danske arbejdsmarked [The Gender-Segregated Danish Labour Market], In: Emerek, R. & Holt, H. (eds) *Lige muligheder: frie valg? Om det kønsopdelte arbejdsmarked gennem et årti [Equal Opportunities: Free Choice? About the Gender-Segregated Labour Market Through a Decade]*, Copenhagen: Det nationale Forskningscenter for Velfærd.

Esping-Andersen, G. (1990) *The Three Worlds of Welfare Capitalism*, London: Polity Press.

ETUI (2017) *Benchmarking Working Europe 2017*, Brussels: ETUI.

Eurofound (2009) Denmark: Flexicurity and Industrial Relations, *European Observatory of Working Life*, September 2009.

Eurofound (2012) *Trends in Job Quality in Europe*, Luxembourg: Publications Office of the European Union.

Eurofound (2017) *Sixth European Working Conditions Survey: 2015, Data Visualization*, Brussels.

Falkum, E., Nordrik, B., Drange, I. & Wathne, C. T. (2017) *Medbestemmelsesbarometeret 2017: Arbeidslivsrelasjoner i endring [Co-Determination Barometer 2017: Labour Relations in Flux]*, Oslo: AFI.

Fernández-Macías, E. (2012) Job Polarization in Europe? Changes in the Employment Structure and Job Quality, 1995–2007, *Work and Occupations*, Vol 39 No 2, pp. 157–182.

FIGE (2013) *Gender Equality Index. Main Findings*, Publications Office of the European Union. doi: 10.2839/96248.

Gustavsen, B. (2007) Work Organization and 'the Scandinavian Model', *Economic and Industrial Democracy*, Vol 28 No 4, p. 1. https://doi.org/10.1177/0143831x07082218.

Hoeller, P., Joumard, I., Pisu, M. & Bloch, D. (2012) Less Income Inequality and More Growth: Are They Compatible? Part 1. Mapping Income Inequality Across the OECD, *OECD Economics Department Working Papers*, No 924, Paris: OECD Publishing. https://doi.org/10.2139/ssrn.2014780.

Høyrup, S. & Møller, K. (2012) *Employee-Driven Innovation*, Basingstoke, UK: Palgrave Macmillan.

Hvid, H. (2001) Dansk arbejdspolitiks gyldne årti [The Golden Decade of Danish Working Policy], *Tidsskrift for Arbejdsliv*, No 4/2001.

Juul, J. S. (2016) *Skattetryk. Danmark har udsigt til det laveste skattetryk siden 1992 [Denmark has the Lowest Tax Burden since 1992]*, Copenhagen: Arbejderbevægelsens Erhvervsråd.

Juul, J. S., Pihl, M. D. & Damm, E. A. (2016) *Danmark på fattigdomskurs [Denmark on Track Towards Poverty]*, Copenhagen: Arbejderbevægelsens Erhvervsråd.

Karasek, R. (1989) *Healthy Work. Stress, Productivity, and the Reconstruction of Working Life*, New York: Basic Books.

Karlsson, J. C., Skorstad, E. J. & Axelsson, J. (2015) On the Track of the Worker Collectivity: Its Various Adventures over the Past 60 Years, *Sage Open*. https://doi.org/10.1177/2158244015575635.

Kettunen, P. (2012) Reinterpreting the Historicity of the Nordic Model, *Nordic Journal of Working Life Studies*, Vol 2 No 4, pp. 21–43.

Kjellberg, A. (2009) The Swedish Model of Industrial Relations: Self-Regulation and Combined Centralisation-Decentralisation, In: Phelan, C. (2009) *Trade Unionism since 1945: Towards a Global History*, Bern: Peter Lang Publishing Group.

Larsen, F., Hansen, T. B., Ellersgaard, C. & Krogh, A. H. (2016) *Kvinder i ledelse [Women in Management]*, Copenhagen: Institut for Menneskerettigheder.

Lysgaard, S. (2001 [1961]) *Arbeiderkollektivet. En studie i de underordnedes sociologi [The Worker Collectivity. A Study of the Sociology of the Subordinates]*, Oslo: Universitetsforlaget.

Madsen, J. S., Andersen, S. K. & Due, J. (2001) *From Centralised Decentralisation towards Multi-Level Regulation: Danish Employment Relations between Continuity and Change*, Copenhagen: FAOS.

Madsen, P. K. (2010) Denmark, In: de Beer, P., & Cheltenham, T. S. (eds) *The Labour Market Triangle: Employment Protection, Unemployment Compensation and Activation in Europe*, Cheltenham, UK: Edward Elgar Publishing, 44–69.

Navrbjerg, S. E. & Ibsen, C. L. (2017) *Arbejdsgiverorganisationer i Danmark: Fra passiv tradition til aktiv tilpasning [Employers' Organizations in Denmark: From Passive Tradition to Active Adaptation]*, Copenhagen: FAOS.

Nergaard, K. (2016) *Organisasjonsgrader, tariffavtaledekning og arbeidskonflikter 2014 [Organization Rate, Tariff Agreement Coverage and Labour Conflicts 2014]*, Fafo-notat, Oslo.

Nielsen, P., Nielsen, R. N., Bamberger, S. G., Stamhus, J., Fonager, J., Larsen, A., . . . & Omland, Ø. (2012) Capabilities for Innovation: The Nordic Model and Employee Participation, *Nordic Journal of Working Life Studies*, Vol 2 No 4. https://doi.org/10.19154/njwls.v2i4.2306.

Nordström, K. A. & Ridderstråle, J. (1999) *Funky Business, Talent Makes Capital Dance*, Covington, GA: Bookhouse.

Pateman, C. (1970) *Participation and Democratic Theory*, Cambridge, UK: Cambridge University Press.

Rokkan, S. (1966) Norway: Numerical Democracy and Corporate Pluralism, In: Dahl, R. (ed.) *Political Oppositions in Western Democracies*, New Haven, CT: Yale University Press.

Scruggs, L. & Allan, J. (2006) Welfare-State Decommodification in 18 OECD Countries: A Replication and Revision, *Journal of European Social Policy*, Vol 16 No 1. https://doi.org/10.1177/0958928706059833.

Sørensen, C. (2010) *Arbejdsmarked og den danske flexicurity-model [Labour market and the Danish flexicurity model]*, Copenhagen: Academica.

Sørensen, O. H. & Holman, D. (2014) A Participative Intervention to Improve Employee Well-Being in Knowledge Work Jobs, *Work & Stress*, Vol 28 No 1. https://doi-org.ep.fjernadgang.kb.dk/10.1080/02678373.2013.876124.

Statistics Denmark (2018) *Labour Force Survey*, Copenhagen.

Svendsen, G. L. H. & Svendsen, G. T. (2016) *Trust, Social Capital and the Scandinavian Welfare State. Explaining the Flight of the Bumblebee*, London: Edward Edgar Publishing.

Vartiainen, J. (2014) *To Create and Share: The Remarkable Success and Contested Future of the Nordic Social-Democratic Model*, Fafo-report 2014:25, Oslo.

Chapter 2

The peculiar history of Nordic working life

Eivind Falkum, Helge Hvid and Per Bonde Hansen

Introduction

The Nordic countries have developed independently, but, in the case of Norway, Denmark and Sweden, largely in parallel. Finland, which today is part of the Nordic model and has contributed significantly to renewal of the model, has historically followed another path to becoming a Nordic country (Sippola, 2015). In the following, we will present key features of the history of the Nordic model by presenting key events in Norway and Denmark, with sporadic reference to Sweden.

The Nordic model had its cradle in the conflicts that arose when wage labour became widespread and the towns grew in the late 19th century. The conflicts led both employees and employers to organize their own interest associations. The conflicts were particularly prevalent in the first decades of the 20th century, leading to extensive institutional building in the labour market. That did not eliminate the labour market conflicts, but from now on, they had an institutional framework in which they could unfold. These institutions are still vital today. We call this period 'from the streets to the negotiation table'.

From the mid-1930s onwards, the institutional framework for regulating conflicts between employees and employers expanded. During the same period, a welfare society was gradually established in intensive interaction between the state, the social parties and other interest groups. The Nordic social democracies dominated the political systems during this period. We therefore call this period 'the social-democratic era'.

From the mid-1980s onwards, the Social Democrats gradually lost their political hegemony. Global competition was growing. International regulation became more comprehensive. The welfare state gradually changed its character. Governance principles, formed by neo-liberal thinking, took over. Pay and working conditions were gradually individualized. The period saw a dissolution of the ties between the trade union movement and the Social Democrats on the one hand, and employers' organizations and the conservative parties on the other. Nevertheless, the social parties and the state have maintained and further developed the central institutions in the Nordic model.

The social parties succeed in combining high levels of economic efficiency with high levels of equality and social security (Kristensen & Lilja, 2011). We call this period the 'neo-liberal era'.

From the streets to the negotiation table

The Nordic labour markets are often said to be characterized by trust, collaboration and consensus. The outset of the process towards a peaceful working life was, however, quite the opposite: serious and protracted conflicts in the labour market.

In the last decades of the 19th century and the first decades of the 20th, the industrialization processes redefined and reorganized the political and economic interests in societies, and thus also the social and cultural interests. Industrialization transformed societies and their institutions, providing completely new ways to produce and distribute wealth.

The exchange economy was still common in the final decades of the 19th century in Denmark and Norway. Industrialization accelerated in the 1890s. Power plants, chemical plants and metallurgical manufacturing plants were established at waterfalls in Norway. In Denmark, primarily shipyards, but also the food, metal and other industries grew in the same period. Paid work became the normal way to make a living, replacing the exchange economy and domestic work for large numbers of the population. Labour relations changed as the more or less feudal work arrangements faded out of societies and history. This was the common background to the transformation of the Nordic societies, although there were national differences in timelines and speed in this development.

Institutionalization of class conflicts in Denmark

In the late 19th and early 20th centuries, Denmark was a pioneer nation in terms of organizing the labour market. Denmark had the highest union density in the world around the year 1900, according to historians. About 50% of skilled workers were members of a trade union (Galenson, 1955). In 1899, employers' associations and trade unions signed a so-called 'basic agreement' that regulated the employer–employee relationship. This agreement has been expanded since then, but has been preserved in essence.

The 'basic agreement' expresses pragmatic sense and consensus, despite the less friendly and peaceful climate that created it. The agreement was created after decades of hard labour conflicts.

In Denmark, the first steps to establishing trade unions were taken in the 1870s. Following a major demonstration in 1872, the leaders of the new labour movement, Louis Pio, Paul Geleff and Harald Brix, were arrested and the International Labour Union for Denmark was banned. Louis Pio was later urged by the police to emigrate to the United States. In the next decade, trade unions were further weakened due to an economic crisis. However, from the mid-1880s the number of workers grew rapidly, as did the trade unions. Now the peasant movement and the labour movement had become so strong that the authorities could no longer pursue unions with unconstitutional interventions.

The trade unions' main strategy was to use what in Danish is called 'omgangsskruen' or in English, the 'wrench': a strike for better pay and working conditions was initiated by the unions at a workplace where the union considered that it would be possible to pressurize an employer. When the union had won one victory, it would proceed to the next employer. The strikers received compensation from the union.

In line with the establishment of the unions, employers began to organize themselves. Employers' response to the 'wrench' was lockouts. If there was a conflict in one workplace, employers implemented lockouts in many other workplaces to make it difficult for the unions to compensate workers for their lost wages.

In 1897, a labour dispute in one major metal enterprise led to a lockout for the entire metal industry. Employers wanted to ensure their right to lead and direct the work, their right to decide whom to employ, and they also defended their right to determine pay and working conditions. The employers lost this conflict, but it led to the national organization of both parties, across all sectors. There were already a large number of sector-specific employers' associations. In 1898, they formed the Danish Employers' Association. In the same year, the Confederation of Trade Unions, with the support of a large number of unions, was established. Now the social parties geared up for battle, and in May 1899, employers started a large lockout to recover what they had lost.

One key demand of the employers was the right to direct and distribute the work. They also wanted to protect their right to hire the labour they considered appropriate. Further demands were an institutionalization of the conflicts in the labour market and collective agreements to be determined through centralized negotiations, with an obligation for both parties to comply with the agreement until it expired. As long as the agreement was in force, strikes and lockouts were not to be permitted. This was something completely new.

These requirements were in contrast to the demands of the workers, who fought for their right to direct and distribute the work. Furthermore, the trade unions were not in favour of centralized negotiations. That would undermine their effective weapon, 'the wrench', which split the employers. The employers, for their part, could not accept 'the wrench' and consequently could not agree to local negotiations.

The conflict became extensive; it lasted for 100 days and included 40,000 workers, which was a large number for a small country of 2.5 million inhabitants, most of whom worked in agriculture and fisheries. The farmers supported the workers with contributions. The conflict gained international attention, and the workers received financial support from all over the world.

However, the unions could not resist the pressure in the long run. The parties made an agreement on 5 September 1899. Both parties proclaimed this a victory. Subsequently, however, most analysts found that the employers were the primary victors.

It was legally confirmed that employers had the right to direct and distribute the work and employ those they deemed appropriate. From then on, it became much more difficult to organize local and spontaneous strikes. A system with centralized collective agreements was established, and the unions were obliged to ensure labour peace as long the agreement was in force. Employers accepted trade unions as negotiating partners and were no longer allowed to prevent employees from organizing in trade unions.

The 'September Agreement' was subsequently strengthened by the establishment of two institutions: a special court and a mediation board. The court could impose sanctions if agreements were not fulfilled by one of the parties. The mediation board was to provide support if the parties could not reach a new agreement when the old one was about to expire. For both these institutions, the national court and the state have played a decisive role.

The main agreement, concluded with the September settlement in 1899, is still the constitution of the labour market in Denmark. However, in the meantime, a large number of modifications and additions have been made to the agreement.

For some of the employers' organizations, the goal of the grand lockout in 1899 was to break the trade union movement. However, they did not succeed; in fact, unions grew in membership and influence in the following years. About 50% of skilled workers were members of a trade union in 1900. Employers' associations also grew, and the level of organized employers was far higher in Denmark than in the other Nordic countries (Galenson, 1955).

Since the September Agreement, employers' organizations and trade unions have become mutually dependent and have had a common interest in maintaining an organized labour market.

The other Nordic countries achieved general agreements similar to the Danish September Agreement, but much later. Norway signed its basic agreement in 1935, Sweden in 1938, and Finland saw a number of similar agreements during the 1960s. Consequently, the conflicts were less regulated for decades in Norway, Sweden and Finland than they were in Denmark. Next, we will briefly present developments in Norway in the first decades of the 20th century.

Institutionalizing class conflicts in Norway

The first employer and union agreement in Norway was signed between some organized employers and the labour union for metal industries in 1902, and revised in 1907. Agreements as tools to solve differences and possible conflicts were already on the working life agenda in the early phases of the industrialization process and the introduction of modernity to the Nordic societies, in parallel with Denmark. However, these first agreements were quickly broken, either by employers' lockouts or by union strikes. Labour conflicts were common from the beginning of the 20th century until the 1930s.

In 1915, a law was passed in Norway to regulate labour conflicts. That law (Arbeidstvistloven) established the national mediator (Riksmeglingsmannen) and the labour court (Arbeidsretten) as public tools to solve differences of interest between employers and employees.

Labour conflicts peaked in Norway in 1930, with 8 million working days lost due to labour conflicts during that year. The situation inspired the prime minister of the Liberal government to conclude that political decisions and labour laws had demonstrated their inability to solve the devastating conflicts between labour and capital, and unions and employers. He invited the parties to a new Labour Peace Committee and suggested that they needed to find out how to avoid conflicts. This process ended in the basic agreement in 1935.

The level of conflicts was very high in the whole of Europe in the early 20th century. In the first place, World War I damaged European economies and nations from 1914 to 1918. The Russian revolution took place in 1917 and introduced the proletarian dictatorship to political governance. The Third Communist International (Comintern) advocated a communist world order from 1919 to 1943. Several national labour movements all over Europe joined Comintern, including the Norwegian Labour Party.

World War I led to economic downturns, ruined food production and brought fear of hunger to European countries, including the Nordics. Simultaneously, inspired by the Russian revolution, labour movements became radicalized. An opposition group in the Norwegian Labour Party insisted on adopting some of the socialist ideas in the political programme, including the idea of organizing workers' councils as a local political force in most areas of society (Debes, 1919). This suggestion was accepted and recognized by the party convention in 1918. The party joined Comintern in 1919. They left Comintern three years later because of disagreements on the centralized power in the international movement. Furthermore, the Norwegian Labour Party lost large numbers of members who disagreed with the association with Comintern (Langfeldt, 1961). The labour union opposed the Labour Party's membership of Comintern. Turning back to the social-democratic platform, the alliance between the party and union recovered and improved. The labour movement now gave priority to the battle of labour interests with employers: to improve wages, working conditions and welfare services.

Liberals and conservatives often criticized the alliance of the Labour Party and the labour union for dominating through their ability to influence politics and the economy simultaneously. However, there was another important alliance in the early 20th century, between the liberal parties in parliament and the employers' associations (Bjørnson, 1990, p. 566). The prime minster in the Liberal government, Gunnar Knudsen, even guaranteed to support employers in case of socialist-inspired attempts of workers to take over private property in 1919, if necessary with armed force. There were at least two occasions when the army was ordered to intervene in labour conflicts: one in 1913 in a mining company in the north, and military actions towards striking workers in 1931 at a plant in the south-east (Johansen, 1977). In the early 1930s, a Conservative government proposed 'worker-hostile' laws to prevent strikes (Bjørnson, 1990). The parliamentary majority turned down the proposal, and following a vote of no confidence, the government had to resign.

The period 1921 to 1931 has been labelled by historians as 'the period of great labour conflicts' in Norway (Ousland, 1949). When negotiations between the social parties and the government took place in the Labour Peace Committee from 1930 until 1935, the relations between worker and employer gradually changed. After the basic agreement in 1935, the climate changed. In the same year, the Labour Party obtained a majority of votes in the general election and formed its second government.

In the 1950s and 1960s, the communist parties called the agreement treachery towards labour class interests and a subordination to capital interests, i.e. a co-optation. Basic agreements are generally considered to be the result of class compromises. The labour unions accept the private property right of employers by signing the agreements. In return, the employers accept the unions as rightful representatives of workers' interests in collective bargaining on wages. This is the fundamental principle of the industrial relations derived from basic agreements.

The Labour Party and the labour union have challenged the private property rights in Norway since their very beginnings. Firstly, their declarations and political programmes, by the Norwegian Labour Party since 1897 and the labour union in 1899, were strongly inspired by socialist conceptions of private property and the need for a social distribution of wealth. Secondly, the labour union demanded to be part of workplace management in the wage negotiations in 1918 (Debes, 1919). The employers' association (NAF) interpreted this as an attack on their administrative prerogative and thereby also the private property rights (ibid.).

The historian Einar Terjesen has, however, argued that the class compromise of 1935 was not a compromise between economic interests and the boundaries of the administrative prerogative, but between different views on a just society and was thus a compromise between market and democracy (Terjesen, 2012, p. 26).

The Norwegian basic agreement of 1935 simply consisted of some rules on how to disagree, in order to prevent differences of interest from escalating into conflicts. The social parties have subsequently revised the basic agreement several times, every fourth year in recent decades.

The social-democratic era

For 40 to 50 years from the mid-1930s, the Social Democrats dominated the governments in Denmark, Norway and Sweden. The Social Democrats had a strong relationship with the trade unions in that period. We call this period the social-democratic era. The boundaries between the labour market parties and the state were largely erased: the state determined the conditions for business and had an influence on wages and working conditions. However, the government did not overrule the social parties. The social parties were heavily involved in the development of government policies.

Social democracies in the Nordic countries dominated the government apparatus from the mid-1930s to the mid-1980s, but with different strengths in Norway, Sweden and Denmark. In both Norway and Sweden, the Social Democrats had an absolute majority in parliament for long periods. In other periods, they had to work with parties to the left of the Labour Party. In Denmark, the Social Democrats formed the largest political party by far, but never had a majority in parliament; for almost the whole period they had to make coalitions with liberal parties in the middle of the political spectrum, which was rather sceptical of the social parties. This meant that the state in Denmark was less involved in matters settled by agreements directly between the social parties.

However, all the Nordic countries (again with Finland as a latecomer) were busy building a social-democratic society. In Sweden, this new society was called the 'Home of the People' (Folkhemmet). In Denmark, the new society was described in the Social Democracy Party Programme of 1934 (Socialdemokratiet, 1934). The programme stated that the goal was still to abolish capitalism, but in the long term. The focus for now should be on the creation of a worthy life for all with a respectable job: workers, officers, self-employed workers, small farmers and agricultural workers. Furthermore, social security should be expanded and the economy regulated. The programme text ends with the following wording:

> Now the time has come. Not for miraculous experiments and unlawful actions (which both Communists and Nazis were responsible for), not for threats and attempts to break down an organized society, but the time has come to create a community of people to oppose lawlessness and to make the construction of a new society the goal of our future work.
>
> (Authors' translation)

The ideal was a society characterized by:

1 Full employment. It presupposed vocational education and labour policy that supported business development.
2 Security. For children and for unemployed, disabled, ill, and elderly people. Housing for all.

3 Equality. Equality in income and wealth. Equality in opportunities through free access to education and healthcare.
4 Enlightenment. Everyone must have access to general education and cultural services.
5 Democracy. Democratization of the economy, democratization of workplaces, democratization of residential areas.

The policies of the Nordic Social Democrats were realized in a dual political system, which Rokkan (1986) labels 'corporate pluralism'. The social parties and other interest groups were involved in the creation, administration and renewal of the democratic policies. The corporate channel, however, included only organized interest groups, but in great numbers and varieties, which are covered by the concept of corporate pluralism (Rokkan, 1986). The political logic was to bring together opposing interests and perspectives in advance, in order to arrive at shared understandings of the problem at hand.

This model has several advantages over normal political decision making where the majority prevails. Firstly, the policy at hand is enlightened by groups with vested interests in it; thus, in principle, it is explored more deeply through a range of different approaches and perspectives. This is assumed to improve planning and implementation. Secondly, not only experts, bureaucrats or the most powerful people in society have a say; the groups that will experience the consequences of the proposed policies should also participate. Those who wear the shoes matter. Thirdly, when groups known to have different attitudes, experiences, knowledge and interests meet each other in such tripartite arrangements, opportunities to negotiate during the elaboration and planning process will enhance abilities and possibilities to agree on solutions in the early stages. Finally, this kind of planning and decision making, when successful, will achieve policies that have support in advance of the final decision, which will increase the possibility of successful implementation of new policies. This is exactly the same logic that is intrinsic to democracy in workplaces as we know it in the Nordics (see Chapters 3 and 4 of this volume).

A possible disadvantage of corporate pluralism, however, may be what the historian Edvard Bull has called 'top level partnership'. According to Bull, the leadership of the Norwegian Confederation of Trade Unions shared a common understanding with government and employers that differed from that of the members and shop stewards in workplaces (Bull, 1979). In addition, we may assume that the top level involvement of the unions strengthened the character of the organizations as social institutions rather than social movements that could play a transformative role in society.

The social-democratic era coincided with the Fordist epoch that occurred throughout the Western world with mass production, mass consumption and welfare states. In the Nordic countries, a specific social-democratic version of Fordism was developed. It balanced out differences and conflicting interests through negotiations and compromises between the social parties (Falkum, 2008).

Naturally, we cannot describe here the whole social revolution that occurred in the era. However, many of the other chapters in this book will illuminate this period within more specific areas: employment and equality have been discussed in Chapter 1. In Chapter 3, we will focus on democratization efforts at the end of the social-democratic era. We will also elaborate further on initiatives taken during that period in other chapters.

Here we will present two examples of positive and negative effects of the social-democratic era. We will describe how the state, trade unions and employers' associations stood together to introduce Taylorism and Fordist production methods in the 1950s, with Denmark as an example (there was a similar development in Norway). We will briefly describe how the state, trade union and employers' organizations subsequently started to find alternatives to the Taylorist and Fordist production systems, by introducing socio-technology, here with Norway as an example (this also took place in Denmark, but later than in Norway).

In the first years after World War II, both the trade union movement and the Social Democrats were of the opinion that Denmark had outdated production facilities. There was a consensus on the need for rationalization in industry. Although rationalization often leads to job losses, and severe rationalization often hits certain professions and trades particularly hard, it was generally supported by the trade union movement. Efforts were made to create rationalizations in collaboration between management and elected representatives of the employees, with particular emphasis on ensuring that the rationalizations were beneficial for both parties.

One step in that direction was the signing of a cooperation agreement between employers' associations and the trade union movement in 1947. Under the agreement, cooperation committees would provide workers with insight into strategic issues and the company's economy, and the two parties would collaborate in the creating of rationalizations that respected and improved the health and wellbeing of workers (Samarbejdsnævnet, 1997). A special agreement between the social parties in Norway in 1946 had similar aims (Bjørnson, 1990).

Taylorist time and motion studies were the most advanced approach to rationalization in the first years after World War II. Work processes were analysed, time measurements were made for the different processes, the tasks were split up to let each one be as simple as possible, and work was paid at piece rate. The trade union movement took an active part in the introduction of Taylorist principles in Denmark and Norway (Christensen et al., 2015). Rationalization consultants were employed by the trade unions. They arranged workshops on rationalization in large companies, and they entered into rationalization agreements in the companies. The workers' education associations held training courses in rationalization. The trade unions in Denmark organized study trips to the United States to learn the most effective approach to rationalization. The Ministry of Commerce supported these visits (Christensen et al., 2015).

Eiler Jensen, who chaired the Danish Federation of Trade Unions (DsF) in the early 1950s, stressed again and again that as long as the modernization of production supported the common good, they would succeed. Rationalization would improve competitiveness, secure employment, increase wages and improve working conditions. Therefore, cooperation on modernization and rationalization was crucial.

However, the Taylorist rationalization encountered significant resistance from the workers. A five-week strike in the Philips television factory in 1954 became iconic. The strike was called because of unrealistically high productivity requirements and humiliating surveillance. The conflict gained great support from workers in other companies, while the trade union movement had to distance itself from the conflict. Throughout the 1950s and 1960s, there were a number of similar conflicts.

The highly controlled and intensive Taylorist work organization met with strong opposition from workers. This led to a demand for a democratization of working life that would have an impact on working conditions, influence corporate leadership and ultimately also involve the influence of workers on investments and priorities through economic democracy. This democratization effort will be presented in more detail in Chapter 3.

Here we will place this democratic movement in a broader historical context. In Norway, initiatives were taken as early as the 1960s to find alternatives to the Taylorist approach to work organization. These initiatives took place in cooperation between labour unions and employers' associations (Thorsrud & Emery, 1964, 1970).

Democracy as a perspective became quite clear in the revision of the basic agreement in Norway in 1966 (Bjørnhaug & Halvorsen, 2009). The basic agreement was significantly expanded. It stipulated a two-stage democratic process in workplaces. Employees' participation in workplace development and work autonomy was introduced as mandatory in workplaces that signed the agreement. This was the first stage. The second stage was an extension and clarification of unions' rights to codetermination in decision making and planning in private enterprises, as further elaborated and analysed in Chapters 3 and 4 of this volume.

Parallel to the revision of the basic agreement in Norway in 1966, an extensive debate about political regulation of work environments arose after a major accident with 23 casualties in a coalmine in Svalbard in 1963. Heiret (2003) argues that this accident, and the following debate, also triggered the revision of the basic agreement. Political parties argued in parliament for making employee board representation mandatory by law during the 1960s. Finally, in 1972 the Limited Companies Act included the proposal that employees could demand to have up to one-third of board members in limited companies, elected from and by all employees, not only union members.

Efforts to democratize working life were continued in the Working Environment Act of 1977. Here, socio-technical principles and socio-psychological requirements were introduced as the basic principles for work organization. Furthermore, the development of the working environment was to take place in a democratic process. Any enterprise with 30 employees or more was required to set up a working environment committee. All workplaces with ten employees or more had to have health and safety representatives elected from and by all employees. This represented a paradigm shift from a focus on work hygiene and health to a focus on social relations and dynamics in workplaces (Falkum, 2008).

As shown earlier, the trade union movement was deeply involved in the development of working life in the social-democratic era through close cooperation with employers. As a result, the trade union movement participated in the development of working conditions characterized by standardization, managerial control and high labour intensity. However, it was also involved in the development of cooperation between autonomous employees as part of the development of democracy in working life.

In the social-democratic era, democratization of daily work and democratization of top management through democratization of the economy were important issues. However, the economy was never democratized; such efforts in Norway ended in 1980. A public proposal to increase employee board representation from 30% to 50% of board members was turned down by unions as well as employers' associations (Nyhamar, 1994, p. 326). In Denmark, efforts to democratize the economy had ended a few years earlier.

Simultaneously, the new market liberalism influenced politics in the Western world. It brought ideas of deregulation of markets, including labour markets, and a new and less interfering role of politics in economic development (Friedman & Friedman, 1980).

However, as we will argue later, there are different varieties of neo-liberalism. The Nordic countries seem to have developed a specific variant of neo-liberalism, yet with significant differences between the countries. For example, it was possible to fulfil the wish of the neo-liberal era for a high degree of flexibility with the experience gained in the Nordic countries on the democratization of work organization.

The neo-liberal era

During the 1980s, the social-democratic project was weakened, and neo-liberal understandings and regulatory principles grew throughout the Western world, including the Nordic countries. In neo-liberal thinking, a belief in planning is replaced by a belief in market mechanisms. The social policy had previously included a wide range of universal rights. These were now diminished or replaced with activities to support the individual's ability and motivation to get a job and be part of the labour market. Social policy changed from welfare to workfare. According to neo-liberal ideology, wage formation should follow supply and demand.

For the United States and the UK, the neo-liberal project was in line with the liberal social model that was already established in these countries. In contrast to these liberal countries are the countries Hall and Soskice (2001) call 'co-ordinated market economies'. Here, pay and working conditions are determined by collective agreements, there is a public infrastructure for education and training, business-level collaboration has been developed and investors have a relatively long-term perspective on their return on capital. In this category of countries, we find Germany, Japan, Austria and the Nordic countries.

In some of these countries, social conditions have deteriorated remarkably during the neo-liberal era. This applies for instance to Germany, where the influential institutions connected to the labour market and social parties have been maintained in traditional industries without significant renewals. However, the rising group of low-paid workers in the service industries and the increasing numbers of highly educated people in the services sector are not included in the institutional protection associated with coordinated market economies (Thelen, 2014). This has created a sharp rise in the numbers of working poor, and an unregulated labour market for the highly educated.

The neo-liberal social order has been heavily criticized (e.g. Standing, 2010). Some of the criticisms are as follows: market relations will surpass all other social considerations; both the state and the private sector are managed within a short-term perspective; individuals are obliged to find a position in the labour market themselves and must accept pay and working conditions that correspond to their market value; and individual competition replaces social solidarity.

Neo-liberalism, however, does not appear in a uniform manner from country to country. Kathleen Thelen (2014) identifies different varieties of liberalization, and she investigates attempts to defend solidarity in different neo-liberal frameworks. Among a wide range of countries, she examines the formation of a neo-liberalism that, to use Wolfgang Streeck's term, can be called 'competitive solidarity' (Streeck, 1999).

This competitive solidarity has developed especially in Denmark, perhaps because both employers and employees have been relatively well organized in all sectors, while social democracy, compared with the other Nordic countries, has remained relatively weak. As a result, the state has played a minor role in the labour market in Denmark compared to the other Nordic countries, and the legacy of the social-democratic society has been less extensive. The social parties therefore have had wider scope to find a compromise between the flexibility employers wanted in order to participate in global competition, and the equality and social security which are the eligibility of employees' organizations.

Competitive solidarity, as it has evolved in the Nordic countries, especially in Denmark, is characterized by:

- *Acceptance of globalization of the economy.* Both employers' associations and trade unions abandon all forms of protectionism. There is full acceptance that the Nordic economies are open economies in global competition. Cooperation between the social parties at company level must help to make companies competitive in the global economy. The awareness and acceptance of global competition among Danish industrial workers is described in Hull Kristensen's book (2003) on the role of employee representatives in multinational companies in Denmark.

- *Flexibility and decentralization*. Flexibility is a key word in the era of neo-liberalism. It is said that the market requires constant adjustments. To increase flexibility, employers now want general agreements on wages and working conditions terminated in favour of decentralized and local agreements. In the first half of the 20th century, employers were in favour of centralized agreements. Now they prefer decentralized agreements. In Denmark, a gradual decentralization of contractual relations occurred in the mid-1980s. The social parties entered into a number of framework agreements. These agreements were then to be implemented locally. A new model for collective agreements was developed, which Due and Madsen call 'centralized decentralization' (Due et al., 1994); here, local agreements were concluded within a centrally defined framework. Over the years, the framework for local agreements has gradually become more flexible. Due and Madsen (2008) now characterize the system of collective agreements as multi-level regulation: it seems that Denmark has succeeded in creating a system of collective agreements where centralized agreements provide some strength to decentralized agreements, and decentralized agreements give strength to centralized agreements. In Norway, this decentralization has not taken place to the same extent. The tripartite system for wage formation is highly centralized in Norway and forms the basis for local negotiations, compromises and solutions to a great extent.
- *Employability*. Education, training and competence development, which will be presented in detail in Part III of this book, are seen as a common concern for the social parties. Agreements and legislation ensure that workers have access to and the right to education and training. This will provide companies with qualified labour and give workers better access to employment. The idea is that even if employees lose their jobs, the employability developed through education and training will make it easy to find a new job. When unemployment is rising, such as after the financial crisis in 2008, and the sudden drop of oil and gas prices in 2014, public and private education and training programmes are normally established to ease the situation.
- *Workfare*. Since the mid-1980s, social policy has increasingly focused on work as the solution. Citizens who cannot support themselves should not just be provided with social benefits. They should be pulled and pushed into education or work. Therefore, a large number of programmes have been established to bring unemployed people and those with health problems into supported employment or education. Both employers and trade

unions are involved in these concrete measures to bring citizens into work. From the mid-1980s, large-scale pension funds, established through collective agreements, are intended to provide workers with reasonable pensions when they leave the labour market.

- *Productivity-enhancing health.* The working environment, particularly the psychosocial environment, has become an object of increasing concern among the social parties. An unhealthy psychosocial working environment can lead to physical and mental health problems and sickness absence. At the same time, a poor psychosocial work environment leads to poor communication, lack of loyalty to the company, a high turnover rate – in short, productivity losses. Therefore, there has been a common interest in improving the psychosocial working environment.

We can hardly conclude that the Nordic model has been a protective buffer against neo-liberalism. On the contrary, the model has widely embraced neo-liberalism, and adapted to it to ensure its own survival: the social parties do not oppose market forces, they accept and adapt to them. The social parties contribute to a regulated and predictable implementation of market mechanisms. By following the neo-liberal trends and seeking to shape the neo-liberal policies, instead of opposing the neo-liberal flow, the trade unions have succeeded in remaining in touch with the entire labour market and have managed to maintain a high employment rate and a high degree of equality.

Does this mean that we can reject the criticism of neo-liberalism? In our opinion, no. Market competition is for many experienced as a life of high speed and unpredictability. In the Nordic region, employees also experience individualization of responsibility for their own working life. Inequality is growing, even in the Nordic countries, only to a lesser extent than in other countries. However, the Nordic experience shows that neo-liberalism can be shaped.

Norway has not until now followed the path of neo-liberalism to the same extent as Denmark. Norway still has centralized wage formation, and the government is in charge of a large part of the labour market and related social policy. On the other hand, Norway has privatized many key companies that were previously run by the state, such as the postal service, railways and the distribution of alcohol. Political governance was replaced with corporate governance structures in hospitals and social services in the early 2000s, as in many other European countries. A Social-Democratic government introduced new public management as a public variety of neo-liberalism in the early 1990s (see Chapter 4 of this volume). In addition, the ban on private intermediation and hiring out of labour was lifted in 2000. Thus, an important part of the regulatory framework that constituted the standard employment relationship was removed. The ban legally protected the bilateral employment relationship consisting of a worker and an employer, where the worker was under the direct supervision of the employer. The bilateral employment relationship was, and still is, the institutional prerequisite for industrial relations consisting of employers and workers (in contrast to the self-employed). However, as mentioned in Chapter 1, the Norwegian variant of the standard employment relationship was not generally dismantled.

Summary of the historical background to the Danish and Norwegian varieties of the Nordic model

Employment relations in the Nordic countries are regulated by a wide range of institutions established through more than 100 years of conflicts, struggles and compromises.

In terms of institutional structure, there are quite significant differences between the Nordic countries. However, there is considerable similarity between them with regard to institutionalized practice. What characterizes all the Nordic countries is a general acceptance that employers and employees have conflicting interests, which entitle both employers and employees to organize themselves collectively.

Often it is possible to resolve conflicts between employers and employees informally through dialogue between management and union representatives. In other cases, conflicts will be resolved at the negotiating table. Finally, sometimes open conflicts break out. Labour market institutions vary considerably between the Nordic countries; however, the institutionalized approach to solving problems is quite similar. The Nordic model is characterized less by a particular institutional structure and more by a particular approach or method. The Nordic model (or approach) was created through tough conflicts between workers and employers in the last decade of the 19th century and the first three decades of the 20th century.

In the subsequent social-democratic era, the development of working life became a central aspect of building a social-democratic society. Employment should be secure, pay should be fair and people should be treated with respect and dignity. In addition, work should be democratic with a high degree of worker influence and with the democratization of business operations and development.

Since the mid-1980s, the social-democratic project has been weakened and the key goal is now to ensure productivity and competitiveness, so that employment and welfare can be maintained. Democracy is no longer a goal in itself, but involvement of employees can be a good means of achieving productivity.

The basic narrative about differences of interest and possible compromises in favour of both parties is still strong. The Nordic approach has therefore created a special version of neo-liberalism. In our view, however, there is a danger that neo-liberal thinking will weaken the Nordic approach to handling labour market problems. If the development of competitiveness is the main common goal, why not let the most skilled experts take care of the development of working life? Why not replace union representatives and working environment representatives with well-qualified HR professionals? Why not transfer the activities previously conducted in the cooperation committees to the HR departments, which can use a professional approach in consulting employees?

The labour market institutions have been maintained. However, we also see the disappearance of some features of these institutions in favour of expert approaches to solving problems (see Chapter 4). This may undermine the Nordic approach to conflict resolution and the building of social relations.

References

Bjørnhaug, I. & Halvorsen, T. (2009) *Medlemsmakt og samfunnsansvar (1935–1969) [The Power of the Members and Social Responsibility (1935–1969]*, Bind 2 i LOs historie 1899–2009, Oslo: Pax.

Bjørnson, Ø. (1990) *På klassekampens grunn (1900–1920) Arbeiderbevegelsens historie i Norge [On the Battlefield of Social Class Conflicts. The History of the Labour Movement in Norway]*, Oslo: Tiden Norsk forlag A/S.

Bull d.y., E. (1979) *Norge i den rike verden: Tiden etter 1945 [Norway in the Rich World after 1945]*, Norges historie. Bd. 14. Oslo: Cappelen.

Christensen, L. K., Kolstrup, S. & Hansen, A. E. (2015) *Arbejdernes historie i Danmark 1880–2000 [The Workers' History in Denmark 1880–2000]*, Copenhagen: Saxo.

Debes, I. (1919) *Økonomisk demokrati. Arbeidernes andel i bedriftsledelsen [Economic Democracy. The Workers' Share of Management in the Companies]*, Kristiania, Norway: Steenske Forlag.

Due, J. & Madsen, J. S. (2008) The Danish Model of Industrial Relations: Erosion or Renewal, *Journal of Industrial Relations*, 50(3). http://journals.sagepub.com/doi/10.1177/0022185608090004.

Due, J., Madsen, J. S. & Jensen, C. S. (1994) *The Survival of the Danish Model: A Historical Sociological Analysis of the Danish System of Collective Bargaining*, Copenhagen: FAOS.

Falkum, E. (2008) Makt og opposisjon i norsk arbeidsliv [Power and Opposition in the Norwegian Working Life], PhD dissertation, Oslo: Universitetet i Oslo.

Friedman, M. & Friedman, R. (1980) *Free to Choose. A Personal Statement*, San Diego, CA: Harcourt.

Galenson, W. (1955) *Arbejder og arbejdsgiver i Danmark [Workers and Employers in Denmark]*, Copenhagen: H. C. Ørsted.

Hall, P. & Soskice, D. (eds) (2001) *Varieties of Capitalism: The Institutional Foundation of Comparative Advantage*, Oxford, UK: Oxford University Press.

Heiret, J. (2003) Et nasjonalt system i en internasjonal verden 1978–2003 [A National System in an International World 1978–2003], In: Heiret, J. et al. (eds) *Arbeidsliv, historie, samfunn*, Bergen, Norway: Fagbokforlaget.

Johansen, P. O. (1977) *Menstadkonflikten 1931 [The 'Menstad' Conflict 1931]*, Oslo: Tiden Norsk Forlag.

Kristensen, P. H. (2003) *Et grænseløst arbejde, en fantastisk fortælling om danske tillidsvalgtes arbejde med at sikre arbejde, indflydelse og fremtid i multinationale datterselskaber [An Unlimited Work, a Fantastic Telling about Danish Shop Stewards' Efforts to Secure Work, Influence and Future in Subsidiaries of Multinationals]*, Copenhagen: Nyt fra Samfundsvidenskaberne.

Kristensen, P. H. & Lilja, K. (2011) *Nordic Capitalisms and Globalization. New Forms of Economic Organization and Welfare Institutions*, Oxford, UK: Oxford University Press.

Langfeldt, K. (1961) *Moskvatesene i norsk politikk [The Moscow Theses in Norwegian Politics]*, Oslo: Universitetsforlaget.

Nyhamar, J. (1994) *Nye utfordringer (1965–1990) Arbeiderbevegelsens historie I Norge [New Challenges (1965–1990). The Labour Movement's History in Norway]*, Oslo: Tiden.

Ousland, G. (1949) *De store kampåra 1921–1931 [The Peak of Class Conflicts 1921–1931]*, Oslo: Arbeidernes faglige landsorganisasjon i Norge.

Rokkan, S. (1986) Norway: Numerical Democracy and Corporate Pluralism, In: Dahl, R. A. (ed.) *Political Oppositions in Western Democracies*, New Haven, CT: Yale University Press.

Samarbejdsnævnet (1997) *Samarbejdsaftalen 50 år [The Basic Agreement 50 Years]*, Copenhagen.

Sippola, M. (2015) Collective Agreements versus Legislation from the Perspective of Values: The Case of Finland, In: *Den nordiske arbejdsmarkedsmodel i global konkurrence*, Copenhagen: Foreningen Norden, 21–31.

Socialdemokratiet (1934) *Danmark for Folket [Denmark for the People]*, Copenhagen.

Standing, G. (2010) *Work after Globalization*, Cheltenham, UK: Edward Elgar.

Streeck, W. (1999) Competitive Solidarity: Rethinking the European Social Model, MPIfG Working Paper 99/8, Cologne, Germany: Max Planck Institute for the Study of Societies.

Terjesen, E. A. (2012) Partsforholdet i arbeidslivet. Kompromiss, allianse, samarbeid eller kamp? [Industrial Relations. Compromises, Alliances, Collaboration or Conflicts?], *Arbeiderhistorie 2012*, Oslo: Arbeiderbevegelsens arkiv og bibliotek.

Thelen, K. (2014) *Varieties of Liberalization and the New Politics of Social Solidarity*, Cambridge, UK: Cambridge University Press.

Thorsrud, E. & Emery, F. (1964) *Industrielt demokrati. Representasjon på styreplan i bedrifter? [Industrial Democracy. Employee Representatives in Companies]*, Oslo: Universitetsforlaget.

Thorsrud, E. & Emery, F. (1970) *Mot en ny bedriftsorganisasjon, Eksperimenter i industrielt demokrati. Fra Samarbeidsprosjektet LO/NAF [Towards a New Organization of Companies. Industrial Democracy Experiments. Report from the Collaboration Experiments]*, Oslo: Tanum.

Part II

Organization and management in a working life perspective

Introduction

Helge Hvid and Eivind Falkum

If the Nordic approach is really to make a difference, it must be felt in everyday life. It is not enough for the Nordic approach to manifest itself in hundreds of meetings, declarations of intent, agreements, laws and regulations. It must also make a difference in people's daily work.

In this Part, we will investigate whether the Nordic approach, characterized by institutionalized conflict and cooperation, has influenced Nordic working life. Thus, we have an ambition to go beyond the perspectives that dominate research in this area. On the one hand, there is a strong tradition of exploring industrial relations but rather independently of organization and leadership. On the other, there is also a strong tradition of studying organization and leadership but detached from the institutional networks that surround jobs and businesses. Various studies of the connection between industrial relations and organization and management are presented in this Part.

Chapter 3: Democracy at work. By Heidi Enehaug, Eivind Falkum and Helge Hvid.

There were strong efforts in the 1960s and 1970s to democratize working life. The objective was firstly to democratize work organization with job designs that supported autonomy and, secondly, to democratize management by employee representatives being heavily involved in management issues. It is argued that these democratization efforts have had a significant effect on working life in the Nordic countries. Democracy in practice is illustrated by a few cases.

Chapter 4: Workplace democracy under pressure. By Eivind Falkum, Ida Drange, Heidi Enehaug and Bitten Nordrik.

Here, the relatively optimistic tone of Chapter 3 is replaced by a more pessimistic tone. The chapter presents studies on the status of co-determination in Norwegian working life. The overall tendency is quite clear. Co-determination is decreasing. However, there are very large differences between different sectors and different types of business.

Chapter 5: International management concepts meeting Nordic working life. By Peter Hagedorn-Rasmussen and Pål Klethagen.

Working life in the Nordic region has been influenced by international production concepts for many decades, which have been adapted to the production, organizational, normative and social contexts in which they entered. In this chapter, it is argued that an active translation of the international concepts is taking place. It is shown how the international concept of lean is translated in the organizational context that adopts the concept. However, it is also demonstrated how the social parties play an active role in this translation process.

Chapter 6: Working environment regulation in Norway and Denmark. By Jan Erik Karlsen, Klaus T. Nielsen and Robert H. Salomon.

Working environment legislation has been more extensive in the Nordic countries than in other countries in two areas. There have been extensive requirements for addressing the working environment in companies, which have included involvement and cooperation and the procedures to be used in local working environment activities. In addition, there are requirements for the psychosocial work environment and the organizational work environment. The chapter presents similarities and differences in regulation. Furthermore, strengths and weaknesses of the regulation of the working environment for everyday practice are discussed.

Chapter 7: New working time and new temporalities: the erosion of influence and rhythms in work. By Henrik Lambrecht Lund.

Flexibility in working hours and location, and flexibility in tasks and relations, is a double-edged sword from a working life perspective. Flexibility can improve work/life balance and create learning opportunities. However, flexibility can also break down rhythms and influence in work. These potential negative issues have scarcely been addressed in the regulation of work. The chapter shows that temporality of working life is an under-regulated area.

Chapter 3

Democracy at work

Heidi Enehaug, Eivind Falkum and Helge Hvid

Democratic work organization to balance differences of interests

As we have described in Chapter 2, the trade union movement gave up the original idea of a democratic working life when they signed general agreements with the employers' associations: in Denmark in 1899, in Norway in 1935 and in Sweden in 1938. It finally confirmed that the right to direct and distribute work lay unambiguously with the employers. Nevertheless, there is hardly any place in the world where employees have more influence on their working conditions than they have in the Nordic countries. In Chapter 1 we mentioned that 85% of employees in Denmark have access to an elected union representative, whose obligation is to represent viewpoints and interests of employees in contact with management.

Some 73% of Norwegian employees and 72% of Danish employees indicate that in their organization there are regular meetings in which employees can express their views about matters of importance at their workplace. No other EU country (except Sweden) is at the same level.

With regard to autonomy at work, learning opportunities and opportunities for employees to apply their own ideas, the Nordic countries also are at the top in the EU (see also Chapter 1, where other indicators of a relatively high degree of influence and participation are mentioned).

Here we will investigate the background for the high levels of influence and participation among Nordic employees. We pay most attention to developments in Norway, where the social parties were already initiating extensive efforts to democratize work in the early 1960s. However, experiences from Denmark will also be included.

We focus on efforts to democratize working life in the last 60 years. In the next chapter (Chapter 4) we will present a recent study of the current state of democracy at work in Norway. However, first we will briefly outline three different approaches to democracy in working life.

Three levels of democracy at work

Unions, employers' associations and the political parties started discussions on democracy at work more than 100 years ago. On the one hand, new market liberalism (Friedman, 2002 [1962]) rejected the desire for democracy at work. The argument was that the whole legitimacy of private companies lies in their ability to generate profits and thus create growth in society. Therefore, the right to take decisions should lie with those who can identify themselves with, and have a personal interest in, profits and growth, namely the owners. Democracy will weaken the focus on earnings, thus weakening the economy to the detriment of us all. We find a similar argument with regard to the public sector. Democratically elected politicians govern public sector institutions, and workplace democracy would be a restriction on parliamentary democracy. In Norway, the basic agreement for employees in government offices and enterprises excluded political issues from autonomy and co-determination arrangements, arguing that it would give governmental employees more political influence than other citizens (Lægreid, 1983).

In opposition to this point of view, we find more conservatively oriented understandings, for instance represented by Emile Durkheim. Durkheim studied the possibilities for creating social cohesion in modern society. For him, the establishment of companies led by both workers and employers was an opportunity to reduce the level of conflict in society (Durkheim, 2014 [1893]). When workers and employers run the companies together, they could settle the many unconstructive labour conflicts. The well-known conservative political scientist Robert Dahl argued for formal and informal democracy in workplaces as an important part of a modern democracy (Dahl, 1985). Pateman (1970) agrees with Dahl when she argues that democracy in the workplace would make citizens able and interested to participate in general democratic processes. The workplace can be a place for learning democracy.

Another argument for the common interest in democracy relates to productivity. Democracy in the workplace has also been economically justified. Democratization of working life can enable workers and employers to work together to improve productivity and quality (Thorsrud & Emery, 1970; Appelbaum et al., 2000; Gustavsen et al., 2010; Ekman et al., 2011). This argument relates to the extensive literature on human resource management. However, in this literature, concepts of motivation replace concepts of democracy at work (Pink, 2009).

Finally, we have the socialist-oriented approach to democratization. Here democracy is a means to strengthen the power of the workers and in that way ensure decent working conditions. Only by gaining power can workers protect themselves against exploitation and alienation at work. There are, however, also representatives from the left wing of the labour movement who argue that so-called democracy at work will weaken the power of labour, since the workers themselves will be co-responsible for the "necessary" exploitation of the workers (Olsen, 1984; Olstad, 2010).

Combinations of conservative-oriented wishes to create harmony and productivity at the workplace and socialist-oriented wishes to defend the interests of workers initiated democratization of working life in many European countries.

Most countries established arrangements that allowed workers to elect shop stewards and safety representatives, giving them the right to negotiate with management on behalf of the employees. Similarly, works councils with union and management representatives discuss and settle issues related to work organization and working conditions, technology and company development (Knudsen, 1995). In many countries, employees have certain options to elect representatives to the company's board of directors.

Finally, many European countries, the United States, Canada and Australia, make efforts to democratize work organization. Employees themselves organize and govern their daily work. The Nordic sociotechnical tradition (Thorsrud et al., 1969) was a source of international inspiration in the 1960s, 1970s and 1980s. The Tavistock Institute in England inspired the development of the Nordic sociotechnical tradition. Trist and his colleagues experimented with self-governing groups (Trist et al., 1963; Thorsrud & Emery, 1964, 1970). Collaboration experiments started in Norway in the 1960s, and the social parties further developed democracy at work during the next two decades.

Democratization of work has not taken place in a linear process, where democracy has increased year by year. On the contrary, there have been some democratic leaps forward in many European countries in some quite short periods. Between these periods, democratization has stagnated. Democratization has taken place in periods when the labour movement was strong and when it was uncertain whether the predominant social structure could survive. This applies to the years after World War I, when the democratization of work took its first steps forward. Democratization at work made significant progress after World War II. This took place in the late 1960s and early 1970s, where there was social unrest and the labour movement was strong.

During these periods, it was possible to make alliances between socialists and conservatives regarding the development of democracy in working life. In some countries, conservative forces dominated these alliances, and employees were now able to elect representatives independent of the trade unions and the labour movement. In other countries, including the Nordic countries, socialist forces dominated the alliances, and the elected shop stewards represented not only the employees of a company but also the trade unions.

Efforts to democratize working life are not unique to the Nordic countries. It seems, however, that the Nordic countries have made the greatest progress in the democratization of working life. We find three levels of democratization in working life:

1 *Democratization of work organization.* Autonomy and learning opportunities for individual workers and for groups of workers.

   Efforts to democratize work organization were largely due to the anti-authoritarian social unrest in the 1960s and 1970s. Internationally, efforts to democratize work organization were referred to in terms of "quality of working life" or "sociotechnical work systems". The Scandinavian countries were strongly involved in this movement.

Efforts to democratize work organization still exist, but strong contradictory trends in work organization hamper the democratization efforts; this will be further discussed in Chapter 4.

2 *Democratization of management.* Workers' representatives are involved in management decisions related to work organization, competence development, introduction of new technology, quality standards, personnel policy, etc.

The first steps to democratize management came about in the years after World War I. Agreements between unions and employers made it possible for employees to elect shop stewards who would be involved in management. Denmark had the first experiences with works councils.

Democratization of management expanded after World War II. Scandinavian countries established works councils in the labour market in general, based on agreements between unions and employers' associations. In both Denmark and Norway, the post-war modernization of industry was implemented through close collaboration between unions and management (see Chapter 2).

Safety representatives with the task of negotiating the quality of the work environment were introduced to the Nordic labour markets in the 1970s. Both employers' associations and trade unions have supported and maintained this aspect of representative democracy at workplaces since then.

3 *Democratization at the strategic level.* Workers combine the roles of owners and employees by buying shares in the companies where they work. This kind of economic democracy is not widespread in Norway, partly as a result of a recommendation by the largest union (LO) to their members not to invest in their own workplace. Employees could lose both their wages and their savings in case of bankruptcy.

In the 1970s, the Scandinavian Social Democrats had a dominant political position. They wanted to use their position to democratize the economy through the creation of employee-managed funds that could eventually have a decisive influence at the strategic level in business. Resistance by employee and union members to such funds proved to be too great, and the Danish and Swedish unions only realized their own pension funds as bases of economic investments. In Norway, pension funds are part of the public social security system.

At the same time, employees at company level were now permitted to elect some representatives to the corporate boards in private companies. In Norway, since a 1972 act (Aksjeloven), workers can demand one-third of board representatives elected by and from all employees in limited companies.

In the following sections, we present the efforts to democratize work organization in Norway. It is characteristic of the Norwegian democratization efforts that they have taken place in an interaction between the social parties who have created the frameworks, researchers who have contributed to the creation and assessment of the content, and the government which has financed research projects and, in some cases, has legislated in support of democracy at work.

Scientific approaches to democracy at work

The idea of democracy at work arose within the framework of the *Quality of Working Life Movement*, an international research agenda that originated in the British Tavistock Institute (Trist et al., 1997). This movement was closely linked to the development of a sociotechnical understanding of organizations, and an international focus on "the importance of autonomy for people's ability to master the demands of working life" (Gustavsen, 2016, p. 1). In 1961, the Norwegian Institute of Industrial Environmental Research, in cooperation with researchers from the Tavistock Institute, started what were called industrial democracy projects (Skorstad, 2002). In 1966, the efforts to democratize working life were further developed when five large manufacturing plants took part in experimental collaboration projects. The Work Psychology Institute (later Work Research Institute) managed the projects under the leadership of Einar Thorsrud. These research and development projects were a new feature of working life at the time, but also a continuation of an already established cooperative tradition (Enehaug, 2018). The social parties shared experiences from production committees in the 1940s, showing that cooperation between them could be mutually beneficial. The basic agreement of 1935 had ended the long line of labour conflicts since the beginning of the 20th century (see Chapter 2 of this volume).

The collaboration experiments developed in the context of a more general objective of democratization of society and working life, and were a criticism of the dominant views on organization. Division of labour and productivity came into focus (Thorsrud & Emery, 1970; Herbst, 1971; Karasek & Theorell, 1990; Gustavsen et al., 2010). The collaboration experiments took place in a working life under cross-pressure; there were demands of specialization and standardization introduced by the rationality movement and supported by logics of planned economy, on the one hand, and demands of free market economy by the Marshall Plan, on the other. By signing the Marshall Plan, the government introduced liberalization of political regulations and free markets in some areas, compared to the plan economy established by the social-democratic government in the first decade after World War II (Bjørnson, 1990; Falkum, 2008). Norway entered an era of mixed economy that affected working life relations with new demands on productivity and efficiency: demands for change, development and innovation.

In the first phase of the collaboration experiments, analyses of different types of representation systems in Norway, Yugoslavia, Germany and the

UK (Skorstad, 2002) showed that "if optimizing the technical system at the expense of the social system, the results achieved will be suboptimal" (Herbst, 1971, p. 12).

Direct democracy (participation) was a necessity, according to Thorsrud and Emery (1964, 1970). Individual participation in development processes was essential to increase the involvement and knowledge of employees in order to reduce alienation at work and simultaneously develop workplaces and productivity. The idea was that individual involvement and autonomy at work would contribute to the development of human resources. Employees' learning capabilities would be enhanced by their participation in decision making, their own "job enrichment", and by "partly self-governing groups". Such learning processes could lead to more interesting work and better working conditions (Heiret, 2003). In other words, there was a need for broader communicative practice when dealing with complex local processes in work organizations (Gustavsen, 2017).

At the Work Research Institute in Norway, the concept of *work organization* was used in relation to autonomy, broad participation and the psychological demands of work (Thorsrud & Emery, 1970; Gustavsen et al., 2010). These demands refer to employee needs to have interesting tasks and varied work processes, to learn and develop competencies, to participate in decision making, to gain managerial recognition, to avoid alienation at work and to fulfil future life expectations at work. Work organization became the central mechanism to link people and environmental factors in companies.

Employee participation in workplace maintenance, as well as the development of jobs and organizations, was the basic methodological principle in the collaboration experiments. Falkum (2008) claims that Thorsrud and Emery (1964) presented both a *management model* and a *model of collaboration*. The collaboration experiments can thus be seen as two-faced: a management face of means and ends, and a collaboration face of employee participation and autonomy at work. As a management model, the collaboration experiments fit in with the early traditions of human resource management at that time (Falkum, 2008). Thorsrud's focus on the autonomy and influence of the individual worker, or groups of workers, as a means to reduce alienation at work and enhance learning and development in work and the workplace in general by direct individual participation, represents a logic that is partly in line with Habermas' (1984) concept of communicative rationality, where communicative actions will ensure that the best argument wins.

There were approaches to democracy at work by other Norwegian social scientists that differed significantly from the collaboration approaches of Thorsrud and Emery (1964). Lysgaard (2001 [1961]) and Holter (1958, 1964) paid less attention to individual participation than the action research programmes. They considered it more important for workers to protect their collective interests. Both Holter and Lysgaard suggested a representative concept of democracy. Unions would represent employees by participation in company decision making (Falkum, 2008).

Thorsrud and the Tavistock researchers were more oriented towards dialogue between managers and employees, and the outcome of development processes, thus more in line with human and labour relations than with the institutionalization of regulatory elements in industrial relations.

Since the early 1960s, this tension between direct participation and representative participation has existed in the understanding of democracy in working life. However, empirical studies seem to show that representative democracy and direct democracy complement each other (see Chapter 4).

The diffusion of workplace democracy

The basic agreements between the employer's confederations and the unions are often described as a prerequisite for democracy at work (Engelstad, 2003; Brøgger, 2007; Falkum & Colbjørnsen, 1997) and as the starting point for mutual recognition of the working life parties (Hasle & Sørensen, 2013). Although the basic agreements paved the way for democracy at work, there were only a few examples of workplace democracy prior to the collaboration experiments in Norway (Maurseth, 1987; Enehaug, 2018).

The social parties in Norway revised and updated their basic agreement in 1966. This new agreement defined democratic tools like works councils and employees' individual rights to participate and influence their work and workplace, i.e. participation and autonomy at work, in line with the ideas of the collaboration experiments of Thorsrud and Emery (1970). The 1966 agreements legitimized individual and direct democracy, as well as collectively oriented, representative democracy, called indirect democracy by some (Ingebriktsen, 1993).

The 1966 version of the basic agreement in Norway was important because of the formal constitution of both individual and collective democratic employee rights. It carried both the structural and the functional approaches from research and workplace studies. It represented the start of a process to institutionalize and legitimize industrial and human relations, in line with Lysaard's and Thorsrud's scientific analyses.

The social parties implemented both representative and direct democracy, both collectively and individually oriented democracy, in many manufacturing industries and plants during the 1960s and 1970s. This first took place in the five large manufacturing plants that participated in the collaborative experiments from 1966 as a permanent effect of that participation (Thorsrud & Emery, 1970). These sociotechnical perspectives and approaches were also present in Denmark, Sweden, Finland, Belgium and the Netherlands. The tradition established individual participation, influence and autonomy at work.

Throughout the 1970s and 1980s, these forms of industrial relations spread to the workplaces, eventually covering most manufacturing industries, through the establishment of works councils, bargaining structures, and organization and management development, in line with the revision of the basic agreement in 1966. Both the individual and collective approaches to workplace democracy were constituted by the basic agreements and further developed in subordinated collective agreements in the different manufacturing industries, such as process manufacturing, mechanical manufacturing industries, and oil and energy. The principles of democracy at work did spread, but at first almost entirely in manufacturing industries.

The social parties in the Norwegian public sector signed their basic agreement in 1980. Originally the state and the unions in the public sector intended to copy the basic agreement in the private sector (LO/NHO). However, only a few months before this plan was to be realized, the participants agreed on another path. The parties made a negotiation-oriented agreement instead of a collaboration-oriented one (Lægreid, 1983). The argument was that collaboration between employees and the state would give state employees more influence in political processes than other citizens could have in political elections, since they would thus participate in political processes and policy making. In this way, employees in the public sector would have rights to information, discussions and negotiations in bodies led and administered by the management. These rights do not cover political issues, and public management defined the issues that were "political". The local government sector also signed its basic agreement in 1980. Later on, basic agreements in private services and commerce were established.

While the 1960s was a decade of development of the individual and collective democratic approaches and of industrial and labour relations, in the 1970s, legal acts and labour laws, decided by the parliamentary system, dominated the institutionalization of industrial and labour relations.

A major accident in a coalmine at Svalbard led to employees' legal right to have representatives on the board of directors of limited companies. The liberal political parties in the national assembly picked up the old debate about employee board representation. They assumed that such representation might have given the board of directors of the mining company the necessary information to prevent the accident. This debate resulted in a new law for limited companies in 1972. Employees obtained the right to demand one-third of the representatives on boards of directors (Hagen, 2010).

In 1980, a public committee, "Skytøen-komiteen", suggested that employees should have half of the members of the boards. However, none of the social parties approved this proposal. The labour union argued that such representation would make employees responsible for board decisions and that they could be co-opted by the private owners (Hagen, 2010). Employers, on the other hand, perceived the proposal to be a new attack on private property rights.

A survey in 2009 concluded that two out of three limited companies had employee board representatives (Falkum et al., 2009). By 2017, register analyses (Hagen, 2017) showed that the number of companies with employee members on the board of directors had been falling dramatically compared to the earlier analyses.

Working environment legislation in Norway has supported democracy at work (see Chapter 5). Since the first working environment regulation in Norway in 1895, the working environment has been very health and medically oriented (Falkum, 2008). With the collaboration experiments and the sociotechnical tradition, social psychological perspectives entered working life. The committee that prepared a new working environment act in 1977 introduced sociotechnical perspectives as well as psychological job demands to the organization of work and workplaces (Gustavsen et al., 2010). The Norwegian Confederation of Trade Unions (LO) strongly supported this new perspective. The national assembly approved the Norwegian Working Environment Act in 1977.

The act stipulated an expansion of democracy at work. All workplaces with ten employees or more were to have health and safety representatives, elected by and for all employees. Workplaces with 50 or more employees had to have work environment councils with management and employee representatives. The law regulates all workplaces, with or without union or employer association membership. In 1980, co-determination at work was defined as a universal right in the Norwegian Constitution.

In Section 12 of the Working Environment Act, the importance of organizational working conditions for health, learning and development surfaced, and it is clear how the psychological job demands formulated through experience in the collaborative industrial experiments directly influenced the legal wording:

> The central issue was – and is – its focusing effect. It brings work organization on the agenda as a theme similar to noise, temperature, unfortunate work postures, hazardous substances, and everything else that can affect the work environment.
>
> (Gustavsen et al., 2010, p. 74)

The expansion of the law to a more holistic understanding of work organization can be said to mark something of a break with former "laws of protection" and a "direct attempt to reconcile ideas from industrial democratic issues with ideas about working environment" (Berg, 1998, p. 36). The act implied a shift in the working environment paradigm. Firstly, by expanding the dominating focus on health and medical issues, such as occupational accidents and diseases, to include attention to psychological and social relations at work. Secondly, by having a strong focus on individual workers and introducing more collective perspectives on work organization, development, and health and safety issues. Thirdly, the Working Environment Act represents a more holistic understanding of "wellbeing" – not just protection from harm but expectations that the needs of people, organizations and society as a whole should be balanced and equated. A viable working environment needed the implementation of a bottom-up-oriented democratic mindset and practice. For Thorsrud, this was about power as:

> [a] force that operates inside conversations rather than outside and that, even if all efforts at new forms of communication between workers and managers were a failure, there is no other way in which the possibility of democracy can be tested.
>
> (Gustavsen, 2018, p. 15)

The construction and institutionalization of democracy at work ended in 1980 (Falkum, 2008). The agreements and laws that institutionalized industrial relations, co-determination and individual and group-based autonomy at work were completed. Revisions arise from time to time in the basic agreement every fourth year.

Democracy at work has a two-pronged legal legitimacy in both basic agreements and labour laws. We hold this to be one of the reasons why the Nordic working life models have seemed to prevail until now, despite labour immigration, globalizing markets, strong standardization of work and continuous technological development of work organization.

The practice of institutional democratic arrangements

Here we will illustrate democracy at work as it was, and still is, practised in Norway. We will present two industrial companies which for a long period actively participated in the efforts to democratize work.

A subsidiary of the Norwegian part of Siemens AG participated in the collaborative experiments of the 1960s. The plant produced electric heaters for households. They organized work in self-governing groups as part of the experiment. This way of organizing work still continued in 1998. At that time, the plant had 110 employees, 1.75 full-time equivalent managerial positions and about 10 self-governed groups of workers. Each group elected one of its members as coordinator. The coordinator shifted from time to time, so that every group member had been in this position after some time. The coordinator was the communication channel between the group and the two managers. The managers were mostly involved with markets, sales and corporate tasks. The groups made all necessary decisions, including planning, production and time schedules needed to fulfil production demands and even new appointments. In 1998, the plant was more profitable than a similar subsidiary in Turkey, despite much higher labour costs. The plant had started this way of organizing work as a participant in the collaboration experiments of the 1960s but dissolved this kind of workers' self-management in 2010 when they adopted corporate models of organization. In this plant, all workers had been group coordinators, and thereby every member had been through a learning process on how to manage and implement plans at work as an example of knowledge building and learning in democratic processes (Falkum et al., 1999).

This was a kind of individualized direct and democratic way of organizing work, compared to collective co-determination through union representatives in company decision making. Some of the five companies that participated in the collaboration experiments implemented similar models of self-managing/self-governing work groups, but mostly as experiments. The Siemens subsidiary is the only participant that ran this model permanently until the beginning of the 2000s. As a way to manage and organize work, the model failed in most of the attempts. However, self-governing groups were supposed to increase individual participation, autonomy, dialogue and productivity. Some attempts succeeded, and some did not. Autonomy is common in Norwegian workplaces as employees have considerable influence on their work situation. However, there are huge differences in how these ideas on labour relations are practised, depending greatly on what managers, unions and employees are able to achieve in collaborative relations. They have to agree on how to understand and implement the models in use. Thus, union–management collaboration as representative democratic arrangements can help the implementation of direct democracy and autonomy at work.

In 1998, the CEO and board of directors of a large corporation in the forestry industry ordered the top manager at a Norwegian paper-mill to reduce costs by 18% within three years. Instead of calling in consultants, he took the problem to the works council at the subsidiary plant. Within three weeks, the council, consisting of shop stewards from all the unions and managerial representatives at the plant, came up with a plan to reduce costs as required:

- To downsize from 700 to 600 employees within the three years, but without dismissals.
- To increase employees with vocational training from 40 to 90% of employees.
- To reduce absence due to work accidents and injuries by 80%.
- To increase profits by NOK 120 million.

The union representatives in the council discussed the plan with their members. They suggested improvements and adjustments. The managerial representatives did the same. The CEO and the works council presented adjustments in a final draft in plenary meetings with all employees. In the end, management and all the unions signed the agreement. This collaboration and the negotiated agreement now became the plan for economic improvement. At the end of the three-year period:

- The downsizing of 100 employees was completed without dismissals, and simultaneously productivity rose by several thousand tons of paper.
- The programme for vocational training showed some results, but far from an increase to 90%.
- In 2003, the plant won an award for the best health, environment and safety (HES) practice and had reduced sickness absence due to accidents by more than the planned 80%.

- Profits increased by NOK 60 million, i.e. half of the planned improvement. This was the result of a huge fall in paper prices on international spot markets.

The board of the corporation was very pleased with the results and encouraged other subsidiaries to copy the project.

Works councils are common in private companies. Union representatives and managerial staff are members. Even some companies without union members establish such bodies to practise democracy at work, especially in small businesses with only a few employees. In the public sector, management arranges meetings with union representatives in order to discuss and eventually negotiate terms of labour or organizational change.

How these collaboration bodies are organized, what they do and the results of their activities vary considerably between companies, even within the same sectors and industries. Representatives from all unions at the workplace participate in such bodies, but practice can vary. These bodies of democracy may be very formal organizations with a strong focus on rules, norms and procedures. They may have formal agendas and protocols for every meeting. However, in some companies, democracy at work can be very informal, with good personal relations between the management and the union representatives (Colman et al., 2011). Thus, case studies and qualitative research are necessary to capture the practical impacts of work life institutions at the workplaces, in addition to data from registers, surveys and process documentation.

Working environment councils are often more formal than works councils. Management and the employee-elected HES representatives have their roles defined in clearer terms. These bodies are responsible for looking into HES problems, discussing solutions for them, proposing measures to handle health and safety issues and ensuring that the company complies with the legal rules and demands. The chairmanship of the working environment councils shifts annually between management and employee representatives. When management chairs the meetings, the employee representatives are secretaries of the council, with the roles reversed at the next meeting.

These are just two examples of companies in Norway that have made great efforts at co-determination as well as individual participation. This democratization took the interests of individuals, organizations and the local community into consideration. However, new organizational models and recipes, new management concepts and the general development of working life in an era of globalization challenge these models (Koch, 2013) (see Chapter 4).

Democracy in Danish working life

Employee influence at the strategic level of companies as part-owners or as members of the company's board of directors has developed in parallel in Norway and Denmark. This also applies to employee influence on management through their elected representatives. In Denmark, democratization of the work organization was considered to be less important than in Norway. Despite this, we find that Norway and Denmark seem to have developed autonomy at work to similar levels. This raises the question: how has democracy in work organization been supported and developed in Denmark? We suggest four factors that may help to explain the relatively high level of democracy in work organization in Denmark:

1 Democratization efforts in Norway and Sweden strongly inspired Denmark. Denmark copied the Norwegian collaborative experiments in the 1970s.
2 Denmark has no research institutions dedicated to the development of corporate democracy as in Norway. However, there has been a proliferation of active working life research at all the universities in the country since the 1970s.
3 The government has only occasionally allocated funds for the development of autonomy in working life (e.g. the fund called "Better Working Life and Productivity" in the 1990s). However, the parties themselves, at the industry level, typically in the context of collective bargaining, have allocated funds, often to a more limited extent, to support the development of autonomy at work.

Compared to other countries, the employees are relatively well organized at company level. This implies that employee representatives are involved in decisions on new technology and organizational changes. Employers' representatives seek to defend employment but also the quality of the psychosocial working environment, including autonomy and learning opportunities at the workplace.

Current challenges for workplace democracy

The current democratic workplace arrangements are practices developed from institutionalized industrial relations. Basic agreements, labour laws, collective bargaining procedures, the organized social parties and the tripartite structures have set the terms for the relations between management, unions and employees. These institutions influence relations, structures and processes at work and thus the organization of work. We have pointed out how democratic arrangements in workplaces are constructed in formal rules, norms and intentions, how they are supposed to work and, not least, how they can vary in practice.

The establishment of the institutional and formal industrial relations took place in a period of strong labour conflicts, class conflicts and disagreements on how to share the values added: the wealth in society. The democratic workplace arrangements that developed throughout the latter half of the 20th century have led to a particular kind of balance between labour and capital interests in the Nordic countries. This balance is fragile and skewed but less so than in other countries and economies. The labour market actors still maintain this fragile balance in the Nordics. The balance provides greater *predictability in politics and economics*, as well as for the social parties on all levels. This perhaps pinpoints the concept of democracy at work, in the Nordic way.

This balance is under pressure from external as well as internal change and development in the Nordic countries, as in most Western countries. The globalization of economies has introduced new markets, competitors and suppliers, and changed economic competition and, thereby, national and industrial economic competitiveness. These economic developments provide new models of organization and management. Some of these models are less compatible with democratic organization at work than others. We address this problem in the next chapter.

Short-term perspectives have become more prominent in recent decades. Shareholder values increasingly dominate parts of the private sector. That makes it more difficult for employee representatives to defend longer-term development of autonomy and learning opportunities at work. The same applies to employee representatives in the public sector, where the institutions focus on achieving short-term goals and quality standards.

The short-term perspective strengthens the growth of precarious working conditions. Employers' demands for a flexible workforce increases employees' financial risks and the predictability of a decent income. The last Part of this book presents research on precarious work.

Foreign owners dominate a growing part of private companies. These owners bring with them new principles of management and organization, and introduce new relations between employees and management alien to the Nordic context. They introduce new production concepts developed under different social conditions from those of the Nordic countries. Chapters 4 and 5 analyse this in detail.

Migrants have entered the Nordics since the large expansion of the EU and its free labour markets in 2004. Migrant workers from East Europe and Asia have taken employment in Norway, especially in building and construction, shipbuilding and low-skilled service industries. They are not used to democratic work organization and industrial relations, and their union density is lower than that of domestic employees.

Within certain sectors, only a minority of the employees are members of a trade union. This is especially true for low-skilled work in the service sector, for instance in hotels and restaurants. Here it is difficult to maintain democratically inspired principles.

New technology increasingly allows for standardization of work in many industries, especially in the oil and gas industries and process manufacturing. Standard operating procedures have replaced the need for specialized education and training in some areas. Work tasks and resource needs are changing. Employees are becoming more replaceable. Employability demands are lower. One might argue that the driving forces of management have taken a U-turn:

new technical solutions involve a renewed focus on standardization, control and surveillance of employees, and the lessons learned in the historical processes of democratization have been left out of the equation. Management becomes a matter of checking that employees are following standard operating procedures instead of facilitating participation, autonomy and learning. In this way, the relations between employees and management are changing and may take a path away from the Nordic democratic organization of work. New technology also paves the way for new solutions, e.g. health technologies have the potential to change elderly care and work conditions in the health sector. The overall consequences of this development still remain to be seen, but European research has already identified polarizing trends in the European working life context:

> On the one hand, we see a neo-Taylorization with the division of work into minor unit operations, more routine work, and increased levels of control at work . . . On the other hand, we see an increased degree of individualization of employees with expert competence who can have a high level of individual negotiating power, given that their expertise is in demand in the marketplace, while at the same time they possess jobs that demand an ever greater degree of autonomy due to complex tasks. [Author's translation]
>
> (NOU, 2010, p. 184)

However, these conditions are not new, and until now, the Nordic democracy model has had the strength to survive the current challenges. On the other hand, as is shown in Chapter 4, democracy in work is on the decline. Nevertheless, as already mentioned, history has taught us that increased democracy usually manifests itself in short periods. Nobody knows when the next sprint for democracy will take place.

References

Appelbaum, E., Berg, P. B., Kalleberg, A. L. & Bailey, T. A. (2000) *Manufacturing Advantage. Why High-Performance Work Systems Pay Off*, Ithaca, NY: Cornell University Press. https://doi.org/10.5860/choice.37-5767.

Berg, A. M. (1998) *Den vanskelige medvirkningen. Arbeidstakermedvirkning i staten 1970–1996 [The Difficult Collaboration. Employee Participation in the State 1970–1996]* (Vol. 5), Oslo: Arbeidsforskningsinstituttet.

Bjørnson, Ø. (1990) *På klassekampens grunn (1900–1920). Arbeiderbevegelsens historie i Norge [In the Class Struggle (1900–1920). The History of the Labour Movement in Norway]*, Oslo: Tiden Norsk Forlag A/S.

Brøgger, B. (2007) Samarbeid som produksjonsfaktor: en introduksjon [Collaboration as a Production Factor: An Introduction], In: Brøgger, B. (ed.) *Å tjene på samarbeid: medvirkning, partssamarbeid, bedriftsutvikling [To Benefit from Collaboration: Participation, Co-Determination, Corporate Development]*, Oslo: Gyldendal akademisk, 11–31.

Colman, H. L., Stemsaker, I. & Tharaldsen, J. E. (eds) (2011) *A Merger of Equals? The Integration of Statoil and Hydro's Oil and Gas Activities*, Bergen, Norway: Fagbokforlaget.

Dahl, R. A. (1985) *A Preface to Economic Democracy*, Berkeley, CA: University of California Press.

Durkheim, E. (2014 [1893]) *The Division of Labour in Society*, New York: Free Press.

Ekman, M., Gustavsen, B., Asheim, B. T. & Pålshaugen, Ø. (eds) (2011) *Learning Regional Innovation. Scandinavian Models*, Basingstoke, UK: Palgrave Macmillan.

Enehaug, H. (2018) Å lære av det gamle, for å forberede seg på det nye. En studie av medvirkningens betydning for organisatorisk utvikling og læring [Learning from the Old, to Prepare for the New. A Study of the Importance of Participation for Organizational Development and Learning], PhD dissertation, Institutt for mennesker og teknologi, Roskilde Universitet, Denmark.

Engelstad, F. (2003) Makt i det norske samfunnet [Power in Norwegian Society], In: Frønes, I. & Kjølsrød, L. (eds) *Det norske samfunn [Norwegian Society]*, Oslo: Gyldendal Akademisk, 42–68.

Falkum, E. (2008) Makt og opposisjon i norsk arbeidsliv [Power and Opposition in Norwegian Working Life], PhD dissertation, Universitetet i Oslo.

Falkum, E. & Colbjørnsen, T. (1997) Corporate Efficiency and Employee Participation, In: Gustavsen, B., Colbjørnsen, T. & Pålshaugen, O. (eds) *Developing Coalitions in Working Life*, Amsterdam: John Benjamins.

Falkum, E., Eldring, L. & Colbjørnsen, T. (1999) *Medbestemmelse og medvirkning. Bedriftsutvikling mot år 2000 [Co-Determination and Participation. Corporate Development towards the Year 2000]*, Oslo: Fafo-rapport 324.

Falkum, E., Hagen, I. M. & Trygstad, S. C. (2009) *Bedriftsdemokraties tilstand. Medbestemmelse, medvirkning og innflytelse i 2009 [State of Corporate Democracy. Co-Determination, Involvement and Influence in 2009]*, Oslo: Fafo-rapporte 2009, 35.

Friedman, M. (2002 [1962]) *Capitalism and Freedom*, Chicago, IL: Chicago University Press.

Gustavsen, B. (2016) *Fred Emery og andre fredianere: teoretisk diskurs i Quality of Working Life-bevegelsen [Fred Emery and other Frisians: Theoretical Discourse in the Quality of Working Life Movement]*, Oslo: Arbeidsforskningsinstituttet, Høyskolen i Oslo og Akershus, 1–10.

Gustavsen, B. (2017) General Theory and Local Action: Experiences from the Quality of Working Life Movement, *Nordic Journal of Working Life Studies*, 7. https://tidsskrift.dk/njwls/article/view/96692.

Gustavsen, B. (2018) *Einar Thorsrud. Contribution to "Thinkers on Organizational Change"*, Basingstoke, UK: Palgrave Macmillan.

Gustavsen, B., Qvale, T. U., Sørensen, B. A., Midtbø, M. & Engelstad, P. H. (2010) *Innovasjonssamarbeid mellom bedrifter og forskning: den norske modellen [Innovation Collaboration between Companies and Research: The Norwegian Model]*, Oslo: Gyldendal Akademisk.

Habermas, J. (1984) *The Theory of Communicative Action. Volume One, Reason and the Rationalization of Society*, Boston, MA: Beacon Press.

Hagen, I. M. (2010) Det mektige mindretallet. Ansatterepresentasjon i styret mellom Corporate Governance og Industrial Relations [The Mighty Minority. Employee Representation in the Board between Corporate Governance and Industrial Relations], PhD dissertation, Universitetet i Oslo.

Hagen, I. M. (2017) Flere styrer: færre ansattevalgte styremedlemmer [More Boards: Fewer Employee-Elected Board Members], *Søkelys på arbeidslivet 4/17 (Vol 34)*, Oslo. doi: 10.18261/issn.1504-7989-2017-04-02.

Hasle, P. & Sørensen, O. H. (2013) Employees as Individually and Collectively Acting Subjects: Key Contributions from Nordic Working Life Research, *Nordic Journal of Working Life Studies*, 3: 9–29.

Heiret, J. (2003) Samarbeid og statlig styring 1945–1977 [Cooperation and Government Management 1945–1977], In: Heiret, J., Venneslan, K. & Bjørnson, Ø. (eds) *Arbeidsliv, historie og samfunn. Norske arbeidslivsrelasjoner i historisk, sosiologisk og arbeidsrettslig perspektiv [Working Life, History and Society. Norwegian Working Relations in a Historical, Sociological and Labour Law Perspective]*, Bergen, Norway: Fagbokforlaget, 109–176.

Herbst, P. G. (1971) *Demokratiseringsprosessen i arbeidslivet: Sosio-tekniske studier [The Process of Democratization in the Workplace. Sociological Studies]*, Oslo: Universtitetsforlaget.

Holter, H. (1958) Disputes and Tensions in Industry, In: Lauwerys, J. A. (ed.) *Scandinavian Democracy. Development of Democratic Thought & Institutions in Denmark, Norway and Sweden*, Copenhagen: The Danish Institute, The Norwegian Office of Cultural Relations, The Swedish Institute, in cooperation with The American-Scandinavian Foundation.

Holter, H. (1964) Ønsker om medbestemmelse og selvbestemmelse på en del norske arbeidsplasser [Desires for Co-Determination and Self-Determination in a Number of Norwegian Workplaces], *Tidsskrift for Samfunnsforskning*, No 1/1964, Oslo: Universitetsforlaget.

Ingebriktsen, B. (1993) *Deltakelse og innflytelse [Participation and Influence]*, IFIM-notat 19/93, Trondheim, Norway: SINTEF.

Karasek, R. & Theorell, T. (1990) *Healthy Work: Stress, Productivity, and the Reconstruction of Working Life*, New York: Basic Books.

Knudsen, H. (1995) *Employee Participation in Europe*, London: Sage Publications.

Koch, C. (2013) When the Blues Meet the Blue Eye, In: Sanberg, Å. (ed.) *Nordic Lights. Work, Management and Welfare in Scandinavia*, Stockholm: SNS Förlag.

Lægreid, P. (1983) Medbestemmingsretten i den offentlege sektor og det politiske demokrati [The Right to Vote in the Public Sector and Political Democracy], In: Bergh, T. (ed.) *Deltakerdemokratiet. Demokrati og samfunnsstyring [Participating Democracy. Democracy and Social Governance]*, Oslo: Universitetsforlaget.

Lysgaard, S. (2001 [1961]) *Arbeiderkollektivet [The Workers' Collective]*, Oslo: Universitetsforlaget.

Maurseth, P. (1987) *Gjennom kriser til makt (1920–1935). Arbeiderbevegelsens historie i Norge [Through Crises towards Power (1920–1935). The History of the Labour Movement in Norway]*, Oslo: Tiden Norsk Forlag.

NOU (2010) *Medvirkning og medbestemmelse i arbeidslivet. [Participation and Co-determination in the Work Life]*. Oslo: Arbeidsdepartemente

Olsen, O. J. (1984) *Makt og motstand: en studie av bedriftsorganisasjon og fagorganisasjon ved Eidanger Salpeterfabrikker 1945–1970 [Power and Resistance: A Study of Corporate Organization and Professional Organization at Eidanger Salpeter Factories 1945–1970]*, The University of Bergen, MORAL-prosjektet 12.

Olstad, F. (2010) Veien fram til hovedavtalen 1899–1935 [The Road to the Main Agreement 1899–1935], In: Bergh, T. (ed.) *Avtalt spill. Hovedavtalen 75 år [Agreed Game. The Main Agreement 75 Years]*, Oslo: LO/NHO.

Pateman, C. (1970) *Participation and Democratic Theory*, Cambridge, UK: Cambridge University Press.

Pink, D. H. (2009) *Drive. The Surprising Truth About What Motivates Us*, New York: Riverhead Books.

Skorstad, E. J. (2002) *Organisasjonsformer. Kontinuitet eller forandring? [Organization Forms. Continuity or Change?]*, Oslo: Gyldendal Norsk Forlag AS.

Thorsrud, E. & Emery, F. E. (1964) *Industrielt demokrati. Representasjon på styreplan i bedriftene? [Industrial Democracy. Board Representation in the Companies?]*, Oslo: Universitetsforlaget.

Thorsrud, E. & Emery, F. E. in cooperation with Trist, E. (1969) *Form and Content in Industrial Democracy. Some Experiences from Norway and other European Countries*, London: Tavistock.

Thorsrud, E. & Emery, F. E. (1970) *Mot en ny bedriftsorganisasjon. Eksperimenter i industrielt demokrati fra Samarbeidsprosjektet LO/NAF [Towards a New Corporate Organization. Experiments in Industrial Democracy from the Collaborative Project LO/NAF]*, Oslo: Johan Grundt Tanum Forlag.

Trist, E., Emery, F. E. & Murray, H. E. (1997) *Volume III: The Socio-Ecological Perspective*, Philadelphia, PA: University of Pennsylvania Press.

Trist, E. L., Higgin, G. W., Murray, H. & Pollock, A. B. (1963) *Organizational Choice: Capabilities of Groups at the Coal Face under Changing Technologies*, London: Tavistock Publications.

Chapter 4

Workplace democracy under pressure

Eivind Falkum, Ida Drange, Heidi Enehaug and Bitten Nordrik

Introduction

Workplace democracy helped to balance the different interests of labour and capital after World War II in Norway. The main intention of the basic agreements in the Nordics was to reduce the high levels of labour conflicts (see Chapters 1, 2 and 3 of this volume). The social partners agreed on how to disagree in order to avoid manifest conflicts. Chapter 3 outlined the establishment, implementation and development of democratic workplace structures from the 1940s. Here we focus on the practice of workplace democracy today.

An analysis of democratic practices at workplaces in Denmark and Norway shows some decrease in employee participation, autonomy and influence in work organization and work situations, as well as co-determination by unions (Dølvik et al., 2015). Hagen (2017) shows a decline in employee representation on company boards. Nordrik and Falkum (2017) show that the role of working environment committees and health and safety representatives has diminished at some workplaces as well.

The global economy and distribution of ownership seem to be introducing new concepts of organization and management that may challenge practices of workplace democracy (Falkum et al., 2017). This chapter presents an analysis of the present situation and possible future of the Nordic working life models with reference to Denmark and Norway. To what degree will the introduction of new and international models of governance and management challenge Norwegian workplace democracy?

Four concepts of governance at workplaces

In a study of co-determination, we developed four main categories of management and governance in use. We defined the four ideal types of governance using theoretical assumptions based on organization and management theories, empirical observations in a series of working life case studies and factor analysis and reliability tests of survey data. The four different ideal types will appear in most companies, but in various degrees (Figure 4.1). The survey allows us to

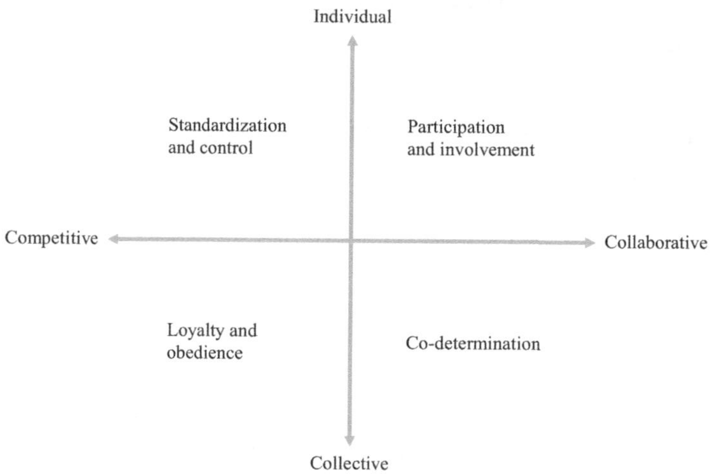

Figure 4.1 Four ideal models of governance

measure the extent to which the different types govern company organization, how they combine and how they are related to each other.

Governance of work organizations rests on a shared understanding of realities at work. Lukes (2005) defines thought control as a major premise of power and the distribution of power in society in his new version of *Power, a Radical View* from 1974. He refers to Foucault (1982) when he emphasizes thought control as a third dimension of power in society. Foucault claimed that the ability to establish shared and institutionalized understandings of realities represented "truth regimes" but also that such regimes are reversible and change over time. Power to define "thought control" and "truth regimes" would dominate the whole organization as a strong form of governance. The shared understandings of realities can determine the direction in organizations but also set some cognitive limitations on what we pay attention to. To establish shared understanding of realities is a basic premise in the governance of organized activities.

The four concepts in the model in Figure 4.1 represent different ways to establish such shared understandings of realities within the work organization. Shared understandings are a cognitive framework for the development of policies, goals and objectives that make all those involved move in the same direction.

Shared understandings of realities and situations can arise from open and free discussions in democratic systems where everyone can participate and contribute to the development of such understandings. In authoritarian systems, those in charge will define how to understand realities. They have the power and legitimacy to make subordinates accept and commit to the understandings presented, irrespective of whether they are false or true. Shared understandings at workplaces may also be the result of planned manipulation of the participants' perceptions and conceptions of realities.

The four concepts in the model represent different ways to make organizations come to shared understandings of realities and situations, to set goals and to implement planned policies in line with these understandings.

Standardization and control refers to models and ideas of standard operating procedures. The standards lead to actions assumed to be rational solutions, according to the ruling understandings of realities. Standardization of processes reduces complexity, increases efficiency and reduces quality variations. Control makes processes predictable and reduces uncertainty at workplaces. The shared understanding is to do as expected without critical questions, as change is introduced from the top down.

Standardization individualizes labour relations between management and employees, as it determines the organization of work instead of managers. Relations between managers and employees become less important since the standards replace some of the managerial orders and commands, and since control of individual performance can be more or less automatic by way of forms, routines and formal procedures, which are often digitalized. Since standards decide what a worker does and thereby what the worker needs to know, external courses may become less important than internal training. In some workplaces, one only needs to know the standards that are easy to learn. In this way, employees become more replaceable than they would be in work organizations based on individual expertise. Lean production, conceived to be an archetypical form of standardization, appears in many shapes (Womack et al., 1990). Standardization of work operations and measures of deviations from the standards are an important example in both manufacturing and the public sector. New public management presented new forms of governance that introduced corporate structures, user/customer orientations and programmes of standardization to public services.

Standardization and control mostly imply individual goals and performance measures, but in a collective perspective they apply to all individuals that participate in identical work operations. Competition between colleagues is supposed to improve performance and productivity. Manufacturing, construction, and oil and gas companies standardize work operations for health and safety reasons, as well as to enhance productivity. The standards in themselves express understandings of realities institutionalized in the performance of actions. Standardization and control are mostly top-down oriented.

Participation and involvement is the individual part of the Norwegian collaborative working life model. Thorsrud and Emery (1964) introduced the terms employee "participation" and "involvement" (medvirkning) to Norway in their design of the collaboration experiments in manufacturing industries (see Chapters 2 and 3). (There is, however, no English word that covers the concept of "medvirkning" exactly). According to this model, individual employees should make improvements in their own work, in their own work situation and at their workplace in general. Some of the companies that participated in the collaboration experiments organized work in self-governing groups. The experiments aimed to increase productivity and reduce alienation of workers in labour processes by increasing individual autonomy at work.

The basic agreement of 1966 stipulated employee rights to participate and thus become involved in workplace development. Participation and involvement were conceived as an individual entitlement to influence the work organization. We introduce the concepts as a model of governance and management at the workplace, and as a way to use close relations, communication and employee autonomy as a toolbox for running and developing the workplace and improving production and productivity.

Thorsrud and Emery (1964, 1970) launched their version of employee participation as a model of collaboration. In Norway, manufacturing companies were the first to implement the model. The experiments introduced participation as a model of collaboration and consensus making, not a model of governance and management. Later studies, however, interpret Thorsrud and Emery's model of participation as a management model and one that was intended to support productivity and efficiency at the company level (Falkum, 2008). This dual interpretation of employee participation and involvement as a model of collaboration as well as management allows for both top-down and bottom-up orientations.

Open communication and dialogue between individual employees and their immediate superiors and colleagues establish a consensus on what to do and how to do it: how to perform the work and organize the workplace, i.e. continuous and collaborative development of shared understanding of realities at the workplace on an individual level. The model allows for different employee and management opinions and understandings. They can solve differences of interests through negotiations between individual employees and their immediate superiors, and in teams of workers responsible for certain tasks, sometimes in self-governed groups. Such negotiated compromises at the individual level are likely to rely on mutual trust and respect, in other words negotiations on equal terms in a democratic manner.

Loyalty and obedience is a model that we have identified in recent studies in social psychology and organization (Ulrich et al., 2009; Ulrich & Ulrich, 2010). We include transformation management in this concept. The models we refer to introduce the values of the owners and top management as the objectives of the company. Value-based management is another label of this model. Employee acceptance of the established values, and commitment to them as norms and guidelines for attitudes, can institutionalize loyalty to the established understanding of realities in a company. This, however, implies that employees obey the managerial policies, goals and decisions. Without employee acceptance of and obedience to the established understanding of realities, loyalty to management will be fragile.

This model may very well produce employee loyalty and obedience based on true employee convictions that the established values represent the "one best way" for the company. In one scenario, this may actually be shown to be the case. In another, employers' understandings of realities are very convincing and employees really believe in them, without proof of evidence. A third scenario is that the employees do not really believe in the managerial values, but the sanctions against opposition lead to loyalty and obedience. Finally, employers may manipulate employees to believe in managerial values, policies and plans that in reality are a construct without evidence. In all these cases, the model is likely to shape employee loyalty in action, while the legitimacy of management may still be false. The three latter cases may lead to unstable relations between management and employees. Unpredictability and social insecurity may be intrinsic to this model when the management–employee relationship is poor.

Relations between management and employees are the main tools in this model. Relations are important, since employees are expected to adopt and commit to proclaimed norms and values. Performance measures support employee commitment to the values of employers by rewarding good and sanctioning bad performance.

Transformation management is about establishing a specified understanding of realities as the truth of a company and its context. Managers use different methods to motivate their employees to perform at their best and to implement managerial decisions and plans as expected. Competition between colleagues will motivate and improve individual performance, according to some studies (Busch et al., 2015). Some of the studies of transformation management introduce the idea that anxiety at the workplace will improve performance (Moxnes, 2012).

Loyalty and obedience, as we define them, represent methods, assumptions and tests in a range of motivation triggers. Busch et al. (2015) distinguish between internal and external motivation. Management may reward improvements and good results with external goods like bonuses. Kuvaas (2006) showed that material rewards had to be very large in order to affect performance and enterprise results significantly. He found that intrinsic motivation had better effects on individual performance. Intrinsic motivation would improve through individual development of competencies, organizational identification and other personal aspects. External motivation is linked to transaction management, while intrinsic motivation is connected to transformation management. Some research has found evidence that transformation management improves performance.

To establish a shared understanding of workplace realities is the main key to ways to govern and manage work organization that involve loyalty and obedience. The model rests strongly on the management–employee relationship, as the employees are expected to commit to managerial goals and values. Companies that apply this model are more likely to be top-down than bottom-up oriented.

Co-determination (medbestemmelse) is the final managerial model. It is the collectively oriented element in the Nordic working life model. Workers are unionized. Democratic structures like wage negotiations, HES committees, employees as board members and works councils are in place. Top and middle managers appreciate unions and include their representatives in planning, decision making as well as the implementation of change and improvement schemes. Democratic structures become the dominant model and principles of the governance, management and organization of companies.

Co-determination is linked to decision making and representative democratic structures. In addition to determining rules of participation and autonomy at work, the Norwegian basic agreement in 1966 established the concept of co-determination as unions' rights to be informed of workplace change and restructuring, and to participate in company decision making in councils that include the workplace parties (Herbst, 1971). Like participation and involvement, we define co-determination as a model of governance and management practised in the Nordic countries. The basic agreements reflect and represent shared understandings of working life realities. The parties negotiated for about five years before they signed the first basic agreement in Norway in 1935. The shared understandings and interests are the result of negotiated compromises that cover most intentions, relations and expectations that the working life parties could agree on.

We define co-determination as a model for governance and management in practice at the workplace. The Norwegian working life model is often said to work in the same way anywhere. However, research gives reason to question this. Management and organization studies show firstly that such models flourish in great numbers and varieties, and secondly that any model will be adapted to the company that uses it (Røvik, 2007). How employers and employees interpret the models will affect their implementation in practice. Studies of mergers and acquisitions show that the parties involved have different interpretations, and that what they had thought of as agreed policies may prove to be false compromises when it comes to implementation (Colman et al., 2011).

Shared understandings of realities are key for governance but not enough alone to make intentions determine results at the workplace. What comes on the company agenda, how decisions are made, how resources are controlled and who has the power to implement policies will all influence the correlation between intentions and results in organizations (Engelstad, 1999; Engelstad & Hagelund, 2015).

Most studies on democracy at work treat employee participation and union co-determination as core elements of the Nordic working life model (Gustavsen et al., 2001; Levin, 2002; Ekman et al., 2011). In this chapter, we define employee participation and involvement and union co-determination as democratically oriented principles and models of governance and management at workplaces. Employee participation and co-determination are managerial and organizational means and tools, not only employee and union rights and obligations, in this perspective.

Measuring the four models

In 2016, we launched an annual survey on co-determination (Medbestemmelsesbarometeret, Falkum et al., 2017). A partnership of five Norwegian unions[1] is funding the survey. We also ran the survey in 2017, and we analyse the present state of workplace democracy in Norway on the basis of the 2017 data. We sent the survey to a sample of 6,000 employees, drawn from a respondent panel of 45,000 inhabitants. Kantar TNS owns the panel, drew the sample and collected 3,054 responses in 2017. The net sample of 51% response is representative of the Norwegian workforce with regard to independent variables such as age, gender, education, job, industry, size of enterprise (number of employees) and region of Norway.

We used the above theoretical discussion and definition of the four forms of governance and management to identify questions in the survey that measured characteristics of each of them. We then ran reliability tests to measure the inter-correlations between the chosen variables. Cronbach's alpha of 0.7 or above meant that the chosen variables could merge in an index to measure each model of governance and management.

Standardization and control were measured using the statements below and the scale 1 = completely disagree to 5 = completely agree, Cronbach's alpha = 0.85:

- "Top management is getting more and more power"
- "The manager role has been bureaucratized during the last decade"
- "Middle managers have low influence on enterprise governance"
- "Management is more and more about control and measuring deviances"
- "Formal guidelines reduce managers' opportunities to use their competencies".

Loyalty and obedience were measured using the scale 1 = completely disagree to 5 = completely agree, Cronbach's alpha = 0.89:

- "Top management does not like discussion of critical issues"
- "Criticism is interpreted as lack of loyalty"
- "We compete with each other"
- "Managers spend a lot of time controlling employees' attitudes"
- "Managers spend a lot of time controlling employees' behaviour".

For participation and involvement, we used the same scale, Cronbach's alpha = 0.69:

- "My immediate superior is open for suggestions when we disagree on facts"
- "My primary manager motivates me to make an effort"

- "Managers lead the enterprise in motivating ways"
- "I have authority to make decisions on work issues".

Co-determination had the same scale, Cronbach's alpha = 0.89:

- "We dare to express our opinions about managerial decisions"
- "The management meets opposition constructively"
- "Top management is open for suggestions when we disagree on facts"
- "The management welcomes critical comments on business performance"
- "Relations between top management and employees are good".

Comparing autonomy at work in 2009 and today

A survey from 2009 contained questions about employee influence at work (Falkum et al., 2009). The 2016 and 2017 co-determination surveys adopted some of these questions and analysed the answers identically for comparison.

Figure 4.2 shows that Norwegian employees have very high influence on their work situation (autonomy). However, it is statistically significantly much lower in 2016 and 2017 than it was in 2009. Autonomy at work has fallen during the last decade. In 2016, we asked the respondents, "In what direction do you think working life is developing?":

- 45% answered, "in a more authoritarian direction"
- 10% answered, "in a more democratic direction"
- 21% said, "don't know"
- 24% said, "no change".

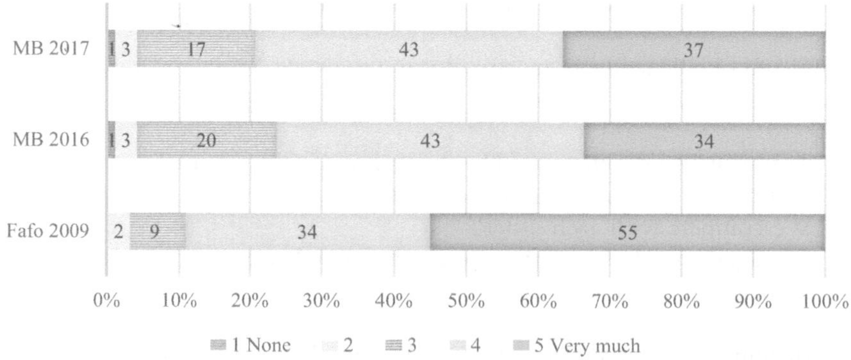

Figure 4.2 Employee-experienced influence on their own labour situation (index of autonomy at work: How much influence do you have on: (1) your work tasks, (2) the quality of your work, (3) performance of your tasks) in 2009, 2016 and 2017

The responses from 2017 showed only insignificant differences from those of 2016.

These results question the common assumption that Nordic working life is stable and democratic. The participants perceived working life to be developing in a less democratic and employee-friendly manner than one would assume from recent studies of the Nordic model (Dølvik et al., 2015).

Formal democratic structures and managerial models in use

Nordic working life is generally supposed to involve collaboration between unions and management that leads to consensus and reduces levels of labour conflicts. Strikes and lockouts have been very few in number in Norway, while Denmark experienced significantly more labour conflicts in the 1990s and 2000s, but these have declined during the 2010s.

Unions and management, despite the common perception of consensus and harmony, often disagree on their respective interests at workplaces. The agreed democratic structures are tools to reach consensus on differing interests, mostly in terms of compromises. Since the late 2000s, however, we observe that a growing number of companies establish democratic structures formally, according to labour laws and agreements, while their actual practice serves managerial interests that differ from the legal and formal democratic intentions (Nordrik & Falkum, 2017).

A comparison of the results of the co-determination survey in 2017 with the workplace democracy survey of 2009 (Falkum et al., 2009) shows only minor and insignificant differences in terms of the presence of formal democratic structures such as unions, negotiated wage formation, works councils, shop stewards, employee-elected HES representatives and working environment committees. However, based on register statistics, Hagen (2017) finds a significant decline in employee representation on company boards.

We find only minor differences between private enterprises with foreign and domestic owners. More surprisingly, employees at workplaces with formal democratic structures (collective bargaining, basic agreements, employee board representation and labour unions) show similar results for influence at work as employees without such structures. As mentioned, 45% of Norwegian employees conceive working life to be moving in an authoritarian direction. How can that be, when we observe no significant change in the presence of most of the formal democratic structures?

In Table 4.1 we see that employee influence correlates negatively with standardization and control, and with loyalty and obedience, but positively with co-determination, and with participation and involvement (autonomy). Most correlations are moderate to strong. Standardization and control show a strong positive correlation with loyalty and obedience, but a negative correlation with co-determination, as well as with participation and involvement.

Table 4.1 Correlations between the four management/governance models and employee influence at workplaces in 2017 (Pearson's R, significance (p, two tailed))

	1	*2*	*3*	*4*	*5*	*6*	*7*
1 Standardization and control	1						
2 Loyalty and obedience	0.67**	1					
3 Participation and involvement	−0.42**	−0.50**	1				
4 Co-determination	−0.50**	−0.60**	0,74**	1			
5 Influence on own work situation	−0.24**	−0.31**	0.44**	0.40**	1		
6 Influence on work organization	−0.25**	−0.22**	0.41**	0.38**	0.53**	1	
7 Influence on governance	−0.31**	−0.20**	0.53**	0.49**	0.46**	0.53**	1

** p = 0.001 (sig.)

Norwegian Police Federation, n = 2890–1096.

Management models such as standardization and control, and loyalty and obedience, seem to be quite incompatible with the working life models practised in the Nordics. Furthermore, Table 4.1 shows consistency in the Nordic model. Employees who have strong influence on their own work situation are more likely to have strong influence on the organization of work and on the governance and organization of their company. These three types of influence correlate positively with co-determination, and with participation and involvement, and negatively with standardization and control as well as with loyalty and obedience. These findings are also valid when we exclude respondents with managerial positions from the analysis. Working life seems to divide into two parts: one dominated by the values and principles in the Nordic collaboration models, and one that applies principles from the Anglo-American concepts of organization, governance and management. What are the contextual boundaries in this division?

Sectors, industries and ownership

The general view of Nordic working life gives the impression that the working life model works in an almost similar way at any workplace. By comparing sectors and industries, we may test this idea of the "one and only way" to practise democracy at work, and perhaps reveal differences.

The difference between employee influence in private and local government enterprises is quite small, while employees in enterprises owned or

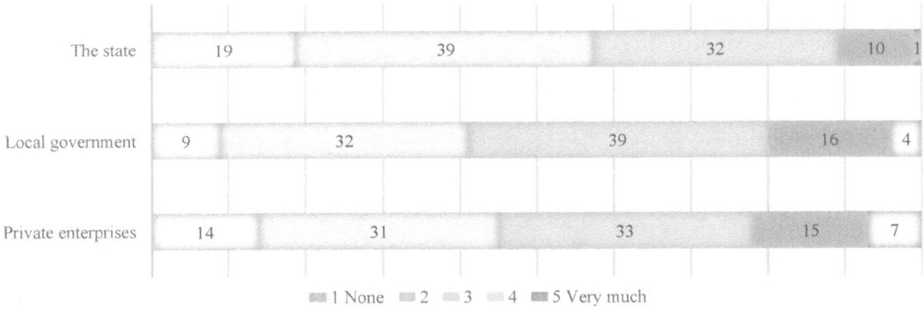

Figure 4.3 Respondents' influence on governance and organization at the workplace (measured by an index consisting of 12 variables: How much influence do you think you have on enterprise decisions on (1) strategies, (2) quality demands, (3) efficiency demands, (4) profitability demands, (5) choice of work technologies, (6) who gets to know what, (7) recruitment, (8) enterprise organization, (9) customer/user relations, (10) cooperation with other enterprises, (11) social responsibilities, and (12) enterprise environmental responsibilities, tested by factor analysis), in percent, n = 2335

organized by the state differ considerably from both of them (Figure 4.3). Respondents employed by the Norwegian state have less influence on governance and organization at their workplace, and this difference is statistically significant ($p < .001$). They experience higher degrees of standardization and control, and lower degrees of co-determination and autonomy at work than do employees in private and local government enterprises. In Figure 4.4, we present differences in degrees of governance and forms of management across industries. The panel data includes 20 different industries, which implies that the numbers of respondents in some of them are quite small. We include only those industries with sufficient numbers of respondents (about 100 or more) to be significant.

Health services have the lowest degree of co-determination and the third lowest degree of participation and involvement. We will comment in more detail on the low ratings in the public sector and connect them to the introduction of new public management in the next paragraph.

The main point in Figure 4.4, however, is the variations in levels of co-determination, and participation and involvement (autonomy) across industries. We use indexes of all the four types of governance and management that we elaborated in the introduction to this chapter. These indexes give robust findings that are statistically significant (Falkum et al., 2017; Falkum & Drange, 2018). Union–employer collaboration and high levels of union co-determination dominated governance and management in the oil and gas industry until 2008, when the largest companies introduced standardization programmes for production and maintenance, including HES issues in North Sea installations (Colman

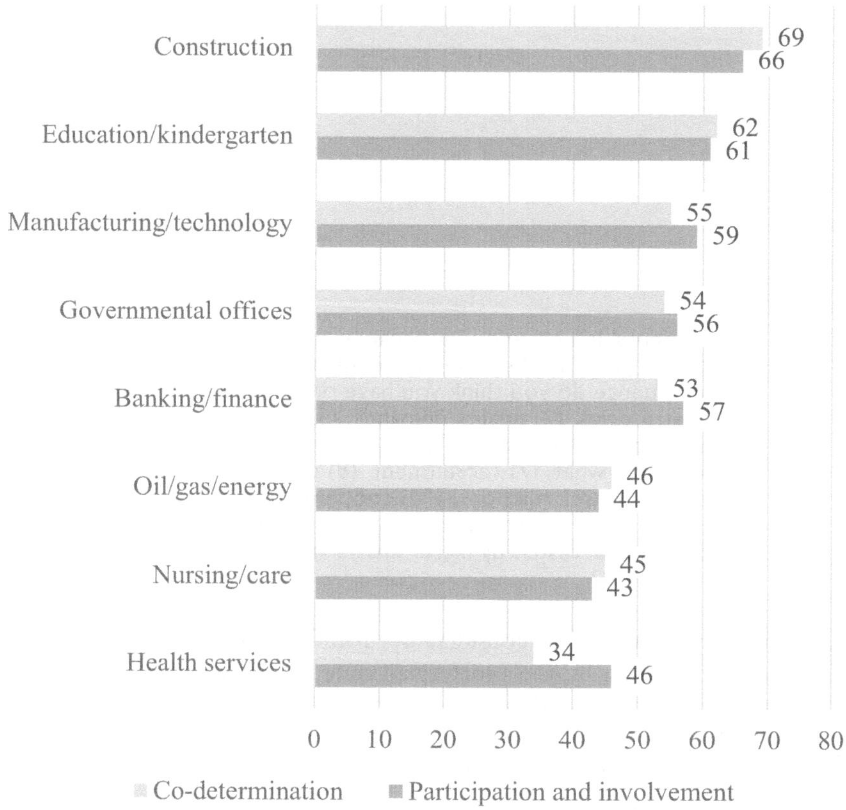

Figure 4.4 Respondents' perceived degree of co-determination and participation and involvement/autonomy (percentage scoring 4 or 5 on a scale from 1 = very small degree to 5 = very high degree, n = 326–93)

et al., 2011). Table 4.1 showed positive correlations between co-determination and participation and involvement, as Figure 4.4 clearly illustrates.

Comparing Figures 4.4 and 4.5, we find that those industries where employees experience a high degree of co-determination, and participation and involvement, seem to show a lower degree of standardization and control, while the levels of loyalty and obedience seem to correlate in the same way, but less statistically significant, when we compare industries (Falkum & Drange, 2018). Figures 4.4 and 4.5 show that governance and managerial forms vary considerably between industries. This variation challenges the idea of "one best way" that "fits all". We need to question the idea of a common working life model in Norway and therefore also in the rest of the Nordics.

A widening range of tools for management, governance and organizing activities is another source of varieties of industrial relations in practice.

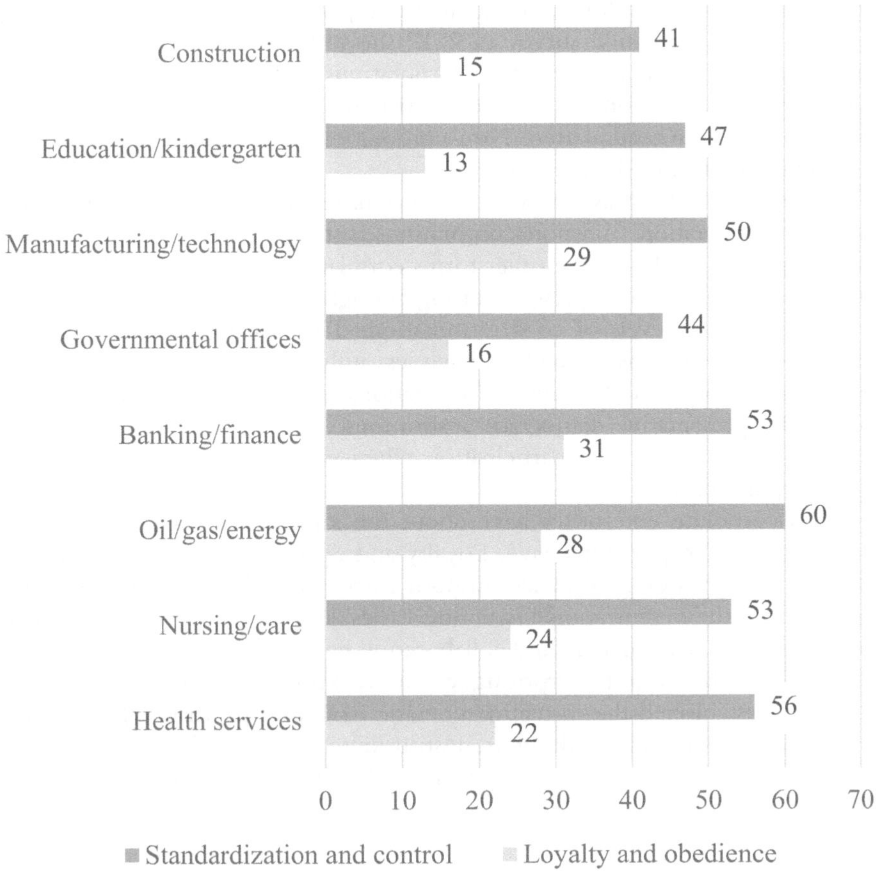

Figure 4.5 **Respondents' perceived degree of loyalty and obedience, and standardization and control (percentage scoring 4 or 5 on a scale from 1 = very small degree to 5 = very high degree, n = 326–93)**

Who owns an enterprise matters. In corporate governance and new public management (NPM) principles, the owners become the most important actors to instruct management and the entire enterprise. Firstly, they will dominate the understandings of realities, environments and surrounding events as inputs to decide strategic intentions and means. Secondly, they will set goals and objectives, such as return on investments, productivity demands and acceptable cost levels. Thirdly, they will decide what to produce, where to produce it, how to produce it and with what resources. Their interests determine the plans, decisions and actions taken by CEOs and top management. The relations between shareholders and top management become the vital and central relationship in a company. In the original Nordic working life models and the stakeholder perspectives, the relations between management, unions and employees dominated companies and organizations.

The co-determination survey in 2017 shows huge differences in governance and forms of management in corporations and other ways to organize enterprises. Corporations are normally a structure of several enterprises that are run from the same headquarters. Non-corporations are autonomous companies and other enterprises (Figure 4.6).

A regression analysis shows that the differences in co-determination between corporations and non-corporations is statistically significant (Falkum & Drange, 2018). The three other forms correlate in the expected directions, but the differences are at present not big enough to be significant. Thus, corporations reduce levels of co-determination. That means that unions, their representatives and their members have less influence in corporate structures than in non-corporate structures. Corporations reduce the roles of collectively oriented representative democratic institutions. There are no significant differences in autonomy and participation when we compare corporations and non-corporations.

Non-corporate enterprises have about the same levels of standardization and control as corporations have. Loyalty and obedience score lower than all three other forms of governance, in both corporate and non-corporate structures. Thus, the organizational structure varies, and they carry different forms of governance, management and collaboration between employers, unions and employees. This is quite surprising when we know that they do not differ in having established the formal democratic structures prescribed by national industrial relations and working life institutions. Institutionalization of democratic structures seems to be no guarantee for the practice of democracy at

Figure 4.6 Distribution of the governance and management models in corporate (workplaces under corporate headquarters) and non-corporate structures (autonomous workplaces) (employees' average scores on a scale from 1 = small degree to 5 = high degree, n = 783–286)

workplaces. What characteristics distinguish corporations from non-corporate enterprises, and will such characteristics explain some of the differences?

- 63% of employees in our survey work in a corporation, nearly twice as many as those in non-corporate enterprises.
- 51% of employees in corporations have domestic owners, compared to 95% of employees in non-corporate enterprises.
- 49% of employees in corporations have institutional owners (foundations or finance institutions), compared to 13% in non-corporations.
- 40% of employees in corporations are in those with 500 or more employees, compared to 7% in non-corporative enterprises.

Figure 4.6 confirms the common assumption that the introduction of corporate governance, and shareholder perspectives, would affect democratic practices and labour relations at workplaces. Differences in ownership, size and site of the headquarters will affect distances and thereby communication lines and labour relations. These characteristics may explain some of the differences in the practical use of governance and management methods, and employee and union influences at work. However, these characteristics are likely to be the result of the introduction of corporate governance and NPM, and not the opposite, i.e. that the introduction of corporate governance and NPM is a result of size, ownership or site of headquarters. They are the owners' preferred ways to govern a large part of working life. The differences still remain when we control for number of employees (size).

Corporations let the owners' interests dominate enterprises according to corporate governance principles (Hagen, 2010, 2015). Relations between owners and management become dominant in the shaping of the understandings of realities, strategic choices and principles of governance and management. In this way, relations between employers, unions and employees will be of less importance in the running of enterprises. Shareholder perspectives take over from stakeholder perspectives through labour relations and the practice of industrial relations at workplaces.

We found that the practice of workplace democracy varies by industries, sectors and by enterprise structures. Models of work and working life have to reflect realities at workplaces in order to support predictability, stability and consensus. Despite the proven varieties of workplace practices, conflicts between employers and unions are still scarce in Denmark and Norway.

Workplace differences by ownership (foreign or domestic)

The co-determination survey reveals only minor differences between companies with foreign- and with domestic-dominant owners in terms of the establishment of democratic structures such as unions, shop stewards, works councils, collective bargaining, basic agreements, HES committees and more. Obviously, they practise these differently, as in for example the use of individual or collective wage negotiations. Foreign owners practise individual wage negotiations more often, according to our respondents. Table 4.2 shows the differences in the use of the four management and governance models.

We tested the figures for several independent variables such as size of the enterprise (number of employees), industry and more. The differences observed in Table 4.2 are statistically significant (Falkum & Drange, 2018). Employees in enterprises with foreign owners score higher on standardization and control than employees in enterprises with domestic-dominant owners. Employees in enterprises with domestic owners score higher on participation and involvement (autonomy) and co-determination than employees in enterprises with foreign-dominant owners.

Foreign owners seem to bring in different models of governance and management than domestic owners, and to practise Norwegian democratic workplace arrangements differently. When a foreign investor buys a domestic company or enterprise, they will often include it in corporate structures with headquarters abroad. That increases distance and possibilities for communication and dialogue. This may affect the relations between the headquarters and the local management, unions and employees, and thereby the model of governance and management in use. In a recent case study (Nordrik & Falkum, 2017), an international corporation implemented corporate standard models of HR systems and business governance that we found partly incompatible with national agreements and labour laws. This may indicate how internationalization and the ongoing globalization of economies can affect national working life models and workplace organization and management.

Privatization of state enterprises

A social-democratic government (Stoltenberg 1) introduced NPM to Norway in the early 1990s. The British Labour Party developed NPM under the reign of Tony Blair (Giddens, 2013). NPM sought to adopt logics of "new market

Table 4.2 Employees' experience of governance and management, dominant owners compared (degree of the four models, average score on a scale from 1= very small degree to 5 = very high degree, (n))

Model	*Domestic*	*Foreign*
Standardization and control***	3.0 (544)	3.4 (285)
Participation (autonomy)***	3.5 (845)	3.3 (405)
Loyalty and obedience	2.6 (401)	2.8 (234)
Co-determination ***	3.5 (737)	3.3 (352)

*** $p <= 0.001$ (significance)

liberalism" from the early 1980s in the public sector. Customer/user orientations in public services, cost control and reduction of public spending were high on political agendas (Christensen & Lægreid, 2007). In parallel with corporate governance in the private sector, NPM put a public variant of owners' governance in charge.

NPM led to the privatization of many public services. Privatization introduced variants of corporate structures as the main way to organize services like telecommunications, railways, the national postal service, the national oil company and more. Parliament established them as "state limited companies" (statsaksjeselskap) by legal acts. The relevant ministry was to hold the general assembly of the new limited company. The general assembly in limited companies represents the shareholders. It elects the board of directors in representative democratic structures. NPM carries principles of corporate governance (Meld. St. 27 (2013–2014)). Today the Norwegian state owns 74 such companies (Nærings- og fiskeridepartementet 13.01.2018).

The public authorities restructured hospitals in a somewhat similar way in the early 2000s. The state now organized hospitals and defined them as health corporations and enterprises, known as "special law companies" (særlovsselskap), i.e. state companies with particular authority. Political decisions transferred the responsibility for hospitals from the 18 counties to 5 state-owned regional health trusts (helseforetak) in 2002. This was a huge reform implemented in a very short time. The Ministry of Health is in charge of the five health regions. The reform introduced corporate structures similar to those of the limited companies owned by the state. However, this was not a Norwegian innovation. The same model applied in Denmark and several other European countries.

We have examined differences in governance and management models in some of the workplaces under governmental authority.

Table 4.3 shows the survey responses on the indexes for the four models of governance and management in different areas of state activities. The figures show the average scores in the different areas on a scale from 1 = very low degree to 5 = very high degree. It also shows statistically significant differences in the degree of participation and involvement (autonomy) and co-determination in the different types of enterprise. Autonomy and co-determination in privatized state-owned limited companies and health enterprises score significantly lower than the other types of enterprise. Universities and university colleges are at the top. Standardization and control scores are highest in health enterprises and state-owned limited companies compared to all the others, significant at the 0.01 level.

These findings may have many different explanations. The restructurings took place in the early 2000s. The privatized limited companies used to have strong labour unions, party collaboration and union influence on the management and business in their period as public enterprises. Since then they have developed their business and reorganized and restructured the enterprise

Table 4.3 The four models of governance and management in different state-owned enterprises (degree of the four models, average score on a scale from 1 = very low degree to 5 = very high degree, (n))

Enterprises	*Standardization & control**	*Participation & interference ****	*Loyalty & obedience*	*Co-determination****
Ministries, directorates, adm.	3.5 (105)	3.4 (162)	2.6 (94)	3.3 (132)
Defence, police	3.5 (52)	3.5 (74)	2.7 (46)	3.2 (62)
Universities, university colleges	3.4 (48)	3.5 (71)	2.4 (36)	3.6 (60)
Health enterprises	3.8 (96)	3.2 (140)	2.7 (75)	3.0 (112)
State-owned limited companies	3.7 (66)	3.1 (93)	2.8 (59)	3.0 (78)

*** $p <= 0.001$

organization and management more frequently. Reallocation of staff, downsizing, expansion into new markets, and mergers and acquisition are taking place continuously in some of them. We know from the surveys in 2016 and 2017 that restructuring correlates negatively with autonomy and co-determination.

Health professions, especially physicians and nurses, held positions of power in their period under the governance of the counties. Disputes with health authorities over budgetary issues and cost control were common. The introduction of the health corporations and enterprise reform was intended to change the situation by establishing governance models that clearly divided management and administrative functions from service provision. It is reasonable to assume that this rearrangement of managerial authority and governance in hospitals would influence professionals' understandings and experiences of co-determination and participation and involvement at work (see Chapter 11 on NPM in this volume).

Privatization of public services was intended to improve them by several processes of change of managerial authority and responsibilities. We believe we have observed this in our findings. One of the main questions in our survey is "In what direction do you think working life is developing?" The possible responses are "In a more authoritarian direction", "In a more democratic direction", "No change" or "I don't know".

In health enterprises, 47% felt that working life was becoming more authoritarian. In state-owned limited companies, the figure was 57%. These scores are higher than in most other areas and industries, except for oil and gas, where 58% thought that working life was developing in a more authoritarian direction.

We have controlled these findings for numbers of employees and other independent variables by regression analysis (Falkum & Drange, 2018). Size matters but not so much to make the correlations statistically insignificant.

We take these findings to indicate that the restructuring of public sector workplaces by the logics of NPM are changing workplace structures and cultures in a less democratic direction.

Consensus or co-optation: pressures on the Nordic workplace models

In this section, we turn to a case study in order to outline how a large multinational corporation in the oil and gas industry avoids co-determination in practice. Here, we reveal corporate actions that undermined industrial relations and the institutionalized formal democratic structures, simply by changing the practices of agreements and labour laws, not the laws and agreements as such (Nordrik & Falkum, 2017). This particular large international corporation decided to implement the same organizational structure and managerial codes of conduct in all subsidiaries and units, irrespective of location. The idea to standardize production processes and maintenance as well as administrative processes, management and formal relations between management and employees seems to have been permeating the oil and gas industries at least since 2008 (Colman et al., 2011).

The Norwegian subsidiary in our case study decided to implement transformation management principles and HR systems based on measurement and control of individual performance, behaviour and attitudes. The corporate headquarters developed large numbers of guidelines and instructions. The Norwegian corporate headquarters introduced the restructuring strategy in the Norwegian plant in 2010. Union representatives, shop stewards and elected health and safety representatives have reported and complained about the lack of participation, co-determination, involvement and consultation with management in the implementation of the corporate HR system. We have documented this with copies of minutes of meetings, letters, emails and 14 formal qualitative interviews and more than 40 conversations with employees, elected HES representatives and union representatives as well as the management of the Norwegian subsidiary and the plant under study.

Elements of the imported HR system

Corporate management introduced a programme for operational excellence in production in 2014 to cut costs and increase productivity by defining social values assumed to improve results. The programme started with an exploration of options to define improvement objectives and goals. It transformed aims and objectives into standard operating procedures as a strategic baseline. Measures of operational results had to agree with defined goals. The local union and the HES representatives claimed that they were not involved in the decision making or the planning of the four phases of this programme as they were entitled to by laws and agreements. Plant management claimed otherwise: that union and HES representatives did participate but none of our interviews with employees and union representatives confirmed that.

A second programme was intended to match capacities and competencies in operational tasks: to define and establish the "critical competencies" in all tasks. Management introduced the programme in 2014. External consultants explored and made the operational design of the programme, including a new schedule of working hours and shifts at the plant. The local union and its representatives claim that they neither participated nor had any influence in this process. Again, the plant management and the top manager of the Norwegian subsidiary claim that the union representatives were involved, although the CEO admits that:

> [t]here have been some problems with the union's co-determination in recent years. But we are now improving industrial relations.
>
> (Interview, 15 November 2016)

The third programme, introduced in 2015, was a verification system that mapped each employee's individual knowledge and competencies. In the "life-saving rules", for instance, there are 12 points of "dos and don'ts" with more than 100 outlined codes of conduct. This mapping system was intended to prevent major accidents by controlling the performance of all tasks in detail. The local union and the plant management disagree on the practice and degree of co-determination and employee participation in this process.

The final element was the introduction of a governance system based on individual employee goals, performance measures and recording of results introduced in 2016. This completed the corporate governance package. Again, the union and HES representatives asked for co-determination and participation in the planning, decision making and implementation, and again managerial and HR staff tell a different story.

Implementation of the HR system came in separate portions but was never introduced as connected strategic elements of a complete system for corporate governance. When management eventually introduced the element of individual performance measures, the links between all four elements finally became obvious to unions and employees like the pieces of a jigsaw puzzle.

Interviews, conversations and email correspondence between employees expressed a shared understanding of this process as planned and implemented stepwise in order to hide the full corporate intentions until the process was irreversible. The final introduction of the individual performance measures became the eye-opener that gave local unions the full understanding of corporate intentions: the introduction of a system of corporate governance based on individual human relations and human resource management principles. The by-passing of industrial relations, collective interests and union influence in decision making and planning was a tactic to fulfil corporate intentions, according to the interviews with unions and employees. All our employee informants labelled these managerial acts as manipulation aimed at reducing the co-determination of unions and employees. The CEO and plant managers refused to accept such interpretations of the processes. Nevertheless, the way management introduced the system seemed to produce negotiation myopia (Martin, 2015, pp. 17–33) among the actors, intentionally or not.

This case study shows how a large multinational corporation set national industrial relations aside by introducing their own corporate governance and management systems, intended to be implemented in all organizational units worldwide. They did so, however, not by challenging industrial relations and working life institutions but by changing the game itself, by introducing new practices that in principle were breaking some of the institutionalized rules, although claiming throughout the process that industrial relations and HES structures were recognized. Corporate managers in the Norwegian subsidiary and at the plant claimed that their new principles were in line with national industrial relations, while the implementation process showed otherwise. The corporate intention to introduce transformation management did not comply with the rules of participation by union and HES representatives. The corporate programmes prescribed individualization of labour relations and individual participation and support for the programmes by employees and union and HES representatives. They ignored collective and representative democratic structures and intentions in practice, while simultaneously stating that they were following the national rules of the game. Lawyers have evaluated the process and concluded in favour of the unions (Nordrik & Falkum, 2017).

Workplace democracy can be formally in place, while practice tells a different story. Such systems, of corporate governance disguised as democracy, diminish the opportunities for employee opposition and union influence. Management presumes that the unions are participating and supporting the corporate programmes in line with the logics of what we have labelled loyalty and obedience, not the logics of co-determination. Corporate governance that rests on subordination more than trust in labour relations may lead to co-optation of unions and false co-determination. Top managers will have the power to define understandings of realities. They will take the support from co-opted unions and employees for granted. Institutionalized industrial relations no longer fit with practice, and corporate practice trumps the working life institutions.

Our survey data tells us, however, that there are still many corporations and enterprises that follow the rules of national industrial relations, domestic as well as foreign enterprises in almost all industries. But cases like the one here occur more frequently than before. The Nordic working life model is under pressure, a pressure that originally stems from the neo-liberalism of the 1980s and the logics of corporate governance and new HR strategies derived from that ideological base. This case study, as well as the survey data, indicate that the collective democratic structures of co-determination are under greater pressure than individual participation, but there are also examples of attempts to transform individual participation and involvement into loyalty and obedience, as in the case here.

Changing the understandings of realities and the game of democracy at work

The research findings presented here challenge the common assumption that the Norwegian working life model is democratic, stable and uniform. This assumption is based on some macro studies of industrial relations and companies in the Nordics (Moene, 2006; Dølvik et al., 2007, 2015). We have questioned these interpretations of institutional impacts with our studies of the practice of democracy at work, using questionnaires with representative samples of employees.

Comparing the identical questions from the surveys in 2009, 2016 and 2017, we conclude that participation and autonomy at work have been falling in the 2010s. In 2009, 89% scored 4 or 5 on the scale from 1 = none to 5 = much. This figure was 12% lower in 2016, and 9% lower in 2017, than in 2009. Individual influence on one's own work situation was one of the features of the Norwegian model of work organization and business development. There is a downward trend in dialogue and collaboration between managers and individual employees, as democratically oriented methods of management. However, the formal democratic structures are still in place and do not seem to change. The institutions of industrial relations remain while the democratic practice of them is declining.

The four methods of governance and management correlate in different directions. Standardization and control correlate positively with loyalty and obedience, and negatively with co-determination, and with participation and involvement. Anglo-American research, studies and practices are the sources of the first two methods, while Norwegian working life institutions and practices have developed the latter two. The four forms of governance represent different methods to shape shared understandings of realities in working life. The standards introduced at workplaces are reflections and operational definitions of certain understandings of the realities of work and the workplace. Some workplaces use the methods of co-determination and individual participation to outline and form the standards. Workplaces that have a high degree of standardization and control combined with a high degree of co-determination and participation reflect these possibilities. These workplaces are few, however, since standardization correlates negatively with co-determination and participation. Workplaces are more likely to introduce standardization and control top-down than bottom-up. Management establishes truth regimes based on its understanding of realities. Standardization and control are methods to make employees accept these understandings.

Participation and involvement score quite high in workplaces with both foreign and domestic owners, in corporations as well as non-corporations and in most industries. We found no significant differences in the practice and distribution of this kind of governance. Participation and involvement relate to Thorsrud's and Emery's ideas of individual participation in company development. In our analysis, we suggested that participation and involvement were a necessary basis for collectively oriented democratic elements such as co-determination, i.e. a foundation for industrial relations in the Nordics. The statistical correlation with co-determination is strong and significant. Participation and involvement correlate negatively with standardization and control as well as with loyalty and obedience.

In companies that practise loyalty and obedience, management defines and shapes realities and convinces employees that their understandings of these realities are true. This form of governance is less widespread than the other three forms. It correlates strongly and significantly with standardization and control, and negatively with the two Nordic forms of governance.

Organization and mobilization of collective interests are the basic premise for co-determination. The social partners constructed the working life institutions in the Nordics through the social-democratic era from 1935 to about 1980 when the neo-liberal era took over. Shared understandings of realities are the result of negotiated compromises at the levels of the workplace and working life in general. The social parties have shaped, maintained and developed industrial relations incrementally, in collaboration with the state. Co-determination is now under pressure from corporate governance and HR systems in the private sector. The state introduced corporate structures to a large part of public services. It is a paradox and a surprising finding that enterprises owned by the Norwegian state practise standardization and control to a higher degree than the rest of working life, and a majority of employees in limited companies owned by the state think that Norwegian working life is developing in a more authoritarian direction.

Working life seems to divide into two parts: one is moving away from democratic methods of organization and management, especially through standardization programmes, while the other part still keeps to the Norwegian working life model. So far, standardization programmes are gaining ground, and levels of co-determination and participation are declining at workplaces that implement such programmes. The case study presented showed an example of how this can happen. The models and methods of government and management from neo-liberal sources can prove to be more or less incompatible with the models and methods developed in Nordic working life.

Practices of the Norwegian working life model are not "one best way". We have shown variations between sectors and industries in their practice of the four models of governance and management. We found that organizational structure also matters, as there are significant differences between corporations and non-corporations. Corporate structures established by privatization of former public services are less democratic and more standardized than other state enterprises. The bumblebee is still flying, but seemingly in less predictable directions under the shifting conditions of the neo-liberal era.

Note

1 Medbestemmelsesbarometeret is funded by Lederne (The Norwegian Organization of Managers and Executives), Legeforeningen (The Norwegian Medical Association (NMA)), Forbundet for ledelse og teknikk (The Norwegian Engineers and Managers Association (FLT)), Forskerforbundet (The Norwegian Association of Researchers (NAR)) and Politiets Fellesforbund (Norwegian Police Federation).

References

Busch, R., Dysvik, A. & Kuvaas, B. (2015) *Produktiv motivasjon i arbeidslivet [Productive Motivation in the Working Life]*, Oslo: Cappelen Damm.

Christensen, T. & Lægreid, P. (2007) *Transcending New Public Management. The Transformation of Public Sector Reforms*, Aldershot, UK: Ashgate.

Colman, H. L., Stensaker, I. & Tharaldsen, J. E. (eds) (2011) *A Merger of Equals? The Integration of Statoil and Hydro's Oil and Gas Activities*, Bergen, Norway: Fagbokforlaget.

Dølvik, J. E., Fløtten, T., Hernes, G. & Hippe, J. M. (eds) (2007) *Hamskifte. Den norske modellen i endring [The Moulting. The Norwegian Model in Change]*, Oslo: Gyldendal Akademisk.

Dølvik, J. E., Fløtten, T., Hippe, J. M. & Jordfall, B. (2015) *The Nordic Model towards 2030. A New Chapter?*, Oslo: Fafo-rapport 2015:7.

Ekman, M., Gustavsen, B., Asheim, B. T. & Pålshaugen, Ø. (eds.) (2011) *Learning Regional Innovation*, Basingstoke, UK: Palgrave Macmillan.

Engelstad, F. (ed.) (1999) *Om makt. Teori og kritikk [On Power. Theory and Critique]*, Oslo: Ad Notam Gyldendal.

Engelstad, F. & Hagelund, A. (eds) (2015) *Cooperation and Conflict the Nordic Way. Work Welfare and Institutional Change in Scandinavia*, Berlin: De Gruyter.

Falkum, E. (2008) Makt og opposisjon i norsk arbeidsliv [Power and Opposition in the Norwegian Working Life], Avhandling til Dr. philos dissertation, Universitetet i Oslo.

Falkum, E. & Drange, I. (2018) *Medbestemmelse og eierskap [Co-determination and Ownership]*, Oslo: Afi FoU resultat.

Falkum, E., Hagen, I. M. & Trygstad, S. C. (2009) *Bedriftsdemokraties tilstand. Medbestemmelse, medvirkning og innflytelse i 2009 [The Condition of the Workplace Democracy. Co-determination, Autonomy and Influence in 2009]*, Oslo: Fafo-rapport 2009, 35.

Falkum, E., Nordrik, B., Drange, I. & Wathne, C. T. (2017) *Arbeidslivsrelasjoner i endring [Labour Relations in Change]*, Oslo: Afi FoU resultat.

Foucault, M. (1982) The Subject and Power, In: Dreyfus, H. L & Rabinow, P. (eds) *Michel Foucault: Beyond Structuralism and Hermeneutics*, Brighton, UK: Harvester, 208–226.

Giddens, A. (2013) *The Third Way and the Renewal of Social Democracy*, Cambridge, UK: Polity Press.

Gustavsen, B., Finne, H. & Oscarsson, B. (2001) *Creating Connectedness: The Role of Social Research in Innovation Policy*, Amsterdam: John Benjamins. doi: 10.1075/dowi.13.

Hagen, I. M. (2010) Det mektige mindretallet. Ansatterepresentasjon i styret mellom Corporate Governance og Industrial Relations [The Powerful Minority. Employee Board Representatives between Corporate Governance and Industrial Relations], PhD dissertation, Universitetet i Oslo.

Hagen, I. M. (2015) Participation and Co-Determination: Why some Arrangements Fail and Others Prevail, In: Engelstad. F. & Hagelund, A. (eds) *Cooperation and Conflict the Nordic Way. Work Welfare and Institutional Change in Scandinavia*, Berlin: De Gruyter.

Hagen, I. M. (2017) Flere styrer: færre ansattevalgte styremedlemmer [More Boards: Fewer Employee Representatvies], Oslo: *Søkelys på arbeidslivet 4/17*, Vol. 34.

Herbst, P. G. (1971) *Demokratiseringsprosessen i arbeidslivet. Sosio-tekniske studier. [Democratization in the Working Life. Sociotechnical Studies]*, Oslo: Universtitetsforlaget.

Kuvaas, B. (2006) Work Performance, Affective Commitment and Work Motivation: The Roles of Pay Administration and Pay Level, *Journal of Organisational Behaviour*, 27(3): 365–385.

Levin, M. (ed.) (2002) *Researching Enterprise Development. Action Research on the Cooperation between Management and Labour in Norway*, Amsterdam: John Benjamins.

Lukes, S. (2005 [1974]) *Power: A Radical View* (second edition), Basingstoke, UK: Palgrave Macmillan.

Martin, C. J. (2015) Negotiation and the Micro Foundation of Institutional Change, In: Engelstad, F. & Hagelund, A. (eds) *Cooperation and Conflict the Nordic Way: Work Welfare and Institutional Change in Scandinavia*, Berlin: De Gruyter.

Meld. St. 27 (2013–2014) Eierskapsmeldingen. /id2009187/.

Moene, K. O. (2006) Den skandinaviske modellen: et skjørt politisk kompromiss eller et stabilt økonomisk system? [The Scandinavian Model: A Fragile Political Compromise or a Stable Economic System?], *Foredrag på konferansen Den nordiske modellen: et forbilde?* Samfunnsøkonomisk institutt, Universitetet i Oslo 24. januar 2006. www.uio.no/info/den_nordiske_%20modellenet_%20forbilde.html.

Moxnes, P. (2012) *Positiv angst. I individ, gruppe og organisasjon [Positive Anxiety. In Individuals, Groups and Organizations*], Oslo: Universitetsforlaget.

Nordrik, B. & Falkum, E. (2017) *SAFE Undersøkelsen 2016 [The SAFE Study 2016]*, Oslo: www.afi.no. OsloMet, Arbeidsforskningsinstituttet.

Røvik, K. A. (2007) *Trender og Translasjoner: Ideer som former det 21. århundrets organisasjon. [Trends and Translations: Ideas that Influence the Organization of the 21st Century]*, Oslo: Universitetsforlaget.

Thorsrud, E. & Emery, F. (1964) *Industrielt demokrati. Representasjon på styreplan i bedriftene? [Industrial Democracy. Representation in Company Boards?]*, Oslo: Universitetsforlaget.

Thorsrud, E. & Emery, F. (1970) *Mot en ny bedriftsorganisasjon, Eksperimenter i industrielt demokrati [Towards a New Company Organization. Experiments in Industrial Democracy]*, Fra Samarbeidsprosjektet LO/NAF, Oslo: Tanum.

Ulrich, D. & Ulrich, W. (2010) *The Why of Work: How Great Leaders Build Abundant Organizations That Win*, New York: McGraw-Hill.

Ulrich, D., Allen, J., Brockbank, W., Younger, J. & Nyman, M. (2009) *HR Transformation: Building Human Resources from the Outside In*, Chicago, IL: McGraw-Hill.

Womack, J., Jones, D. & Roos, J. D. (1990) *The Machine That Changed the World*, New York: Productivity Press.

Chapter 5

International management concepts meeting Nordic working life

Peter Hagedorn-Rasmussen and Pål Klethagen

Introduction

Management concepts travel across contexts. Protagonists present management concepts as universalized knowledge that fulfils desirable goals by following the ideas and prescriptions proposed. But what happens when decontextualized knowledge developed in one context travels across contexts and is recontextualized? In this chapter, we explore how international management concepts travel into the Nordic working life – and to what extent international management concepts challenge the work environment and transform inherent principles in the Nordic Working life Model (NWM). In the first section, we sketch out what we understand as NWM in order to explore how this interacts with international management concepts. We then identify two rough theoretical perspectives in the understanding of management concepts and organizational transformation. *The first perspective* aligns to the idea that management concepts represent universalized knowledge that is *transferred across context and transforms organizations*. This perspective, which we label *Transfer*, includes two opposing approaches: one is that of the proponents and advocates of specific managerial concepts; the other is that of those who critically scrutinize management concepts and the outcomes they produce. The second theoretical perspective we label *Translation*. The translational approach adheres to the idea that management concepts *can never be transferred without also being translated*. Each has implications for understanding the relationship between management concepts and organizational transformation.

This leads us to the second section of the chapter, in which we explore the travel of Lean into Nordic working life. We begin by sketching out Lean, and then, by means of earlier literature studies, ask what can be said about the influence of Lean on work environment and health. While these studies reach beyond the scope of the Nordic countries, we reflect upon their implications for Nordic working life and implications for the principles and characteristics implied in NWM. This leads us to explore in more depth some of the translational processes of Lean into the Nordic countries, including the role of researchers and social parties. We present three cases of translational processes in Norway and Denmark.

Although the exploration of the relationship between international management concepts and the work environment has general implications, this chapter is rooted within the industrial area. Our delimitation includes the role of consultants in translating managerial concepts (Hagedorn-Rasmussen, 2001; Holmemo et al., 2016). In the following paragraph, we define what we mean by Nordic working life and summarize principles and characteristics that signify what we have chosen to give the problematic label NWM.

The NWM and work environment

Why is it problematic to speak of an NWM? Asking whether the NWM is challenged by international management concepts might be an odd question, given the model is itself a result of a historical international melting pot. Just some of the threads from which the Nordic model has been woven are the origin and institutionalization of social parties that acknowledge differences in interests; the systematization of a "model" that is in an ongoing process of becoming by means of negotiation, possible conflicts and democratic participation at many levels; the historical role of origin and cooperative dissemination of Taylorism in the aftermath of World War II; and the integration of ideas from sociotechnical studies in the UK. This texture is still in the becoming but also forms the context of contemporary industrial organization and the working life in Nordic countries. Democratic institutions and practices in the form of formal representation as well as participatory, employee-involving practices have been institutionalized as strong principles and characteristics of the Nordic working life, although also continually contested. In the following sections, we thus focus on the emergence and institutionalization of principles and characteristics of the NWM with specific emphasis on the sociotechnical influence, on democracy and on work organization. This complements Chapter 3, which provides a broader introduction to the Nordic working life tradition.

In both Denmark and Norway, rebuilding after World War II was assisted by the Marshall Plan, which brought North American thinking on organization and management with it. Rationalization and Tayloristic principles in general seemed to prosper in the Nordic countries (Hvid et al., 2003, p. 12). Even though Taylor's principles came late to the Nordic countries, when first introduced during the 1940s they were quite strongly implemented, likely due to an improved cooperative relationship (Burchardt, 2001, p. 79). Trade union representatives and work councils supported the search for techniques for increased, efficient and quality-based production in order to raise the general standard of living (Johansson, 2013, p. 243). Work tasks became fragmented and labour-intensified. Highly specified and controlled work roles allowed for little participation in terms of development and maintenance of skills, and very little freedom to take initiatives, perform judgements or make decisions (Gustavsen, 1990, p. 40).

In the UK, the coal mine studies targeted the downsides of mechanizing the industry. Today, these studies are often applied as a somewhat esoteric reference point within the field of working life studies and organization theory. The scene of what later became such an influential stream of thought, the sociotechnical school at the Tavistock Institute, was set by Eric Trist and Ken Bamforth (the latter had been working in the mines for 18 years). In "Some Social and Psychological Consequences of the Longwall Method of Coal-Getting", Trist and Bamforth describe how the "outstanding feature of the social pattern with which the pre-mechanized equilibrium was associated" had deteriorated (1951, p. 6). The loss of responsible autonomy within the smaller groups who had previously worked in the coal mines was associated with the shift towards a work organization with large groups with very little or no autonomy. The key learning points from these studies was that, when changing the work organization, social and technical systems had to be considered in combination. It exhibited how innovations in the *work organization* increased productivity as well as the social quality of working life, greater cohesiveness in groups, greater personal satisfaction and a decrease in sickness and absenteeism (Trist & Bamforth, 1951).

The researchers behind the studies had ambitions of reforming working life in order to create an industrial democracy, but in the UK such a movement proved difficult to establish. In Norway, on the other hand, such studies found fertile ground; the research program *Industrial Democracy* was established in 1962 and became a source of inspiration in the formation of Nordic working life in the decades that followed. The Industrial Democracy program "grew out of a widespread public discussion of alienation in industry and utilization of human resources" (Thorsrud & Emery, 1970, p. 187) and was led by Thorsrud and Emery, aiming at a democratization and sharing of social power of all those engaged in industry (Thorsrud & Emery, 1970, p. 188). The programme's first phase was concerned with employee representatives on company boards, while the second phase consisted of field experiments on employees' "opportunities to participate in determining how they did their work" (Thorsrud & Emery, 1970, p. 187).

The programme documented the somewhat conflicting roles of the representatives on boards which had been instigated in the 1950s. The boards prioritized the economic prosperity of the firm (Thorsrud & Emery, 1970, pp. 189–191), thus externalizing issues relevant for working conditions. Here, work councils were seen as sites for negotiation of a more practice-oriented influence, in which employees were capable of handling problems in the concrete work settings. The insights from the first phase led to focus on some basic needs in the following experiments, for example:

> [r]easonably demanding job content, a need to learn on the job, a need to have a minimum opportunity for decision-making, a need for some minimal degree of social support and recognition, and to relate what he does and produces to his social life.
>
> (Thorsrud & Emery, 1970, p. 194)

These ideas and principles came to inspire and permeate projects and programmes around the Nordic countries, thus giving strength to the formation of an idea, almost reified as NWM, although always in its becoming. This was not without challenges. The Industrial Democracy programme was a reaction to decades of joint practices based on Tayloristic principles. Likewise, the sociotechnical approach during the 1970s was criticized for neglecting the power relations within companies. In this process, the Norwegian professor Bjørn Gustavsen, who was also at the Norwegian Work Research Institute, played a significant role. By means of action research into the continuation of experiments on work organization, he emphasized the role of language and dialogue. Technology policies came to play a role, and a revitalization of the idea of equal cooperation was strengthened and gave birth to new legislation strengthening employee rights at company level (Hvid et al., 2003, p. 12). Concepts like *The Developmental Work* arose in the 1990s in Sweden and Denmark and were propagated by unions and also disseminated by researchers (Hvid et al., 2003, p. 12). As such, Nordic working life was in an ongoing transformation. Although the nature of this *becoming* had its own dialectic character, the formation of a line of principles and characteristics thrived. It thrived to a degree that the NWM became a concept in "such a wide spectrum of areas as management, user-friendly technology development, industrial democracy, group-work, welfare legislation, and industrial relations. Many observers even came to Scandinavia to study the future" (Byrkjeflot, 2003, p. 29). Byrkjeflot emphasizes how this climaxed in the mid-1980s, when international management concepts became more important. In the following section, we will probe the landscape of management concepts before we turn to explore their travel into the Nordic working life.

Transforming by transferring: management concepts that travel across contexts

Managers apply management concepts in order to cope with organizational complexities. Management concepts consist of a coherent set of ideas and heuristics that include a *theory of practice* on how to succeed within a specific area (Hagedorn-Rasmussen, 2000; Koch et al., 2003; Kamp et al., 2005). Examples could be Total Quality Management (Deming, 2000; Hagedorn-Rasmussen, 2000), Diversity Management (Kamp & Hagedorn-Rasmussen, 2004), Organizational Learning (Senge, 1990; Bottrup, 2001), Business Process Reengineering (Koch et al., 1999; Moltu, 2003; Hagedorn-Rasmussen, 2000; Hammer & Champy, 2009) or Lean (see later) to mention but a few. The *theory of practice* prescribed by each of these is based on experiential evidence. The concepts and their inherent tools intend a transformation of work organization that includes important modes that affect working life, often with (un)intended effects on work environment and health, as well as principles and characteristics implied in NWM: autonomy, scope of tasks, decision latitude, involvement, job demands, development of skills and competences, reward system, are affected by the "improvements", "innovations", "reengineering"and "value streaming" that flow from the implementation of concepts and the tools.

The concepts thrive as a result of the need for complexity reduction experienced by managers in a complex world of information overflow. In the introduction of management conceptual literature, the claim most often repeated is that the world is changing ever more rapidly. The subsequent claim is that those who are likely to survive are those who follow the philosophy and tools prescribed by this particular book. This becomes a self-fulfilling prophecy (Grey, 2008), followed by a fear among managers of missing out and an inclination to adopt socially legitimized management concepts (Rosenzweig, 2014). This leads to the understanding of the management industry as a fashion industry (Abrahamson, 1996; Benders & Van Veen, 2001; Björkman, 2013), in which makers become masters and gurus of management (Huczynski, 2012) who offer the ideas by which organizations become ever more isomorphic as a result of ongoing imitation of one another (DiMaggio & Powell, 2000).

The proponents of management concepts conform to a realistic philosophy of science that makes strong claims about the opportunities for successfully transforming organizations. By far, most of the management concepts are rooted in a North American context and lend themselves to the isomorphism of organizational practices internationally. This led Clegg and other postmodern inspired organizational scholars to apply the acronym NATO, *North American Theory of Organization*, to describe contemporary organization theory (Shenhav, 2003, p. 203). Managerial concepts might have roots in other contexts, but the potential for becoming a leading star surges when they are reinterpreted and vitalized in the North American context.

Critical perspectives on management concepts

Strong claims for positive outcomes in terms of organizational transformation stem from these prescriptive ideas. However, a notable field of critical research shares the idea of Transfer, in which concepts are perceived as knowledge that *does* transform organizations directly. But the critical approach reached quite the opposite conclusion with regard to the consequences of the transformations: from the earlier Labour Process Theory and later Critical Management Studies, management concepts have been explored as means of managerial control (Braverman, 1974; Burawoy, 1979), while others have highlighted their effect on discipline and redistribution of power (Lukes, 1974; Clegg, 1989). In the legacy of these critical approaches, management concepts are considered as part of the instigation of regimes that cause a deterioration in the work environment; intensify work; reduce autonomy at work (Skorstad, 2013); and influence identity, subjectivity, meaning and politics in organizations (e.g. Knights & McCabe, 1998, 2000, 2002), thus being more subtle but ever more advanced means of control.

Also in the Nordic countries, criticism of and concerns over the possible influence of mainstream management thoughts on working life have been put forward. The Norwegian social anthropologist Tian Sørhaug stayed at the Norwegian Work Research Institute (AFI). Sørhaug, who had also been Director of AFI, stayed there during the times of Thorsrud. He writes on the influence of US consultants in the aftermath of World War II (as part of the Marshall Plan) and argues that the influence of the US consultants was seen to clash with the ideas outlined and practised within the programme on Industrial Democracy in Norway, in which a sharing of social power in industry of all who are engaged in industry was seen as a means to de-alienate the industry (Sørhaug, 1996, p. 188). US consultants, Sørhaug wrote, had a far more hierarchical perspective on management, in which robust organization equated to a clear, straightforward, authoritarian leadership. Likewise, the influence from Japan increased (Gustavsen et al., 2010; Skorstad, 2011). Both authors emphasize the difference between Japanese and Norwegian approaches to involvement, implying a critique of transferring concepts and ideas from one context to another. During the 1980s, an instrumental approach to involvement as a means of creating ever more efficient and flexible companies superseded that of involvement as a driver for democracy and equality. This made critical researchers conclude that, for instance, Lean equals "loss of autonomy and further intensification of work" (Skorstad, 1994, p. 429). Gustavsen et al. (2010) specify that working life research in Norway was weak at the end of the 1980s. This created an open space for influences from other sources. The prescriptive management literature expanded (Peters et al., 1982) and provided a source for inspiration and influence. *The Machine that Changed the World* (Womack et al., 1990) was a bestselling book that paved the way to success for Lean as a specific management concept.

What the critics and proponents share is a belief that decontextualized management concepts *work* across contexts: by transferring decontextualized knowledge, it is possible to transform organizations. Proponents argue for the sake of improvements, quality and efficiency in terms of company goals. Critics argue there is a negative influence on the work environment, which may be said to stem from the *externalization* of variables, principles, practices and characteristics such as autonomy, psychosocial work environment, balanced job demands, learning opportunities and whole tasks, not to mention democracy and participation. Such ideas are externalized from the agenda and from the mental maps that managers (and consultants) apply as sense-making heuristics (Weick, 1995; also see Simon, 1971). The critique unmasks the flaws and failures following from such externalization by interpreting, analysing and describing the complex dynamics of power and discipline associated with the practice of these mental maps.

Contexts and concepts: a translational perspective

These approaches imply an almost causal relationship between concept and transformation, including – from the critics – an implied negative impact on working life. But each of these perspectives might neglect the complexity and micro-sociological processes implied in the 'transfer' of universalized knowledge. A *neo-institutional* approach was formulated in which the need for more critical examination of the micro-sociological processes of organizational change was suggested (Czarniawska & Joerges, 1996), presumably to uncover a much more diverse, complex and rich understanding of organizational change. Sometimes this is referred to as the *Scandinavian neo-institutional approach* and sometimes as the *pragmatic neo-institutional approach*. Czarniawska and Joerges (1996), together with other colleagues, explored the travel of ideas and challenged the notion of how management concepts unilaterally influence organizational transformation. An important contribution was that ideas themselves are also transformed by literally, as well as metaphorically, going through the process of translation. This idea provided a rich ground for research on different perspectives on translation studies (Czarniawska & Joerges, 1996; Røvik, 2007; see also Spyridonidis et al., 2014). Any transfer of a managerial idea from one context to another implies translation. The idea is woven into the context and cannot be moved without its fundamental content being translated.

As a contributor to the pragmatist Scandinavian neo-institutionalism, Norwegian professor Kjell Arne Røvik (2007) provides an account of translation within sociological studies. He distinguishes between two paradigms (Røvik, 2007, p. 251). The early paradigm of translation predominantly emphasized *literal* translation, in which the author is obliged to translate word by word: the aim is to reproduce the text as precisely as possible. The translator's obligation is to be loyal to the text and only the text. Metaphorically, this would be tantamount to an organizational change process guided by a managerial concept, including tools/heuristics, which is implemented 1:1.

This standard of translation was challenged during the 1980s. The challenge contended a *cultural turn*, in which the translator was "expected now to consider the receiving culture" (Røvik, 2007, p. 252). The original idea of an author, Røvik argues, is intimately linked to the cultural context in which it is produced. If you transfer the text to another cultural context, the meaning of the original text is likely to get lost in translation. Translation needs to include co-authorship on the part of the translator in order to bring the ideas to life in the new context.

Any consultant, management guru, manager or employee who participates in dissemination of a managerial concept becomes part of the translation process and, consequently, a potential co-author. If you practise the managerial concept 1:1, and are true *only* to the text, you are likely to expect cultural clashes of meaning. If you, for instance, take a managerial concept that originates from a culture in which the group is the smallest foundational social unit (e.g. Japan) and transfer this to a cultural setting in which the smallest social unit is the individual (e.g. the United States or the Nordic countries), the actual practice is likely to have very different processual outcomes. Likewise, taking a concept that represents a coherent meaning system founded on specific institutionalized power structures will obviously have significant implications depending on whether this is practised within an *authoritarian* or *egalitarian* organizational culture.

Several important observations can be extracted from this: first, translation happens, no matter what; second, translation is contextually and culturally bound; and third, translation can happen more or less explicitly and more or less consciously. It is reasonable to suggest that contextual clashes between ideas/concepts and new contexts can be eased by means of reflective action. Explicit translation, ongoing learning, participatory (re)design of tools that embed practices within the "receiving" context, and reflection as part of this, are important. Røvik does not suggest normative approaches, but he does take up the idea of reflecting on distinct capabilities for the sake of better translation. If knowledge and ideas are supposed to be transferred from context to context, critical resources and skills will make a profound difference. Being a skilled translator is about the ability to practise a distinct set of deeds. Four essential characteristics of a translator are being *knowledgeable and multi-contextual*; *courageous and creative*; *persistent*; and *resilient/strong* (Røvik, 2007, pp. 319–337, our translation).

Transfer or translation by means of management concepts

We have presented two distinct theoretical perspectives on the potential influence of management concepts: Transfer and Translation. Both proponents and critics assume that management concepts transform organizations. Proponents apply them as knowledge that provides opportunities for competitive success, but seldom, if ever, consider democracy, autonomy and representation – as well as the working environment or health – as legitimate issues. Ironically, the critical approach shares the assumption that management concepts are decontextualized knowledge that is transferred and transforms organizations. But the critics argue that management concepts cause a deterioration in the work environment and health and are a means of control and discipline. This perspective implies a strategy of critique and resistance: "Within such a context resistance will appear as a more probable reaction than creative involvement" (Skorstad, 1994, p. 429).

The second theoretical perspective, the translational approach, is less inclined to accept the implied causal relationship between concepts and transformation. Instead, it emphasizes the need to enquire into micro-sociological processes to understand the processual complexity and the social dynamic of the symbolic interaction that shapes practices and outcomes. This perspective opens a different room for agency that may lead to positive – or less negative – outcomes in terms of work environment and health associated with the travel of ideas into Nordic working life.

In the next paragraph, we explore the travel of Lean into Nordic working life. First, we sketch out the concept of Lean. Then we draw on earlier research to explore the relationship between Lean and the work environment. Here, we broaden our scope from the Nordic to an international perspective but reflect on the findings' possible implication for Lean and the work environment in the Nordic countries. Last, we follow the idea of Translation and enquire into cases that can be seen as expressions of translation in order to understand possible strengths and weaknesses of such creative involvement.

Lean meeting the NWM

Lean refers to the production system and management concept which, in its broadest terms, focuses on eliminating waste. The historical roots go back to Sakichi Toyoda (1867–1930), who established *Toyoda Automatic Loom Works* and automated the process of looming. To reduce waste, he invented a device that automatically stopped the machines when a problem occurred. This principle was coined *jikoda*, and it became a "red thread" in the later Toyota Production System. In the decades following, different fundamental principles and tools that later became associated with Lean were developed. For instance, in the late 1940s, Taiichi Ohno at Toyota developed with a "common sense" approach just-in-time production. Also, the single-minute exchange of dies (SMED) was invented as an important means of reducing the time taken to shift between different products (Holweg, 2007, p. 422).

The Japanese economy expanded during the 1960s and 1970s, becoming something of an admired wonder whose competitive abilities challenged the Western world (Björkman & Lundqvist, 2013, p. 19). The export of Japanese cars increased dramatically and paved the way for joint ventures between US and Japanese car manufacturers. This accelerated the knowledge exchange, resulting in visits to factories in Japan and the United States, that had already occurred in the earlier development of different tools mentioned earlier. The popularity of Lean surged *after* being (re)discovered in the North American setting, when quality engineer John Krafcik worked on a joint venture between Toyota and GM (New United Motor Manufacturing) in California. However, it was when Krafcik went to MIT to do an MBA (Krafcik, 1988; Björkman & Lundqvist, 2013, p. 23) and turn the GM-NUMMI into research data with Womack and others that it surged as a management concept (see Holweg, 2007 for a more detailed account of the genealogy of Lean). Lean was "born" as a management concept that was presented as *universalized knowledge*, and *The Machine That Changed the World* (Womack et al., 1990) became one of the bestselling management books in decades.

Today, Lean is often associated with a set of tools; for instance, Value Stream mapping, Kaizen, 5S, 5 Whys, Go to Gemba and SMED. *Value Stream Mapping* is a means of carefully identifying work flows that create value and those that can be apprehended as waste; *Kaizen* is a means of systematically conducting continuous improvement; *5S* is five Japanese words beginning with the letter 's' for processes that help organize work in order to achieve efficiency that have been creatively translated into several other languages to keep the 5S's (in English, the words are translated as *Sort*, *Set In Order*, *Shine*, *Standardize* and *Sustain*); and the *5 Whys* is a technique applied to find the root cause of a problem.

But what does Lean not include? In the general philosophy, among the fundamental principles and known tools of Lean, there is no mention of democracy, quality of working life, meaningfulness, autonomy, whole tasks, balanced job demands, learning, or other themes that we met within the sociotechnical thinking and the principles and characteristics that were institutionalized historically in the emergence of NWM. In the Nordic countries, vast investments in programmes have been made to reform working life. As a consequence, as Björkman and Lundqvist point out (2013, p. 33), role models should be chosen carefully; the authors emphasize that Japan has never invested in the humanization of working life to institutionalize it in the same way that Nordic countries have. Likewise, Sandberg emphasizes that Lean production can never "be the ultimate goal and form for human productive activity. Some 'fat' is needed to make the workplace a decent place for human activity, a place where you can unfold as a human being" (Sandberg, 2007, p. vii). The "fat" includes an inclusive orientation towards some characteristics, principles and practices that have been institutionalized historically. Learning is important for the experience of balancing job demands with an experienced control (Thorsrud & Emery, 1970; Gustavsen, 1990; Hagedorn-Rasmussen & Elsborg, 2016) and is a necessary "fat" mark of a resilient, inclusive organization.

Are Lean mean? Leaning against "science"

We have found only one survey that looks into the role of Lean on the (psychosocial) work environment and related issues *within the Nordic countries*: Leanus – a contraction of "Lean uden stress", which means "Lean without stress" – was a Danish research project that followed the interventions within ten companies introducing Lean. We will return to that later in the chapter. Leanus applied a survey that included the ten participating companies within the specific research programme. Looking internationally, we found three international literature studies, summarizing and making inferences about the relationship between Lean and work environment. However, we also found Norwegian surveys that focused on the *adoption of Lean* in Norway that we return to at the end of this paragraph.

First, we look into three international literature studies which have investigated possible effects of Lean on the work environment and health. Like the first of our two presented theoretical perspectives, Transfer, the research design is based on the idea that it is possible to establish a causal relationship between a management concept (independent variable) and its consequences (dependent variables). It should be emphasized that these studies do not address Nordic working life specifically. However, the findings do provide us with important insights into the relationship between Lean and its travel into organizations, from which we can make inferences about Nordic working life.

In 1999, Landsbergis et al. published a survey of the literature on the impact on worker health of Lean production and related new systems of work organization. They identified 38 studies, of which 20 were published in peer-reviewed journals covering mostly the United States, Canada and England, with one in Finland. Of these, 13 were in the auto industry, 13 in other manufacturing industries, 11 in the health care industry and 1 in telecommunication. They concluded that, in general, the introduction of Lean production does cause some challenges in terms of the work environment: "Increases in decision authority and skill are very modest or temporary, and decision latitude remains low. Thus, such work can be considered to have job strain" (Landsbergis et al., 1999, p. 122). But they also emphasize exceptions to these deteriorating influences: "The exceptions to these general conclusions tend to appear in groups of workers who participated in the implementation of new work systems, or in which worker influence was secured through a collective bargaining agreement" (Landsbergis et al., 1999, p. 122). Toivanen together with Landsbergis (2013) conducted a literature survey covering the period from 2000 until 2011. They identified 15 relevant studies, 14 in peer-reviewed journals and 1 book covering 9 different countries. Although ambiguous, the studies documented an increase in work pace as well as an increase in work intensity. In line with the prior literature study, this literature study documented higher levels of stress, as well as a deterioration in wellbeing, fatigue and tension among employees within Lean production with manual work (Toivanen & Landsbergis, 2013, p. 97). Their study shows that "Lean production practices are often related to intensification of work pace and job demands, relatively low influence and only modest or temporary increase of influence in work" (Toivanen & Landsbergis, 2013, p. 97, our translation). Some of the studies accounted for the role of unions, and two of those suggested that the involvement of unions lessens the risk of stress on the job.

Almost simultaneously, Hasle et al. (2012) published a literature study which overlaps with Toivanen and Landsbergis (2013). In contrast to Landsbergis et al.'s (1999) study, Hasle et al. make greater efforts to consider the scope and context of Lean more clearly. The review likewise predominantly suggests evidence for negative effects on work environment, employee health and wellbeing when we look into manual work with low complexity. But it is also argued that the assumed causal relationship inherent in the research design is overemphasized and needs to be revised, because Lean takes many forms in terms of context, implementation and practice. These differences, they concluded, will have different effects: "In order to understand the effects of Lean on the working environment, we must examine the workings of Lean as a socio-technical system where the causal relations with the working environment are a matter of contextual and practical interpretation" (Hasle et al., 2012, pp. 845–846).

In the Norwegian surveys on adoption, Heien (2012) focused on organizations with more than 100 employees and found that 48% of the responding organizations had implemented Lean. Storsveen (2016) and Moum and Bordewich (2017) did not select respondents based on size but found adoption rates of 21.8% and 19.5% respectively. Storsveen (2016) further investigates the role of consultants who play an active role in implementing Lean. Only 23.9% of respondents have implemented Lean *without* the help of consultants, and, even more interesting for the scope of this chapter, the consultants primarily related to top and middle management (50.3% and 45.8% respectively) against employee representatives (13.5%), which confirms the idea of Lean not being particularly inclusive in terms of employee involvement.

The literature studies in general identify some negative consequences of the introduction of Lean on the work environment, etc. However, it also seems as if processes of translation can take place. We infer that such understandings of the interpretive flexibility of Lean also open the way for active strategies of translation. In the following sections, we will investigate cases in which translation of Lean has occurred.

Translating: the strategy of enacting work environment and NWM

Translation occurs regardless of whether you engage consciously in the process or not. As such, translations are likely to occur arbitrarily if not reflected. The quality of translation is likely to depend on the strategy and action undertaken.

Historically, the social parties and researchers have, in general, taken an active (though different) role in translating management concepts. In Norway, the Lean Forum was established in 2009 to create a Norwegian Lean model (Rolfsen & Ingvaldsen, 2013, p. 263), followed by reflections and discussions on whether unions as well as employee representatives became co-opted by managerial ideas and manipulated by consultants and Lean experts (Rolfsen & Ingvaldsen, 2013). Researchers suggest that it is important that companies take ownership of the concepts and develop them for their own purposes, and they encourage them to invite unions to do the work of "appropriation" (Ingvaldsen et al., 2012). In Denmark, the development of and research on Lean occurs in local experiments across sectors (Edwards et al., 2010). In Sweden, a national research and development programme has been financed by several different national funds (Abrahamsson & Sederblad, 2013, p. 324) following the line of investments in programmes that also consider work environment and working life. These cooperative efforts do not mean that Lean has been embraced unconditionally. Arguments against Lean and other management concepts, being an instrument of the reduction of autonomy, intensification, etc. (described earlier in the section "Critical perspectives on management concepts") have also influenced the approach in a dialectic process of becoming which has characterized the NWM.

In the following sections, we provide a renewed analytical perspective on three earlier projects that all represent the travel of Lean into the Nordic working life. The three projects are exemplary cases. It is our understanding that they strongly elucidate processes of translation. First, we investigate *Lean Operations* in Norway. In short, we start out by describing the introduction of Lean in Norway and then focus specifically on the research project Lean Operations. We investigate one specific case study within Lean Operations that provides insights into some of the translational dynamics, when Lean travels into organizational practice. After this, we turn to the second project, *Leanus*, mentioned earlier. This Danish intervention research programme explored how Lean was introduced within ten distinct companies. One of the ideas was to explore opportunities for introducing Lean *without stress*. We interpret this as an example of intentionally exploring the opportunities of translating Lean. This section ends with the third project that was designed to explore opportunities for the development of vocational training of production employees: what skills and qualifications do production employees need when Lean and other managerial and production concepts are introduced in industrial companies? What do the employees need to know to make sense of managerial ideas in the everyday practice of work organization and practices? One of the authors of this chapter participated in this project. These three projects enlighten various aspects of opportunities for actively engaging in translation as a strategy, while keeping in mind the need for critical scrutiny.

Engaging with Lean Operations

For a long period, the circulation of Lean among Norwegian organizations was limited (Levin et al., 2012). Apart from the process industry and automotive part manufacturers, diffusion was limited (Rolfsen, 2014). The concept started to attract interest among a diverse set of industry and sectors in 2008 and 2009, and, in the following decade, reports on Lean started to appear in printed media (Madsen et al., 2016). Work researchers with ambitions of diffusing and developing NWM had an ambivalent attitude towards the concept (Gustavsen et al., 2010; Skorstad, 2011; Levin et al., 2012). Lean was acknowledged as a concept that could potentially improve productivity and quality, but it could also lead to intensification of work and reduced autonomy (Skorstad, 2011) and reduced capabilities for learning because of standardization and reduced slack. As the concept gained popularity, researchers from institutions with a long tradition within NWM decided to take part in a research project aimed at developing a Norwegian approach to Lean. This project, Lean Operation, lasted from 2010 to 2014. The project arranged an annual two-day conference with about 500 participants (between 460 and 580 participants in the period from 2012 to 2017).

Lean Operations was probably the first Norwegian research project in which working life researchers engaged with a managerial idea potentially in conflict with the NWM. Working life researchers and companies went together to explore opportunities for a Norwegian translation. Lean influenced the way researchers, companies and social parties worked together across sectors. Working life researchers actively explored ways of transforming the management concept and "adapting" aspects of the concept to the institutional context within Norway. The intention was to develop knowledge on the functioning of Lean within Norwegian working life, as well as making a research-based contribution to the participating companies. The case studies from the project show that Lean could both conflict with NWM or be a useful tool for improvement based on broad participation. It also showed that the effects of Lean could differ over time within the same organization, as exemplified by Bygdås and Falkum (2012). They conducted a case study, Lean in the Sunset, in which they investigated the role of Lean during a period of economic success as well as decline. The case study presented two distinct approaches to Lean applied at REC Herøya.[1] In the first version, up until 2008, management introduced an instrumental version of 5S that enforced a top-down, rule-oriented approach with a strict interpretation of creating order (Bygdås & Falkum, 2012, pp. 5, 23). The implementation of Lean was met with significant resistance and had limited or no results. A combination of the financial crisis and increased competition from China created a "burning platform". The factory was at risk of going out of business, and a restructuring took place. The executive group was replaced, and new initiatives were taken. A second, and very different, approach to Lean was presented, although still decided by management. The new plant manager had a long history of producing results in collaboration with workers from the process industry. A new trade union representative was also elected, also with process industry experience in both fighting and collaborating with management in crisis situations.[2] The innovative approach was far more inclusive and cooperative. Employee representatives were included in:

> [p]lanning and decision on how the methods of improvement should appear and be applied. Even though much of this was already defined in RBS, Six Sigma and other tools that where applied, had to be translated and adapted to the context.
>
> (Bygdås & Falkum, 2012, p. 30, our translation)

This led to a quite distinct process that supported and engaged employees; for instance, absence caused by injuries decreased by 88%, complaints about inferior quality reduced by 95% and production cost per wafer reduced by 44% (Bygdås & Falkum, 2012, p. 11). Comparing the two approaches of Lean shows how "differences seem far more striking than the resemblances" (Bygdås & Falkum, 2012, p. 29, our translation). While management decided both initiatives, they differed in terms of creating an inclusive and cooperative approach with employees. Bygdås & Falkum conclude that:

> Lean is not necessarily an impediment to the Norwegian cooperative model. On the contrary, it documents that work towards continuous improvement conducted as a translation of Lean may benefit from letting managers, employee representatives and employees become equal actors.
>
> (2012, p. 29, our translation)

They conclude that REC Herøya succeeded in reaching their goals, precisely because they spent time creating a mutual understanding of what they needed to do, how and by whom. The study documents the importance of translation and draws attention to the need for participation by employees and the potentially devastating effects of a narrow, control-oriented approach.

Lean without stress

In 2010, researchers from Danish Technical University, National Research Centre for the Work Environment, and Aalborg University published the results of their research project *Lean and Work Environment* (Edwards et al., 2010), referred to as Leanus. The foreword is written by the CEO of the Confederation of Danish Industry and Secretary of the Central Organisation of Industrial Employees in Denmark. The researchers worked together with ten very distinct organizations (design, construction, accounting, logistics, machine producer, waste treatment company, surgery, cancer department, domiciliary care, and bank) and followed them before, during and after their implementation of Lean. Compared to other researchers within the work environment, the programme is optimistic about the opportunities for bringing in issues related to employee involvement and influence (Edwards et al., 2010, chapter 5). For instance, they emphasize the general claim of Womack et al. (1990) that employees will find greater challenges in work, since the idea of Lean is to instigate responsibility down the organizational ladder (Edwards et al., 2010, p. 113). Whether their expectations were confirmed is a complex subject to address. Leanus did measure the development of the psychosocial work environment during the process within each company with quite ambiguous results ranging from significant improvement to significant deterioration; in summary, four had positive changes in the psychosocial work environment, five had no changes and one had negative changes (Edwards et al., 2010, pp. 89–90). With regard to involvement, 56% of employees who experienced the introduction of Lean answered (in the follow-up survey) that they had experienced having some influence on Lean activities. The baseline survey documented that, in general, the answer from employees experiencing involvement was 50%. The result is interpreted as a positive result (Edwards et al., 2010, pp. 119–120). It could be argued that these results occur within a project in which the attention to the issue of work environment, involvement and so on was expected to be significant. Consequently, it would be reasonable to expect a greater increase.

In general, the results reflected a large diversity across companies. The companies took very distinct approaches to adopting the Lean practices, partly given their primary tasks but also because of other institutional settings. The researchers suggested that the companies differed with regard to two axes in their approach to the practice of Lean: *pragmatic vs dogmatic* approach, and *shortsighted vs longsighted* approach, creating Sporadic-Lean, Tool(based)-Lean, Standard-Lean and Transformation-Lean (Edwards et al., 2010, pp. 53ff). The Transformation-Lean approach (pragmatic/longsighted) included a more learning-oriented approach that also implied continuous translation of tools, etc. The more dogmatic came close to a fundamentally tool-based approach (Edwards et al., 2010, pp. 53 ff). The researchers also emphasize how Lean may be apprehended as a process of learning (Edwards et al., 2010, p. 157), implying a longsighted pragmatic perspective and emphasizing the translational process.

The researchers concluded that there is no straightforward way to judge the influence of Lean on the work environment: it *is* possible to have a positive work environment with Lean and even improve, but they rush to state that the question is too simple. It is necessary to look behind how employees and managers interact with Lean and how they transform it (Edwards et al., 2010, p. 183). The research project created a foundation for the companies, together with the researchers, to explore strengths and weaknesses, and possible clashes between distinct institutional logics of Lean meeting variants of the Nordic working life, and also enlighten some opportunities and barriers for translating Lean with regard to work environment, involvement, etc.

Equipping production employees to meet the future management concepts

Under the headline *Skilled Employees in a World of Production and Management Concepts*, the Danish Ministry of Education financed a joint project between the Educational Secretariat for Industry (Industriens Uddannelser, IU) and a consultancy firm specialized in analysing the need for vocational training and education within different sectors (Clematide et al., 2011).[3] IU is an independent institution comprising Dansk Metal (the Danish Metalworkers Union), 3F (United Federation of Danish Workers) and DI – Dansk Industri (the Confederation of Danish Industry). Thus, IU embodies the NWM insofar as it is a joint effort in which the employers and employees are represented in exploring the need for and developing vocational training and education to support the needs of the future industry. The project aimed at producing an analysis which could provide the foundation for developing vocational training within industrial education to equip future skilled employees to participate in confronting Lean, Performance Management and other production and management concepts. Recently, they have conducted a similar project on team structure and group organization in industrial companies in Denmark (Voxted, 2017), in which they concluded that teams are influenced by Lean team thinking, but that it also works in reverse (Voxted, 2017). Strengthening the vocational training within specific areas will provide processes of translation that contextualize the managerial ideas.

Based on an analysis of how six industrial companies adopted Lean and Performance Management, the project explored how the ideas travelled into each company. In particular, the project focused on how industrial employees interacted in the processes of adopting and translating the managerial concept, including how the organizations created room for participation, levels of autonomy and so on. The six qualitative case studies included interviews with skilled and semi-skilled employees, managers with responsibility for training and development, and production managers and shop stewards. The employees were interviewed in focus groups in which their approach to adopting Lean and Performance Management was explored. By means of a literature survey, an interview guide was developed to explore distinct approaches to Lean and other management concepts. Themes explored in the interviews included: To what degree does the company emphasize employee involvement? To what degree is Lean practised as a cultural, processual change or as a more tool-oriented approach? To what degree are Lean practices and tools performed by the employees as part of the ongoing work, or are Lean practices and tools a matter for experts and managers?

The results showed a high degree of variety in ways of translating Lean. Three ideal typical configurations were presented in the study, here labelled *ManagingLean*, *ApplianceLean* and *CulturLean*. In *ManagingLean*, the company worked in a very tool-oriented way with selected Lean tools. It was managers, above all, who enacted Lean roles, and employee involvement was relatively slight. *ApplianceLean* was much like *ManagingLean*, although employees had a high degree of involvement. The involvement was focused on applying their knowledge, feeding it in to make continuous improvements. The involvement did not transgress those process improvement initiatives selected by management. In the last configuration, *CulturLean*, Lean tools were seen as important in order to make process improvements. However, the tools were selected cooperatively by employees and management, while the selected tools reflected the opportunity of sense-making, given the context. Employees enacted the Lean roles, and employee involvement was, in general, high. This included what to adopt from Lean, how to adapt the Lean tools to make sense within the context and how to actually perform the tools in everyday practice.

Based on the analyses, skills which were important in working with and confronting the production and management concepts were identified: 24 skills in 7 different areas, such as technical-professional, methodological, organizational, communicative, IT, numeracy and personal competencies. These were skills and competencies that may be important when employees are introduced to new managerial ideas and concepts that will benefit from a constructive critical examination by professional and knowledgeable employees. The committees related to each of the distinct industrial educational areas within IU adopted these insights and systematically reviewed teaching plans and curricula to see if improvements were needed.

This project illustrates not only how the social parties within IU enacted a translational strategy but also how the employers and employees enact various aspects given the opportunities for translation, e.g. in work councils. It also directs attention towards the role of vocational training as a potentially valuable resource for translation.

The three examples show different cases of translation in which the social parties, employees, employers and managers at company level, as well as researchers, enact roles as translators implying some degree of co-authorship. The cases do give – although not in depth – ideas on how this co-authorship may include principles and characteristics otherwise externalized by the agenda provided by Lean. While this is no guarantee of a positive outcome, it does stress the interpretive flexibility of Lean that is open to some degree of translation.

Conclusion

In this chapter, we have explored what happens when decontextualized knowledge travels into Nordic working life; specifically, the extent to which international management concepts challenge the work environment and transform inherent principles in the NWM. First, it is important to stress that the NWM is a social construction – *a model*; second, it is in an ongoing process of becoming; and third, it is to some degree normative, insofar as the principles and characteristics that signify it are far from permeating all the institutions that constitute everyday working life in the Nordic countries. Moreover, it is a model that reflects a historical process of institutionalization which is open for translation. However, these reservations considered, we would argue that it is possible to speak of a loosely coupled NWM even in its becoming. This, in particular, is characterized by an institutionalization that – to a larger extent than represented among mainstream management in general and managerial concepts specifically – emphasizes what we have labelled principles and characteristics of the NWM, such as, for instance, democracy, participation, responsible autonomy, together with a reasonably demanding job content and the availability of learning opportunities at work.

Most managerial concepts in general, and Lean more specifically, tend to externalize these at the expense of a narrower, instrumental focus on organizational goals and the related core in the managerial concept. As such, our findings suggest that *Lean does challenge the work environment and the NWM*. It is documented that Lean *within specific contextual circumstances* is likely to externalize important issues with regard to the work environment and the NWM. However, the degree and appearance of influence are ambiguous. Context matters. In general, the causal idea that to some extent is implied in the research question – and propagated by both proponents and critics of management concepts – has inherent flaws that need to be considered. The practice of Lean (like other management concepts) is very diverse. This emphasizes the need for sensitivity towards the translational and contextual aspects of managerial concepts and the transformation of organizations. Strategies of active translation are likely to pave the way for more positive outcomes. Furthermore, it is concluded that, historically, the social parties, together with researchers within the field of work environment in the Nordic countries, have been engaged in such processes of translation, and that this is an inherent part of the model. This calls for continued strategies of active translation. However, likewise it is stressed that there is a need for balancing this with a continuous critical examination of the outcome of the introduction of international management in the work environment and the principles and characteristics implied in the NWM. When relating to managerial concepts, researchers, as well as social parties and actors at company level, may take on at least two distinct roles: the critical role and the translational role. It is important to balance those two roles in a continuation of strategies for developing a sustainable future work environment.

Notes

1 REC Herøya produces wafers, and the market changed dramatically during this period. However, the case emphasizes the distinct transformations that Lean undertook during this period. In the period of success up until 2008, the price of wafers increased. However, the financial crisis and increasing competition from China challenged the company (Bygdås & Falkum, 2012, p. 7).
2 The change of trade union representative is not mentioned in the report.
3 One of the authors participated in the project, conducting a literature review, case studies and analysis.

References

Abrahamson, E. (1996) Management Fashion, *Academy of Management Review*, 21(1): 254–285.

Abrahamsson, L. & Sederblad, P. (2013) Avslutning [Conclusion], In: Sederblad, P. (ed.) *Lean i arbetslivet [Lean in Working Life]*, Stockholm: Liber AB.

Benders, J. & Van Veen, K. (2001) What's in a Fashion? Interpretative Viability and Management Fashions, *Organization*, 8(1): 33–53.

Björkman, T. (2013) Management: Still a Fashion Industry, In: Sandberg, Å. (ed.) *Nordic Lights. Work, Management and Welfare in Scandinavia*, Stockholm: SNS, 91–125.

Björkman, T. & Lundqvist, K. (2013) Lean ur historiskt perspektiv [Lean in a Historical Perspective], In: Sandberg, Å. (ed.) *Nordic Lights. Work, Management and Welfare in Scandinavia*, Stockholm: SNS, 18–47.

Bottrup, P. (2001) *Læringsrum i arbejdslivet: et kritisk blik på Den Lærende Organisation [Learning Room in Work Life: A Critical Perspective on The Learning Organization]*, Copenhagen: Forlaget Sociologi.

Braverman, H. (1974) *Labor and Monopoly Capital*, New York: Monthly Review Press.

Burawoy, M. (1979) *Manufacturing Consent*, Chicago, IL: University of Chicago Press.

Burchardt, J. (2001) Introduktion af nye ledelsesformer: da Scientific Management kom til Danmark 1905–1920 [Introduction of New Managerial Styles: When Scientific Management Came to Denmark 1905–1920], *Tidsskrift for Arbejdsliv*, 3(4): 69–90.

Bygdås, A. & Falkum, E. (2012) Lean i Solnedgang. Vekst og Fall i RECs Waferfabrikk på Herøya. [Lean in Sunset. Growth and Decline in REC's Waferfactory at Herøya], *Arbeidsforskningsinstituttet*, 18/2012. https://doi.org/10.7577/afi/rapport/2012:18.

Byrkjeflot, H. (2003) Nordic Management: From Functional Socialism to Shareholder Value, In: Czarniawska, B. & Sevón, G. (eds) *The Northern Lights: Organization Theory in Scandinavia*, Stockholm: Liber AB, 17–39.

Clegg, S. R. (1989) *Frameworks of Power*, London: Sage.

Clematide, B., Hagedorn-Rasmussen, P. & Stahl, N. (2011) *Faglærtes kompetencer i en verden af produktions- og ledelseskoncepter [Skilled Employees in a World of Production and Management Concepts]*, Research report, Undervisningsministeriet (Danish Ministry of Education).

Czarniawska, B. & Joerges, B. (1996) Travels of Ideas, In: Czarniawska, B. & Sevón, G. (eds) *Translating Organizational Change*, Berlin: Walter de Gruyter, 13–48.

Deming, W. E. (2000) *Out of the Crisis*, Boston, MA: MIT Press.

DiMaggio, P. J. & Powell, W. W. (2000) The Iron Cage Revisited: Institutional Isomorphism and Collective Rationality in Organizational Fields, In: Baum, J. A. C. & Dobbin, F. (eds) *Economics Meets Sociology in Strategic Management*, Bingley, UK: Emerald Group Publishing Limited, 143–166.

Edwards, K., Bojesen, A. & Nielsen, A. P. (2010) *Lean og arbejdsmiljø: et dynamisk spændingsfelt [Lean and Work Environment: A Dynamic Tension Field]*, Copenhagen: L&R Business.

Grey, C. (2008) *A Very Short Fairly Interesting and Reasonably Cheap Book About Studying Organizations*, London: Sage.

Gustavsen, B. (1990) *Strategier for utvikling i arbeidslivet [Strategies for Development in Worklife]*, Oslo: TANO.

Gustavsen, B., Qvale, T. U., Sørensen, B. A., Midtbø, M. & Engelstad, P. H. (2010) *Innovasjonssamarbeid mellom bedrifter og forskning [Innovation Cooperation between Companies and Research]*, Oslo: Gyldendal Norsk Forlag AS.

Hagedorn-Rasmussen, P. (2000) Ledelseskoncepter fra idé til social dynamik: politiske processer på tværs af organisatoriske grænser. En analyse af sammenhænge mellem koncepter, forandringer og arbejdsforhold [Management Concepts from Idea to Social Dynamics], PhD dissertation, Roskilde University, Denmark.

Hagedorn-Rasmussen, P. (2001) Ledelseskonsulenters formning af forandringsprocesser, [Management Consultants Shaping Change Processes], *Tidsskrift for Arbejdsliv*, 3(2): 33–51.

Hagedorn-Rasmussen, P. & Elsborg, S. (2016) Forandring som læreproces [Change as Learning Process], In: Hagedorn-Rasmussen, P., Pries-Heje, J., Bødker, K., Scheuer, J. D. & Elsborg, S. (eds) *Robust organisationsforandring [Robust Organizational Change]*, Frederiksberg, Denmark: Samfundslitteratur, 185–202.

Hammer, M. & Champy, J. (2009) *Reengineering the Corporation: Manifesto for Business Revolution*, London: Nicholas Brealey Publishing.

Hasle, P., Bojesen, A., Langaa Jensen, P. & Bramming, P. (2012) Lean and the Working Environment: A Review of the Literature, *International Journal of Operations & Production Management*, 32(7): 829–849.

Heien, V.-A. A. (2012) *Lean: Utbredelsen blant norske produksjonsbedrifter [Lean: Distribution among Norwegian Manufacturing Companies]*, Ås, Norway: Norwegian University of Life Sciences.
Holmemo, M. D. Q., Rolfsen, M. & Ingvaldsen, J. A. (2016) Lean Thinking: Outside-In, Bottom-Up? The Paradox of Contemporary Soft Lean and Consultant-Driven Lean Implementation, *Total Quality Management & Business Excellence*, 29(2): 148–160.
Holweg, M. (2007) The Genealogy of Lean Production, *Journal of Operations Management*, 25(2): 420–437.
Huczynski, A. (2012) *Management Gurus*, Oxford, UK: Routledge.
Hvid, H., Møller, N., Kristensen, T. S. & Smith-Hansen, L. (2003) Developmental Work, In: Hvid, H. & Hasle, P. (eds) *Human Development and Working Life: Work for Welfare*, Aldershot, UK: Ashgate, 11–39.
Ingvaldsen, J. A., Rolfsen, M. & Finsrud, H. D. (2012) Lean organisering i norsk arbeidsliv: slutten på medvirkning? [Lean Organisation within Norwegian Working Life: End of Participation?], *Magma*, 4: 42–50.
Johansson, S. (2013) Lean och det svenska fackföreningsrörelsen: ett tudelat förhållande [Lean and the Swedish Union Movement: A Twofold Relationship], In: Sederblad, P. (ed.) *Lean i arbetslivet [Lean in Working Life]*, Stockholm: Liber AB, 241–258.
Kamp, A. & Hagedorn-Rasmussen, P. (2004) Diversity Management in a Danish Context: Towards a Multicultural or Segregated Working Life?, *Economic and Industrial Democracy*, 25(4): 525–554.
Kamp, A., Koch, C., Buhl, H. & Hagedorn-Rasmussen, P. (2005) *Forandringsledelse: med koncepter som ledestjerne [Change Management: With Concepts As Leading Star]*, Copenhagen: Nyt Teknisk Forlag.
Knights, D. & McCabe, D. (1998) Dreams and Designs on Strategy: A Critical Analysis of TQM and Management Control, *Work, Employment and Society*, 12(3): 433–456.
Knights, D. & McCabe, D. (2000) 'Ain't Misbehavin'? Opportunities for Resistance under New Forms of 'Quality' Management, *Sociology*, 34(3): 421–436.
Knights, D. & McCabe, D. (2002) A Road Less Travelled: Beyond Managerialist, Critical and Processual Approaches to Total Quality Management, *Journal of Organizational Change Management*, 15(3): 235–254.
Koch, C., Hagedorn-Rasmussen, P. & Vogelius, P. (2003) New Management and Working Life: The Forced Marriage, In: Hvid, H. & Hasle, P. (eds) *Human Development and Working Life: Work for Welfare*, Aldershot, UK: Ashgate, 41–65.
Koch, C., Vogelius, P. & Manske, F. (1999) Er ledelseskonceptet Business Process Reengineering vejen til et bedre arbejde? [Is the Management Concept BPR the Road towards Better Work?], In: Hvid, H. (ed.) *Ressourcer og velfærd i arbejdslivet [Resources and Welfare in Working Life]*, Copenhagen: Frydenlund, 46–56.
Krafcik, J. F. (1988) Triumph of the Lean Production System, *Sloan Management Review*, 30(1): 41–52.
Landsbergis, P. A., Cahill, J. & Schnall, P. (1999) The Impact of Lean Production and Related New Systems of Work Organization on Worker Health, *Journal of Occupational Health Psychology*, 4(2): 108–130.
Levin, M., Nilssen, T., Ravn, J. & Øyum, L. (2012) *Demokrati i arbeidslivet. Den norske samarbeidsmodellen som konkurransefortrinn [Democracy in Working Life. The Norwegian Cooperation Model as a Competitive Advantage]*, Bergen, Norway: Fagbokforlaget.

Lukes, S. (1974) *Power: A Radical View*, New York: Palgrave Macmillan.

Madsen, D. Ø., Storsveen, M., Klethagen, P. & Stenheim, T. (2016) The Diffusion and Popularity of Lean in Norway: An Exploratory Survey, *Cogent Business & Management*, 3(1): 1–21.

Moltu, B. (2003) 'BPR på norsk!' Managementkonseptet Business Process Reengineering (BPR) som kulturell praksis [BPR in Norwegian. BPR as cultural practice], PhD dissertation, NTNU.

Moum, J. V. & Bordewich, I. O. (2017) *Lean: Glasur eller ingrediens? En studie av hvordan styringsverktøy oversettes og implementeres eksemplifisert gjennom en studie av Lean i Norge [Lean: Glaze or Ingredient? A Study of How Management Tools are Translated and Implemented Exemplified by a Study by Lean in Norway]*, Trondheim, Norway: NTNU.

Peters, T. J., Waterman, R. H. & Jones, I. (1982) *In Search of Excellence: Lessons from America's Best-Run Companies*, New York: Warner Book.

Rolfsen, M. (2014) *Lean blir norsk: Lean i den norske samarbeidsmodellen [Lean Becomes Norwegian: Lean in the Norwegian Collaboration Model]*, Bergen, Norway: Fagbokforlaget.

Rolfsen, M. & Ingvaldsen, J. (2013) *Fackföreningsrörelsens förhållande till lean i Norge [Trade Union Movement's Relation to Lean in Norway]*, In: Sederblad, P. (ed.) *Lean i arbetslivet [Lean in Working Life]*, Stockholm: Liber AB, 259–274.

Rosenzweig, P. (2014) *The Halo Effect. . . and the Eight Other Business Delusions that Deceive Managers*, New York: Frem Press.

Røvik, K. A. (2007) *Trender og translasjoner: ideer som former det 21. århundrets organisasjon [Trends and Translations: Ideas That Shape the 21st Century Organization]*, Oslo: Universitetsforlaget.

Sandberg, Å. (2007) Volvo Kalmar: Twice a Pioneer, In: Sandberg, Å. (ed.) *Enriching Production: Perspectives on Volvo's Uddevalla Plant as an Alternative to Lean Production.* Online at http://mpra.ub.uni-muenchen.de/10785/. Originally published 2004, Aldershot, UK: Ashgate, 87–101.

Sederblad, P. (ed.) (2013) *Lean i arbetslivet [Lean in Working life]*, Liber AB: Stockholm.

Senge, P. (1990) *The Fifth Discipline*, New York: Century Business.

Shenhav, Y. (2003) The Historical and Epistemological Foundations of Organization Theory: Fusing Sociological Theory with Engineering Discourse, In: Knudsen, C. & Tsoukas, H. (eds) *The Oxford Handbook of Organization Theory*, 183–209, Oxford: Oxford University Press.

Simon, H. A. (1971) Designing Organizations for an Information-Rich World, In: Greenberger, M. (ed.) *Computers, Communications, and the Public Interest*, Baltimore, MD: University of Johns Hopkins Press.

Skorstad, E. (1994) Lean Production, Conditions of Work and Worker Commitment, *Economic and Industrial Democracy*, 15(3): 429–455.

Skorstad, E. (2013) Organizational Change and Resistance in Norwegian Working Life, In: Sandberg, Å (ed.) *Nordic Lights. Work, Management and Welfare in Scandinavia*, Stockholm: SNS.

Skorstad, E. J. (2011) *Omstillinger i arbeidslivet: Importerte moter og nasjonale tradisjoner [Changes in Working Life: Imported Fashions and National Traditions]*, Oslo: Gyldendal.

Sørhaug, T. (1996) *Om ledelse: makt og tillit i moderne organisering [About Management: Power and Confidence in Modern Organizations]*, Oslo: Universitetsforlaget.

Spyridonidis, D., Currie, G., Heusinkveld, S., Strauss, K. & Sturdy, A. (2014) New Developments in Translation Research, *International Journal of Management Reviews*, 16(2): 245–248.

Storsveen, M. (2016) *Utbredelsen av Lean i Norge: en spørreundersøkelse [The Dissemination of Lean in Norway: A Survey]*, Ås, Norway: Norwegian University of Life Sciences.

Thorsrud, E. & Emery, F. E. (1970) Industrial Democracy in Norway, *Industrial Relations*, 9(2): 187–196.

Toivanen, S. & Landsbergis, P. (2013) Lean och arbetstagarnas hälsa [Lean and Workers' Health], In: Sederblad, P. (ed.) *Lean i arbetslivet [Lean in Working Life]*, Stockholm: Liber AB, 84–102.

Trist, E. & Bamforth, K. (1951) Some Social and Psychological Consequences of the Longwall Method of Coal-Getting, *Human Relations*, 4(1): 3–38.

Voxted, S. (2017) *Analyse af udviklingen i teamstrukturen i industrien og afledte kompetencebehov [Analysis of the Development in the Team Structure Within the Industry and Deduction of Needs for Skills and Qualifications]*, Report, IU. https://iu.dk/public/dokumenter/01.PDF_bladreformat/Analyser/Analyse%20udvikling%20af%20teamstruktur%20(FINAL).pdf (last accessed 25 September 2018).

Weick, K. (1995) *Sensemaking in Organizations*, New York: Sage.

Womack, J. P., Jones, T. D. & Roos, D. (1990) *The Machine That Changed the World*, New York: Palgrave Macmillan.

Chapter 6

Working environment regulation in Norway and Denmark

Jan Erik Karlsen, Klaus T. Nielsen and Robert H. Salomon

The initial development of labour law legislation

Across industrialized countries, there is more or less consensus that working life needs regulation in order to become safer and enhance protection, health promotion and welfare for employees.

In Denmark, the Parliament passed the first labour protection law in 1873. The aim was mainly to reduce child labour in factories. Following this legislation, Denmark established its first labour inspectorate. The issue of child labour in the tobacco industry was clearly addressed in their first annual report. Later, accident protection was also included in the legislation, and in 1901, a more general industrial labour protection law was introduced in Denmark. The labour inspectorate was then established as an independent agency, in fact the first independent agency in the Danish governmental system, which indicates the salience of the issue.

Labour law developments in Denmark inspired early Norwegian labour law work. Norway did not follow Denmark until 1885, when the Government appointed a commission to prepare a law. Child labour was also a main issue in Norway. Finally, in 1892, the first factory inspection law was approved by Parliament (Karlsen, 2018). This first law covered factory workers, but other groups of workers also had some legal rights, such as miners, who had been covered by a law since 1842. The aim of the first protection laws in both countries was accident protection and reduction of health hazards in the factories, and the focus was on technical solutions.

In Norway, the regulation of working hours was also an important issue at that time. The emergent workers' associations pushed for a regulation, supported by the liberal bourgeoisie, who were also in favour of reduced working hours. The main arguments for reduced working hours were: (1) improved health and welfare, (2) greater possibilities for workers to improve skills, (3) improved working methods (productivity) and (4) opportunities for workers to take part in democratic processes in society (Byrkjeland, 2006).

There were several attempts to include working hours in the legislation of 1892, but without initial success. It took 23 years before the standard working day was fixed at 10 hours and included in a revision of the 1909 legislation. In Denmark, working hours were regulated in collective agreements rather than legislation.

The labour protection laws until the 1970s

The Norwegian labour protection law of 1936 had a wider scope and coverage than previous legislation and can be characterized as a general labour protection law. There were also attempts to change the Danish labour protection law in the 1930s. However, these attempts were fruitless at first, and World War II postponed the process further. Finally, in 1954, Denmark managed to introduce a new labour protection law. This new legislation covered most of the labour market in Denmark. There were three complementary laws covering: (1) trade and office work, (2) agriculture and (3) miscellaneous industries including industrial production and construction.

The revision and extension of the labour protection laws in the 1950s were also influenced by activities and policies outside the Nordic countries. Included in the new regulatory regime was the national implementation of conventions of the International Labour Organization (ILO) such as the Labour Inspection Convention of 1947. This illustrates how national legislation was influenced by and adjusted to international legislation and conventions.

Occupational health and safety back on the agenda in the 1970s

Several European countries, including Denmark and Norway, revised their Occupational Health and Safety (OHS) legislation during the 1970s. The revisions were partly inspired by the British Lord Robens' report (Lord Robens, 1972) and a general upsurge in radical political thinking among students and workers following the 1968 movement. In addition, an accumulation of problems stemming from the success of Taylorism, expansion of mechanization and the increasing use of chemicals in many industries, ran concurrently with a growing knowledge of the risks associated with work in modern workplaces.

In Denmark, left-wing students wrote a series of reports on various aspects of the working environment, such as "the painters report", "the slaughterhouse report" and "the brewery report". It was not high science, but the reports made it clear that there were serious challenges for both trade unions and labour inspections to overcome. The "painters report" was particularly successful. Soon, the health problems of organic solvents were almost eradicated, and Denmark was a pioneer in that issue. A commission to prepare a new OHS act issued four reports, including one that proposed wellbeing as a significant and novel OHS issue. However, when the act was finalized, the four reports did not play a decisive role, and wellbeing was not included in the legislation. In the comments to the act, which in Denmark have legal significance, wellbeing was explicitly exempted from the legislation. The act, adopted in 1975 and effected in 1977, was named "The Working Environment Act". It signalled a shift from individual protection from harm to a concern to make the general workplace environment risk-free. All Nordic countries adopted this new term, working environment, as a substitute for OHS during the 1970s.

In Norway, the development of the working environment legislation was partly influenced by the cooperation experiments in Norwegian industry, which began in the late 1960s and continued into the next decade. In these experiments, the main employers' association and the largest labour union agreed on field experiments in different sectors, including an iron plant, a paper and pulp factory, a factory making electric ovens and a large Norwegian process industry company (Thorsrud & Emery, 1970). The experiments were later expanded to the hotel and restaurant, offshore and shipping industries. The experiments took place with the participation of the workers, in order to improve work processes and maintenance work and routines.

The field experiments showed interesting results, improving both productivity and the working environment. Important questions were also raised, e.g. who will benefit from the productivity increase: the owners, the management, workers who took part in the experiments or all workers? Such questions are also relevant today. The field experiments also created an important training ground for industrial democracy, e.g. allowing for the organization of work in self-governed groups as alternatives to assembly line work. To disseminate the experiences from these experiments to other workplaces and the industrial sector in general was a challenge (Gustavsen, 1992). One important follow-up activity was the introduction of self-governed groups in the Swedish Volvo car factory. In fact, Swedish employers were very active in reforming industrial work in this period (Agurén & Edgren, 1979). In Norway, the dissemination effect was smaller than hoped for, although the idea of worker participation was followed up in many sectors. However, the potential of involving workers in improvement of production processes was also relevant for the improvement of the working environment. This insight was brought into new Norwegian legislation in 1977.

Until 1977, working environment legislation was based on factory inspection and workers' protection laws. The basic elements of these laws were continued in the new 1977 legislation. However, several new elements were also included. While the former legislation was protective (and thus reactive), the new law focused also on the development of a sound working environment, which enabled a higher quality of work combined with increased productivity.

The Norwegian 1977 legislation included five new characteristics (Karlsen, 2018, pp. 174–179):

- A holistic perspective: none of the factors of the working environment should be considered in isolation; the working environment should be examined as an interplay between various factors.

- Continuous improvement: the employer has a continuous task to ensure a sound working environment. In reality, this is a request for continuous improvement of the working environment.
- Psychological and social conditions: to include psychological factors was quite novel. The relevant paragraph was criticized for being too vague. However, it was argued that such a paragraph had an educational function in encouraging managers to consider social and psychological factors.
- The use of lay opinion: workers are not experts on working environment in general but can be assumed to have good knowledge of their own working environment as they experience it in their daily operations. The act allowed for whistle blowing by employees when things were not in order and for employees to participate in continuous efforts to improve the working environment.
- Worker participation: one of the aims of the act was to strengthen working environment efforts in each company with a focus on its particular challenges. Direct and representative participation by the workers was a prerequisite for improvement of the working environment locally. This principle was built into the main mechanisms for improving the working environment today.

The legislation in Denmark presented some of the same features, but not all of them. It had a holistic perspective. Indeed the name, the Working Environment Act, signalled a shift away from individual environmental risk factors towards the all-encompassing situation in which work was taking place. Further, worker participation in activities initiated to mitigate OHS problems and improve the working environment was in focus in the Danish legislation. However, despite the proclamation in the first paragraph of the act that the aim was to create "a safe and healthy working environment which is at all times to be in accordance with the technical and social development of society" (*The Danish Working Environment Act*, 1975), the notion of continuous improvement is not a very prominent feature of the Danish legislation.

The distinct difference between the countries is, however, the rules concerning the psychological and social environment. In principle, the psychosocial working environment has been included in the Danish legislation since the 1970s, due to the general aim of the act cited here and due to other general references in the act and underlying executive orders. Nevertheless, not until a 2012 amendment to the act were there specific references to the psychosocial working environment in the paragraphs of the act, and even today, there is no particular executive order relating to these aspects of work in Denmark.

Present working environment in Norway and Denmark versus the EU

Before we discuss the more contemporary developments of working environment regulation in Norway and Denmark, let us consider the status of the quality of the working environment.

Data collected in the *European Working Conditions Survey* (Parent-Thirion et al., 2016) and processed in the study (Aagestad et al., 2017) addresses similarities and differences between working conditions and health in Norway and the EU, including Denmark. Most of the working environment factors described in their report reveal significant similarities between Norway and the other Scandinavian countries. Across Europe as a whole, it is especially the Netherlands, but also Switzerland, that share characteristics with Denmark and Norway with regard to working conditions, health and wellbeing in the workplace (Table 6.1).

Flexible and predictable working hours, a shorter working week and a high prevalence of part-time work, especially among women, are key characteristics of the Norwegian and Danish labour markets. Such factors are conducive to a good *work–life balance*. Around nine in ten Norwegian and Danish workers report enjoying an overall good work–life balance. In the EU, the figure is eight in ten. However, in some respects, e.g. working hours decided by the company, as illustrated in Table 6.1, the differences between the European and Danish and Norwegian workers are greater.

The *psychosocial and organizational* working environment is in general more positive in Norway and Denmark than in the EU. As many as 94% of Norwegian workers, 91% of Danish and 86% of EU workers are satisfied with their working conditions. The majority of Norwegian and Danish workers feel that the organization they work for motivates them to do a good job.

Compared with their EU counterparts, a smaller proportion of Norwegian and Danish workers suffer *mechanical exposure* such as painful working positions

Table 6.1 Major working environment indicators for Denmark, Norway and EU28, 2015, percentages

Working environment factors	*Denmark*	*Norway*	*EU28*
Work–life balance; working hours decided by the company (in %)	37	39	61 (EU15)
Psychosocial and organizational working environment; overall satisfaction with working conditions	91	94	86
Work autonomy; decide or change:			
Ordering of job tasks	85	82	68
Work methods/applications	83	84	69
Work pace	84	83	71
Participation in health, safety and environment	90	91	73
Health and safety at risk	19	15	23
Quality of work:			
positively challenging working environment	39	38	21
poor quality job	10	8	20

Source: Aagestad et al. (2017, various tables).

and repetitive hand or arm movements. Norwegian and Danish workers are less likely than the EU average to experience exposure to *chemical* risk factors in the workplace, although they report being more exposed to *biological* hazards. Norway and Denmark perform well on almost every quality of work factor compared with the EU. Almost two in five workers in Norway (38%) and Denmark (39%) find themselves in the "'high flying' job quality profile" (Parent-Thirion et al., 2016, pp. 130–131), translated in Aagestad et al. (2017, p. 16) as a "positively challenging working environment". In the EU, the figure is 21%. Conversely, the relative number of people in the "poor quality job" profile in the EU generally is 20%, whereas in Norway and Denmark the figures are around 10%.

Parent-Thirion et al. (2016) conclude that working conditions for EU workers have generally improved. However, as Aagestad et al. (2017, p. 13) summarize:

> [a] number of challenges remain, especially in relation to working conditions amongst specific groups of workers and in terms of gender, age and business size. There is also an accumulation of risk factors in certain occupations and sectors.

The main conclusion of Aagestad et al. (2017, p. 13) is that working conditions in Norway are good compared with the EU, although in Norway, too, some challenges exist in certain occupations and sectors. As the various figures above indicate, the situation in Denmark shows similar characteristics.

A closer look at working environment changes and trends since the late 1990s in Norway reveals some improvements and some challenges, as summarized in Table 6.2.

These figures are probably too positive. Norway also has a grey and black labour market in the hotel and restaurant sector, construction work and

Table 6.2 Selected working environment indicators among employed persons 18–66 years, percentages

Year	*1996*	*2006*	*2016*
Exposed to dust, gas or steam most of the time	14	8	4
Pain in neck, shoulders or upper back, due to work	14	11	10
Often or always feel motivated and engaged in own work	n/a	89	85
Feel mentally weary when returning home from work, weekly	29	14	19
Experience bad relationship between employees and management, often or from time to time, employee	34	37	31

Source: Statistics Norway https://www.ssb.no/en/statbank (2017).

services such as car washing, cleaning, etc. These workers have temporary jobs, often without any written contract. They are at risk of losing their job and will often hesitate to take part in surveys and are therefore underrepresented in these tables.

The chosen physical working environment measures show a promising trend. In 2016, 85% often or always felt that they were motivated and engaged in their own work, a slight decrease since 2006. It is interesting to notice that the percentage of employees who weekly feel mentally weary when they return home from work decreased from 1996 to 2006 but rose again in 2016. The relationship between employer and employee has (according to the employees) been nearly stable during the 1996–2016 period.

We see a similar picture in Denmark. However, in Denmark an official working environment strategy adopted in 2011 by the government did set three reduction goals to be met in 2020: 25% fewer serious accidents, 20% fewer employees with excessive psychosocial stress and 20% fewer with excessive musculoskeletal stress. When measured in 2016, the figures were approaching the target for accidents, but in the other two areas, the figures had gone up rather than down. Excessive psychosocial stress showed an increase from 14.5% (2012) to 16.9% (2016), while for musculoskeletal problems the figures rose from 9.7% to 11.1% (same years) (Det Nationale Forskningscenter for Arbejdsmiljø, 2017).

The overall picture is one of better working conditions in Norway and Denmark than in most other countries. The situation varies with the sector and the particular aspect of the working environment. Perhaps there is a challenging lack of overall progress, especially when stipulated goals are moving further away rather than being approached.

The regulatory institutional settings, more specifically the legal regulation and the labour inspection authorities, are far from the only important contextual factors to take into account when discussing this status and these developments. Nevertheless, the rosy picture painted suggests we should take a closer look at some of the specificities of working environment regulation in Norway and Denmark, as we shall do in the rest of this chapter.

Psychosocial working environment: different routes for Norway and Denmark?

For years, Norway has been at the forefront of regulating the psychosocial and organizational aspects of the working environment. The work by Thorsrud and Emery (1970) lists a set of six psychosocial factors of importance for the working environment, apart from salary and safety:

- Job content – challenging and varied
- Continuous learning at work
- Opportunity to make decisions related to own work

- Social support and recognition
- Positive relations between work, outcome and outside world
- Prospects for a desirable future.

It is important to emphasize both positive and negative aspects of working life. Social support from management and colleagues when needed, and the possibility to take part in the design of one's own work, will influence job satisfaction, motivation and learning.

In general, Norwegian managers and workers realize the value of a good psychosocial working environment. However, there are differences between sectors of the economy (Eiken et al., 2008). An increasingly important aspect of the psychosocial working environment is conflict mediation. Table 6.2 reveals that almost one-third of employees experience a bad relationship between themselves and management, often or from time to time. Some of the bad relationships have the character of *cool conflict*. That is a conflict where the conflicting parties are represented by someone else, e.g. a union, and where there are formal rules for handling the conflict. Wage formation through negotiations is an example. Usually, such conflicts do not become personal since the negotiating parties are acting on behalf of others. The same statistics cited also reveal that 8% are often or sometimes involved in unpleasant conflicts with management or other employees. At least 1 to 2% of these conflicts are *hot conflicts*. A hot conflict is a conflict between an employee and manager or between employees where there is a dispute about job performance, role interpretation, communication, recognition, support, etc. Such conflicts are common in knowledge work when employees invest their personality in their job and have to cooperate with others to get the job done (Heen & Salomon, 2018; Sørensen & Grimsmo, 2001).

There are formal rules in the Working Environment Act to handle bullying and harassment but no clear rules to deal with other types of hot conflicts. Hot conflicts can be handled by psychological approaches offering individual or group therapy. Both approaches may work. Serious hot conflicts will sometimes end up as a court case. If not mediated, they will end up in a "win–lose" situation where the winner takes all. Labour court cases may last for two to three years and are very burdensome for all involved. Hot conflicts may also be mediated in an organizational context where the parties try to find out if the conflict is related to the working environment or the work organization.

It is not recommended to solve all hot conflicts by legal means because of the excessive costs in time, money and a protracted indeterminate situation. It is therefore necessary to develop local mediating mechanisms at the workplace to deal with hot conflicts. Participatory processes to improve the working environment and establish internal codes of conduct are examples of what can be done locally.

In Denmark, it has taken a long time for the psychosocial working environment to become integrated into the legal framework and regulatory practice.

The most symbolic element was the 2012 reformulation of the Working Environment Act to include the following paragraph:

> § 1a. This Act shall cover the physical and psychological working environment.

The prime mover of this amendment was the Confederation of Professionals in Denmark (FTF), most of whose member unions cover the public sector.

In the mid-1990s (see also Rasmussen et al., 2011) when the government had shifted from right to left, the Danish Working Environment Authority started to issue notices relating to the psychosocial working environment. This paved the way for a committee, primarily consisting of representatives of the social parties. This committee, known as the "methods committee", finalized their work with a report that, despite its legally unconventional status, has dominated the field since. The parties agreed to differentiate between two types of problems (Metodeudvalget, 1995):

- Problems that are directly related to general decisions concerning the company and related to the interplay between management, employees and their representatives, in addition to conditions outside the company, i.e. problems which do not directly or indirectly stem from the individual job function.
- Problems directly or indirectly connected with the individual work situation.

Based on this distinction, the Working Environment Authority is only allowed to issue notices related to the second group of problems, and local working environment committees in companies are not supposed to deal with the first group of problems but should transfer them to the local cooperation committee. This arrangement has been in operation since 1995, and although it has been renegotiated recently, it is continuing almost unaltered.

As Rasmussen et al. (2011) demonstrate, the Danish Working Environment Authority has worked with tools to focus and streamline methods of inspecting the psychosocial working environment. But a comparison of notices in this field with all notices issued by the Authority reveals figures for 2011, 2014 and 2017 of only 2.2%, 2.8% and 2.3% (based on figures available on the website of the Authority: arbejdstilsynet.dk/da/). The majority of psychosocial notices concern the risk of violence from citizens, rather than stress-related problems. It is clear that the relative focus on the psychosocial problems has not grown over this period. There is widespread recognition that psychosocial problems are difficult to regulate through traditional command-and-control regulation (e.g. Jespersen et al., 2016), but the low numbers and lack of growth are still surprising, given the political and public attention.

Concurrent working environment regulation models

Labour law rules are based on various notions of what constitutes the challenges of working life and how they can be solved. In other words, they are subject to political awareness processes and can be changed due to new knowledge and under the impact of new discursive ways to articulate the problems, the field and the conflicts. Graver (1995) suggests the concept of regulatory models in relation to the judicial rules of working life. His three models largely coincide with clear historical epochs. The period from 1892 to 1936 saw a "parliament model" based on public governance; the "organizational model" from 1936 to 1977 is based on the regulation of opposing interests of the social parties; and the "company model" coincides with the introduction of the two working environment acts in the mid-1970s, based on consensus and reflexive, participatory democratic ideals. These terms indicate that different parts of:

> [l]abour law regulation rest on different models of how behavioural patterns between actors in companies unfold when problems and conflicts are to be solved.
>
> (Graver, 1995, p. 149, own translation)

At the turn of the century, a new model has emerged, based on market principles rather than on reflexive practices. We can see this fourth regulatory model with the introduction of internal controls in Health, Safety, and Environment (HSE) work in companies in Norway from 1992, which gained further momentum with the phasing in of these HSE requirements into the Working Life Act of 2005 and subsequent Working Environment Act of 2006. In Denmark, the primary manifestation of this model is the introduction from 2004 of a scheme whereby companies can exempt themselves from regular labour inspection if they become certified according to an OHS management standard. In the international arena, the emergence of this model is visible in the literature (e.g. Frick et al., 2000). This model we may term a "market model".

In Norway in particular, new regulations on working hours and more leeway for precarious employment contracts indicate a change towards market regulation rather than institutional arrangements. Firstly, the *market model* signals stronger management-based internal control than previous legislation. Secondly, the government's motivation is to develop an inspection-regime-based second-order inspection – a regime anticipated to be both cost-saving and deregulating. Thirdly, the companies themselves need to identify the actors among their stakeholders (shareholders, suppliers, customers and interest organizations) that will influence HSE work in addition to the company's own employees.

In Denmark, the market model is synonymous with the phasing out of a compulsory occupational health service that applied to certain sectors, representing about 40% of the labour market. At first, this was accompanied by a stricter inspection regime under which all companies were to be inspected, or rather screened, within seven years; that is hardly a market model, although it was argued that it created more equal market conditions. After the first screening round, in which almost all workplaces were visited, the labour inspection authorities returned to a sampling approach, now termed risk-based inspection.

We can now expand Graver's (1995) models of labour law regulation regimes into four types, as shown in Table 6.3.

In today's working life, all four models are operating side by side, but they have different impacts when problems and conflicts are to be resolved. Declining endorsement, support and influence for unions indicates that the regulatory importance and impact of the *organizational model* will decrease. Some general considerations of the welfare, health and safety of vulnerable groups, and the regards for the external environment, suggest that the regulatory function of the *parliament model* ought to be expanded to ensure appropriate minimum working environment standards. Enhanced competencies, improved insight into the solution of technical issues, social processes and interaction, as well as more realistic management theories, suggest that the *company model* will need greater leeway in future regulatory regimes. Local problem solving and common interests of employers and employees should be in focus.

In the following two sections, we shall dig deeper into some aspects of working environment regulation that have constituted major differences between the Norwegian and Danish regulatory systems since the 1990s.

Table 6.3 Models of working environment regulation regimes

Themes	*Parliament model*	*Organizational model*	*Company model*	*Market model*
Regulatory principles	Authority execution Concise rules	Lateral regulation Procedural rules	Tripartite regulation In-house co-determination	Bilateral checks and balances Self-inspection
State interest	Delimitations of industrial work	Mitigate conflicts Accountability	Increase productivity Democratization	Deregulation Cost-saving
Types of interaction	Intervention Regulation	Institutionalized conflict resolution	Consensus on goals, frames and means	Market-based stakeholders
Examples	Factory Supervision Act Working hours regulation	Labour Dispute Act Basic Agreement Worker Protection Act	Working Environment Act Companies Act	Internal control regulations Working Life Act

Source: Karlsen (2018, p. 270). In the typology, the examples pertain mostly to Norway.

In Norway, internal control has been a dominant strategy. At first, this was seen by some as an overly bureaucratic way of dealing with the problems (Skaar et al., 1994), more tailored to the oil industry than ordinary land-based workplaces. Indeed, both Sweden and Denmark were inclined to follow similar strategies but finally chose to do it differently. In Denmark, there is very little that resembles the internal control regime, perhaps with the exception of those companies that chosen to have a certified OHS management system. Sweden chose what could be seen as a middle road between the Norwegian and the Danish strategy: Systematic Work Environment Management (Walters et al., 2011, chapter 6).

The Danish case is a transformation of the EU requirement of risk assessment by management in relation to OHS. In Denmark, this has become the workplace assessment that in most cases is not performed by management but by the local working environment committee, which includes both managers and employee representatives.

The Norwegian case: internal control

In the Norwegian context, a central and vital regulatory vehicle since 1992 has been the Internal Control Regulations (regulations relating to systematic health, environmental and safety activities in enterprises, hereafter IC-HSE Regulations). Arguably, in Norway, internal control, with its broad spectrum of company obligations, is deemed a road to sustainable working life. Internal control is:

> Systematic measures designed to ensure that the activities of the enterprise are planned, organised, performed and maintained in conformity with requirements laid down in or pursuant to the health, environmental and safety legislation.
>
> (Karlsen, 2011, p. 58, own translation)

Because the capacity for the labour inspectorate to actually inspect workplaces is always relatively limited, the work necessary to create and maintain a safe and sound working environment needs to be performed by people at the workplace. Based on this assertion, the labour inspection should focus on the quality of the system or organization dealing with working environment issues in the workplace rather than the quality of the working environment in itself. This is the core thinking behind internal control.

The system, i.e. rules and procedures, put in place by management has to be documented and made easily accessible for management and workers. It should identify health, environment and safety problems and produce an action plan for improvements. Companies are requested to follow up with an annual review of the OHS status, based on a written procedure.

The implementation and follow-up of an internal control varies considerably between companies. The largest companies, especially in the petroleum sector, have comprehensive written procedures, while smaller companies may have a written internal control document prepared by an external consultant and then placed on a bookshelf without being much consulted.

The IC-HSE Regulations cover practically all companies and employees (270,000 units, employing 2.7 million employees) in Norway. These regulations encompass much more than OHS; in fact, eight different laws, five ministries and eight regulatory agencies administer the regulation and supervision of the HSE situation in companies. Businesses are obliged to document their efforts always to stay above the minimum level set out in the HSE legislation. This legislation actually requires companies not only to reach the minimum standards but also to continuously improve their HSE level beyond this limit. The IC-HSE Regulations also require companies to adapt to new, more bureaucratic management routines, principles and systems.

Despite this interactive and joint strategy of OHS management, the Norwegian regime has not yet led to step-change improvements in occupational health, environmental quality and safety. This may reflect the paradoxical situation of the government-enforced self-regulation regime: in theory, it is an ideal framework for OHS improvement, but in practice it has yielded rather mediocre and modest upgrading. The proclaimed zero visions and continuous improvement assertions are still mostly political ambitions. On the other hand, we could argue that the status of working environment quality could have been inferior if these regulatory instruments did not exist. We should not forget that the Norwegian working environment (and arguably the Danish) is still world class.

The Danish case: workplace assessment

In Denmark, workplace assessment is a compulsory procedure for all companies and has to result in a written document. It must be renewed at least every third year, or when work processes change.

The rules on workplace assessment are, as mentioned, a Danish transformation of the EU OHS Framework Directive (89/391/EEC). According to Jensen and Riis (2002, p. 73), risk assessment as outlined in the directive was considered by both employers' organizations and unions as too bureaucratic and "was perceived as an expert-based, systematic approach, out of line with the Danish tradition of emphasizing local activities as the prime driving force in preventive actions". However, the unions were in favour of written assessments in all workplaces, while the employers were opposed to demands for written documents and wanted only "risky" jobs covered. "Workplace assessment" as a term and future practice became a compromise that both parties could accept.

A core element in the thinking was that the assessment was to be performed in cooperation between management and representatives of the employees. The workplace assessment as a practice has now become one of the major activities of working environment groups and committees in many workplaces.

There is a high degree of freedom in how to perform a workplace assessment. Today's version of the rules, however, include a requirement for five different elements: mapping of the working environment, assessment of the problems, considerations of sick leave, an action plan to prioritize the problems and guidelines for follow-up work. This is a fairly standard version of a plan-do-check-act cycle, but with much leeway in practice.

In Denmark, 14% of all workplaces visited by the Danish Working Environment Authority in 2017 received a legal notice due to their lack of a workplace assessment (based on figures available on the website of the Authority: arbejdstilsynet.dk/da/). Although the risk-based sampling strategy followed by the Authority of picking out the "bad apples" would suggest that the actual average is lower, there is no doubt that many companies have no workplace assessment procedure, or a very weak version of it. Even when workplace assessment is in operation, it is no guarantee that the working environment is of high quality and continuously improving. Indeed, Jensen and Riis (2002), among others, suggest that the system of employee participation and workplace assessment is almost exclusively reactive and unable to tackle more difficult problems, such as those related to the psychosocial working environment. Yet again, the situation had no system been in place, is open for speculation.

In this context, another trend is important. In a situation where the former occupational health service system with its professional OHS knowledge has been phased out, many workplaces, particularly larger, well-organized companies but also medium-sized construction firms, are now introducing in-house working environment professionals (Seim et al., 2016). Their role varies; some include employee representatives in their work, while others reduce the representatives to data providers and ambassadors for their systems. The role of the representatives as people who promote the legitimate interests of the workforce and participate in an informed dialogue with management is perhaps under threat.

Trends, threats and opportunities in the new working life

The changes in today's working life in Denmark and Norway affect ways of solving health challenges at the individual workplace. The concept of working environment actually reflects opinions on, and use of, safety delegates and the involvement of new forms of control and regulatory regimes in the solution of the entire range of HSE challenges. New types of expertise, especially system comprehension and the ability to handle formal HSE schemes, are required, which results in new formally qualified occupational groups.

Arguably, each of these change drivers promotes trends, and trends offer both threats and opportunities (Karlsen, 2018), as outlined in Table 6.4.

Table 6.4 Trends, threats and opportunities

Trends	*Threats*	*Opportunities*
Local adaption of theories of working environment	Health effects are overlooked, and learning gains from other sectors and countries are overridden	There is involvement in working environment efforts in individual companies
A new concept of working environment emerges	The working environment profession is diluted and marginalized	The working environment is encapsulated in corporate development
The safety delegate system loses its significance	The working environment loses its competent spokespersons	The working environment is linked to individual daily work
Internal control of HSE as a major form of regulation	Working environment work gets stuck in ineffective routines	An alternative local cause of understanding working environment is being developed

Source: Karlsen (2018, p. 310).

The first trend we can observe is that working environment efforts are increasingly being tailored to the character of the individual. The threat is that certain companies will ignore both short-term and long-term workplace threats and fail to invest in preventative, health-promoting and inclusive working environment measures. On the other hand, some companies will use their working environment to create a reputation that also serves their business interests.

The second trend is that the working environment concept is gaining ground and is gradually expanding. This may mean that the working environment's traditional priority in the overall HSE work is becoming weakened, and new challenges such as resource management and external environmental conditions are receiving the most attention. On the other hand, the possibility opens for HSE (including working environment) to be more closely integrated into the overall business development of a company.

A third trend is that safety delegates and working environment committees are again becoming a kind of "empty democracy". This means that the working environment loses its competent spokespersons because their contribution becomes irrelevant to the company's operation and strategy. However, if the HSE work is linked to daily work, i.e. everyone is engaged in HSE improvements, this trend can promote a more sustainable production system.

The fourth trend is linked to the very idea that companies should have more rights to control themselves in the HSE field. There is a risk of creating a new corporate bureaucracy. HSE work will then become a clearer part of the employer's governance, and internal control will be a management tool in line with other models and tools the company uses. The optimistic side is that internal control of HSE is actually perceived as the most promising model for modern and effective management and that this gives rise to a new understanding of the connection between optimal and safe production and the HSE threats that the production can lead to. Changes in the tasks and duties of the safety delegate system will enhance the link between elected and professional involvement in the operations of a company, to the benefit of HSE quality.

Some concluding remarks

A rationale of the Danish and Norwegian working environment regulations since the 1970s was to encourage the emergence of a favourable in-house safety climate in companies, which in turn might influence safety behaviour and safety culture. The regulatory model, being both innovative and future-oriented, was based on a three-pillared system, involving employer, employees and the government. It was genuinely different from those found elsewhere in Europe and has influenced the principles later enshrined in the EU framework directive on the working environment. However, as briefly sketched in this chapter, it has a distinct history, a blurred present and possibly a bleak future.

On the other hand, Norway and Denmark have a better working environment than most countries. However, both countries are facing some challenges of a political nature and some challenges that companies have to deal with themselves. The direction of the work of the labour inspectorates is influenced by the development of the open European labour market, international migration, open economies, restructuring processes in most industries and the influence of international management and control systems, such as lean management.

As described in other chapters of this book, the labour migrations and the open economy have increased the number of precarious workers operating in the grey market. There also seems to be an increase in social dumping and economic crime. It has been necessary to focus more on physical OHS factors, especially in the construction industry where migrant workers from Eastern Europe and elsewhere work at high risk without the necessary safety equipment. According to a report evaluating the Norwegian Labour Inspection Authority, this development has led to a shift of attention by the Authority from preventative OHS measures to economic crime and social dumping (Wathne et al., 2017). Obviously, this is necessary, but it is given priority at the cost of broader preventative OHS work.

Although both Norway and Denmark score well on working environment quality, there are distinct differences between the strategies the countries pursue in relation to the psychosocial working environment, and how the labour inspection authorities interact with companies and try to motivate them in their working environment and HSE efforts. Norway has been a distinct leader in terms of the psychosocial working environment, or organizational working environment as it has been very appropriately termed in Norwegian.

Denmark has also started to deal with these issues, but much later, and in a situation where the problems just seem to grow rather than being contained by policy interventions.

In relation to company motivation, Norway has followed a formal high road with its internal controls that make the Labour Inspection Authorities take a step back by inspecting how companies deal with their problems rather than inspecting the results of the companies' efforts. At the same time, the working environment in Norway has been integrated with a number of other issues, such as fire prevention and the external environment. In Denmark, a low road was deliberately taken, but a road with a strong emphasis on employee representatives, as workplace assessments are performed by working environment groups and committees, which are cooperative organs in the companies. More recently, many employers in Denmark seem to be shifting their preferences by moving in the direction of more integrated management systems that take the working environment more seriously and at the same time tend to squeeze out the participatory aspects of the "low road".

Frustratingly, neither of the different national models seems to have found the direct road to serious continuous improvements in the working environment. It is more like continuously counteracting, what Jens Rasmussen (1997) has termed a "migrating toward accidents". A migration that is due to management's continuous strive for effectivity and competitiveness, which often pushes the working environment in a negative direction.

This leaves us with some open-ended questions: Is counteracting the negative trends enough? Or do we have the wrong focus or the wrong model in Norwegian and Danish working life? Can we optimize the strategies we have adopted, or perhaps learn from each other?

Perhaps, we should focus on the reasons why most of our daily work operations in fact are going well, rather than on deviations, mishaps and accidents. Should we shift our focus from non-compliance and minimizing risks to the ability to respond, monitor, learn and anticipate reasons for adjustments, in order to achieve a safer workplace? Is organizing for resilience a more viable and sustainable model than organizing for safety (Hollnagel, 2014)?

Alternatively, is the opposite approach more reasonable? After all, two recent systematic reviews (performed in Denmark and Norway, but referring primarily to US studies: Andersen et al., 2017; Johannessen et al., 2017) find stronger effects of legislation and inspection with sanctions compared with measures like guidance, training, campaigns, etc. Should the present working environment regulation leave its "soft" and supervisory position and move into a harder regime where companies are constricted by tougher regulation and stricter control?

In short, does the conceptual opacity of our current understanding of workplace safety, in combination with the "discursive blindness" fuelled by the current organizational safety literature, distract our attention away from the fact that "we are not improving health and safety" as we would like to?

References

Aagestad, C., Bjerkan, A. M. & Gravseth, H. M. U. (2017) *Arbeidsmiljøet i Norge og EU: en sammenligning [The Working Environment in Norway and the EU: A Comparision]*, Oslo. http://hdl.handle.net/11250/2466019.

Agurén, S. & Edgren, J. (1979) *Annorlunda fabriker: mot en ny produktionsteknisk teori [Different Factories: Towards a New Production Technical Theory]*, Stockholm: Tekn. avd., Sv. arbetsgivareförен. (SAF).

Andersen, J. H., Malmros, P., Ebbehøj, N. E., Flachs, E. M., Bengtsen, E. & Bonde, J. P. (2017) *Systematic Literature Review on the Effects of Occupational Safety and Health (OSH) Interventions at the Workplace*, Copenhagen. https://arbejdstilsynet.dk/~/media/AT/at/16-Om-Arbejdstilsynet/09-Publikationer-om-Arbejdstilsynet/Review-effekter-virkemidler pdf.pdf.

Byrkjeland, M. (2006) *Kortare arbeidstid: Eit oversyn over diskusjonen om arbeidstidsforkortingar i Noreg 1880–2006 [Shorter Working Hours: A Review of the Discussion about Reductions of Working Hours in Norway 1880–2006]* (Stein Rokkan Centre for Social Studies No. 7), Bergen, Norway. http://hdl.handle.net/1956/1894.

Det Nationale Forskningscenter for Arbejdsmiljø (2017) *Notat: Belastningsindeks for psykisk arbejdsmiljø og muskelskeletbesvær 2016 [Note: An Index of Strains Due to Psychosocial Working Environment and Musculoskeletal Disorders 2016]*. www.arbejdsmiljoforskning.dk/~/media/Projekter/AH2016/Opgrelse-af-belastningsindeks-for-psykisk-arbejdsmilj-og-muskelskeletbesvaer-2016.pdf.

Eiken, T., Tynes, T., Grimsrud, T. K., Sterud, T. & Aasnæss, S. (2008) *Psykososialt arbeidsmiljø: delrapport [Psychosocial Working Environment: Subreport]*, Oslo: Statens arbeidsmiljøinstitutt. https://brage.bibsys.no/xmlui/handle/11250/288520#.W0XZqdhz0qc.mendeley.

Frick, K., Langaa Jensen, P., Quinlan, M. & Wilthagen, T. (2000) *Systematic Occupational Health and Safety Management: Perspectives on an International Development*, Oxford, UK: Pergamon, Elsevier Science.

Graver, H. P. (1995) Reguleringsmodeller i arbeidsretten [Regulatory Models in Labour law], In: Olberg, D. (ed.) *Endringer i arbeidslivets organisering [Changes in the Organization of Work Life]*, Oslo: Fafo, 131–153.

Gustavsen, B. (1992) *Dialogue and Development: Theory of Communication, Action Research and the Restructuring of Working Life*, Assen, the Netherlands: van Gurcom.

Heen, H. & Salomon, R. H. (eds) (2018) *Varme konflikter i arbeidslivet: organisatoriske perspektiver og håndteringsmetoder [Hot Conflicts in Working Life: Organizational Perspectives and Methods of Intervention]*, Oslo: Gyldendal Akademisk.

Hollnagel, E. (2014) *Safety-I and Safety-II: The Past and Future of Safety Management* (2nd edition), Aldershot, UK: Ashgate.

Jensen, P. L. & Riis, A. H. (2002) Denmark: Transforming Risk Assessment to Workplace Assessment, In: Walters, D. (ed.) *Regulating Health and Safety Management in the European Union: A Study of the Dynamics of Change*, Brussels: P.I.E.- Peter Lang, 59–80.

Jespersen, A. H., Hasle, P. & Nielsen, K. T. (2016) The Wicked Character of Psychosocial Risks: Implications for Regulation, *Nordic Journal of Working Life Studies*, 6(3). doi: https://doi.org/10.19154/njwls.v6i3.5526.

Johannessen, H. A., Løchting, I., Bakke, B., Nielsen, M. B., Skyberg, K. & Mehlum, I. S. (2017) *Effekter av myndighetstiltak på arbeidsmiljø og helse: en systematisk kunnskapsoppsummering [Effects of Government Measures on Working Environment and Health:*

A Systematic Summary of Knowledge], Vol 18 No 5, Oslo: Statens arbeidsmiljøinstitutt. https://brage.bibsys.no/xmlui/handle/11250/2469616#.W1G4uh8BrxI.mendeley.

Karlsen, J. E. (2011) *Metoder for HMS-regulering [Methods for HSE Regulation]*, Oslo: Cappelen Damm Akademisk.

Karlsen, J. E. (2018) *Visjoner for det gode arbeidsliv: Arbeidsmiljøloven i samfunnsvitenskapelig lys (Vision for a Good Working Life: The Working Environment Act in Social Scientific Light)*, Oslo: Cappelen Damm Akademisk.

Lord Robens (1972) *Safety and Health at Work: Report of the Committee 1970–1972*, London.

Metodeudvalget (1995) *Psykosociale risikofaktorer i arbejdslivet: Rapport fra et af arbejdsministeren nedsat udvalg [Psychosocial Risk Factors in Working Life: Report by a Committee Appointed by the Minister of Labour]*, Copenhagen.

Parent-Thirion, A., Biletta, I., Cabrita, J., Vargas Llave, O., Vermeylen, G., Wilczyńska, A. & Wilkens, M. (2016) *Sixth European Working Conditions Survey: Overview Report*. https://doi.org/10.2806/422172.

Rasmussen, J. (1997) Risk Management in a Dynamic Society: A Modelling Problem, *Safety Science*, 27(2–3): 183–213.

Rasmussen, M. B., Hansen, T. & Nielsen, K. T. (2011) New Tools and Strategies for the Inspection of the Psychosocial Working Environment: The Experience of the Danish Working Environment Authority, *Safety Science*, 49: 565–574.

Seim, R., Møller, N. & Limborg, H. J. (2016) Professionelle og medarbejderrepræsentanter: nye roller i arbejdsmiljøarbejdet [Professionals and Working Environment Representatives: New Roles in Local Working Environment Activities], *Tidsskrift for Arbejdsliv*, 18(1): 18–33.

Skaar, S., Lindøe, P. H., Jersin, E. & Tinmannsvik, R. (1994) *Internkontroll: ørkenvandring eller veien til det forjettede land [Internal Control: A Walk in the Desert or the Path to the Promised Land]*, Trondheim, Norway: SINTEF IFIM.

Sørensen, B. A. & Grimsmo, A. (2001) *Varme og kalde konflikter i det nye arbeidslivet [Hot and Cold Conflicts in the New Working Life]*, Oslo: Tiden Norsk Forlag.

The Danish Working Environment Act, Act no. 681 of 23 December 1975, on Working Environment (1975), The Danish Parliament.

Thorsrud, E. & Emery, F. E. (1970) *Mot en ny bedriftsorganisasjon: Eksperimenter i industrielt demokrati [Towards a New Company Organization: Experiments in Industrial Democracy]*, Oslo: Tanum.

Walters, D., Johnstone, R., Frick, K., Quinlan, M., Baril-Gingras, G. & Thébaud-Mony, A. (2011) *Regulating Workplace Risks: A Comparative Study of Inspection Regimes in Times of Change*, Cheltenham, UK: Edward Elgar.

Wathne, C. T., Nordrik, B., Fossen, Ø., Enehaug, H., Falkum, E. & Ingelsrud, M. H. (2017) *Et arbeidstilsyn i endring [A Labour Inspection under Transformation]*, Oslo. www.hioa.no/content/download/143739/4052533/file/r2017-06_EtArbeidstilsynIEndring.pdf.

Chapter 7

New working time and new temporalities

The erosion of influence and rhythms in work

Henrik Lambrecht Lund

Introduction

The overall aim of this chapter is to identify some of the advantages and disadvantages of working time flexibility. This is done by pursuing three underlying purposes.

The first purpose of this chapter is to contextualize the way in which questions of working time manifest themselves when working hours are shaped in accordance with the Nordic industrial relations model and the Nordic model of working environment traditions. This is necessary to understand why the chapter's illustrative case deviates, including how it differs from the Nordic model approach and from the recent tendency to give employees more autonomy. It provides a basis for understanding the ability of the Nordic model to create quality in working life but also a number of challenges and paradoxes. One of the challenges is that trade unions are entering into collective agreements with employers' associations about flexible work hours that can create new workloads that are difficult to find solutions for in the collective agreements and in general. In addition, a lack of solutions in the collective agreements must be seen in light of the fact that daily work is subject to the right of employers to direct and distribute work. However, this is not unambiguous. These rights can be challenged, e.g. through demands for autonomy related to structuring working hours or through local agreements to manage flexible hours to suit the specific work in question.

The second purpose of the chapter is to identify some of the new types of psychosocial stressors that arise when flexible work hours erode the rhythms of everyday life at work. Here, a qualitative perspective on time at work is used, inspired by the sociology of time. We look into the time-related conditions and circumstances in work that go beyond the linear clock measurement of time in minutes, hours and days.

The third objective of this chapter is to include an illustrative case study that captures the challenges and dilemmas of psychosocial stressors when long hours of work with high autonomy are changed to a fixed organization of working hours. Further case studies conducted with colleagues and other researchers will also be used to identify relevant concepts and state of the art knowledge.

Working time, historically and in the contemporary flexibility agenda

The length of the working day has been a key area of conflict between unions and employers' associations since the establishment of the labour movement. In 1889, the mantra of the workers' second international congress was eight hours of work, eight hours of free time and eight hours of sleep. This became for many years the main demand of May Day demonstrations worldwide. The main argument for the claim was that everyone has the right to freedom in their lives. Everyone should have the right to be with their family, take part in social activities and have time for political participation in society. In the years after World War I, the labour movement had become strong enough to allow the demand to be met in a large number of countries. In Denmark, in 1919, the labour unions and employers' associations agreed on an 8-hour working day and a 48-hour working week. Since then, working hours have been negotiated in periodic collective agreements between the unions and employers' associations. Unlike many comparable countries, the state has not passed legislation on working hours, with the exception of this chapter's illustrative case. The Nordic countries are thus differentiated by the fact that working time is determined only by the unions and employers' associations, which also means that hours are not regulated in companies without such agreements. Since 1919, when the first agreement on working hours was established, the hours have gradually been reduced. In 1986, an agreement was reached on a 37-hour working week, which was finally implemented in 1991. Since then, weekly working hours have not been reduced, but holidays have been extended and are now six weeks, and maternity leave has been extended to one year. These changes are also the result of agreements between the unions and employers' associations. In addition to general agreements on the number of working hours, a large number of agreements on how time at work is structured have been made. Such agreements, which are mostly industry-specific, cover timing of hours, fixed breaks, overtime rules, including prohibition of systematic planned overtime, as well as compensation for overtime in the form of payment or leave, financial compensation for atypical working hours, annual leave, rules on working hours with atypical employment terms, availability allowance, etc.

Since 1990, there have been no strong demands from the trade union movement to reduce the standard weekly working hours from 37. This may be because working time has become far more flexible than earlier, which has hampered traditional regulation of working time in collective agreements. A number of agreements previously aimed at limiting working time flexibility. However, many of these directives have been weakened or terminated, mostly according to the wishes of employers. The unions have allowed more employer-required flexibility in working time in return for other benefits. Another important reason why trade unions have allowed a greater degree of flexibility in working hours is that many members have wanted it. Working hours thus constitute a problem that is difficult to regulate and handle with previous approaches taken in this area (Thomas, 2006). One of the problems is that flexible working hours in self-organized work are associated with longer working days (Albertsen et al., 2007).

The different forms of flexible working hours

The limitation of work in time and space is a relatively new phenomenon. For farmers, fishermen and craftsmen in pre-industrial society, there were no established boundaries between work and leisure. Productive activities and free time were integrated and often the same thing to the pre-industrial worker. As Thompson describes, it took almost 100 years in England to discipline workers to their industry's time structure. To check in every day at the same time and place, concentrate on work throughout the working day and then go home at the same time every day did not seem particularly natural or attractive. It was therefore necessary for capitalism to punish those who could not or would not subordinate to the specific industry time structure. Thompson argues that the modern era of industrialization in England created totalitarian time discipline because the emergence of capitalism needed synchronization of labour. He describes how the entire life of the employee was embedded in the capitalist era, supported by a new cultural and religious work ethic (Thompson, 1967).

With the focus on flexibility in recent decades, there has evolved a certain fracturing, or perhaps a renewal, of the time structure of industrialization. In the 1980s, the growing demand for employers' flexibility was perceived by the unions as an opportunity to humanize work, which explains the Nordic unions' positive participation in some aspects of the creation of flexible work (Hvid & Moeller, 2001). More flexible forms of production required the development of new skillsets and greater autonomy for employees (Piore & Sabel, 1984; Kern & Schumann, 1984). It was also possible to make flexible working time arrangements that provided for the needs of leisure time. Later, flexible work was internationally identified as the very source of social decline and cultural erosion (Sennett, 1998; Beck, 2000). In Denmark, the darker side of flexibility has also been identified, for example, short-term employment. But this has been somewhat moderated through the solutions of unions and employers' associations, labour market welfare policies such as unemployment benefits and the flexicurity model to avoid long-term unemployment by e.g. using labour education institutions to try to support employees' return to regular standard employment.

In addition to these points, it has always been difficult to clarify what the concept of flexibility covers. It has mostly developed into an interest-driven struggle about what is definitely not flexible. From the beginning, employers pointed out that what were perceived as rigid collective agreements were barriers to flexibility. Employee arguments were that many companies were stuck in bureaucratic and Taylorist organizational structures that prevented people from developing and flourishing at work.

The main difference between the Nordic working week and that of other EU countries is not the number of hours but the flexibility of working time. Parallel with the development of flexible organizational forms, employees gain more influence on scheduling working hours and have more autonomy to adjust hours in response to their own needs and the needs of the work. This Nordic design of working hours has been created in a relation between agreements on working time and influence and participation at work in accordance with the sociotechnical tradition (see Chapter 3). Flexible working time has been seen as potentially creating more autonomy in work. Workers are not forced to follow certain management-based divisions of work and daily routines; rather, they can adapt their work to what makes sense in relation to the overall workflow. In addition, they can adapt their work to reduce strain. Sociotechnical methods created the basis for the spread of autonomy in the workplace and are now influencing the development of flexible working hours.

According to the European Working Conditions Survey database,[1] Denmark is the EU country where employees have greatest influence on their working hours, followed by Norway, Sweden and Finland. In Denmark, 65% of employees have a say in how their working hours are set. In particular, many workers in the Nordic countries state that they can adapt their working hours within certain limits, e.g. different types of flexible working arrangements. For Danish workers, the figure is 40% and in Norway it is 44%. For comparable countries like Germany and Hungary, the figures are only 20% and 15%, respectively. Denmark and Norway are also the countries where most employees report being very satisfied with their working hours. In Denmark, the figure is 47%, in Norway 44%, while the EU average is 26%. Almost all employees in Denmark (91%) and in Norway (94%) are either very satisfied or satisfied with their working hours. Some 76% of Danish and 82% of Norwegian employees find it easy to take care of personal or family matters during working hours. However, in relation to this, there are still groups of workers in Denmark who do not have any influence on their working hours. In today's society there are still people who have no possibility to make choices on how to spend their time (Goodin et al., 2008).

Advantages of flexible working hours and temporal autonomy

This section focuses solely on the possible benefits for employees and employers of employee autonomy and self-management of working hours. Criticism and negative aspects of this are addressed in the following section.

The most widely used form of influence on working hours is flexitime. For Danish employees working with different kinds of flexitime arrangements, there are possible benefits in terms of quality of life. Flexitime represents a move away from the disciplinary time structure of industrialization. Individuals do not all have to come to work or go home at the same time each day. Often, they can also save up hours to get more time off, either in their daily work or as longer holidays. The working day can be organized according to domestic and family needs and provide greater opportunity to pursue leisure activities. Workers may have other reasons for choosing flexitime, such as sleep, finances, health, personal capacity, opportunity to study, etc. They may wish to control their working hours to enhance the timing of individual duties and activities. Collective agreements on flexible working time may give employers certain rights to apply more working hours in peak periods and to decrease worker capacity when there is less work. Flexibility thus gives employers the opportunity to optimize the use of working time. For employees, it can prevent them having to waste time waiting for tasks.

It can be emancipatory for employees to have working time governed by tasks rather than an obligation to clock in and out. For employees, it is primarily about temporal freedom, i.e. being able to perform their work independently of time and place, and thus having control over where and when they work. For instance, this may allow employees to work when they feel most energetic. Many of those who work with self-managed flexibility are often driven by a conviction that they themselves can find the most suitable temporal framework for their work. Work is less governed by external controls, measures, rules and trivial working days, and more by the tasks at hand and tasks that appear, thus creating meaningful utilization of time. In this way, work released from time and space also mitigates the time discipline of early industrialization. For employers, flexible solutions allow for better handling of unpredictable situations and less disturbance of the flow of products or services. One solution might be that employees themselves choose what tasks they want to solve. Flexible working time also implies that employees need not wait for each other. If a task meets temporary barriers in the organization, the employee can switch to another task. For employers, it also can provide flexible access to labour.

Turning now to shift work, we must consider its influence on working hours in the light of its problematic nature in relation to work–life balance and leisure time activities. Its harmful effect on health is also a key factor (Albertsen et al., 2007). A previous project focused on 13 workplaces in the health sector where changes had been made to the shift work structure in an attempt to give employees greater influence over their own working hours. The project was conducted in collaboration between Roskilde University and the Danish National Research Centre for the Working Environment. It was a qualitative and quantitative longitudinal intervention study over three years (Hvid et al., 2011; Nabe-Nielsen et al., 2013; Albertsen et al., 2014; Hansen et al., 2015). Each workplace tested an IT system for scheduling. The main purpose of these IT systems was to make working hours more flexible while giving employees more say in setting their own working hours, prioritizing when they wanted to work and when they wanted time off. The benefit for the employees was that they experienced an improvement in work–life balance. The benefits for employers were that they could create improved working conditions and a more attractive workplace, thus maintaining and recruiting sufficiently qualified labour. The schedules were generally set without management having to intervene. These benefits made the companies choose to continue using the IT systems after the end of the research project.

However, autonomy related to working hours can be illusive because of high demands, performance standards, workload, obligations, collaboration, etc.

Psychological strain related to autonomy due to flexibility creating fluid temporality

As a basis for a critical interpretation of the disadvantages and dilemmas of flexible working hours and for an analysis of the illustrative case study, this section presents the development of a conceptual framework using the core concepts of the sociological study of time and space. As Gabriella Paolucci argues, changing working hours expresses a new postmodern temporal condition where desynchronization dominates contemporary society, and time is experienced as fragmented due to the complexity created by different temporal regimes (Paolucci, 1996). This puts a temporal perspective on the characteristics and quality of time related to flexible working hours. Clock units of time cannot give us an understanding of the quality of time; we need qualitative concepts of time to tell us whether time has been intense, uninteresting, fragmented, slow, fast, chaotic and so on. Some qualitative perspectives on time are already well known in working environment research, for example, pace and intensity.

The concept of rhythms is central to the sociology of time. It originated as an inspiration from Henri Lefebvre (Lefebvre, 2004). His idea was that rhythms can be used to understand everyday life, as they form a kind of background structure. It is meaningful to analyse working time and temporalities from such a perspective in order to prevent strain and create rhythms in work. Linear time, such as clock time and fixed timing of working hours, separates the past, present and future. When clock time has passed, it does not return.

However, the time structure of work is also rhythmic. Employees perform similar activities every day, rhythmically structured in time and space. Sometimes they repeat themselves with small variations. Rhythms are tied to work and social life; they define human life and our interaction with those around us. When these rhythms are challenged, it can affect our social life, our biorhythms, and our cognitive and mental capacities. Routine and practices cannot be maintained without rhythms; thus, missing rhythms at work can lead to overuse of human resources, involving strain that makes it difficult to create meaning and time structures (Hvid et al., 2008). Flexible working time and fluid temporality can challenge everyday rhythms.

Flexible working hours can obstruct the time-based synchronization of colleagues, thus creating problems for the common rhythms that we support in stabilizing our own rhythms and in interaction with colleagues. Flexible working hours can make it difficult to coordinate time. In the earlier example of workers having control over their working hours in shift work, it was found that opportunities for mutual learning were reduced because there was no longer a common meeting time. In some cases, it was impossible to transfer oral knowledge from one shift to another shift, as there were no longer any joint handover meetings. This loss of time-structuring rhythms can also weaken social relationships between colleagues. An interesting finding was that many employees prioritized their working time in ways that maintained certain time structures in their everyday lives. Employees setting their own working hours establish new rhythms but not common rhythms. Employees are separated in time and space. Failing to maintain some structures during working hours can be problematic for employees both socially and in terms of social support as a buffer against psychosocial stressors. From an employer's point of view, flexible working hours may also have negative consequences. If colleagues rarely meet, workplace culture can be weakened, as can common norms, values and practices. Opportunities to share experiences can decrease, learning can become individualized and employees may need greater support from management.

Even employees having far-reaching influence over their own working time do not necessarily have an effect on the demands of their work. This can result in a decoupling of demands and resources, as the demands may erode the freedom associated with self-management of working time. Thomas Hylland Eriksen's (2001) concept of 'fast time' and Hartmut Rosa's (Rosa, 2013) concept of 'acceleration' can help us understand the dynamics and mechanisms that can lead to flexible working hours and autonomy becoming a burden in the psychosocial working environment. Hylland Eriksen discusses conflicts between time systems as conflicts between fast and slow time. Hartmut Rosa argues that the acceleration of contemporary Western societies due to technology, social change, competition and the pace of life is leading to alienation. It can be difficult to hold onto rhythms when time accelerates. Fast time can lead to more desynchronized colleagues and fragmentation of tasks. Time can be characterized by many urgent tasks. Slow time enables long-term planning, which supports our ability to maintain rhythms. Flexible working time and quickly changing temporalities can create unpredictability in everyday life, which can cause family and leisure activities to be subjected to work. Therefore, fluid temporality can result in work being done at times that challenge the family's basic rhythms. It can also be harder to commit to firmly structured spare-time activities. In addition, acceleration can increase intensity, both at and outside work. Employers using flexible working arrangements to optimize labour can create such high demands that it causes a chronically high pace. The natural breaks that previously existed in work may be filled up, leaving less time for socializing with colleagues (Fritz et al., 2013). Employees find themselves unable to complete required tasks because new, more urgent work is always cropping up. This can lead to stacking of tasks and difficulty in finding time to immerse oneself. Thus, flexible working time does not necessarily result in a better balance and less strain (Grönlund & Gro, 2007). This is also described as 24/7 work where employees are always available for work needs that may arise. Hence working time is not measured in hours.

The above-mentioned European Working Conditions Survey shows that approximately a fifth of employees in Denmark decide on their working time without demands on time and place. To illustrate the possible disadvantages of flexible working hours, I will draw on a case study by the Finns Oili-Helena Ylijoki and Hans Mäntylä (2003) and re-interpret their results. They conducted a study on self-management of time among university academics, presented in their article 'Conflicting Time Perspectives in Academic Work'.

The two researchers found that the university employees have a utopian pursuit of 'timeless time' (Ylijoki & Mäntylä, 2003) marked by immersion, and slow time where they forget time and place and experience smooth workflow. Teaching duties, development projects, dissemination of knowledge in society, administration, meetings and interaction with colleagues and managers all fragment the research and thus obstruct the necessary immersion.

Immersion and the state of 'timeless time' require slow time for longer periods, which is made difficult when employees are expected to engage in university organizational processes. In this way, organizational tasks, teaching and research often become a time-consuming chaos without rhythm and with daily time conflicts both relationally and between different types of task. Researchers are expected to be passionate about their work, which can be translated into high performance requirements. Work is assignment-controlled time where employees' time-based practice is often so individual that there is limited common experience with co-workers' working hours.

Work is usually done in individualized and weak rhythms, with nobody knowing how much and when others work, or how busy they are, all of which makes it difficult to help each other. Such employees are thus left with a very personal choice about the place of work in their life. Demands in this kind of work are diffuse and complex, which in turn increases the workload and makes it difficult to prioritize time spent on the various tasks. Some tasks will be poorly executed, while others will be over-performed, depending on the employee's allocation of time for each task. This can make it difficult to develop a temporal practice with common rhythms.

During periods of writing and immersion, which may take place at home and are usually not fragmented by meetings, teaching and administration, researchers can establish their own rhythms and experience timeless time. But these rhythms are vulnerable because they are personal and not embedded in collective rhythms. Self-managing researchers tend to intervene in each other's rhythms because they are rarely at the same stage in their work processes. There is temporal disorganization between academic staff in their everyday work, creating many disturbances and interruptions, even though work immersion is a prerequisite for achieving results (Spurling, 2015). The above-mentioned challenges can be enhanced when researchers participate in different research projects and work with other complex interpersonal relationships. This can result in researchers finding themselves in a constant state of planning where timing and management of time become a key skill. This is 'time work' in constantly changing circumstances determined by the way the work manifests itself.

Further, the flexible time management of the university from semester to semester must be included in the management of researchers' own time. The challenge for temporal autonomy is thus to be in the right place at the right time in order to complete the tasks on time, without wasting time and without becoming a colleague perceived as a person who creates barriers to the solution of others' tasks. Researchers can be expected to align themselves with the organizational 'common', which can make them postpone their major writing tasks repeatedly.

Acceleration and long working days can also be linked to the darker sides of working at universities. In many cases, work takes place in a highly competitive environment. There is constant competition for recognition, publication, research funding and student evaluations. This can easily push researchers to make their work take up as much space as possible in their lives. Many other jobs have the same lack of clear boundaries (Allvin et al., 2011).

Working according to self-managed time can make it difficult to develop a practice where weekends are kept free from work and colleagues do not pressure each other to complete tasks for which they themselves are responsible. Work that is released from time and space will in some environments create an 'online culture' (Agger, 2011). Lack of temporal practice thus affects life as a whole; it is difficult to realize personal time preferences, in terms of both working life and life outside work. There is no longer any balance measured in hours in the work–life relationship; rather, there are complex interactions between the two spheres (Felstead et al., 2005). Work–life balance is not only a matter of hours but also of energy and vitality (Brannen, 2005). Work without formal or informal upper limits on working hours has a time structure that may pervade the person's entire life, and it can be difficult to distinguish between work and free time. A work–life balance can be considered as the control of temporal boundaries (Perlow, 1999).

Old and new temporalities related to teachers' working hours

I will now present the pros and cons of flexible and fixed working hours for teachers and their work-related temporality. Teachers in Denmark are a particularly interesting case here, because in recent years they have experienced extensive conflicts about working time. The case of teachers makes it possible to examine both positive and negative aspects of flexible and fixed working time arrangements and the relationship between working hours and temporality at work. First, I present the conflict about teachers' working hours, as it has played out within the Nordic negotiation model. Then I investigate the way in which changed working hours have influenced temporal autonomy and thus also the Nordic tradition of influence on an employee's work.

From profession-driven working time to management time control: the Working Time Act

The regulation of working hours for teachers has historically played a key role in the policy strategies of the teachers' union to achieve better working conditions without long working days but also professional autonomy. The fact that professional autonomy has played a key role in the negotiations is somewhat atypical. As mentioned, it is a topic where management rights also matter. Control of their own working time has always played an important part in teachers' professional identity. Professional autonomy included both self-management of time and self-management of teaching methods, and scheduled teaching time was the only regulated time. But even this scheduled teaching was most often planned by a team and subject to some restrictions on the hours allocated to different subjects.

The allocation and management of the remaining time were handled by the individual teacher and the team to accommodate lesson preparation and other work. It is difficult to calculate the distribution of hours between teaching, preparation and other work before the change in working time in the 2013 Working Time Act (WTA), because it varied from school to school, depending on the nature of the work and a large number of local agreements. Local agreements are important as the labour unions and employers' organizations have sought decentralized framework agreements to create flexibility in working time, thus avoiding bureaucratic calculation of working time. Similarly, teaching time can be difficult to identify when using teaching methods such as experiments, projects and interdisciplinary processes. A cautious estimate is that preparation and time for other work constituted half of the total working hours before the WTA.

Previous cutbacks in preparation hours created political mobilization and radicalization of the teachers' union, as union awareness was raised among teachers during periods of school cutbacks. During these periods, there was always a demand for a settlement with unpaid hours. After each period of political mobilization against deterioration, teachers have returned to a profession-oriented union strategy and identity under the new conditions. Within this strategy, the requirements are embedded in the teachers' ambition to take professional responsibility for the national development of the schools as individual teachers, as local working community and as national trade union.

As described in an earlier chapter of this book, Denmark has a strong tradition of labour market regulation through collective agreements between employer organizations and employee unions. For teachers, the negotiation of the 2013 collective agreement failed to create a result before the existing agreement expired. The longest labour market conflict ever seen in the public sector arose. The core of the conflict was the allocation and timing of teachers' working hours. The conflict lasted 25 days and was nationwide. It was an 'employer lockout'. Local Government Denmark represented the employers (the local authorities in charge of the schools), and since the teachers' union is considered to be the strongest public-sector union and union density was at that time 96% of the workforce, all schools were effectively shut down during this period. There was widespread union activism. The media was filled with accusations about who was to blame: employer, teachers' union or government? The problem for the government was that, in parallel with the negotiations, it wanted to introduce a new reform of public schools that included longer school days. Within the existing collective agreement, it meant a considerable supply of new labour to schools, which should be seen in conjunction with general public-sector cutbacks. After the 25 days of conflict, the government intervened and forced the new working time through by law, since there was no indication that the labour market partners were going to reach a solution. This was considered unacceptable political interference in the collective bargaining negotiations in relation to the Nordic model. Historically, intervention by the government is seen as problematic because it can destabilize the Nordic model of industrial relations. This could mean that labour unions and employers' associations would consider whether there are benefits in creating a breakdown in the negotiations, if they think government intervention will be to their advantage. It could also make it legitimate for the government to indicate a desired result of the negotiations. Implementation of an agreement through legislative intervention has historically been handled by the already existing collective agreement or a proposal by a mediator being passed as law. Even these cases have historically been very rare. In the case of the teachers, the government decided to follow the employers' demands. As stated, this is a remarkable intervention in the Danish context and has been criticized from all sides by supporters of the Nordic negotiation model.

A distinctive feature of the conflict was that it was very emotional. It was not a classical labour market conflict about working hours, salary or other benefits. Teachers felt mistreated in relation to their professional integrity, and there was deep mistrust and massive demonstrations both during and after the conflict. The Nordic model is based on compromise and consensus where nobody is entirely happy but both parties are equally satisfied. After the final negotiations with the government and the employer, the chairman of the teachers' union declared: 'Friends, we lost'. They were furious about the mistrust associated with the indication that teachers were incapable of managing their own working time. The result was complete managerial control over working time and a demand that teachers spend all working hours at the school, including preparation time.

The case study

The case study is based on a variety of qualitative data collected within a two-year period before and after the WTA, although different methods were used before and after the WTA. The studies before the WTA were somewhat 'classical' qualitative workplace studies, with empirical data collected at 2 schools involving 10 days of observation at each school and 20 interviews. The interviews focused on how working hours and temporalities were embedded in workplace culture, values, norms and practices. There were also questions about where and how preparation was done, individually and in teams. We observed execution of teachers' work as well as meeting culture and practices, and we conducted short debriefing interviews both during and after the observations (Kamp et al., 2011).

The insights and knowledge after the WTA came from own consultant assignments such as workshops and seminars where teachers were invited to interpret changes in the temporalities of work and in the psychosocial work environment. The starting point in these workshops was a presentation of the results from the studies before the WTA. This is ongoing work and we have now completed about 30 seminars and workshops, with 20 to 150 teachers participating in each. The workshops have been conducted with employee representatives, school managers, union consultants, politically elected representatives from the union and teachers at local schools. We developed a dialogue method for the workshops where we 'translated' some of the complex concepts and research questions from the sociology of time into everyday language and structured it to fit the workshops. In some of the workshops we used four dichotomies: (1) 'slow time' (e.g. questions about opportunities for immersion and thoughtfulness) versus 'fast time' (e.g. questions about tasks conducted at a high pace); (2) 'synchronization' (e.g. questions about coordinated work with efficient cooperation on the core tasks) versus 'desynchronization' (e.g. questions about poor cooperation and coordination and lack of understanding of co-workers' tasks); (3) 'flow and timeless time' (e.g. questions about organized work with smooth workflows) versus 'fragmentation' (e.g. questions about interruptions, disruptions and tasks that interfere with each other); and (4) 'productive time' (e.g. questions about time for the important tasks) versus 'unproductive time' (e.g. questions about barriers to performing the best teaching, events where energy is taken out of the work, time spent on unimportant tasks). The approach was to ask the teachers to reflect on the character and quality of time as it manifests itself in concrete work situations. The interpretation of all the studies was framed thematically using concepts from psychosocial work environment research and sociology of time research (Lund, 2017).

Findings

We examined the rhythms of teachers' work and how they were affected by the new WTA organization of work time. We sought insights into how teachers are trying to create more rhythms in their daily work and the barriers to establishing those rhythms. The WTA has made it more difficult for teachers to time their work. Based on the studies before the WTA, it could be assumed that at least some fixed working hours would make it easier to establish rhythms, but this was not the case in relation to the WTA.

The WTA challenged the timing of work. Teachers in the workshops used the example of preparing a lesson. Before the WTA, they would do it as close to the lesson as possible. They found that this reduced their mental workload and provided a more natural order of work. For example, in one workshop, a teacher talked about sometimes being obliged to prepare on Monday for a lesson to be given on Thursday. The reason could be that Monday has an opening in the schedule, but if the opening is one hour and the preparation only takes half an hour, time is wasted. In addition, if preparation takes longer than one hour, the teacher will have to wait until a new opening appears in the schedule before going back to it. Often there are no more scheduled gaps before the class, which results in poorly prepared teaching. Since the WTA, work is characterized by a lack of processes with time allotted for every purpose, which disrupts rhythm and flow. Before the WTA, this attempt to follow the principle of one task at a time often resulted in days with long hours and often team meetings in the late afternoons, evenings, weekends and vacations. On other days, teachers had short but very intense hours at school. They found it difficult to find time for concentration and preparation at school and therefore took work home. They reported that they worked many more hours than was expected of them before the WTA and that too many teachers suffered from stress and chronic fatigue. It was difficult to find rhythms in work, family life and social activities.

Structuring of time for preparation and teaching was disturbed by the WTA. It created a rigid scheme where every activity is compressed into an 8 a.m. to 4 p.m. working day. After the first study, we brought up the problem of the long working days and lack of time structures. The consequence of the WTA was that the shorter working days did not reduce the strain. Working in the evening when it can be avoided is difficult to recommend from a working environment perspective, but with teachers' work, it was actually a way of organizing tasks in a logical progression. It was a process that moved forward, often fragmented by disturbances and changes, but nevertheless with a timely logical and chronological process. This at least created cognitive meaning despite the chaos. Since the WTA, the timing of work is determined not by the work content but by the fixed working hours. The result is compressed workdays with high pace and intensity. There could sometimes be a reasonable time allocation for a task, but the teachers said that their work was all about timing, and a lack of timing led to exhaustion and inferior teaching. In the workshops it was often said that it is a daily struggle not to deviate from a good standard of teaching and not to give poorly prepared lessons. Before the WTA was implemented, teachers could decide when to do their preparation, often preparing, e.g. Thursday's work on Wednesday evening and working until they were satisfied that everything was finished. The consequence was many days with long hours, which became even more of a norm with the addition of emails, text messages and phone calls in the evening and early morning to do last-minute preparation in the teams.

The changes in working hours created major changes in synchronization and contained dilemmas regarding teachers' work–life balance. Before the WTA, the need for time coordination created a culture in which it was an ideal to be accessible around the clock. Teachers saw time synchronization with colleagues as necessary for pupils' learning processes, and this ideal was not limited to colleagues but also applied to parents and pupils. Since the WTA, it is in principle not possible to contact teachers after working hours. Before the WTA, working time organized by tasks was demanding on the teachers, creating periodical fluctuations in working hours and intensity. Since the WTA, teachers argued that fixed hours limited their opportunities for coordination in line with their professional needs, causing them to experience the work as more demanding and to find working life at school more uncertain due to lack of synchronization with colleagues. This is another paradox, as one would think that it had become easier since the introduction of fixed working hours, as everyone is present at school at the same time.

Before the WTA, the most demanding tasks in terms of professional immersion were performed outside school. Hence, teachers reported huge problems in balancing work and family life. For example, one said:

> I told my family, I'm not here this weekend. I'll be up to eat, but apart from that, I'll be in the basement. And that was simply to be allowed to concentrate and get finished. . . I ended up not really seeing anyone else. My daughter in year 7 replied at the time, 'What? Again? So you're not home today either?' And that's the point where I stop up and think, that's actually true. How many times have I said to her, I'm going to be home late tonight, and when I come home, I will need to sit down and work.

The fluid boundaries between working life and leisure time were seen as a problem by most participants in the study. The rest saw it as a way of life they chose when becoming a teacher. It would seem natural to see the WTA as an advantage for one's work–life balance. However, it is not so straightforward, because teachers report being more mentally and emotionally drained after work since the WTA because of the many hours spent in a very intensive environment. They are also more concerned about upcoming poor teaching after work hours. This should be seen in light of the more compressed time spent at school. It is obvious that if tasks are not removed in a shortened working day, work will become more compressed. It had become difficult to time one's work and led to fragmentation of rhythms, desynchronization with colleagues and accelerated work. In the workshops, the teachers constantly reminded each other that they should not work outside the school or exceed weekly hours. Since the WTA, the workday is over when one goes home, no matter how much work is unfinished. As time passed, more and more teachers in the workshops stated that they were doing extra work at home.

There are many types of task for teachers. Each requires a certain mindset that can only be achieved if time has suitable characteristics and quality. A particular task can be so different that it takes time to prepare mentally for it. It is especially hard to move back and forth between teaching and preparation. Many teachers experiencing rapid transitions between tasks found it cognitively demanding, leading to an experience of fragmented, unproductive and wasted time. This is putting pressure on teachers, because since the WTA, teachers have to finish preparation within fixed timeframes, instead of juggling with time until they are professionally satisfied with the outcome or happy that they are meeting the needs of the team. As one teacher commented: 'We often allocate things between us and then you just have to finish the work. You need to continue until the work is done. If you don't, someone else is going to miss it in their work'. It was therefore easier for teachers to create a rhythmic relationship between instant effort and slow time when the tasks and the end of the working day were fluid. One reason why the WTA cannot bring about rhythms can be traced back to the rigid time structures within a chaotic working day. Plans of when and where to do tasks outside teaching often fail. There is a teaching deadline, but the day is unpredictable. The temporalities are brutal in the sense that a teacher cannot create a connection between the necessary quality of time and the task within the new time regime. This is not just due to lack of time but also due to poor timing between tasks, including preparation, planning and coordination. Finding time and space for immersion is difficult and was so even before the WTA. Teachers saw the WTA as an opportunity to structure common breaks, but it did not happen. The breaks are increasingly used for preparation and acute ad hoc tasks.

WTA is based on the principle that it is the school manager who allocates time for each teacher's work. In practice, this was impossible and therefore different standards developed locally contrary to the intention of the WTA. The WTA did not allow for this possibility. Before the WTA, teachers had substantial control over their time because the time to do tasks was allocated to the teams beforehand. It was important that this time was allocated as time norms, not clock time, i.e. time had an elastic form managed through collectively professional priorities. This enabled teachers to make decisions on schedules and timing of work more easily. Some teachers used these opportunities to make work-related decisions on a daily basis. Following the WTA, each teacher typically already has scheduled time standards for tasks before the team becomes involved. As mentioned earlier, one would think that such time structures would help to sustain rhythms. This is true in relation to limiting the time spent on boundaryless, ongoing and never-ending tasks, such as extra care for special needs pupils or improving aspects of one's teaching or the school in general. Teachers generally report that they work fewer hours since the WTA but that does not change the fact that work is still highly complicated. The WTA gives a false impression of reduced complexity. Its demand for more interesting teaching for pupils combined with fixed working time has become a double bind for teachers and, according to the teachers in the workshops, at the cost of innovative teaching.

In the interviews, it became clear that the ideal type of teacher is self-managing, competent, passionate, enthusiastic and dignified. These values came from management, but even more from the employees themselves. Being that kind of teacher is therefore not a matter of choice; it is a requirement and one that is linked to the trust of being able to manage working time without management control. It is also a self-accelerating culture. Before the WTA, there were values and a culture of passionate participation, which meant that teachers put pressure on themselves. As one teacher said:

> You need to get involved. You can't allow yourself to sit back and take orders, just saying, 'Yes, fine, it doesn't really worry me'. The way that teacher team meetings work, you just need to get involved and give something. You can't sit back and relax.

Efforts to divide work often failed and led to increased workloads. Plans and the ideal of cross-disciplinary teaching led to drained energy and long hours, including many additional tasks and team meetings. Down to the last minute there was ad hoc planning as teachers coincidentally collided. Breaks were often filled with work-related activities, such as brief meetings, coordination, appointments, planning, extra activities and dealing with pupils' social problems. Cross-disciplinary teaching is naturally more unpredictable than traditional blackboard teaching.

Conclusion

High autonomy associated with flexible working time and workers' management of time is particularly common in the Nordic countries. It is also a phenomenon that demands that the Nordic model must be able to mediate opposing interests when working time becomes more flexible. When there is a common interest in improving the working environment, for example because that will facilitate recruitment of labour, autonomy over time management appears to be a factor that improves working life quality. Common interests focusing on a better working environment and labour optimization show more ambiguous results, as does flexible working time in boundaryless work. This chapter shows that in general it can be problematic to argue that flexible working time arrangements are positive or negative for the working environment. Our previous research project in the field of shift work shows the most benefits of flexible working hours and that it enhances quality of life. The Finnish studies show that the problem of excessive demands cannot be solved with far-reaching autonomy in relation to flexible working hours. The case of the teachers shows that flexible working hours are necessary to succeed in teaching work. Here, fluctuating temporality and situational working time seems preferable.

If we ignore the project about shift work, much of the empirical evidence suggests that acceleration of work, time conflicts between tasks, fragmentation, increased intensity and unpredictability are not solved by flexible working hours. The changes in work brought about by many forms of flexibility create new temporalities that subsequently need to be handled.

The WTA in the teachers' case is unfavourable to the working environment. Fixed working hours are not suitable for hyper-flexible schools with constant changes in work and often chaotic everyday situations. The quality of work and the psychosocial working environment were negatively affected. Teachers seem to need flexible working time to shape their work, as for them job-crafting is a daily necessity.

The WTA contradicts the earlier description of Denmark as a place with the ideal aim to give employees maximum autonomy over their working time, to the extent that the work allows it. The cases of the teachers and the researchers both indicate that employees, to a large degree, accept long hours as long as professional autonomy is maintained at work. This means that autonomy related to flexible working time supports their professional ideals but does not protect them from the stressors of flexibility. Work has changed, and it is now no longer meaningful to organize work based on regular working hours, but limits must be established that support rhythms and stability in working life and elsewhere. All studies in this chapter show that when flexible working time is applied in specific work situations, mechanisms and dynamics arise that lead to dilemmas and paradoxes that can cause mental strain. One of the ways to enhance the working environment would be by establishing routines, habits and synchronization in everyday work, i.e. creating more rhythms in work.

The research has studied work and flexible working time from a temporal perspective. It is argued that lack of rhythms is a good predictor for mental stress in contemporary work. It is necessary to seek new theoretical grounds and empirical knowledge to understand this. There is a need for studies on various types of work where rhythms potentially can create a less stressful work environment. On the basis of this chapter, it is suggested that future research on working time attempts to involve the interaction between working time and qualitative perspectives of time. In this way, it should be possible to capture all the most important temporal relationships in work that create new stressors in the psychosocial working environment and provide new opportunities for quality in working life.

Note

1 www.eurofound.europa.eu/data/european-working-conditions-survey.

References

Agger, B. (2011) iTime: Labor and Life in a Smartphone Era, *Time & Society*, 20(1): 119–136.

Albertsen, K., Garde, A. H., Nabe-Nielsen, K., Hansen, Å. M., Lund, H. & Hvid, H. (2014) Work–Life Balance among Shift Workers: Results from an Intervention Study about Self-Rostering, *International Archives of Occupational and Environmental Health*, 87(3): 265–274.

Albertsen, K., Kauppinen, K., Grimsmo, A., Sørensen, B. A., Rafnsdóttir, G. L. & Tómasson, K. (2007) *Working Time Arrangements and Social Consequences: What Do We Know?*, Copenhagen: Nordic Council of Ministers.

Allvin, M., Aronsson, G., Hagström, T., Johansson, G. & Lundberg, U. (2011) *Work Without Boundaries, Psychological Perspectives on the New Working Life*, Hoboken, NJ: Wiley-Blackwell.

Beck, U. (2000) *The Brave New World of Work*, Cambridge, UK: Polity Press.

Brannen, J. (2005) Time and the Negotiation of Work–Family Boundaries: Autonomy or Illusion?, *Time & Society*, 14(1): 113–131.

Eriksen, T. H. (2001) *Tyranny of the Moment: Fast and Slow Time in the Information Age*, London: Pluto Press.

Felstead, A., Jewson, N. & Walters, S. (2005) *Changing Places of Work*, New York: Palgrave Macmillan.

Fritz, C., Ellis, A. M., Demsky, C. A., Lin, B. C. & Guros, F. (2013) Embracing Work Breaks: Recovering from Work Stress, *Organizational Dynamics*, 42(4): 274–280.

Goodin, R. E., Rice, J. M., Parpo, A. & Eriksson, L. (2008) *Discretionary Time: A New Measure of Freedom*, Cambridge, UK: Cambridge University Press.

Grönlund, A. & Gro, A. (2007) Employee Control in the Era of Flexibility: A Stress Buffer or a Stress Amplifier?, *European Societies*, 9(3): 409–428.

Hansen, Å. M., Nabe-Nielsen, K., Albertsen, K., Hogh, A., Lund, H., Hvid, H. & Garde, A. H. (2015) Self-Rostering and Psychosocial Work Factors: A Mixed Methods Intervention Study, *Applied Ergonomics*, 47: 203–210.

Hvid, H., Lund, H. L., Garde, A. H., Hansen, Å. M., Albertsen, K., Møller, J. & Ajslev, J. Z. N. (2011) Frit valg som aflastning og belastning: selvvalgt arbejdstid i døgnbemandet arbejde [Free Choice as Relief and Workload: Self-Selected Work Hours in Shift Work], *Tidsskrift for Arbejdsliv*, 13(3): 81–97.

Hvid, H., Lund, H. & Pejtersen, J. (2008) Control, Flexibility and Rhythms, *Scandinavian Journal of Work, Environment and Health, Supplement*, 6: 83–90.

Hvid, H. & Moeller, N. (2001) The Developmental Work, *Human Factors and Ergonomics in Manufacturing*, 11(2): 89–100.

Kamp, A., Lund, H. & Hvid, H. (2011) Negotiating Time, Meaning and Identity in Boundaryless Work, *Journal of Workplace Learning*. doi: 10.1108/13665621111128655.

Kern, H. & Schumann, H. (1984) *Das Ende der Arbeitsteilung? Rationalisierung in der industriellen Produktion, Bestandsaufnahme, Trendbestimmung [The End of the Division of Labour? Rationalization in Industrial Production, Inventory, Trend Determination]*, 3. Aufl, München: Beck.

Lefebvre, H. (2004) *Rhythm Analysis, Space, Time and Everyday Life*, London: Continuum.
Lund, H. (2017) Time and Control in Teachers' Work: The Erosion of Rhythms, *Advances in Intelligent Systems and Computing*, 596: 22–35.
Nabe-Nielsen, K., Lund, H., Ajslev, J. Z., Hansen, Å. M., Albertsen, K., Hvid, H. & Garde, A. H. (2013) How do Employees Prioritise When They Schedule Their Own Shifts?, *Ergonomics*. doi: 10.1080/00140139.2013.815804.
Paolucci, G. (1996) The Changing Dynamics of Working Time, *Time & Society*, 5(2): 145–167.
Perlow, L. A. (1999) The Time Famine: Toward a Sociology of Work Time, *Administrative Science Quarterly*, 44(1): 57–81.
Piore, M. & Sabel, C. (1984) *The Second Industrial Divide, Possibilities for Prosperity*, New York: Basic Books.
Rosa, H. (2013) *Social Acceleration, A New Theory of Modernity*, New York: Columbia University Press.
Sennett, R. (1998) *The Corrosion of Character: The Personal Consequences of Work in the New Capitalism*, New York: Norton.
Spurling, N. (2015) Differential Experiences of Time in Academic Work: How Qualities of Time Are Made in Practice, *Time & Society*. doi: 10.1177/0961463X15575842.
Thomas, M. (2006) Union Strategies to Re-Regulate Working Time, *Just Labour*, 9 (Autumn): 1–15.
Thompson, E. P. (1967) Time, work-discipline, and industrial capitalism, *The Past and Present Society*, 38(1): 56–97.
Ylijoki, O. H. & Mäntylä, H. (2003) Conflicting Time Perspectives in Academic Work, *Time & Society*. doi: 10.1177/0961463X03012001364.

Part III

Learning, inclusion and equality

Introduction

Helge Hvid and Eivind Falkum

Minimum wages are relatively high in the Nordic countries. In spite of that, the employment rate is also high, including among young people. At the same time, mobility in the labour market and social mobility are quite high. The educational system plays a crucial role in making this possible. However, learning opportunities at work and opportunities for further education and training also play an important role.

All the Nordic countries have a comprehensive education sector. Education is free, and universal student grants partially cover living costs while studying. Much of the education and training system is managed in close cooperation between the state and the social parties.

It has to some extent been possible to create a positive feedback circle between high-quality production, jobs with autonomy and learning opportunities and continuous upgrading of skills. There are, however, many dilemmas related to education, training and learning, which are dealt with in the following chapters. Courses that are directed at the immediate needs of workplaces create relevance but reduce mobility and flexibility. Should inclusion be ensured by adapting the education of students to the demand, or should companies be encouraged to adapt their work organization and job designs to the supply?

These dilemmas are handled differently in the Nordic countries.

Chapter 8: Young people's access to working life in three Nordic countries: what is the role of vocational education and training? By Christian Helms Jørgensen.

This chapter contains a general discussion of the importance of the Nordic education system for the quality of work and for social mobility, based on literature studies. In addition, vocational education and training are investigated in three Nordic countries, Sweden, Norway and Denmark. Dilemmas in the field are presented. The major differences between the systems are described, and ongoing initiatives are identified that may overcome some of the dilemmas.

Chapter 9: Bargaining for continuing education: a Norwegian case of 'lifelong learning unionism'. By Anders Underthun and Ida Drange.

Unions and governments initiated lifelong learning and continuing education programmes after the recessions in the late 1980s. 'Lifelong learning unionism' was created. The chapter presents a case study of a new way to establish and provide continuing education to members of a union. The aim is twofold: firstly, to improve the employability of the individual members, and secondly, to strengthen the position of the union in collectively oriented bargaining and negotiations.

Chapter 10: Tackling increasing marginalization: can support-side approaches contribute to work inclusion? By Kjetil Frøyland, Angelika Schafft and Øystein Spjelkavik.

Some citizens find it hard to find employment. This is especially true for citizens with serious learning disabilities and mental health issues. The chapter examines different approaches to bringing this group into work. It is pointed out that the most effective one is a support-side approach, where efforts are made to qualify citizens, to create appropriate working conditions and to provide support to companies.

Chapter 8

Young people's access to working life in three Nordic countries

What is the role of vocational education and training?

Christian Helms Jørgensen

Introduction

The high quality of working life in the Nordic countries is closely associated with their well-educated working populations. A highly and broadly skilled labour force has been essential for the Scandinavian development path, based on high-quality production in small open economies (Kristensen et al., 2015; Senghaas, 1985). The Nordic universal welfare states provide free and public education at all levels, which contributes to the low levels of educational inequality. Their comprehensive compulsory school systems reduce social and gender selection in education, promote social mobility and contribute to high female employment rates. The high level of female employment is also supported by the universal provision of public welfare services in the fields of education, health, childcare and eldercare. The expansion of education for these welfare sectors has opened up educational opportunities for women, whose average level of education now exceeds that of men. Therefore, the high quality of working life and the low levels of inequality in the Nordic labour markets can partly be attributed to the organization of education as a key element in the Nordic welfare states. However, this model of the welfare state and labour market is under increasing pressure from globalization, neo-liberal deregulation and technological change. Social inequalities are increasing, and indications of social polarization and labour-market dualization are emerging (Melin, 2014).

In the Nordic labour markets, young people constitute a vulnerable group that generally experiences higher levels of unemployment than adults and older workers, particularly in periods of economic downturn (Albæk et al., 2015; Halvorsen et al., 2013). Compared to adults, young workers face considerably higher risks of being in part-time and/or temporary jobs and have lower earnings and labour-market security (Segendorf, 2013). This situation draws attention to the issue of how young people gain access to working life in the Nordic countries. This chapter focuses on the role of initial vocational education and training (VET) at upper-secondary level in Denmark, Norway and Sweden. In these countries, VET includes between one-third and one-half of the members of every youth cohort. VET at this level aims mainly at 16- to 19-year-olds, but in Norway and Denmark it also includes adults. The question examined here is how VET provides access to working life for young people. This includes a broader investigation of the links between VET and the world of work.

VET is important because the effects of globalization, outsourcing of production, labour migration and automation/informatization are particularly strong for jobs at the lower end of the skills' hierarchy. A strong VET system with high standards is essential in order to counteract the increasing dualization of the labour markets. However, VET in the Nordic countries increasingly relies on school-based training that is organized separately from the world of work. A crucial question to be examined in this chapter is how VET connects with the labour market in Denmark, Norway and Sweden. The chapter starts with a discussion of different ideas on the relationships between education and work, including the concept of a Nordic transition system. Next, it examines young people's transition into working life and examines how the tensions between the social demands of young people and the requirements of the labour market are managed. In particular, it examines young people's transition into working life in two selected industries: health care and construction. Finally, it examines three new, innovative institutions set up to mediate between VET and working life.

The chapter draws on the results from a comparative research project on VET in the Nordic countries, which includes analyses of the historical and current development (Jørgensen et al., 2018; Jørgensen & Tønder, 2018; Michelsen & Stenström, 2018). For each of the four Nordic countries included in the project, five different research reports were published (www.Nord-VET.dk); these provide the empirical basis for this chapter. Two of the reports compare the development of VET for the health sector and the construction sector, based on a common design and research questions.

Conceptualizing the links between VET and working life

Diverse theoretical approaches have been developed to study the links between VET and working life. The influential research approach of Maurice et al. (1986) emphasized the institutional complementarities between the VET system, the organization of work and the system of industrial relations. Together, they constitute specific national configurations of institutions that shape the organization of work at the local level (a *societal effect*). This approach has highlighted the qualities of occupational work for the autonomy and professionalization of intermediate positions (skilled workers) in the organization of work (Gallie, 2009).

The literature on collective skill formation (Busemeyer & Trampusch, 2012) makes a distinction based on the extent of employer engagement in skills' formation. In this respect, the VET systems of the Nordic countries come out differently from each other. While the Swedish and Norwegian systems are seen as state-led models, the Danish system is categorized as a model of collective skill formation with high employer engagement. Although this categorization correctly points to the diversity of the Nordic VET systems, it is questionable. The Swedish VET system has been strongly marketized since the early 1990s, and the Norwegian system is based on apprenticeships with strong employer involvement, similar to the Danish VET system.

Comparative research on VET systems offers another conceptualization of their links with working life. The concepts of *standardization*, *stratification* and *vocational specificity* proposed by Jutta Allmendinger (1989) have been widely used. High *standardization* is associated with strong regulation and with uniformly high standards of training. All the Nordic VET systems are classified as highly standardized in international comparisons (Pfeffer, 2008). In Denmark, the setting of the standards is left to the labour-market organizations, while this is mainly the responsibility of the state in Sweden. Strong national standardization of vocational qualifications enables their high portability in the labour market. Occupational standardization promotes the matching of VET programmes to job profiles in occupational labour markets. This matching smooths students' transition to work. However, since the late 1980s, the three Nordic countries have decentralized the regulation of VET to make the programmes more flexible and adaptable to local labour markets. This has tended to weaken the matching of VET with the national standards for occupational work set by the labour-market organizations.

The level of *stratification* concerns the extent of tracking, division and selection of students in the VET system. While the Nordic education systems and labour markets have generally low levels of stratification, the Nordic VET systems differ significantly. In Sweden, VET was integrated into a unified school system with the reforms in 1971 and 1991. In contrast, Denmark has maintained a strong division between the *gymnasiums* (academically oriented upper-secondary institutions), which prepare youngsters for higher education, and the VET system, which is based on apprenticeships that prepare them for occupational work. Norway represents a mixed system, with a unified school for the first two years, followed by a division of students into two tracks: either one year of higher-education preparatory programmes or two years of apprenticeships. The higher level of tracking and stratification in Denmark is associated with a higher level of inequality in educational attainment. The strong integration of VET with general education in Sweden is associated with VET's weak links to working life.

Last, in relation to the *specificity* of the qualifications provided, the Nordic countries have given priority to broad and general skills in order to improve the subsequent flexibility and mobility in working life and to prepare for lifelong learning. However, the three Nordic VET systems also differ significantly in this respect. The Danish apprenticeship system emphasizes specific vocational skills, and the school-based Swedish system gives priority to general and generic qualifications. While specific qualifications are expected to have only short-term value in the labour market, they are known to promote fast and direct transition to skilled work (Bol & Van de Werfhorst, 2013). Therefore, this involves a trade-off that has been managed differently in the Nordic countries. All Nordic VET systems have limited the specificity of qualifications and emphasized the role of general qualifications. The number of programmes and specializations has been diminished in order to reduce the risk of locking the students into a specific job or occupation (Jørgensen & Tønder, 2018).

To sum up, the research emphasizes many similarities between the Nordic countries regarding welfare-state and labour-market models – but differentiates between their VET systems, especially with respect to their links to the world of work.

VET and the Nordic model of working life

Working life in the Nordic countries is generally considered to be of a high quality and allows for high levels of autonomy and opportunities for self-development (Gallie, 2009). In a cross-European comparison, Dobbin and Boychuk (1999) term this a 'skill-governed' Nordic work model in contrast to the 'rule-governed' work model in Britain. The breadth and depth of skills provided by the Nordic VET systems are important for the high quality of work and for the high levels of job discretion found in these countries. Comparative studies of production regimes have demonstrated the close interdependence of the national production regimes, labour-market models, and dominant forms of work-organization and VET systems (Gallie, 2003, 2009; Streeck, 1992). Therefore, the search for a single causal factor to explain the emergence of the Nordic model of working life is less appropriate than studying the interaction of multiple, complementary institutions and policies: a configurational causation (Thelen & Mahoney, 2015).

Six of the key institutions involved in this Nordic institutional configuration will be emphasized. First, the centralized wage bargaining in the Nordic countries has resulted in compressed wage structures and relatively high minimum wages, which includes young and unskilled workers. Second, the high wage levels encourage employers' investment in labour-saving technology and innovation, and their preference for employees with high levels of skills (Busemeyer, 2015). Moreover, the strong employment protection in the Nordic countries (except Denmark) gives employers incentives to engage in the training of low-skilled workers and to employ highly skilled labour. Third, the low cost of high skills encourages employers to move up-market and to pursue strategies for 'diversified quality production' (Sandberg & Movitz, 2013; Streeck, 1992). Fourth, the low levels of unemployment and the high levels of social security provided by the Nordic welfare states have strengthened the power position of employees in relation to employers. Fifth, strong trade unions have restrained employers' use of direct control and degrading forms of management and have facilitated the development of non-hierarchical work organizations (Edlund & Grönlund, 2010). These flat organizations have supported the collaboration between employers and employees on innovation, upgrading of skills and workplace learning (Kristensen et al., 2015). This has promoted trade-union strategies to support the technological modernization of work and the upgrading of their members' skills (Lansbury, 2015; Thelen, 2014). The low-skill differential and low-power distance in work organizations improve knowledge-sharing between the planning level and the executing level. Finally, this consensual and skills-driven development is reinforced by public policies. International comparison shows that the level of public spending on education and further training is high in the Nordic countries. In addition, an extensive active labour-market policy has given high priority to getting the unemployed back into employment through retraining, mobility support, etc. (Kananen, 2016). Although the Nordic VET systems have varying levels of employer involvement, they are all strong and highly standardized and enjoy high levels of state support.

These are some of the key interactional effects regarding skill formation and working life in the Nordic countries. They interact to create positive feedback cycles between the improvement of high-quality production, the extension of job discretion and the continual upgrading of skills (Kristensen et al., 2015). The Nordic countries are, however, not homogeneous: there are substantial differences between industries and countries, and systems of skill formation differ significantly (Jørgensen et al., 2018). Moreover, reforms inspired by neo-liberalism since the 1990s have involved marketization, decentralization and deregulation, which have weakened the provisions of the welfare state and contributed to increased social inequality (Kananen, 2016; Melin, 2014). In addition, the effects of globalization challenge the foundation of the Nordic model by shifting the balance of power in favour of the employers and by intensifying the instability and insecurity of working life. This involves new social risks, particularly for vulnerable groups in the labour market, such as young people trying to gain access to working life (Harsløf et al., 2013). The next section investigates how VET adjusts to the changing skills requirement in working life, and how the tensions between young people's educational demands and the supply of work and training placements are regulated.

Balancing social demands with labour-market requirements

In all the Nordic countries, the governments have set the goal that all young people should complete at least upper-secondary education to prepare for the future requirements of working life. VET systems are required to deliver the specific skills and knowledge that are relevant to working life. However, it is also generally believed that young people should be allowed to make their own choices regarding education and work. Thus, the relationship between the VET systems and working life is about balancing young people's demands for education with the labour-market requirements for skilled labour. Due to differences in the governance of the Nordic VET systems, each has given priority to one or the other side of this relationship. In the statist VET system in Sweden, the main priority for upper-secondary school is to provide educational opportunities for all young people. The supply of education by the municipalities is not dependent on training placements provided by the companies. Meanwhile, the Danish and Norwegian apprenticeship systems are more sensitive to the requirements in the labour market, and the labour-market organizations have a stronger role in the governance of VET. In addition, the capacity of the apprenticeship systems depends on the supply of training placements offered by employers. Students in these systems spend more time searching for an apprenticeship, dropping out, or shifting into another form of education. A much higher proportion of 21-year-olds in Sweden have completed upper-secondary education compared to the two countries with apprenticeships (Albæk et al., 2015).

The supply of training placements depends on the employment situation of the training companies and the industries. This close link between the situation in the training market and that in the labour market tends to reduce the risk of mismatch. However, while the apprenticeship system balances the supply of and demand for skilled labour, these systems also generate mismatches. During a recession, companies typically stop taking on new apprentices, and an upturn is often followed by a shortage of skilled labour. This can last for years, as the training of new apprentices typically takes four years.

In all three countries, students' transition to the world of work has been postponed. Before the reforms in the 1970s to 1990s, young people went straight into apprenticeships after completing compulsory school. Today, they must attend school-based training before they can take up an apprenticeship. In Denmark, the school-based course lasts one year and in Norway two years. In Sweden, students must complete a three-year *gymnasium* programme before they can gain access to the post-secondary apprenticeships that are organized by the labour-market organizations in some industries.

In Denmark, many of the most popular VET programmes limit access to the first school-based courses using quotas in order to match the number of students to the number of apprenticeships available. If apprenticeships are not available, the vocational schools in Denmark and Norway offer school-based training. In Norway, the county councils (*fylkeskommunene*) are responsible for all upper-secondary education. The extent to which they adjust the number of students they enrol to fit the demand in the labour market is quite minimal, as the size of the programmes is more dependent on the capacity of the schools (Høst, 2012). As a result, mismatches between students' chosen forms of education and the demand for labour are common. In Norway, the unsuccessful search for apprenticeships is a common reason why students drop out of vocational programmes or shift to general programmes in the third year. In Sweden, until the early 1990s, the capacity of the vocational programmes was determined by the government's assessment of the future demand for labour. Since the introduction of free school choice and the decentralization of regulation, the capacity of VET programmes has mainly been determined by the demand of the students, which increases the risk of mismatch in the labour market (Olofsson & Panican, 2012). This examination has focused on the matching of VET to the requirements of working life. The next section turns to young people's transition from education to work in the three Nordic countries.

A Nordic transition regime

In international studies of young people's transition from education to work, the concepts of *transition system* (Raffe, 2008) and *transition regime* (Walther, 2006) have gained influence. These ideas refer to the institutional structuring of the pathways from education into working life, including the critical points of choice and selection in students' transitions. This approach is useful for exploring the strengths and weaknesses of the institutional regulation of the relationships between the VET system and the world of work. The risks and opportunities for students after completing VET vary considerably, depending on the institutional architecture of the education system and the labour market. Previous research has demonstrated the institutional embeddedness of school-to-work transition (Andersen & Van de Werfhorst, 2010; Müller, 2005; Raffe, 2014). For example, youth unemployment is considerably higher in Sweden, which has a mainly school-based VET system, than it is in Denmark and Norway, where VET is based on apprenticeships (Albæk et al., 2015).

In the typologies of comparative research, the Nordic countries are categorized as representing a universalistic transition regime (Pohl & Walther, 2007). This regime provides strong and multi-dimensional support for young people's transition to working life and reduces the insecurities and risks associated with this (Walther, 2006). The institutional qualities of the Nordic countries – particularly high minimum wages, high skills' requirements and strong employment protection – are claimed to limit young people's access to employment. However, a review by Tamesberger (2017) emphasizes that these institutional conditions can also improve the employment rate of young people. Brzinsky-Fay (2017) shows that institutions influencing youth unemployment unfold their effects only in combination with other institutions. The Nordic countries have given high priority to keeping youth unemployment low through a mixture of social support, activation, training and coercion (Jensen, 2015; Kananen, 2016). The social security resulting from the welfare provisions allows young people to try out different opportunities, make changes and re-orientate their lives. This process of finding their way tends to prolong the transition from initial education to full-time, permanent jobs

(Walther, 2006). In the Nordic countries, young people move away from their parents and become financially independent at an earlier age than in other European countries. A high proportion of young people are engaged in part-time work while they are in education. More than half of the age group of 15- to 19-year-olds are in part-time employment; in Denmark, this figure exceeds 80% (Segendorf, 2013). The Nordic transition regime is often characterized as a collectivist system. However, the universal rights to welfare benefits encourage individual independence and release young people from dependency on the family and the market. Since the late 1990s, neo-liberal reforms have affected the Nordic transition regimes. In all three countries, access to social benefits has been restricted and tied more closely to work obligations (Lorentzen et al., 2014). In Denmark and Sweden, the level and duration of welfare benefits have been reduced for young people, and financial benefits have been made contingent on participation in activation measures (Bengtsson, 2014; Kananen, 2016).

The well-organized Nordic labour markets and the low rates of youth unemployment have constrained the growth of a secondary, low-wage youth labour market (Jensen, 2015). Studies indicate that it has become more difficult for young people to gain access to employment in the Nordic labour markets since the financial crisis, with the exception of Norway (Albæk et al., 2015). Low-skilled jobs that used to be accessible for early school-leavers have disappeared due to the outsourcing of labour-intensive production, new technologies and immigration (Segendorf, 2013). Researchers find that, in most European countries, the transition from education to a stable position in the labour market has become more demanding, prolonged and less transparent (Walther & Plug, 2006). In Denmark, Norway and Sweden, the average age of establishment in the labour market had increased from around 20 years in the early 1990s to 28 years by 2016 (OECD, 2016).

International comparison shows that the employment rates of young people in the Nordic countries are high and that youth unemployment is low (when excluding students, see Albæk et al., 2015). However, youth unemployment rates have been growing since 1998 – except in Norway, due to its continual high growth rates. Young people's opportunities for getting full-time, permanent jobs without any post-compulsory education have been reduced (Madsen et al., 2013). Almost all young people continue in upper-secondary education after completing compulsory schooling. More than half of young people enrol in general education that prepares for higher education, and between one-third and one-half of the members of each cohort enrol in VET with the aim of gaining access to a meaningful working life of high quality. The VET system in general is in a key position to prepare young people for working life and to support their access to the world of work. However, the Nordic VET systems and their linkages to working life differ considerably. In addition, we find significant differences in each country between sectors and industries; two such examples are examined in the next section.

Transition to work in the health-care and construction sectors

This section presents a comparison of young people's transition to the world of work in two different sectors: health care and construction. These sectors have different traditions for VET and different links between education and working life. The health-care sector is a predominantly female field of public employment, where VET developed in connection with the expansion of the welfare state in the post-war period. In the public health-care sector, young people's transition to work is much less affected by shifting economic cycles than it is in the construction sector. Construction is part of the private sector and has mainly male employees, a long and strong tradition of well-organized craft unions and a VET system based on apprenticeships. In both sectors, occupational training has been integrated into a national VET system in all three countries, though with some differences between them. In Norway and Denmark, apprenticeships are integrated into the public upper-secondary VET system. In Sweden, the state-led VET system is mainly school-based and has a post-secondary apprenticeship system in the construction industry (Fjellström, 2014). In both sectors, young people's transition to the world of work is challenged: in the health-care sector, by problems of recognition and by a tradition of recruiting adults; and in the construction sector, by the inflow of migrant labour from the newer EU countries. The investigations are based mainly on two comparative reports produced as part of the Nord-VET project and on two chapters in a book on the Nordic VET systems for construction (Olsen et al., 2018) and health care (Høst & Larsen, 2018).

Transition to work in the health-care sector

The introduction of VET in the health-care sector is an example of a fruitful educational upgrading of the formerly unskilled female health-care workers, who previously comprised the majority of employees in the care sector (Høst & Larsen, 2018). In the 1960s, new education for auxiliary nurses began to be established in all three countries. They soon became very popular, particularly among adults with work experience. The auxiliary nurses tried without success to become integrated into the professional nurses' organizations and so formed their own bodies (Høst & Larsen, 2018). The establishment of vocational education for the subordinate health-care workers was driven by a combination of political objectives. One such objective was to raise the quality of the public-sector health services; another was to provide post-compulsory education for all, including women; and a third was to improve the quality of work and the respect for predominantly female health-care work. In Denmark, the new occupational group established its own jurisdiction independent of the nurses. In the other two countries, the auxiliary nurses had a more clearly defined subordinate position to the nurses, with less autonomy (Høst & Larsen, 2018).

In all three countries, auxiliary-nurse education was replaced by a new and broader VET programme for health-care workers, when they were integrated into the public VET system.

The introduction of vocational education for health-care workers has contributed to the upgrading of formerly unskilled and unrecognized female health-care work. This education supported the establishment of health-care workers as an independent occupational group, which has gained recognition and become one of the largest VET programmes in all three countries. From the very beginning, the VET programme for health-care workers attracted many adults. Also, a large proportion of its participants are from ethnic minorities; the programme has been very efficient at integrating these students into working life (Høst & Larsen, 2018).

Students' transition from VET to working life demonstrates some common challenges in all three countries but also some differences between them. In all three, political measures have been taken to give young people priority in the VET programme for health-care workers. However, employers have continued to recruit mainly experienced adults. Consequently, it is difficult for newly educated health-care workers to gain access to full-time employment in Norway and Sweden. This helps explain why a large proportion of the students in these countries prefer to continue studying. In Denmark, health-care workers have maintained a position in the hospitals, though it is declining, and they generally have access to permanent, full-time employment after completion. Two-thirds of young employees are in permanent jobs, and the proportion of part-time employment has been decreasing (PASS, 2017).

Previously, the training of auxiliary nurses was closely connected to the hospitals, and the connection between education and work in this period was very strong (Høst & Larsen, 2018). Gradually, the auxiliary nurses lost their position in the hospitals, where nurses became the dominant group. This has happened because of technological modernization, rising skill requirements and struggles between the occupational groups. Consequently, the new education for health-care workers has a broad profile that is oriented towards eldercare in the municipal sector, which is considered less attractive by young people. In addition, the subordinate health-care work has been subjected to the measures of New Public Management – with standardization, time control, intensification of work and reduced autonomy.

In Norway, county councils' organization of apprenticeship training is not based on an interest in recruitment. After completing VET, few of the students are offered employment in the public institutions, which prefer to employ unskilled adults in part-time positions and rely on informal training at work (Høst et al., 2014b). In addition, the nurses have succeeded in blocking the employment of health-care workers in hospitals. Consequently, in Norway most of the newly educated health-care workers have access only to part-time and temporary employment in the less attractive primary sector. A large proportion of the students in the health-care programme in Norway do not start an apprenticeship after the second year but instead utilize the opportunity to shift into a third year that gives them access to higher education. In the school-based Swedish VET system, the health-care worker programme is broad and preparatory, and does not award final occupational competence, which makes the transition to work difficult. The adult education programme for health-care workers attracts more students than does the programme for young people. In Sweden, the transition from VET to working life is also difficult. As employers prefer adults with work experience over newly educated health-care workers, less than half of all students are established in the labour market three years after graduation (SCB, 2012). In Denmark, a reform in 2015 made education for health-care workers more age-homogeneous – similar to the situations in the two other Nordic countries – and adults above the age of 25 years are now referred to separate courses. In spite of this, adults still make up two-thirds of the students in Danish health-care worker education.

Despite their educational upgrade, health-care workers remain a low-waged, subordinate female field of staff at the lower rungs of the educational hierarchy. And VET for health-care workers still contributes to reproducing the highly gender-segregated working life in the health-care sector. However, the differences between Denmark and Norway demonstrate the scope for policy to improve the status and quality of health-care work by securing full-time, permanent employment and job autonomy for this group of skilled employees. The development in Norway demonstrates the limits of public educational policy for the upgrading of health-care work. In general, the transition to working life from the VET programme for health-care workers represents a paradox. Forecasts of the demand for labour predict a long-term shortage of health-care workers due to the demographic shift, but newly educated health-care workers in Norway and Sweden today find it difficult to gain access to full-time permanent jobs.

Transition to work in the construction sector

Vocational education for the construction sector is one of the largest fields of VET measured in terms of the enrolment of students in all three Nordic countries. It has traditionally provided access to well-paid and well-respected employment for a large group of young people, mainly men, including students with low grades in compulsory school. The construction industry demonstrates some of the negative consequences for working life of the liberalization of the European labour markets (Friberg & Eldring, 2013).

The trade unions in the construction sector have historically been very strong, and the organization of work has been dominated by self-managing teams. A high level of autonomy of skilled workers has been achieved through collective negotiation at the local level between teams and employers. In all three countries, the construction industry has a strong tradition of craft-based and occupational work, which creates close links between the VET programmes and working life. These links are strongest in Denmark and Norway, where the apprenticeship programmes are closely linked to occupational job profiles. In the school-based Swedish VET system, the programmes are broader and leave more of the specific skills to be acquired in post-secondary apprenticeship training. In Denmark, a strong tradition of craft unionism – rather than industrial unionism – has reinforced the occupational organization of work.

The construction industry in the three Nordic countries has been strongly affected by the opening of the labour markets to migrant labour from the ten new member states of the EU since 2004. The migrant workers have more precarious and insecure working conditions and lower wages, and they are less often unionized or covered by collective agreements than are native workers (Friberg & Eldring, 2013). Particularly in the construction industry, where the employment of posted and temporary workers is very high, this constitutes a serious challenge for the Nordic model of labour relations.

The consequences of this situation have been most pronounced in Norway, which has received by far the highest share of Central and Eastern European labour migrants. Norway has been a preferred target for migrant labour because of high wages, low unemployment and somewhat weaker regulation than the two other Nordic countries. In Norway, temporary staffing agencies have organized a 'migration industry' that provides flexible, low-wage migrant labour, which undermines organized labour relations (Friberg & Eldring, 2013). As an effect of the influx of migrant labour with low skill levels, the organization of work has changed to become more segregated, with separate fields of work for migrant labour and with reduced autonomy and stronger hierarchies (Haakestad & Friberg, 2017).

Young people's transition from VET to the world of work in the construction sector has been affected by this development. First, employers' engagement in apprenticeship training has declined as a result of their access to flexible, low-wage migrant labour. Employers have shifted recruitment policy so that skilled, native workers and apprentices are replaced by migrant workers. In addition, the foreign subcontractors and temporary staffing agencies that allocate a significant part of the migrant labour force do not take responsibility for apprenticeship training. Second, the employment of migrant labour tends to change the organization of work in a neo-Taylorist direction, which reduces the demand for skilled workers (Haakestad & Friberg, 2017). Third, the quality and conditions of work – and the wages – are affected negatively by the migrant labour, which reduces the attractiveness of VET for this sector among young people. This contributes to a shortage of skilled labour, which stimulates the vicious circle of hiring migrant labour and Taylorization of the work organization. The construction industry in Norway has been affected much more strongly by this development than its counterpart in Denmark, where the collective agreements are stronger and the financial crisis was more severe. In Sweden, the temporary staffing agencies are subject to stronger regulation, and the higher unemployment rates among native young people and settled immigrants have reduced employers' demand for foreign labour (Friberg & Eldring, 2013). The construction sector is one of the largest in the VET system. It has provided opportunities for occupational employment that is highly respected for a large group of young men. In all three countries, the liberalization of labour regulation, together with the import and exploitation of foreign labour, threatens a traditionally important pathway to the world of work for young people who do not opt for higher education.

Challenges for young people's transition from VET to work

Due to the continual expansion and extension of school-based schooling in all the Nordic countries, young people's transition from school to work has been postponed. Compulsory schooling has been prolonged, and vocational students' encounters with working life are preceded by preparatory, school-based training of varying duration. Moreover, the priority in education policy has shifted from citizenship to focus more on employability (Blossing et al., 2014; Kananen, 2016). The governments in all the Nordic countries increasingly emphasize VET as a measure to include disadvantaged young people and to support their transition to working life.

The apprenticeship systems of Denmark and Norway have been modernized and have expanded into new sectors. The Swedish VET system has included longer periods of work-based learning and introduced a new apprenticeship programme in 2011. However, the integration of work-based learning in VET raises a variety of challenges. One is them is the matching of students' demands for training to the supply of training placements in companies. The capacity of the apprenticeship system is unstable, because it follows economic fluctuations, resulting in frequent mismatches between the demand for and supply of training. A significant proportion of the students in VET are unable to find training placements, and employers' practices for hiring apprentices can be selective and discriminate against minority groups (Helland & Støren, 2006). This state of affairs is difficult to reconcile with the political aim of providing post-compulsory educational opportunities for all young people.

In general, modern working life offers good opportunities for learning, because of the persistent changes in the production process and the organization of work. However, access to work-based learning in VET is subject to structural constraints, and companies are raising the entry requirements for gaining access to workplace learning (Jørgensen, 2015). When the production process becomes knowledge-intensive and automated, work becomes more abstract and requires higher levels of codified knowledge. In addition, the production process becomes increasingly distributed and specialized. Consequently, each company concentrates on specific operations in global supplier chains and can offer only a small part of the wide range of vocational qualifications involved in learning an occupation. Moreover, the slack in supply chains is being reduced, and the delivery schedules are being made tighter. Work processes are under constant pressure to improve intensity, efficiency and quality, which leaves less room for young people learning from experimentation, trying things out and making mistakes. In addition, volatile markets reduce the planning horizon of companies and limit the possibility of engaging in three-year apprenticeship contracts. Companies increasingly focus on short-term shareholder values that reduce their propensity to make long-term investment in a skilled workforce (Casey, 2012). The strength of these changes and their effects differs between industries, but they indicate that the role of companies in providing work-based training in VET is becoming more restricted.

These challenges are in conflict with the growing political interest in the Nordic countries of strengthening work-based learning in VET and improving the transition to the labour market. These countries do, however, offer interesting examples of institutional innovations to improve the connection between VET and the world of work. The next section explores some new institutions that mediate between VET and working life in Denmark, Norway and Sweden.

New mediating institutions between VET and the world of work

The shift from a vocational school to working life is a profound and risky transition for vocational students. In Denmark and Norway, it is integrated into the vocational programmes, while in Sweden it takes place after the completion of the mainly school-based VET programmes. There is a general recognition of the value of work-based learning in VET but also a broad concern about the quality of work-based training and the availability of training placements. As the primary objective of work is not learning but production, the apprentices' learning is secondary to the requirements of production. Considering the challenges for work-based training mentioned earlier, securing high-quality training is a critical challenge in apprenticeship systems.

Another critical challenge in the Norwegian and Danish apprenticeship systems is that students have no guarantee of obtaining an apprenticeship placement. Although students receive support from vocational schools, the main responsibility for obtaining an apprenticeship lies with the individual students. In Denmark and Norway, a considerable number of students do not succeed in obtaining their desired apprenticeships; this makes them discontinue the VET programme. This situation demonstrates two basic weaknesses of the apprenticeship system at the systemic level: the subordination of learning to production and the individualization of the responsibility for securing training placements.

In all three countries, these weaknesses have been addressed in numerous reforms and initiatives. Most initiatives focus on the individual student by providing supporting measures for the most vulnerable students, as described in

Chapter 10 by Frøyland, Schafft and Spjelkavik in this volume. Placing systemic problems with the individual student and identifying these students as vulnerable can, however, have unintended negative consequences (Jørgensen, 2016). Interestingly, innovative initiatives have also been taken at the institutional level in the form of new intermediary institutions that address the systemic weaknesses mentioned. These institutions are local training agencies (LTAs) in Norway, training centres in Denmark and vocational colleges in Sweden.

Norwegian local training agencies

LTAs in Norway are local associations of companies that train apprentices. They represent an interesting case of the development of local institutions for collective skill formation in a period characterized by deregulation and marketization in other countries. The purpose of LTAs is to improve the quality of training, to relieve the companies of the administrative tasks related to apprenticeship training and to prevent future local skills shortages. LTAs are private associations that are owned and managed by the training companies. In 2013, the average LTA had three full-time employees, comprised 77 member firms and offered a total of 118 apprenticeships (Høst et al., 2014a). The number of LTAs expanded strongly after the reform of VET in 1994, which integrated apprenticeships into the public VET system. The reforms of VET have raised the standards for both quality and administration by requiring continual assessments, quality reports and individual training plans for the apprentices (Høst et al., 2014a).

The main objective of LTAs is to coordinate and strengthen employers' interests in apprenticeship training. This is achieved by supporting and supervising the training of apprentices in the member companies; it includes regular visits to the companies, interviews with the apprentices and administration of the electronic training portfolios (Nore & Lahn, 2014). LTAs also organize supplementary school-based training for the apprentices and training of the workplace trainers. In addition, they engage in the recruitment of young people to apprenticeships and of companies to provide opportunities for training.

The financing of the 340 LTAs derives mainly from public subsidies to the companies that take responsibility for training apprentices (Proba, 2016). State funding has been crucial for LTAs' continual expansion to become contractual partners in 80% of all apprenticeships in Norway and to include more than 80% of all training companies. The local engagement of employers in LTAs has been decisive in the huge growth in the number of apprenticeships since the 1980s. LTAs have been successful in managing the common long-term interests of the employers in training. They have assumed the role of local mediators between the training companies and the public authorities. In addition, they assist in mediation in the case of conflicts between apprentices and training companies. The growth and professionalization of LTAs are backed by regional and national networks of LTAs that organize knowledge-sharing and mutual support (Høst et al., 2014a). The trade unions have opposed the inclusion of LTAs in the formal governance system for VET, because LTAs represent only the employers. LTAs have, however, become a significant local institution in the Norwegian system of collective skill formation. They represent a remarkable innovation that deals with some of the weaknesses of the apprenticeship system, including the quality of in-company training and the long-term supply of apprenticeships and skilled workers.

Danish training centres

Similar to students in the Norwegian VET system, young people in Denmark can start in the first school-based course of most VET programmes without having an apprenticeship contract. During this course of 6 to 12 months' duration, they must obtain a training contract in order to complete the programme. However, a shortage of apprenticeships has hindered many students' transition to work-based training. Therefore, from 1993, students have been offered alternative, school-based training during periods of economic recession. School-based training was offered only as a compensatory measure, and students using it were required to continue searching for a company-based apprenticeship contract. As this measure gained a poor reputation among students, it did not prevent students from dropping out of VET. Therefore, a reform in 2013 introduced a new and permanent institution, the training centres (*praktikcentre*) to offer full-time school-based training in VET and to help students obtain apprenticeships. Now, when VET students are unable to get an apprenticeship in a company after completion of their basic course, they can sign a contract with a training centre. In contrast to the Norwegian LTAs, which have only a weak link to the vocational schools, the Danish training centres are closely connected to the vocational schools. The running of the 50 Danish training centres is financed by the state, and the allowance paid to the students is financed by the employers' training levy, known as the 'AUB' (*Arbejdsgivernes Uddannelsesbidrag*).

The main purpose of the training centres is to provide training for students until they obtain a permanent training placement in a company. An additional aim is to coordinate students' multiple training placements in companies that do not offer a full three-year apprenticeship contract. The training centres supplement this with school-based training to ensure that the students acquire all the skills required to complete the VET programme. In order to increase the supply of training opportunities, the training contracts can be organized flexibly as short-term contracts or combined training contracts (for two or more companies). In some industries, such as construction, one-third of the training contracts are for short training placements. The curricular requirements and final exam in the training centres are similar to those in ordinary apprenticeships. The proportion of students in the training centres has remained steady – at over 10% of all students – since the crisis in 2008 (according to 2017 figures: www.uvm.dk).

The fact that individual students have responsibility for obtaining apprenticeships, and that there is a recurring lack of training placements, have been weaknesses of the apprenticeship system for decades. The training centres take over some of the responsibility for students' successful transition to working life. The centres have a coordinating function for multisite firm-based training and for supplementary training that they provide themselves. They also shift the problem of securing apprenticeships from being an individual responsibility to being an institutional task for the training centres. This role has similarities with that of the Norwegian LTAs, though the Danish training centres are engaged only weakly in supervising the quality of in-company training.

Swedish vocational colleges

When the Swedish VET system was integrated into the state-led upper-secondary comprehensive schools through reforms in 1971 and 1991, its connection to the world of work became very weak. In an attempt to change that situation, the government introduced a new apprenticeship programme in 2011 but received only limited support from employers. The new 'Vocational Colleges' (*Yrkescollege*) present a different picture. The 'Technical Colleges' (*Teknikcollege*) were initiated in 2004 by the main industrial employers' organization and the main union for employees in industry (Olofsson, 2015). Based on decentralized cooperation, this new institution has reactivated an old cross-sector alliance between industry and the unions to promote VET (Persson & Hermelin, 2018). The Technical Colleges are managed by the Industry Council (*Industrirådet*), which comprises the largest organizations in the industrial labour market. A similar initiative was taken some years later to establish 'Health Colleges' (*Vårdcollege*) for the health-care sector. A common aim of the Vocational Colleges is to improve the quality of VET and to make it more attractive for young people in order to secure the supply of skilled workers. The colleges are primarily a certification scheme for high-quality VET in collaboration with VET providers, labour-market organizations and public authorities. The colleges are established as institutions for regional collaboration on vocational training and include a variety of partners. An association of companies in collaboration with at least three municipalities and vocational schools can be certified as a Vocational College. They must meet ten quality requirements, which include high-quality learning environments, state-of-the-art equipment, systematic quality control and an infrastructure for collaboration between vocational schools and employers.

The colleges represent a new form of cooperation on skill formation between training companies, municipalities and vocational schools. By 2017, the Technical Colleges included 150 certified educational providers and 3,000 companies in Sweden (www.teknikcollege.se). The number of certified Health

Colleges has exceeded 100. The colleges are primarily engaged in improving the quality of training and the supply of skilled labour. Training in the colleges is organized in accordance with the vocational curricula defined by the state in collaboration with the labour-market organizations. Due to the extensive decentralization of Swedish upper-secondary schools, the colleges can adapt VET programmes to the requirements of local companies. Like the Norwegian training agencies, the colleges are employer-driven, but – in contrast to these – rely on formal cooperation with the vocational schools and public authorities. The colleges represent a shift in the Swedish VET system from being state-led towards a collectivist system of skill formation (Olofsson, 2015). Although research on the results of the colleges is limited, there are indications that these institutions have contributed considerably to improving the connections between vocational schools and employers, and to smoothing students' transition from VET to working life (Olofsson & Persson Thunqvist, 2018).

Conclusion

The VET systems in Denmark, Norway and Sweden are important elements in the configuration of institutions that have resulted in a high quality of working life for people in those countries. Positive interaction effects between VET, working life and public policies have contributed to producing high levels of autonomy at work and low levels of insecurity and labour-market dualization. By providing high-quality intermediary skills for young people who are not opting for higher education, VET is important for the high level of social equality in these countries. Youth employment rates are high, and youth unemployment rates are low in the three countries examined. They can be seen as representatives of a universal transition regime due to the common qualities of their welfare states and their shared policies for social inclusion and support for young people. However, the opportunities for young people to gain access to working life differ between the three countries.

All three VET systems are highly standardized, which improves the matching of qualifications with jobs and the portability of VET qualifications to and within the labour market. In the Norwegian and Danish apprenticeship systems, the specificity of qualifications is high, which improves the students' transition to employment. Sweden has most consistently implemented the Nordic model of education, with the state prioritizing equal access for all to education, in the spirit of democratic citizenship. This is in conflict with entrusting the training of students in upper secondary education to private employers. In all three countries, the extent of work-based training in VET has been reduced since the 1970s. The Swedish VET system developed into a state-led and mainly school-based system, which made students' transition to working life difficult and prolonged. In the Norwegian and Danish apprenticeship systems, students' transition to working life is quite smooth, because it takes place as an integral part of vocational education. However, not all students gain access to apprenticeships.

Examination of the health-care sector has demonstrated that the establishment of new VET programmes for health-care workers has contributed to improving the quality of and respect for subordinate female work. In Norway and Sweden, however, it is difficult for health-care students to gain access to full-time, permanent employment due to employers' continued preference for older workers. The Norwegian case shows the limited effects of the state's educational initiatives if employers and other labour-market organizations (in this case, nurses) do not support the upgrading of the subordinate occupational group.

Examination of the construction sector has shown how the liberalization of the European labour market threatens the quality of skilled construction work. This is especially the case in Norway, where the influx of migrant labour has been very high. Following the increasing employment of cheap labour from the newer EU member states, the organization of work has changed in a Taylorist direction, and the autonomy of the formerly strong occupational groups is being eroded. This has initiated a vicious circle of degradation, where employers' engagement in apprenticeship training is decreasing while the shortage of skilled labour is increasing. The comparison of the construction and health-care industries demonstrates considerable differences between these sectors regarding the links between VET and working life. Therefore, national 'regimes' of VET and working life can include considerable internal diversity.

Since the late 1990s, work-based training has been strengthened in VET programmes. This has included the establishment of new intermediary institutions that deal with some of the risks and gaps in young people's transition from VET to working life. The responsibility for these intermediary institutions lies with the public school system (in Denmark), employers (in Norway) or collaborative organizations (in Sweden). These intermediary institutions have the common aims of supporting students' transition from VET to working life and of matching the demand for and supply of training placements. These new institutions are interesting because they improve the Nordic transition systems in relation to three weaknesses. First, they shift responsibility for obtaining an apprenticeship from the individual student to the intermediary institution. In Norway and Sweden, these institutions have engaged employers in providing high-quality training placements for the students. Second, the Swedish and Norwegian institutions in particular supervise and support the quality of workplace training. Third, in Norway and Denmark, the intermediary institutions coordinate the students' multiple training placements in different companies and provide supplementary school-based training to compensate for the increasing specialization of the companies. Last, these initiatives can contribute to raise the esteem of VET and the enrolment of young people in such programmes.

These institutions help close a gap in the current Nordic transition systems by extending support to students in their transition from VET to working life. The organization and focus of the new intermediary institutions differ, but all represent collective and long-term interests in securing highly skilled workers for the future. The Norwegian and Swedish institutions are especially remarkable, because they have developed in a period of neo-liberal deregulation and weakening of collectivist institutions in the labour market.

References

Albæk, K., Asplund, R., Barth, E., Lindahl, L., von Simson, K. & Vanhala, P. (2015) *Youth Unemployment and Inactivity*, Copenhagen: Nordic Council of Ministers. doi: 10.6027/TN2015-548.

Allmendinger, J. (1989) Educational Systems and Labour Market Outcomes, *European Sociological Review*, 5(3): 231–250.

Andersen, R. & Van de Werfhorst, H. G. (2010) Education and Occupational Status in 14 Countries: The Role of Educational Institutions and Labour Market Coordination, *The British Journal of Sociology*, 61(2): 336–355.

Bengtsson, M. (2014) Towards Standby-Ability: Swedish and Danish Activation Policies in Flux, *International Journal of Social Welfare*, 23(1): 54–70.

Blossing, U., Imsen, G. & Moos, L. (2014) *The Nordic Education Model*, Dordrecht, the Netherlands: Springer. doi: 10.1007/978-94-007-7125-3_11.

Bol, T. & Van de Werfhorst, H. (2013) Educational Systems and the Trade-Off between Labour Market Allocation and Equality of Educational Opportunity, *Comparative Education Review*, 57(2): 285–308.

Brzinsky-Fay, C. (2017) The Interplay of Educational and Labour Market Institutions and Links to Relative Youth Unemployment, *Journal of European Social Policy*, 27(4): 346–359.

Busemeyer, M. R. (2015) *Skills and Inequality: Partisan Politics and the Political Economy of Education Reforms in Western Welfare States*, Cambridge, UK: Cambridge University Press.

Busemeyer, M. R. & Trampusch, C. (eds) (2012) *The Political Economy of Collective Skill Formation*, Oxford, UK: Oxford University Press.

Casey, C. (2012) Organizations and Learning: A Critical Appraisal, *Sociology Compass*, 6(5): 389–401.

Dobbin, F. & Boychuk, T. (1999) National Employment Systems and Job Autonomy: Why Job Autonomy is High in the Nordic Countries and Low in the United States, Canada, and Australia, *Organization Studies*, 20(2): 257–291.

Edlund, J. & Grönlund, A. (2010) Class and Work Autonomy in 21 Countries: A Question of Production Regime or Power Resources?, *Acta Sociologica*, 53(3): 213–228.

Fjellström, M. (2014) Vocational Education in Practice: A Study of Work-Based Learning in a Construction Programme at a Swedish Upper Secondary School, *Empirical Research in Vocational Education and Training*, 6(1): 1–20.

Friberg, J. H. & Eldring, L. (eds) (2013) *Labour Migrants from Central and Eastern Europe in the Nordic Countries: Patterns of Migration, Working Conditions and Recruitment Practices*, TemaNord 2013: Nordic Council of Ministers, 570. doi: 10.6027/TN2013-570.

Gallie, D. (2003) The Quality of Working Life: Is Scandinavia Different?, *European Sociological Review*, 19(1): 61–79.

Gallie, D. (2009) Institutional Regimes and Employee Influence at Work: A European Comparison, *Cambridge Journal of Regions, Economy and Society*, 2(3): 379–393.

Haakestad, H. & Friberg, J. H. (2017) Deskilling Revisited: Labour Migration, Neo-Taylorism and the Degradation of Craft Work in the Norwegian Construction Industry, *Economic and Industrial Democracy*. doi: 10.1177/0143831X17735671.

Halvorsen, B., Hansen, O. J. & Tägtström, J. (2013) *Young People on the Edge (Summary): Labour Market Inclusion of Vulnerable Youths*, Copenhagen: Nordic Council of Ministers. https://doi.org/10.6027/TN2013-547.

Harsløf, I., Scarpa, S. & Andersen, S. N. (2013) Changing Population Profiles and Social Risk Structures in the Nordic Countries, In: Harsløf, I. & Ulmestig, R. (eds) *Changing Social Risks and Social Policy Responses in the Nordic Welfare States*, London: Palgrave Macmillan, 25–49.

Helland, H. & Støren, L. A. (2006) Vocational Education and the Allocation of Apprenticeships: Equal Chances for Applicants Regardless of Immigrant Background?, *European Sociological Review*, 22(3): 339–351.

Høst, H. (ed.) (2012) *Tradisjonelle utfordringer: fornyet interesse [Traditional Challenges: Renewed Interest]*, Copenhagen: Nordic Council of Ministers. https://doi.org/10.6027/TN2012-503.

Høst, H. & Larsen, L. (2018) Vocational Education for Health Care Workers in the Nordic Countries Compared, In: Jørgensen, C. H., Olsen, O. J. & Persson Thunqvist, D. (eds) *Vocational Education in the Nordic Countries: Learning from Diversity*, Abingdon, UK: Routledge.

Høst, H., Skålholt, A., Reiling, R. B. & Gjerustad, C. (2014a) *Opplæringskontorene i fag- og yrkesopplæringen–avgjørende bindeledd eller institusjon utenfor kontroll? [The Training Offices in the Subject and Vocational Education-critical Link or Institution Outside Control]*, Rapport 51/2014, Oslo: NIFU.

Høst, H., Skålholt, A., Reiling, R. B. & Gjerustad, C. (2014b) *Hvorfor blir lærlingordningen i kommunal sektor annerledes enn i privat sektor? [Why Is the Apprenticeship Scheme in the Municipal Sector Different Than in the Private Sector?]*, Oslo: NIFU.

Jensen, C. S. (2015) The Nordic Labour Market(s) and the European Union, In: Grøn, C. H., Nedergaard, P. & Wivel, A. (eds) *The Nordic Countries and the European Union: Still the Other European Community?*, Abingdon, UK: Routledge, 226–240.

Jørgensen, C. H. (2015) Challenges for Work-Based Learning in Vocational Education and Training in the Nordic Countries, In: Jørgensen, C. H., Wallo, A., Toiviainen, H., Haake, U. & Bohlinger, S. (eds) *Working and Learning in Times of Uncertainty*, Rotterdam: Sense Publishers.

Jørgensen, C. H. (2016) Shifting Problems and Shifting Policies to Reduce Student Drop-Out: The Case of Vocational Education Policy in Denmark, In: Bohlinger, S. T., Dang, K. A. & Klatt, M. (eds) *Education Policy: Mapping the Landscape and Scope*, Frankfurt am Main, Germany: Peter Lang, 325–353.

Jørgensen, C. H. & Tønder, A. H. (2018) Transitions from Vocational Education to Employment in the Nordic Countries, In: Jørgensen, C. H., Olsen, O. J. & Persson Thunqvist, D. (eds) *Vocational Education in the Nordic Countries: Learning from Diversity*, Abingdon, UK: Routledge.

Jørgensen, C. H., Olsen, O. J. & Persson Thunqvist, D. (eds) (2018) *Vocational Education in the Nordic Countries: Learning from Diversity*, Abingdon, UK: Routledge.

Kananen, J. (2016) *The Nordic Welfare State in Three Eras. From Emancipation to Discipline*, Abingdon, UK: Routledge.

Kristensen, P. H., Lilja, K., Moen, E. & Morgan, G. (2015) Nordic Countries as Laboratories for Transnational Learning, In: Strang, J. (ed.) *Nordic Cooperation: A European Region in Transition*, Abingdon, UK: Routledge, 183–204.

Lansbury, R. D. (2015) Trade Unions, Vocational Education and Workplace Training: International Trends, *E-Journal of International and Comparative Labour Studies*, 4(2): 1–25.

Lorentzen, T., Angelin, A., Dahl, E., Kauppinen, T., Moisio, P. & Salonen, T. (2014) Unemployment and Economic Security for Young Adults in Finland, Norway and Sweden, *International Journal of Social Welfare*, 23(1): 41–51.

Madsen, P. K., Molina, O., Møller, J. & Lozano, M. (2013) Labour Market Transitions of Young Workers in Nordic and Southern European Countries: The Role of Flexicurity, *Transfer: European Review of Labour and Research*, 19(3): 325–343.

Maurice, M., Sellier, F. & Silvestre, J. J. (1986) *The Social Foundation of Industrial Power*, Cambridge, MA: MIT Press.

Melin, H. (2014) The Nordic Model and Social Inequalities, In: Eißel, D., Rokicka, E. & Leaman, J. (eds) *Welfare State at Risk*, Dordrecht, the Netherlands: Springer, 105–119.

Michelsen, S. & Stenström, M.-L. (2018) *Vocational Education in the Nordic Countries: The Historical Evolution*, Abingdon, UK: Routledge.

Müller, W. (2005) Education and Youth Integration into European Labour Markets, *International Journal of Comparative Sociology*, 46(5–6): 461–485.

Nore, H. & Lahn, L. C. (2014) Bridging the Gap between Work and Education in Vocational Education and Training: A Study of Norwegian Apprenticeship Training Offices and E-Portfolio Systems, *International Journal for Research in Vocational Education and Training*, 1(1): 21–34.

OECD (2016) *Education at a Glance 2016*, OECD indicators, Paris: OECD Publishing. doi: 10.1787/eag-2016-en.

Olofsson, J. (2015) *Yrkesutbildning i förändring: från lärlingsutbildning till yrkescollege [Vocational Training in Change: From Apprenticeship to Vocational College]*, rapport No 18, Stockholm: Ratio.

Olofsson, J. & Panican, A. (2012) Den svenska yrkesutbildningsmodellen [The Swedish Vocational Education Model], In: Høst, H (ed.) *Tradisjonelle utfordringer: fornyet interesse [Traditional Challenges: Renewed Interest]*, Copenhagen: Nordic Council of Ministers. https://doi.org/10.6027/9789289330220-5-no.

Olofsson, J. & Persson Thunqvist, D. (2018) The Modern Evolution of VET in Sweden (1945–2015), In: Michelsen, S. & Stenström, M-L. (eds) *Vocational Education in the Nordic Countries: The Historical Evolution*, Abingdon, UK: Routledge.

Olsen, O. J., Persson Thunqvist, D. & Hallqvist, A. (2018) Building and Construction. A Critical Case for the Future of Vocational Education, In: Jørgensen, C. H., Olsen, O. J. & Persson Thunqvist, D. (eds) *Vocational Education in the Nordic Countries: Learning from Diversity*, Abingdon, UK: Routledge.

PASS (2017) *Udviklingsredegørelse 2017*, Copenhagen: PASS.

Persson, B. & Hermelin, B. (2018). Mobilising for Change in Vocational Education and Training in Sweden: A Case Study of the 'Technical College' Scheme, *Journal of Vocational Education & Training*, 1–21. doi: 10.1080/13636820.2018.1443971.

Pfeffer, F. T. (2008) Persistent Inequality in Educational Attainment and Its Institutional Context, *European Sociological Review*, 24(5): 543–565.

Pohl, A. & Walther, A. (2007) Activating the Disadvantaged. Variations in Addressing Youth Transitions across Europe, *International Journal of Lifelong Education*, 26(5): 533–553.

Proba (2016) *Opplæringskontorenes rolle og finansiering [Role and Funding of Training Offices]*, Rapport 2016-10, Oslo: Proba samfunnsanalyse.

Raffe, D. (2008) The Concept of Transition System, *Journal of Education and Work*, 21(4): 277–296.

Raffe, D. (2014) Explaining National Differences in Education–Work Transitions, *European Societies*, 16(2): 175–193.

Sandberg, Å. & Movitz, F. (2013) Contested Models: Productive Welfare and Solidaristic Individualism, In: Sandberg, Å. (ed.) *Nordic Lights: Work, Management and Welfare in Scandinavia*, Stockholm: SNS Förlag, 31–90.

SCB (2012) *Etablering på arbetsmarknaden tre år efter gymnasieskolan [Establishment in the Labour Market Three Years After Upper Secondary School]*, Temarapport, Örebro: Statistics Sweden.

Segendorf, Å. O. (2013) *Unga i arbete i Norden. Ungas väg mot etablering på arbetsmarknaden i de nordiska länderna [Young in Work in the Nordic Region. Young People's Path towards Employment in the Nordic Countries]*, TemaNord, Copenhagen: Nordiska Ministerrådet, 572.

Senghaas, D. (1985) *The European Experience: A Historical Critique of Development Theory*, Oxford, UK: Berg.

Streeck, W. (1992) *Social Institutions and Economic Performance: Studies of Industrial Relations in Advanced Capitalist Economies*, London: Sage.

Tamesberger, D. (2017) Can Welfare and Labour Market Regimes Explain Cross-Country Differences in the Unemployment of Young People?, *International Labour Review*, 156(3–4): 443–464.

Thelen, K. (2014) *Varieties of Liberalization and the New Politics of Social Solidarity*, Cambridge, UK: Cambridge University Press.

Thelen, K. & Mahoney, J. (2015) Comparative-Historical Analysis in Contemporary Political Science, In: Thelen, K. & Mahoney, J. (eds) *Advances in Comparative-Historical Analysis*, Cambridge, UK: Cambridge University Press, 3–36.

Walther, A. (2006) Regimes of Youth Transitions. Choice, Flexibility and Security in Young People's Experiences across Different European Contexts, *Young*, 14(2): 119–139.

Walther, A. & Plug, W. (2006) Transitions from School to Work in Europe: Destandardization and Policy Trends, *New Directions for Child and Adolescent Development*, 113: 77–90.

Chapter 9

Bargaining for continuing education

A Norwegian case of 'lifelong learning unionism'

Anders Underthun and Ida Drange

Introduction

The principle of universal access to higher education has a strong position in the Nordic countries (Ahola et al., 2014) and is often combined with the principle of lifelong learning, understood as how adults continue to seek skill and education upgrading throughout their careers. Rubenson (2006) emphasizes that the Nordic countries combine these two elements, since they demonstrate high participation in lifelong learning and a lower degree of inequality in access to lifelong learning than in many other countries. This implies that adults can quite easily upgrade skills and qualifications throughout their careers. Figures for Norwegian adult learning indicate that much learning occurs after individuals have entered working life (Aspøy & Tønder, 2012; Bjørkeng, 2013). At the same time, Statistics Norway shows in its latest review of the 'Learning Monitor' that fewer adults participated in formal education in 2016 than in 2008 (Zachrisen & Bjugstad, 2016), which echoes Rubenson's (2006) concern about weakening institutions for lifelong learning in the Nordic countries.

A key objective of lifelong learning is to improve the worker's position in the labour market by strengthening the *employability* needed in a more mobile and flexible labour market. For the individual, employability is about the prospect of gaining and maintaining stable employment, for instance by getting a new job if the current employment relationship ceases, or making it easier to reach higher career goals (Drange et al., 2018). The literature also highlights that higher employability can make it easier to cope in a more uncertain job market because of increased confidence in finding a different job (Wittekind et al., 2010; Berglund et al., 2014). Employability may be a more appropriate goal for the individual than the more traditional goal of keeping the current job (job security). In one way, this entails that the responsibility of maintaining labour market involvement is more individualized. However, the shift towards employability also has a collective dimension, and trade unions across the world have become more involved in policy developments and bargaining measures that seek to improve members' access to skill upgrading (Jason & Mark, 1998; Winterton, 2006). The idea of empowering union members through education and skill upgrading is further included in a broader discussion in the field of industrial relations on union revitalization and union strategies in the 21st century (Frege & Kelly, 2003).

In this chapter, we ask how *continuing* education (CE) can be part of a new bargaining agenda for trade unions in a less stable labour market. More specifically, we explore how lifelong learning can become an important item on bargaining agendas as well as a feature of general union policy and strategy. We first discuss the more general prospects of 'lifelong learning unionism' in Norway by looking at the emergence and aftermath of the Norwegian 'competence reform' (see i.e. Payne, 2006) in the late 1990s and early 2000s. We then present a case study of the lifelong learning strategy of the Norwegian Engineers and Managers Association (*Forbundet for Ledelse og Teknikk* [FLT]). Members of this trade union are mainly technical staff and mid-management in competitive industries, many of whom have undergone significant restructuring due to the decline in oil prices since 2015 (Underthun et al., 2017). In this way, the case study describe workers who tend to rely on continuous skill enhancement to secure employability.

FLT is arguably a leader in 'lifelong learning unionism' in a Nordic context and has managed to secure a collective agreement with the Norwegian Confederation of Enterprise (NHO), where NOK 1.10 per hour is allocated to a fund for CE. The union has also established its own education and training company (Addisco) in order to facilitate CE for its members and to develop appropriate courses in close cooperation with education providers in Norway and Sweden. The empirical part of the chapter is based on interviews with leading FLT union officials and members. We also conducted interviews with the Norwegian Confederation of Trade Unions (*Landsorganisasjonen* [LO]), the NHO and members of parliament in 2016–2017. Survey data from two member surveys in the FLT conducted in 2012 (Bergene et al., 2013) and 2016 (Underthun et al., 2017) supplement the interview data.

In the following sections, we review perspectives on the revitalization of trade union strategies and why *employability* has become a more important feature of current labour market dynamics. We then continue with a discussion on the possibilities and limitations of lifelong learning unionism in the Nordic countries.

Lifelong learning and the new agenda for employability

The basic definition of employability addresses the individual's ability to maintain a stable relationship with the labour market. This definition can be taken further to include *upward* and *basic* employability (Drange et al., 2018) and *internal* and *external* employability (Sanders & de Grip, 2004; De Cuyper et al., 2012). There is thus a difference between keeping one's job (basic employability) and getting a *better* job (upward employability). Similarly, the prospect of a new job in the same firm (internal employability) is different from the individual's prospects for employment elsewhere in the labour market (external employability).

According to human capital theory (Becker, 1994), education makes workers more attractive. Education is thus an investment to reduce the risk of unemployment or to increase wage bills. In this perspective, self-assessed employability will increase with higher education levels. However, Becker argues that employees and employers have different motivations for enhancing the (formal) skills of employees. For employers, it is not rational to invest in general skill enhancement that makes the employee attractive to other employers. Therefore, employers will mainly cover the cost of education and training that increase productivity in their own business and which have low transfer value to other employers. The cost of general education and training that primarily benefits the individual must therefore typically be borne by the worker (Becker, 1994, p. 34). This difference is also evident in bargaining outcomes. For example, according to the Basic Agreement between the LO and the NHO (NHO & LO, 2014), employers in Norway are obliged to provide employees with the training required to carry out their current job. Postgraduate and CE programmes that are primarily in the interests of the individual, for example in order to strengthen external employability, are not the responsibility of employers. This difference is crucial in a labour market where *mobility* is a major imperative to improving the skills and formal qualifications needed for changing jobs.

Lifelong learning as union revitalization

Union membership levels in Europe have been on the decline since the 1980s (Waddington, 2015). This is also true of the Nordic countries, although unionization rates have fallen less than in many other European countries (Jensen, 2017). Another positive note for Norway is that there seems to be considerable potential for organizing more members, particularly among young workers (Steen et al., 2017).

The literature on union strategies and union revitalization focuses on the variety of strategies that unions can employ to counter decline and the ways in which they can gain or regain strength in a changing economic and political landscape (Frege & Kelly, 2003). There are differences in the strategic directions of unions. A typical distinction is that made between the organizing model and the servicing model of unionism (Heery et al., 2000). The organizing model is a model that emphasizes the importance of building a union movement, both through internal organizing and empowerment of existing members, and through highly active organizing drives to recruit new members (Getman, 2010). This model is often associated with *social movement unionism*, a type of unionism that extends beyond typical priorities, such as wages, pensions and working conditions, to broader social engagement. The servicing model, on the other hand, is a union strategy that aims to satisfy the needs of members, for instance through resolving workplace conflicts or securing different kinds of benefits. Tufts (2009) argues that it is important to look beyond the organizing vs. servicing model dichotomy when analysing union strategies. Rather, unions change the composition of priorities with changing economic and political landscapes. For instance, Tufts argues that union responses to labour market changes in the hospitality sector in North America can be seen as a form of 'Schumpeterian' unionism, a term that hints at the profound organizational shifts associated with the fall of Fordism and the emergence of alternative and more flexible work structures.

In an introduction to a special issue on union revitalization in the *European Journal of Industrial Relations* from 2003, Frege and Kelly (2003) identify six concrete strategies or responses that unions typically employ in revitalization efforts, although with the important proviso that these strategies will vary considerably with contextual differences (Clegg, 1975). First, *organizing* is about the acquisition of new or retention of existing members. As Frege and Kelly note, the bargaining power of a union will always be related to the number of members. Second, they point out that *organizational restructuring* as internal reorganization or mergers with other unions may be an important way to regain strength or keep up with labour market changes. Third, Frege and Kelly point to *coalition building*. This strategy can be a part of social movement unionism as discussed earlier, but the type of coalition depends on the type of leverage or the branding as a societal actor desired by the union (cf. Hyman, 1997). Fourth, Frege and Kelly argue that *partnerships with employers* is a strategy for finding compromise in industrial relations. Strategies related to coordinated wage formation and negotiated compromises in the Nordic countries (cf. Chapters 1 and 2) are an example of a strong focus on collaboration and negotiation that perhaps goes beyond the notion of partnership. However, a common goal for social partnerships or social collaborations as a union strategy is to improve collective agreements. Frege and Kelly also note that this strategy relates to attempts to erode negative images of union militancy. Fifth, *political action* as a union strategy may result in more preferable legislation or policy developments that directly or indirectly may benefit union members. Finally, Frege and Kelly point to *international links* for dealing with transnational corporations, or for increasing the effectiveness of political lobbying at various levels, such as the EU level.

How then are skill upgrading and CE related to union revitalization? UK scholars have paid some attention to lifelong learning. Payne (2001) suggests that the issue of *learning* has become an emerging item on union agendas as part of a reflexive union modernization that acknowledges the need to rethink priorities in a changing labour market. Findlay and Warhurst (2011) argue that this learning agenda has become a new tool in the union toolkit for multiple union strategies; both the organizing model and the servicing model of unionism may incorporate a learning agenda. However, these authors assert that the learning agenda is more associated with a mutual gains perspective (with employers) and is not an oppositional kind of unionism. Moreover, Rainbird and Stuart (2011) point out that the learning agenda in the UK has not been a union initiative as such, but rather a response to state initiatives for promoting skill upgrading. In the same vein, Rainbird and Stuart assert that other formal collective agreements related to lifelong learning remain uncommon in the UK.

The Norwegian competence reform and trade union initiatives for lifelong learning

Following the economic downturn in the late 1980s and early 1990s, trade unions and employers in Norway had to find a middle ground in wage settlements, and it was during this period that skill and education enhancement came to the fore in policy debates in Norway as one of the elements in what has become known as the 'solidarity alternative' (Hågensen, 2005). Stuart and Teige (2010) argue that the LO had a key political role in promoting lifelong learning in the mid-1990s. At the confederation level, the strategy of political action and lobbying (Frege & Kelly, 2003) for lifelong learning was thus emerging. Following a suggestion by the LO, a public committee was set up in 1996–1997 to work towards a joint action plan for skill enhancement in the workplace, the so-called 'Buer Committee'. An important recommendation from the green paper (KUD, 1997) prepared by the committee was that work experience would count as prior learning for admission to higher education. Furthermore, the committee recommended a statutory right to educational leave for employees interested in taking CE courses. In line with the LO's action plan, the committee also recommended that the Norwegian Educational Loan Fund should begin to offer loans and grants to adult workers in CE. This was soon implemented, and the white paper entitled *Competence Reform* was published in 1998 as a further development of the lifelong learning agenda (KUD, 1998).

Hagen and Skule (2008) argue that the competence reform had important effects in the Norwegian work and educational systems. The reform strengthened adult education through statutory rights to primary and secondary education, a statutory right to leave from work for education and more flexibility for adult education from the Norwegian Educational Loan Fund. Moreover, the so-called Competence Development Programme has led to a number of new training opportunities instigated by the state (Døving et al., 2006). However, lifelong learning as a union strategy also extended to partnerships with employer organizations, even in the years before the competence reform. A major bargaining breakthrough was that employers agreed to take responsibility for funding CE and training through the Basic Agreement, Section 18–3 (NHO & LO, 2014) as part of the negotiations in 1994 (Stuart & Teige, 2010). This remains an item in the Basic Agreement between the LO and the NHO. However, the employers' responsibility for CE remains limited to courses that are 'in accordance with company needs' (NHO & LO, 2014, Section 18–3) and not necessarily CE that is in the broader interest of the employee. In an employability perspective, the Basic Agreement is thus oriented towards *internal* employability by securing skill enhancement that decreases the risk of redundancy for employees. It also stipulates that the employer has the power to choose who will receive CE and the type of CE required. In this way, Section 18–3 of the Basic Agreement does not express an explicit need for concrete union initiatives for CE.

In the mid-1990s, there were also examples of education as a reason for industrial action. In 1996, the Electrician and IT workers union went on strike for 56 days to achieve better rights to *any* training, to be paid for by employers (Hagen & Skule, 2008). However, the strike was unsuccessful, as the employers refused to accept the premise that the individual worker could choose the type of training/CE (Stuart & Teige, 2010). The employers rather insisted that the training/CE had to meet the concrete needs of the employer. Teige and Stuart point out that the strike showed how difficult it would be to get employers to fund CE. The strike also illustrates the dilemmas of CE as a way of securing external employability. At the same time, the strike showed the potential for lifelong learning unionism within the LO.

A crucial bottleneck for lifelong learning as part of a union agenda in the late 1990s was the issue of *co*-funding of CE that would grant more power to the employee (Payne, 2006). Who would pay for CE, and was there a place for funding mechanisms in concrete bargaining deals where both employers and employees would have to concede other priorities? As part of the competence reform in the late 1990s, the Government recommended shared funding solutions between the social partners, the state and the individual (Payne, 2006). Even though the LO was positive to the idea of putting lifelong learning on bargaining agendas, the former leader of LO, Yngve Hågensen (2005), has described the disputes between sectoral unions on this issue. Stuart and Teige (2010) also claim that the greatest challenge for the competence reform was the trickling down of the idea of lifelong learning as a union strategy to the sectoral level. For example, the Norwegian Chemical Workers' Association and the Norwegian Iron and Metal Workers Union did not want to prioritize funding mechanisms for CE at the expense of the wage struggle. Other unions, such as the Electricians and IT Workers' Union, the Norwegian Graphic Workers' Federation and the FLT were more sympathetic to the idea of making CE a top priority in bargaining. Given the discrepancies between its federations, the LO had to give priority to wage struggle and demands for a fifth holiday week in their negotiations with the NHO in the late 1990s and early 2000s (Hågensen, 2005). After many years of wage moderation, the majority of federations in the LO were against the idea that education would be set against wages.

Partly as a response to the disputes between sectoral unions, the framework negotiations between the LO and the NHO placed more emphasis on work-related learning than formal education in the period following the competence reform. The negotiations continued to emphasize skill enhancement that was instrumental in maintaining or improving *internal* employability, ensuring that members kept skill levels up to date as required by their employers. Payne (2006) argues that it was easy for the social partners to reach a consensus on work-related skills, while funding for formal education was more demanding. Although there were internal disputes within the LO on the matter of CE funding, there was a more general negative attitude in the NHO. Payne (2006) states that the NHO refused to pay for CE that did not directly meet the immediate needs of the employers, and employers were also sceptical of granting time off to pursue CE that might make their employees attractive to other employers. According to Bowman (2005), the combination of this opposition from the employers' side and the split position within the LO eliminated much of the potential of the competence reform as a platform for lifelong learning as a dominating union strategy.

Improving the access to CE remains modest as a strategy at the LO level, and we would not label the LO's strategies as a case of lifelong learning unionism. The LO nevertheless supports CE initiatives from members through modest scholarships from the LO Education Fund,[1] but LO officials admit that the confederation is in a development phase of revitalization:

> We [LO] have not completed our profile when it comes to continuing education . . . we are in the process of discovering and realizing that competence enhancement should be accessible to all [members].[2]

It is also important to remember that the LO as a confederation mainly operates through political action, coalition building and international links (Frege & Kelly, 2003), while it is more up to the sectoral federations to decide on specific organizing strategies, servicing strategies and concrete bargaining through partnerships and struggles with the employers' side:

> [i]t's difficult for the LO to dictate what the federations should prioritize . . . giving priority to CE in collective agreements is interesting . . . but ultimately it's about priorities . . . it's about different ways to ensure income and employment.[3]

However, some federations within the LO system have given high priority to CE. In the next section, we argue that the FLT can be seen as an example of lifelong learning unionism.

The CE fund of the FLT and NHO: lifelong learning unionism for real?

The FLT was founded in 1951. As part of the LO, the association emerged to organize mid-management and technical staff in their struggle for professional rights. Previous to this, these workers had been organized outside the LO, as the idea of organizing *management* was controversial in a union perspective. At the same time, it was important for managers in intermediate positions to fight for their rights as workers, and they therefore found it appropriate to be part of the LO. However, Wilhelmsen (2011, p. 13) argues that education became an important organizational principle for the FLT from the 1970s onwards, as higher qualifications often implied a transfer from a different union in the workplace to the FLT. At the same time, vertical agreements made it difficult for the FLT to organize some of the highly educated groups of workers, including engineers.

However, it was not only organizing principles that made education an important policy area for the FLT. The members often found themselves in an 'educational dilemma' because they did not necessarily have the formal qualifications considered sufficient to fill the role of a foreman or mid-level manager. For example, a typical career step would be from skilled operator to foreman, which involved work that required higher organizational or managerial skills. It is therefore not surprising that the FLT has been one of the federations in the LO which has emphasized the need for adult learning (Wilhelmsen, 2011). In addition to promoting social mobility among members, the federation has also been a proponent of strong social partnerships and strong workplace interaction and co-determination between employers and employees in a way that reflects the 'Nordic' model of work organization (Gustavsen, 2007).

Wilhelmsen (2011) writes that the former FLT leader, Magnus Midtbø, was almost alone in pursuing CE while other federations chose different union priorities. As part of the difficult 1992 negotiations, Midtbø managed to secure a deal with the NHO where NOK 0.30 per hour was allocated to a fund for CE. Wilhelmsen (2011, p. 69) refers to the conclusion from the negotiations: 'The parties agree that the future of the companies will depend on maintenance and renewal of employee skills'. It is also stated that: 'the fund implies that an amount per hour will go to an education fund meant to be available for FLT members that are covered by this agreement'. In the negotiations, the FLT was granted responsibility to administer the fund, despite the fact that it was co-funded by the concessions made by both the employer and the employee side. The lawyer who represented the NHO at the time[4] points out that the FLT was given this role because the scheme was controversial within the NHO system.

The FLT education fund has been renewed as an item in the collective agreement between the FLT and the NHO in bargaining rounds for 25 years and amounted to NOK 1.10 per hour for each FLT member in 2016 (NHO et al., 2016). This amounts to NOK 2,145 per year per member and a total of about NOK 20 million per year. Grants from the fund can be as large as NOK 50,000[5] per year, and members can receive grants several times. In fact, the FLT encourages members to apply several times for different courses that they can combine as diplomas or university degrees. By 2017, close to 7,600 grants from the FLT/NHO CE fund had been awarded. In 2016, 499 out of 775 applicants received grants.[6] FLT officials state that most members have received a grant as long as the applications have been in accordance with the guidelines. A typical reason for rejection is that a member applies for a type of course that the employer has to cover because of Section 18–3 of the Basic Agreement between the LO and the NHO. As such, the FLT/NHO CE Fund is more important for *external* employability as the aim of the fund is to improve general qualifications. According to the statutes,[7] the aims of the FLT/NHO CE fund include:

> [t]o help to eliminate inequalities and promote gender equality so that education can take place regardless of geographical conditions, age, gender, economic or social situation.

Unlike a situation where the employer chooses the person that will receive support for CE, the FLT/NHO CE fund supports education according to the preferences of the members. Although access to the fund is limited to members with a collective agreement at their workplace, support can also be granted to those who have lost their job/collective agreement within the last two years.

The scheme remains unique in Norway and the Nordic countries in general (Olberg et al., 2017). It is also unique in international terms, as co-funding of substantial CE grants has not been a typical feature of the learning agenda in industrial relations (Winterton, 2006; Stuart, 2007). The only parallel in Norway is the Norwegian Organization of Managers and Executives (*Lederne*), a union that negotiated the same bargaining deal with the NHO as the FLT did in 1992 (Wilhelmsen, 2011).[8]

Addisco: organizational restructuring and building a servicing strategy

Within a few years of the establishment of the FLT/NHO CE fund in 1992, the fund grew in popularity, and it became clear that the FLT had to embark upon organizational restructuring (Frege & Kelly, 2003), as the funding mechanism itself did not suffice as a broader strategy of lifelong learning (Underthun et al., 2017). In 1999, the FLT established Addisco as an education company owned by the union.

Addisco was established to develop and offer education services to meet members' needs. The organizational restructuring was part of building a stronger servicing strategy for lifelong learning within the FLT. The company is currently offering and arranging courses for FLT members[9] through formal cooperation with higher education institutions such as Bergen University College, the University of Bergen and Stockholm University. Addisco also has the role of the formal administrator of the FLT/NHO CE fund. This means that Addisco not only provides services to members who choose courses through

Addisco but also to those who prefer to enrol in courses outside the Addisco system. Addisco currently owns the education in collaboration with higher education institutions, as well as the 'AddiscoLearning' platform. Addisco's principles are very much in line with the overall statutes of the CE fund, and it places a particular emphasis on the importance of formal qualifications through obtaining higher education credits. Moreover, as part of its servicing strategy, Addisco helps FLT members with all the administrative chores of combining CE with full-time jobs. Teaching is largely based on intensive weekends, and Addisco takes care of all travel arrangements, university enrolment and reading lists. Addisco also promotes collaboration between students. Wilhelmsen (2011) argues that an important premise for establishing Addisco was that this would build a stronger 'knowledge' brand, which would be important in both a political sense and as an organizing strategy. We agree with this and would add that the establishment of Addisco as an organizational extension of the FLT represents a revitalizing step towards lifelong learning unionism.

Lifelong learning as an organizing strategy

As an organizing strategy, the focus on lifelong learning in the FLT seems to have been successful. Bergene et al. (2013) argue that the FLT/NHO CE fund is an important explanation for the growth of the federation in recent decades. In a union revitalization perspective, it is particularly interesting to see how important the focus on lifelong learning has been to younger members of the FLT (see Figure 9.1). Whereas older members are more concerned about traditional union values such as solidarity and family traditions of joining a union, the younger members seem to have reflected upon the importance of access to CE opportunities.

One of the FLT members we interviewed was particularly interested in formal qualifications and external employability as effects of CE:

> I discovered the educational opportunities [in the FLT/Addisco] and I see the way society is changing . . . you get clear evidence that you need to have education if you are going to change jobs. They look at your papers . . . so I'm taking these courses to strengthen my competitiveness in the future.
>
> (Quote from Underthun et al., 2017)

In a union revitalization perspective (Findlay & Warhurst, 2011), the lifelong learning strategy of the FLT/Addisco leans more towards a servicing strategy than an organizing strategy,[10] but in interviews with members and staff of the FLT, we also had the clear impression that the union wanted to build a movement based on the idea of social mobility, employability and lifelong learning. As such, the member who receives a CE grant is not only a student of CE but also carries the idea of lifelong learning as collective empowerment.

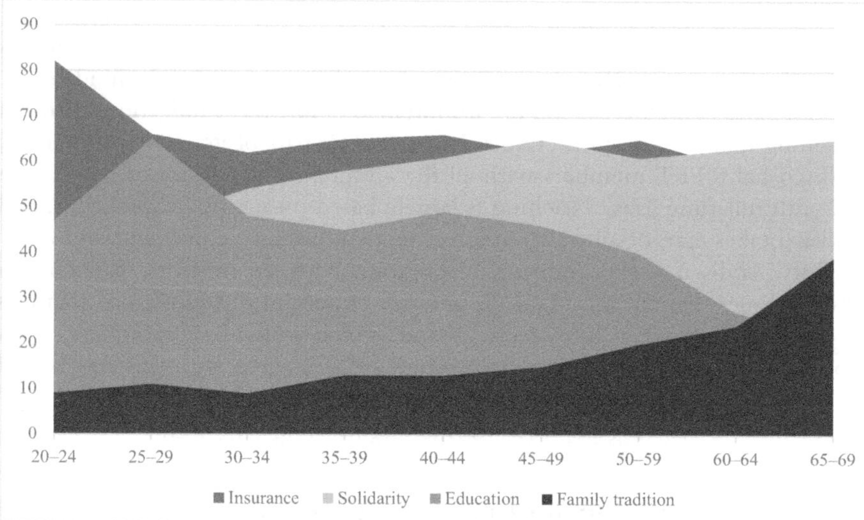

Figure 9.1 The most important reasons for joining the FLT union (Bergene et al., 2013) (N=3250)[11]

The strategy of conceding wages for an education fund clearly also requires a constant legitimization strategy, and the building of a lifelong learning movement has obviously been an important means of legitimizing the wage concession within the FLT and the LO. The FLT has also managed to retain the CE fund in the collective agreement with the NHO despite a lack of enthusiasm from the NHO for a broader co-funding scheme for CE (Underthun et al., 2017). But what about the effects on social mobility and employability? Based on a survey of FLT members, Underthun et al. (2017) show that those who take CE courses generally score higher on upward employability and external employability. In other words, members who have completed CE courses think it is easier to find work elsewhere, at least in a similar kind of job. Although important in the internal legitimization of the lifelong learning union strategy, this finding also explains some of the scepticism from employers. To them, CE represents a risk of losing employees, although it could also imply higher productivity and important skills for the firm (cf. Becker, 1994). Underthun et al. also find that the CE fund and Addisco as a service mechanism for CE seem to attract workers with lower levels of education compared to those that have funded CE from other sources. In other words, those with lower educational backgrounds are more likely to complete CE courses through the FLT/Addisco than other funding sources and higher education institutions. Although the effect is moderate, we would argue that it is important in a union revitalization perspective, as union initiatives can counter patterns of unequal access to lifelong learning.

Concluding discussion

In this chapter, we have discussed the prospects of a type of union revitalization that heralds the importance of lifelong learning as a way of ensuring the employability of workers in more flexible labour markets. Lifelong learning can be integrated in union strategies and priorities in different ways (cf. Frege & Kelly, 2003). As an organizing strategy, lifelong learning unionism can be a way of building awareness and identities around how CE can empower members. Enhancing qualifications is of course a way of formal empowerment, but the lifelong learning agenda can also be about building a movement based on the emancipatory power of education. By building this kind of movement, the members of a union also become responsible for carrying the ideals and principles related to why lifelong learning is important, and the idea of a movement is also a way of legitimizing lifelong learning as a union priority. As a servicing strategy, lifelong learning unionism implies a union that builds robust systems for facilitating education in a way that makes membership attractive to existing and new members. As such, this corresponds to the organizational restructuring necessary to transform a union to include a more integrated lifelong learning agenda. Lifelong learning unionism can also be expressed through promoting education in collective bargaining agreements, and in this chapter, we have shown that this can be achieved through concessions from both sides of the negotiating table. A somewhat less risky form of lifelong learning unionism is *political* action, understood as ways in which trade unions promote political change to support adult education. It is nevertheless an important strategy for initiating change. The Norwegian competence reform was dependent on this kind of initiative from the LO. Finally, lifelong learning unionism typically also includes *coalition building*, both in a political sense and in the sense of building partnerships with higher education institutions in order to create new spaces for lifelong learning. *International links* include networks with other unions in other contexts that also promote lifelong learning, as well as links to higher education institutions abroad.

Although lifelong learning unionism may include all these different forms of union strategy, they do not necessarily exist at the same time. The strategies can also vary from simply being *responsive*, for instance by responding to legal changes at the national level (cf. Winterton, 2006), or *proactive*, as exemplified by the FLT's initiative to include the funding of CE in the collective agreement with the NHO in 1992. In a Nordic perspective, it is also interesting to see initiatives for lifelong learning as an example of *compromise* in industrial relations. The FLT/NHO CE fund was established in the middle of an economic crisis with limited prospects for wage increases. The social parties were willing to make concessions within a bargaining context that was known as the solidarity alternative (Hågensen, 2005). However, only the FLT and the Norwegian Organization of Managers and Executives took advantage of the bargaining that led to the establishment of sizeable funding mechanisms for CE in collective agreements. The accord was an important spark in transforming the FLT as a 'lifelong learning union', leading to organizational restructuring, new coalitions and, importantly for a union, more and younger members. The case study of the FLT also suggests that lifelong learning unionism may improve the employability of members, thus facilitating job changes and labour market flexibility.

As a case of lifelong learning as a bargaining item that implies financial concessions from employers and employees, the FLT/NHO CE fund is not representative of Norwegian industrial relations in general. The employer side has been reluctant to engage in negotiations because they argue that the responsibility for funding CE is already regulated through the Basic Agreement between the LO and the NHO (NHO & LO, 2014). On the employee side, it has been challenging to balance lifelong learning with traditional struggles related to wages, pensions and holidays (Payne, 2006). As Payne argues, there have been clear limits to lifelong learning in industrial relations. At the same time, political efforts to promote CE have had an important impact on the Norwegian work and education system (Hagen & Skule, 2008). Adults now have a statuary right to primary and secondary education. Employees also have the right to educational leave, and the Norwegian State Educational Loan Fund has become adapted to adult education. In February 2017, the Government, the social partners and the voluntary sector launched the new National Competence Policy Strategy. It is too early to say how strong the initiative will become or how much the social partners are willing to invest, but it is clear that lifelong learning has become a major impetus for union revitalization.

Notes

1 www.lo.no/Om-LO/Artikler-om-LO/LOs-utdanningsfond/.
2 Interview with LO official, 1 February 2016.
3 Interview with LO official, 2 February 2016.
4 Interview with NHO Lawyer, March 2016.
5 Corresponds to about EUR 5,200 per year.
6 Data from the FLT administration, personal communication in January 2017.
7 The guidelines are available at www.flt.no.
8 Like FLT/Addisco, Lederne has also taken initiatives to build coalitions with higher education institutions, for instance with Oslo Metropolitan University.
9 Addisco also admits non-FLT members to CE courses, but the bulk of the students enrolled in Addisco courses are FLT members.
10 See https://flt.no/artikler/personal-benefits/ for a description of membership benefits.
11 'Education' is based on the question 'How important was the access to continuing education schemes to your decision to join FLT?'

References

Ahola, S., Hedmo, T., Thomsen, J.-P. & Vabø, A. (2014) Organisational Features of Higher Education: Denmark, Finland, Norway & Sweden, *NIFU Working Paper*, 14/5, Oslo: NIFU.

Aspøy, T. M & Tønder, A. H. (2012) Utredning om forskning på voksnes læring [Review of Research of Adult Learning], *Fafo-notat 2012:17*, Oslo: FAFO.

Becker, G. S. (1994) *Human Capital: A Theoretical and Empirical Analysis with Special Reference to Education*, Chicago, IL: The University of Chicago Press.

Bergene, A. C., Steen, A. H., Egeland, C. & Drage, I. (2013) Hva kan forklare medlemsveksten i Forbundet for Ledelse og Teknikk [What Explains Membership Growth in FLT?], *AFI-Rapport 2013:13*, Oslo.

Berglund, T., Furåker, B. & Vulkan, P. (2014) Is Job Insecurity Compensated for by Employment and Income Security?, *Economic and Industrial Democracy*, 35: 165–184.

Bjørkeng, B. (2013) Ferdigheter i voksenbefolkningen [Skills in the Adult Population], *Rapporter*, 42/2013, Oslo-Kongsvinger: Statistisk Sentralbyrå.

Bowman, J. (2005) Employers and the Politics of Skill Formation in a Coordinated Market Economy: Collective Action and Class Conflict in Norway, *Politics and Society*, 33: 567–594.

Clegg, H. A. (1975) Pluralism in Industrial Relations, *British Journal of Industrial Relations*, 13: 309–316.

De Cuyper, N., Makikangas, A., Kinnunen, U., Mauno, A. & Witte, H. D. (2012) Cross-Lagged Associations between Perceived External Employability, Job Insecurity, and Exhaustion: Testing Gain and Loss Spirals According to the Conservation of Resources Theory, *Journal of Organizational Behavior*, 33: 770–788.

Døving, E., Ure, O. B., Tobiassen, A., Tobiassen, A. E. & Hertzberg, D. (2006) Kompetanseutviklingsprogrammet 2000–2006: Sluttevaluering [The Competence Development Program 2000–2006: Final Evaluation], *SNF Rapport, 32/2006*, Bergen, Norway: Samfunns- og Næringslivsforskning AS.

Drange, I., Bernstrøm, V. H. & Mamelund, S.-E. (2018) Are You Moving Up or Falling Short? An Inquiry of Skills-based Variation in Self-Perceived Employability among Norwegian Employees, *Work, Employment and Society*, 32: 387–406.

Findlay, P. & Warhurst, C. (2011) Union Learning Funds and Trade Union Revitalization: A New Tool in the Toolkit?, *British Journal of Industrial Relations*, 49: 115–134.

Frege, C. M. & Kelly, J. (2003) Union Revitalization Strategies in Comparative Perspective, *European Journal of Industrial Relations*, 9: 7–24.

Getman, J. G. (2010) *Restoring the Power of Unions: It Takes a Movement*, New Haven, CT: Yale University Press.

Gustavsen, B. (2007) Work Organization and 'the Scandinavian Model', *Economic and Industrial Democracy*, 28: 650–671.

Hagen, A. & Skule, S. (2008) Kompetansereformen og livslang læring: Status 2008 [The Competence Reform and Lifelong Learning: Status 2008], *Fafo-report 2008:07*, Oslo: Fafo.

Hågensen, Y. (2005) *Gjør din plikt, krev din rett! [Do Your Duty, Demand Your Rights!]*, second edition, Oslo: Aschehoug.

Heery, E., Simms, M., Simpson, D., Delbridge, R. & Salmon, J. (2000) Organizing Unionism Comes to the UK, *Employee Relations*, 22: 38–57.

Hyman, R. (1997) Trade Unions and Interest Representation in the Context of Globalisation, *Transfer: European Review of Labour and Research*, 3: 515–533.

Jason, H. & Mark, S. (1998) Bargaining for Skills: Trade Unions and Training at the Workplace, *British Journal of Industrial Relations*, 36: 459–467.

Jensen, C. S. (2017) Political Attitudes and Trade Union Membership in the Nordic Countries, *European Journal of Industrial Relations*, 23: 381–395.
KUD (1997) NOU 1997:25, *Ny kompetanse: Grunnlaget for en helhetlig etter- og videreutdanningspolitikk [New Competence: The Foundation for a Coherent Policy for Continuing Education]*, Oslo: Kirke-, Utdannings-, og forskningsdepartementet.
KUD (1998) St. Meld. nr. 42 (1997–98), *Kompetansereformen [The Competence Reform]*, Oslo: Kirke-, Utdannings-, og forskningsdepartementet.
NHO and LO (2014) Hovedavtalen LO-NHO 2014–2017 [The Basic Agreement between LO and NHO 2014–2017]. www.nho.no/siteassets/nhos-filer-og-bilder/filer-og-dokumenter/arbeidslivspolitikk/hovedavtalen_lo_nho_2014–2017.pdf?id=63088.
NHO, LO and FLT (2016) *Collective Agreement between The Confederation of Norwegian Enterprise, The Norwegian Confederation of Trade Unions and the Norwegian Organization of Managers and Executives (FLT)*. http://tariffavtaler.nho.no/getfile.php?TA_Nr=198&TA_Radnr=13772.
Olberg, D., Steen, J. R. & Tønder, A. H. (2017) Tariffavtalene som virkemiddel i kompetansepolitikken [Collective Agreements as Instruments of Competence Policy], *Fafo-report 2017:14*, Oslo: Fafo.
Payne, J. (2001) Lifelong Learning: A National Trade Union Strategy in a Global Economy, *International Journal of Lifelong Education*, 20: 378–392.
Payne, J. (2006) The Norwegian Competence Reform and the Limits of Lifelong Learning, *International Journal of Lifelong Education*, 25: 477–505.
Rainbird, H. & Stuart, M. (2011) The State and the Union Learning Agenda in Britain, *Work, Employment and Society*, 25: 202–217.
Rubenson, K. (2006) The Nordic Model of Lifelong Learning, *Compare: A Journal of Comparative and International Education*, 36: 327–341.
Sanders, J. & de Grip, A. (2004) Training, Task Flexibility and the Employability of Low-Skilled Workers, *International Journal of Manpower*, 25: 73–89.
Steen, A., Nergaard, K. & Drange, I. (2017) Organisering av de uorganiserte [Organizing the Disorganized], *R&D-result 2017:06*. www.hioa.no/Om-HiOA/Senter-for-velferds-og-arbeidslivsforskning/AFI/Publikasjoner-AFI/Organisering-av-uorganiserte, Work Research Institute, Oslo & Akershus University College of Applied Sciences.
Stuart, M. (2007) Introduction: The Industrial Relations of Learning and Training – A New Consensus or a New Politics?, *European Journal of Industrial Relations*, 13: 269–280.
Stuart, M. & Teige, B. K. (2010) Trade Unions and the Norwegian Competence Reform, *Labour & Industry: A Journal of the Social and Economic Relations of Work*, 21: 513–527.
Tufts, S. (2009) Hospitality Unionism and Labour Market Adjustment: Toward Schumpeterian Unionism?, *Geoforum*, 40: 980–990.
Underthun, A., Drange, I. & Borg, E. (2017) Partssamarbeidets kompetanseeffekter: En analyse av Forbundet for Ledelse og Teknikks støtteordning for etter- og videreutdanning og utdanningsselskapet Addisco [The Competence Effects of Industrial Relations: An Analysis of the FLT CE Fund and the Education Company Addisco], *AFI-report 2017: 03*. www.hioa.no/Om-HiOA/Senter-for-velferds-og-arbeidslivsforskning/AFI/Publikasjoner-AFI/Partssamarbeidets-kompetanseeffekter, Work Research Institute, Oslo & Akershus University College of Applied Sciences.

Waddington, J. (2015) Trade Union Membership Retention in Europe: The Challenge of Difficult Times, *European Journal of Industrial Relations*, 21: 205–221.

Wilhelmsen, L. S. (2011) *Forbundet for Ledelse og Teknikk: Mer enn et fagforbund, men fremfor alt et fagforbund [FLT: More Than a Union, But First and Foremost a Union]*, Oslo: FLT.

Winterton, J. (2006) Social Dialogue and Vocational Training in Europe: Are We Witnessing the Emergence of a European Model?, *Journal of European Industrial Training*, 30: 65–76.

Wittekind, A., Raeder, S. & Grote, G. (2010) A Longitudinal Study of Determinants of Perceived Employability, *Journal of Organizational Behavior*, 31: 566–586.

Zachrisen, O. O. & Bjugstad, H. K. (2016) *Livslang læring 2008–2016: Resultater fra Lærevilkårsmonitoren [Lifelong Learning 2008–2016. Results from the Learning Monitor]*, Oslo-Kongsvinger: Statistisk Sentrabyrå.

Chapter 10

Tackling increasing marginalization

Can support-side approaches contribute to work inclusion?

Kjetil Frøyland, Angelika Schafft and Øystein Spjelkavik

Introduction

Labour market participation, self-sufficiency and a small population passively receiving welfare benefits have long been key policy goals across the Nordic welfare states. These states are characterized by an active labour market policy as one major ideology, high levels of employment among women and the elderly, and a large proportion of people working part-time. Public authorities have had a more active and responsible role than social parties and the labour market in promoting work inclusion, but formal agreements between the social parties such as "Inclusive working life"[1] in Norway and its Danish counterpart "The accommodating labour market"[2] also commit them to promoting and increasing work participation. Although the Nordic welfare states are particularly generous with social security and rights-based benefit schemes (Esping-Andersen, 1990; Ministry of Labour and Social Affairs, 2017), increasing levels of motivation and work ethics still prevail. There is a strong consensus among the social parties that the maintenance of the Nordic model presupposes a population actively involved in all aspects of societal processes, not least in working life. Nordic Active Labour Market Policies (ALMP) are grounded in a belief that work participation reduces poverty and inequality, increases the welfare level of society as a whole and that everybody who is capable ought to participate in work and contribute to the value production of society (Hvinden, 2008; Halvorsen & Hvinden, 2009; Stjernø & Øverbye, 2012). As such, active citizenship through work participation is the norm in the Nordic countries (Ministry of Labour, 2012).

However, despite the presence of ALMPs, commitments by the social parties and a strong work ethos, the percentage of the working age population outside the labour market has grown. From 1995 to 2010, the proportion of the Norwegian working age population who received various forms of incapacity benefits increased from 13 to 20% (Ministry of Finance, 2010). Whereas the disability rates among the elderly decreased slightly, there was a clear increase within the age group 18–24. An increasing number of young people with mental health issues drop out of school and become marginalized

(Anvik & Gustavsen, 2012), and this trend is shared across the other Nordic countries (Wulf-Andersen et al., 2016). Even though many people with mental illness want to work and unemployment rates have been comparatively low,[3] an increasing number are offered disability benefits (Berge & Falkum, 2013; Kinn et al., 2016). The various Welfare and Employment Services across the Nordic countries are now facing problems in helping clients with comprehensive support needs into employment (Spjelkavik et al., 2011a). In Norway this situation is further backed up by OECD data (2009) showing that the Norwegian disability employment rate is mediocre compared to OECD countries and below other Nordic countries. Thus, the Nordic welfare states – characterized by dialogue, collaboration between the social parties and an active welfare state – are now facing increased difficulties achieving work participation and citizenship for all.

Can the Nordic welfare states perform better? In this chapter we discuss prerequisites, conditions and opportunities for improved quality of work inclusion. We start out with the supply-side oriented model of Vocational Rehabilitation (VR) that has dominated the Nordic countries, where the idea is to train and prepare people with reduced work capacity to be job-ready before entering the labour market. We then focus on demand-side approaches that pay attention to the role of employers and their needs for compensation and support. We argue that neither of these approaches have so far been successful. Instead we point towards a "support-side approach" that seems to be emerging within the employment and welfare services. This support-side approach is characterized by public services that more proactively support clients and collaborate closer with employers. We discuss possible advantages and challenges related to this approach, as well as its potential to contribute to a more inclusive working life in the Nordic countries.

Observations and analyses in this chapter are based on data and findings from various evaluations and research and development projects from the last decades, exploring approaches to improve work inclusion of vulnerable citizens (carried out by the public employment and welfare services in Norway and other Nordic countries). Several findings from these studies were summed up by a group of researchers and practitioners in 2014, coining the concept "inclusion skills competence" (Frøyland & Spjelkavik, 2014). This concept implies increased attention to the role of the support system in the use of ordinary workplaces as a means to achieve work inclusion for the more disadvantaged and vulnerable jobless citizens.

The challenge of work inclusion

ALMPs aim to transition working-age beneficiaries off passive benefits and into the labour market. The content of ALMPs differs between countries and in their target groups (Frøyland et al., 2018); however, they often include groups with low employment rates such as low-skilled or poorly educated individuals, young citizens with significant problems, people with disabilities, disadvantaged women or immigrants, or those near retirement age. A common trend in the more recent international ALMPs is the inclusion of more marginalized target groups as well (Van Berkel et al., 2017a).

Lessons from supply-side and demand-side approaches

In the Nordic countries, as in many Western countries, the traditional mainstream strategy for labour market inclusion of people with substantial support needs has been vocational training in discrete, sheltered facilities (Frøyland & Spjelkavik, 2014). The basic idea of "train then place" is to increase clients' productivity and employability, allowing them to fit in with employers' anticipated expectations. In practice this is often done by teaching clients "the rules of working life" and "the importance of being motivated for work", trying to raise their self-awareness of how to interact with others, how to avoid inappropriate behaviour, and to understand employer expectations. In sum, a common feature of ALMPs and corresponding activation programs is that they are based on "supply-side fundamentalism" linking joblessness and marginalization almost exclusively to individual failure and lack of employability (Peck & Theodore, 2000; McQuaid & Lindsay, 2005; Bonvin & Galster, 2010; Ingold & Stuart, 2015). As such, supply-side approaches belong to the "medical model" of VR. Based on the assumption that employers' preferences are to hire the most productive workforce available, supply-side approaches aim at repairing and preparing the individual to become ready for work. Assessment tests are used to decide each individual's level of work capacity, their entitlement to temporary benefits and, as a basis for referral to more or less compulsory participation in activation and qualification programs, aiming to improve individual employability.

However, the intended effect of such supply-side-oriented approaches has been poor (Eichhorst et al., 2008; Ministry of Labour, 2012, p. 6; Hauss, 2014; Martin, 2015). Instead of reducing exclusion, there has been a tendency towards permanent exclusion, illustrated by a growing number of young people on disability benefits (NAV, 2017). Activating individuals with supply-side approaches has had little impact on the overall transition from passivity to paid jobs.

Due to the inefficiency of merely focusing on the supply side, there has been an increased focus on employers' needs as well as their social responsibilities, in particular, approaches aimed at activating employers by measures such as legal obligations, incentives and various kinds of service and assistance to employers (Falkum et al., 2014; Frøyland et al., 2018). In Norway, a tripartite agreement on Inclusive Working Life (IA) was launched in 2001, and its latest renewal was in 2014. One of its major objectives is to increase the employment rate of people with disabilities by supporting and strengthening employers through a variety of support measures available for companies that sign an IA agreement.

One example of such measures is a personal IA contact officer who "is assigned at the respective local workplace centre to build a working relationship through which helpful information can be made available in a timely way to employers" (OECD, 2009, p. 24). Evaluations of the Norwegian tripartite agreement have shown that although some companies work actively to reduce sick leave and exclusion of employees with acquired impairments, there are hardly any activities aimed at recruitment of people with disabilities (Ose et al., 2009, 2015; Ingebrigtsen & Moe, 2015).

In Denmark, employment policies and the delivery of ALMPs have been delegated to public job centres at the municipal level since 2007. Whereas Norway strengthened the role of the social parties through the Inclusive Working Life agreement, in Denmark the role of the social parties in the formulation and administration of employment services was marginalized through this process (Ingold & Valizade, 2017, p. 532). Still, recent Danish employment policy reforms have turned towards more employer-oriented measures rather than qualification and guidance as a part of training courses for clients. Companies are expected to play a greater role in helping disadvantaged people towards employment (Jakobsen et al., 2015, p. 34). This means that Danish ALMPs as well have added an increasing interest in demand-side approaches to the dominating supply-side focus. Danish employers are apparently more likely to participate actively in the delivery of ALMPs than employers in other countries (Bredgaard & Halkjær, 2016, p. 50). However, Ingold and Valizade (2017) found that although the literature suggests that Danish ALMP agencies have the potential to increase employers' recruitment of disadvantaged groups, they mainly provide information about jobseekers to companies and about job vacancies to jobseekers instead of acting as "matchmakers". The study also found that the effect of ALMPs on recruiting disadvantaged groups was rather marginal.

Employers' attitudes and experiences

Studies of employers' willingness and attitudes to employ jobseekers with disabilities or mental health issues have been carried out in many countries (i.e. Hand & Tryssenaar, 2006; Waterhouse et al., 2010). These studies reveal that a number of employers are willing to employ these individuals, but they fear that they do not have the required level of knowledge, understanding and ability, in particular regarding vulnerable employees' social and emotional skills (such as not being able to handle critique, lack of flexibility and tantrum control, trouble with socializing or lack of motivation). They also fear that these employees will require a lot of time-consuming attention, that they will have poor working capacity or be unstable and frequently absent.

Holt et al. (2013) found that approximately one-quarter of Danish employers believe that the employment of people with mental illness makes colleagues insecure, is a burden on their employees' social work environment and is a financial burden on the employer. Around a third believe that the employment of people with a mental disorder means poorer quality of work. At the same time, analyses show that over half of the businesses have some sort of objection to recruiting persons with mental disorders (Holt et al., 2013, p. 22).

Andreassen (2009) shows that Norwegian employers consider it to be their responsibility to facilitate employees who acquire a disability while being employed, but they do so to a much lesser degree when it comes to the recruitment of new employees. Falkum (2012) found that employers were afraid of difficulties maintaining production goals because of a possible lack of capability among disabled employees to manage tasks and remain stable at work. Employers also had worries about social and emotional issues, and about costs associated with hiring persons with such challenges. Some employers fear that hiring an employee with a disability will affect the work environment in a negative way by placing high demands on colleagues and contributing to dissatisfaction and stigma (Schafft & Spjelkavik, 2014).

Several studies have shown that companies' "own positive experiences" and "needs of their work force" are among the circumstances that lead them to consider employing (more) people with reduced workability (Unger, 2002; Lauveng, 2008; Jakobsen et al., 2015). Jakobsen et al. found that businesses that already had employees with reduced work ability expressed that they considered hiring persons with reduced work ability more often than other companies did. A majority of businesses expressed that public financial support for employing a person with reduced work ability also made a difference. However, lack of financial support did not explain why some companies failed to hire people with reduced work capacity. According to Jakobsen et al., the main reasons given were the insufficiency of required qualifications, the need for extra adjustments and follow up, or that employers were unsure whether persons with reduced capacity would perform well. Lauveng (2008) found that leaders (or managers) that have personal relationships with employees, friends or relatives with mental illness are more willing to hire persons with such diagnoses. Employers who have previously employed persons with disabilities are also less likely to view such engagements as risky (Unger, 2002; Svalund & Hansen, 2013; Falkum & Solberg, 2015).

Holt et al. (2013) revealed that more than 50% of small Danish private businesses had never been contacted by a job centre, and many had no knowledge of applicable support schemes, such as the financing of in-house resources in terms of a mentor for a person with reduced work ability. They also found a positive correlation between whether the company had been contacted by a job centre and whether they had a person employed with public support.

Other research has shown that jobseekers with high support needs are more likely to find jobs in companies characterized by a culture of inclusion and diversity, and an atmosphere characterized by recognition and concern (Kirsh, 2000a, 2000b). Gilbride et al. (2003) reported that employers who are open to hiring people with disabilities are characterized by openness to diversity and equal treatment of disabled and non-disabled employees, a focus on seeing the capabilities of an employee instead of their impairments, and the ability to manage and supervise a diverse workforce. According to Vornholt et al. (2013), these employers have important roles in the socialization of individuals with disabilities since they represent the organizational culture and serve as models for the employees.

A small number of studies suggest that inclusion of vulnerable persons can actually contribute to an improvement in the work environment. Hartnett et al. (2011) claim that employers can benefit from engaging employees with disabilities via an increased ability to retain quality employees in the company, an increase in company profitability, workforce diversity and avoidance of costs associated with hiring and training new employees. These findings also suggest that work inclusion can be viewed as a learning process for both employer and employee. Work inclusion can improve the organizational climate and culture by improving interactions with co-workers, increasing overall company morale and bettering overall company productivity (Solovieva et al., 2011). For employers, hiring persons with mental health issues may improve their leadership role (Ramvi et al., 2013). An inclusive work environment is not only a prerequisite for the inclusion of vulnerable citizens but can also be a result of it. Diversity in itself can contribute to more tolerance and wellbeing throughout the work organization. Experiences with an employee who often struggles can help the management and colleagues become more capable of coping with other employees' problems (Schafft, 2014).

Reading the literature leaves one with the impression that while employers in general are willing to employ people with disabilities, many of them have insufficient knowledge of support schemes (Holt et al., 2013; Jakobsen et al., 2015). Others may have the knowledge, but it has not "translated into workplace practices and cultures" (Rudstam et al., 2013, p. 44). In Norway as in Denmark, corporate social responsibility mainly seems to mean prevention of absence among already employed persons and not inclusion of the jobless (Andreassen, 2009; Falkum, 2012).

The emergence of support-side approaches

In recent years there has been a growing interest in changing the Norwegian ALMP towards a more systematic utilization of ordinary workplaces based on a "place then train" approach instead of pre-vocational training (Ministry of Labour, 2012; Frøyland & Spjelkavik, 2014). Instead of the widely used placement approaches in activity measures, several have been launched where actors in the employment and welfare services follow up both clients and employers in situ (Spjelkavik, 2016; Spjelkavik et al., 2016; Frøyland & Spjelkavik, 2017). In addition to the supply-side focus, a more systematic demand-side focus seems to be under implementation. There is growing attention towards developing a working life that opens up for diversity and better understanding of how work participation can be a means to avoid marginalization, social inequality and poverty. There is a greater recognition that meaningful work can improve opportunities for recovery, social inclusion and citizenship (Antonovsky, 1987; Bell et al., 1996; Borg et al., 2013).

Overall, this recognition has directed attention towards the need for developing social identity in work environments through facilitation and social support, which in turn may increase work participation of people with support needs. There is growing attention around supporting the actual workplace processes in inclusion efforts. These developments are at least partially inspired by approaches to work inclusion, including various Supported Employment (SE) programs that hold neither the jobless individuals nor the employers responsible for the lack of inclusion, but rather emphasize the role and responsibility of the support services.

Bond et al. (2001) defined SE as an "approach to helping people with disabilities participate as much as possible in the competitive labour market, working in jobs they prefer, with the level of professional help they need" (p. 313). Others have described SE as a "way to help those with disabilities who are unable to successfully gain or retain employment on their own to enter the labour force with dignity and inclusion with others in society" (Wehman, 2012, p. 139). SE not only aims for quick placement or job inclusion but also job retention and achieving full community integration (Riddell et al., 1999).

Different versions of SE have developed, targeting various client groups such as persons with serious mental challenges, learning disabilities, autism, as well as other kinds of disabilities. Although often referred to as "the SE method", SE also has quite a varied content in the Nordic countries (Spjelkavik et al., 2011b; Spjelkavik, 2012). Frequently used versions of SE include a five-stage process developed by the European Union of Supported Employment (EUSE), Customized Employment (CE) and Individual Placement and Support (IPS).

A wide range of studies have documented excellent results in job inclusion approaches based on SE (Burns et al., 2007; Bond et al., 2008; Cimera, 2011, 2012). Research on IPS has in particular produced documentation showing good effects (Drake et al., 2012; Luciano et al., 2014; Nøkleby et al., 2017). For example, Bond et al. (2008) found that the employment rate was 61% for IPS compared to 23% for controls based on an analysis of 11 randomized controlled trials. However, an evaluation of IPS in Norway (Reme et al., 2016) showed that the national results – as for Europe in general – were not as good as the results in the United States. The reasons for these differences have not yet been properly investigated, but elements such as the welfare state model, laws and regulations, and access to available jobs are all likely to be relevant. Bonfils et al. (2017) claimed that there is a need for more comparative studies to find out what kind of impact a welfare state model has on the implementation of this particular approach.

The "SE method" as such is not our main focus of interest, but some key characteristics shared by the different versions of SE are relevant. First is the understanding that work and well-matched labour market participation "is considered beneficial to health and well-being, and is seen as a route to possible recovery from mental illness as well as to normalization and equal worth" (Frøyland et al., 2018, p. 10). Second, work in SE means employment in the ordinary labour market with "valued roles" and competitive wages, *not* in sheltered workshops. The major target group is disadvantaged jobseekers, including "hard-to-place" vulnerable citizens with more complex challenges and support needs, whom employers consider risky to employ (Frøyland & Spjelkavik, 2014). Furthermore, work capacity is viewed as a relational concept shaped and transformed by the united resources and efforts of the person, their co-workers, employer and support givers as well as the requirements of the job. In addition, and probably most importantly, SE follows a "place then train" approach, rapidly addressing workplaces and matching jobseekers to suitable and ordinary work tasks in line with a "job fit principle", while at the same time providing long-term quality support at the workplaces. The support system is characterized by simultaneous interventions from several possible agencies such as the employment services, mental health agencies or others, depending on the challenges and support needs of the individual or the workplace. The support system targets the individuals, co-workers and employers, with the aim of facilitating productive and sustainable work relationships.

Some international researchers have advocated for approaches that combine demand-side and supply-side strategies to operate together in order to integrate the most disadvantaged citizens in work (McQuaid & Lindsay, 2002; Ray et al., 2009; Goodwin-Smith & Hutchinson, 2014).

The support-side approach adds more comprehensive and fine-grained ideas about how to facilitate learning and inclusion at the actual workplace to supply- and demand-side approaches. Whereas supply-side placement practices are mostly aimed at the individual to be trained, taught and qualified, support-side approaches hold that employers, HR managers and co-workers also have a need for learning, and that approaches for inclusion of people with comprehensive needs are not sufficient if they do not address the work organization as a whole (Schafft, 2005).

Utilizing the workplace as a means of learning

As we showed earlier, knowledge about and experience with people with disabilities seems to reduce negative attitudes towards the inclusion of this group. Co-workers learn what it takes to include a colleague with special needs, as well as what they do not need to fear. It is therefore vital that employers and businesses gain experience in managing the physical, psychological and social problems of their employees in a constructive way, and that they become familiar with jobseekers who have substantial support needs.

Work experience placements can represent important arenas for training and learning for the individual and the employer/work organization, as well as a means for trying out different kinds of work and tasks, and/or for determining the right workplace for the individual. A tailor-made job can involve developing work tasks that take into account the individuals' needs for facilitation and follow-up, and will contribute to mastery, participation and inclusion. By trying different kinds of work and work environments, even an individual without any work history can access opportunities to gain valuable work training, experience and competence that he or she would otherwise not have gained. One of the strengths of work experience placement is that the jobseeker is placed within a real work setting in a relationship with colleagues at a workplace. For some young adults in particular, a placement like this might be their first encounter with working life (Frøyland, 2016, 2018). Taking in jobseekers to train in real job settings by working for free for a period of time represents an opportunity for the employer and jobseeker to get to know each other. Such relationships can serve as "door openers" that may lead to employment for jobseekers.

However, a placement in itself does not necessarily lead to employment. Research shows that even though employers are often positive towards giving people with mental health or social challenges the opportunity for work experience practice, they seldom hire them in paid jobs (Schafft & Spjelkavik, 2014; Ekspertgruppen, 2015; Spjelkavik, 2016; Hyggen, 2017). Most employers cannot facilitate successful learning processes on their own. In order for placements to be successful and eventually lead to a job for vulnerable, disadvantaged or less productive citizens, the support-side approach focuses on the need for well-functioning and accessible support services to make sure that placements take the form of "place then train" and not just "place and pray". Comprehensive support is essential to avoid experiences of defeat for both client and workplace.

The employment specialist as a facilitator

An essential feature of SE approaches is the role of employment specialists to support and assist both the employer and the employee in finding jobs or work tasks that represent a match between both parties' interests and skills (EUSE, 2014). They provide professional guidance to the employee and the employer. A long-term relationship of trust between the employee, the employer and the employment specialist over a period of time after the job has been established has been demonstrated as decisive for success (Frøyland & Spjelkavik, 2014). Wage subsidies and other financial support schemes also play important roles, but the major reason seems to be the affirmation that the employment specialist retains a proactive role in the inclusion process, so that responsibility is not left to employers alone (European Commission, 2011).

A study among a sample of Nordic employers revealed their need to receive relevant information about the jobseeker, so as to be prepared for any potential future problems (Spjelkavik et al., 2011a). A majority of them had experienced that the person they hired was not that useful to the company in terms of productivity, and that the company needed to spend extra resources on supervision and follow-up. Most companies, however, considered the benefits large enough to keep them employed. The majority of these employers also had observed that the employees themselves benefitted from being in the company in terms of wellbeing, quality of life and personal development. The employers felt that frequent visits to the workplace was an important prerequisite for the employment specialist in order to be able to provide relevant advice, understand the employee and the company, and to find out what actions could be taken to solve practical problems.

In a Swedish study, Gustafsson et al. (2013) found that the employment specialist played three important roles: a broker, a supervisor and a problem solver. They also found that specialist effort in the follow-up work influenced an employer's willingness to cooperate. The approaches that employers perceived as most successful were the creation of security, responsibility for the workforce being conveyed and the pursuit of trust with employers.

Key concepts in Norwegian ALMP are recruitment assistance to employers and employment assistance to jobseekers, and traditional ALMP is characterized by matching jobseekers to available jobs, accompanied by limited follow-up (Ekspertgruppen, 2015). Such assistance, which we have labelled "promotion of job opportunities", is better suited for jobseekers with minor support needs and is insufficient when the jobseeker needs high levels of social follow-up and practical adjustments, and/or when it is unclear what the appropriate work tasks may be or how much the individual can work (Spjelkavik & Thingbø-Støldal, 2014). Follow-up from this perspective means providing support and time for the development of coping strategies and job matching in the workplace. Table 10.1 illustrates the difference between the type of support traditionally provided by the employment services and the kind of job development that appears to be required for persons with substantial support needs (Spjelkavik et al., 2016).

Job development in this perspective is about developing coping strategies as well as working conditions so that the tasks are adapted to the individual, rather

Table 10.1 Two types of employment support

Promotion of job opportunities	*Job development*
Obtain recruitment assignments	Identify client's interests and support needs
Identify the best candidate among jobseekers	Find suitable workplace, arena for development
Match and present candidates' CVs for employer	Training, qualification at work
Interview	Organize coping and natural supports
Appointment	Appointment or education

than the individual being adapted to the tasks. The aim is to allow the individuals to develop on their own terms and to adjust the tasks in such a way that the work relationship meets the needs of both employer and employee. Inclusion is understood as individual learning and development in a relational process that takes place in the interactions between employees in the workplace. An inclusion process in a "place then train" perspective should not be understood in terms of arranging job opportunities or competing for available jobs, but rather as a development process where interpersonal relationships among all employees in the workplace are important for the process of inclusion, not just the relationship between the jobseeker and the employment specialist (Folkenborg, 2014). The role of the employment specialist is not only to find the right place for the individual but also to find job openings and recruitment strategies in cooperation with employers. A primary aim is to find ways of organizing work and tasks in order to secure both individual and structural diversity. Work tasks may need to be customized to the individual – they may even need to be individually carved out. The result might be a "non-normal job" in a "normal work environment". From this perspective it is insufficient to look for individual qualifications that match the given job requirements; instead, more flexible job requirements are necessary that respond to the individual prerequisites.

Within the support-side approach the employment specialist is a vital "matchmaker" in the facilitation of such inclusionary processes, by collaborating both with the employer and the client while at the same time ensuring other necessary professional and financial support. However, individualized support from an external employment specialist in a workplace can be stigmatizing and as such contribute to social exclusion instead of inclusion (Frøyland, 2016). An important issue is therefore to develop support in ways that minimize stigma. The ability of employment specialists to contribute to the facilitation of natural supports – meaning support activated among co-workers at the workplace – can be vital (Murphy et al., 2005; Drake et al., 2012; Corbière et al., 2014; Frøyland & Kvåle, 2014; Klethagen & Spjelkavik, 2018).

Employment and welfare services as "matchmakers"?

Van Berkel et al. (2017b) recommend more research on ALMP agencies' "matchmaker" roles in order to counteract organizational factors that impede the hiring of disadvantaged jobseekers. However, such support-side approaches put heavy burdens on the shoulders of employment specialists. To what extent can the Employment and Welfare Services themselves carry out this role for jobseekers with comprehensive needs?

The Norwegian Labour and Welfare Service (NAV) has overall national responsibility for the organization of ALMP.[4] Traditionally, much of the practical follow-up of clients with higher support needs has been purchased from external service providers. While the aim of the reform of the Norwegian Labour and Welfare Administration (2006–2010) was to merge the Social Security Service and Public Employment Service to a joint state and municipality agency (Andreassen & Aars, 2015), the reform actually reinforced this division of labour within the principal–agent model of New Public Management (Ministry of Labour, 2012). However, we do find examples within NAV that assign the core "matchmaker" role to NAV itself. One project (2012–2016) in particular has demonstrated that NAV offices can perform follow-up services themselves instead of purchasing them from external vocational service providers.

The project was carried out at five local NAV offices. Instead of using external providers, the NAV offices were tasked with following up clients themselves, using the same resources and guidelines as those utilized by external service providers. The evaluation (Spjelkavik et al., 2016) concluded that the supervisors at the NAV offices quickly discovered that many of the clients had greater than anticipated support needs. They faced serious challenges related to the follow-up of clients in cooperation with employers. Gradually the participating NAV offices developed a more rapid placement approach, with more proactive follow-up in the workplace and increased cooperation with employers. The overall effect of the project was a 39% increase in transition to work compared to external service providers. The evaluation linked this effect to organizational and competence-related factors. The project was organized as specialized teams within the NAV offices who had thus developed better knowledge and skills in practical and operational work inclusion endeavours. The supervisors' approach to follow-up became more adapted to the individual client's needs and interests in order to find the workplace that best suited the client. In addition, the time the supervisors spent on follow-up at the workplace and in cooperation with employers increased significantly during the project period.

Although this was not the initial intention, the project developed as an implementation of the employment specialist model of SE. An expert function was established at the NAV offices for work inclusion of clients with comprehensive needs that required close cooperation with employers. Instead of understanding work inclusion as a pre-vocational "matchmaker" challenge, the project became an example where the "street-level bureaucrats" (Lipsky, 2010) became employment specialists that collaborated with employers to create safe venues for their clients' personal progression in the workplaces, and provided support to develop jobs in accordance to the individual client's needs. Thus, the public employment and welfare services obtained employment specialists that facilitated follow-up of both clients and employers in ways that seemed to strengthen the possibilities for mastering and coping at work (Spjelkavik et al., 2016).

This approach places less weight on the consultation of clients in offices and instead emphasizes the active role of support-givers by providing outreach services, transport services and coaching at work, as well as assistance with adjustments and organizing of work tasks through proactive collaboration and support for employers. After the project, the annual state budgets for similar follow-up approaches to be performed at the NAV offices have been increased. These recent "insourcing" experiences may indicate the development of a new follow-up approach in the NAV offices and a change of perspective within the public Welfare and Labour administration. In Denmark various agencies are responsible for delivering ALMPs and "modifying companies' HRM policies and practice, in order to facilitate the labour market inclusion of vulnerable groups" (Van Berkel et al., 2017b, p. 507). The Norwegian experiences have demonstrated that this facilitating role, as well as the responsibility and performance of work inclusion measures for even the most vulnerable citizens, could very well (and perhaps preferably) be a routine task undertaken by the public employment and welfare services.

Inclusion skills competence

Within support-side approaches, the task of supporting clients with extensive needs so that they can participate in regular work requires a particular competence. This competence is primarily comprised of social, health-related or educational knowledge about a client's support needs and relevant guidance methods for utilizing an ordinary workplace to develop work participation. "Inclusion skills competence" in practice means applying knowledge about a given individual client, supporting this particular client in finding suitable work openings at the workplaces, as well as cooperating with and supporting employers. Performing inclusion skills competence means exploring employment opportunities in the local community, i.e. identifying which industries and companies might fit the client's requirements and vocational interests, as well as identifying which workplaces are able to provide work tasks and opportunities for job matching and job development. Inclusion skills competence requires knowledge about an employer's expectations and requirements as well as the individual's support needs in an employment situation. As many vulnerable clients are in need of support from different actors within their support systems (i.e. psychologists, social workers or special teachers), coordination of the involvement of relevant support agencies is also an important aspect of inclusion skills competence (Frøyland & Spjelkavik, 2014; Spjelkavik, 2016). In sum, inclusion skills competence contributes to the establishment of work relationships and provides the support that maintains them.

Inclusion skills competence marks a shift in thinking about and organizing work inclusion efforts: from sheltered preparation prior to entering the labour market, to approaches that facilitate mastery and personal progression at work sites through practical learning in collaboration with an employer and work organization. Inclusion skills competence requires that the multifaceted competence necessary for user-oriented assistance (already found in several professions in the health and social field) be actively used *within* the workplace. As such, inclusion skills competence highlights the local context and the progression of work relationships within an organization, as well as the support system surrounding the individual and their workplace. Inclusion skills competence challenges both supply-side and demand-side approaches by stressing the importance of a support-based and capability-enhancing focus on both client and employer.

Practical solutions related to work inclusion and job retention should be found at the workplace, in the work organization and in particular in the ability of the support services to assist the client and the employer in developing a sustainable work relationship. Figure 10.1 illustrates the role of the support system.

Sufficient job matching, job development and employment are the results of an inclusion process. Inclusion skills competence means creating a joint project between the employer, the employee and support staff. This project might include activities such as assigning a job specialist to the task and clarifying the responsibilities of the job specialist, jobseeker and employer. These activities and responsibilities may be summed up in an overall inclusion plan describing the purpose and contents of the work tasks, necessary adaptation, training, duration and plan for follow-up.

The tasks of the support system related to the individual are illustrated by the left arrow in Figure 10.1. Examples of relevant activities are mapping the interests of the jobseeker, personalized help to deal with social, mental or physical challenges, career guidance, user involvement and individualized follow-up.

The right arrow illustrates support directed towards employers. Examples of relevant activities are mapping the employer's opportunities and prerequisites, mapping the workplace by learning about the working environment and surroundings, current work tasks, and also investigating whether the workplace

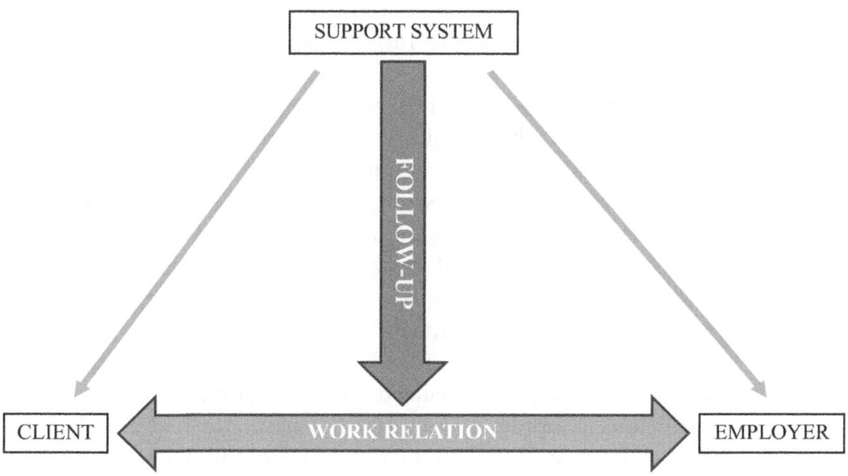

Figure 10.1 The role of the support system

has the psychosocial requirements needed to meet the individual's needs for adaptation and facilitation.

Support givers need to be available and able to provide information about schemes, as grants are often offered to reduce perceived risks among employers as well as individual jobseekers. They need to follow the development of the working relationship closely and be ready to act when needed, or make sure that others do. These may include actors located outside the workplace that can affect the work ability.

The crucial element is illustrated in Figure 10.1 by the arrow in the middle: "Follow-up". This kind of follow-up is what distinguishes inclusion skills competence from other forms of work-oriented rehabilitation in ordinary workplaces. This means making an effort to establish and strengthen a work relationship in situations where the individual or job candidate is not "the perfect employee". Performing inclusion skills competence means facilitating learning through experiences for employers, employees and jobseekers. This means exploring needs and opportunities for facilitation, relevant support schemes, employment conditions, job carving or creation in order to match work tasks to the particular individual and to identify and support natural supporters at the workplace. For some individuals long-term support is needed. Such follow-up can involve insight or disclosure of a disability or other conditions that may affect employability. It can mean advising employers and colleagues as to how they should deal with the employee in case of problems and/or how to talk about and discuss difficult issues, as well as how to create social support, tolerance and understanding.

Towards a more inclusive work-life?

In this chapter, we have described the emergence of the support-side approach to work inclusion. It is an approach where demand-side and supply-side strategies operate together to integrate the most disadvantaged populations into employment.

The support-side approach is characterized by services that proactively support and carry out knowledge-based follow-up of both clients and employers. The support-side approach therefore requires a combination of skills and knowledge from different professions, from evidence-based methods for work inclusion, knowledge about psychosocial work environment issues and inclusion management. Successful work inclusion for vulnerable citizens presupposes dialogue and cooperation between employee, employer and a proactive support system. Our major message in this chapter is:

1 Despite the fact that many marginalized jobseekers are in need of upgrading and qualification, supply-side approaches have not had a sufficiently positive effect on work inclusion in the Nordic countries. Some have found jobs, but these are primarily individuals with minor support needs, and the long-term effect has been poor.

2 Even though some companies have performed well in work inclusion, demand-side approaches have so far not significantly improved the effects on work inclusion for vulnerable citizens in the Nordic countries.
3 Support-side approaches draw knowledge from both supply-side and demand-side orientations, acknowledging the need for training and qualification but suggesting that these interventions take place within the workplace, proactively supported by public employment and welfare services.

  - From supply-side approaches, the support-side approach brings along the need for upgrading and qualification. In the integrated model of the support-side approach, the effect is improved by moving these efforts from sheltered or pre-vocational arenas to the workplace.
  - From the demand-side approaches, the support-side approach highlights the need for employer support, including human and financial support. In the integrated model of the support-side approach, the normative demand for an employer's social responsibility is understood as a responsibility fulfilled through the practices of job development for marginalized and vulnerable individuals.

The support-side approach is an integrated and cooperative model to promote work inclusion, in the sense that the supply-side efforts take place at workplaces and in a close interaction with employers and the support system. As such, the support-side approach has much in common with the Nordic model in terms of promoting dialogue, the collaboration of social parties, and a strong and actively interventionist welfare state. The best-documented support-side oriented practices are found in "place then train" approaches guided by employment specialists. For some reason, such approaches have barely been recognized in the supply-side and demand-side debate.

Established structures for cooperation and dialogue between the social parties on the national level, such as the Norwegian "Inclusive working life" or the Danish "Accommodating labour market" can play vital roles by highlighting work inclusion of vulnerable groups. However, such agreements have so far not been sufficient to promote the required cooperation between employees, their union representatives, employers and governmental support agencies at the company level.

We believe that implementation of the support-side approach in ALMPs and in the social parties' recognition of what is needed is a prerequisite for increased work participation among hard-to-place and vulnerable citizens. This most probably means a form of institutionalization of "Inclusive Working Life" that promotes employment specialists in the public employment and welfare services, and, further, that views work as a means to recovery, social inclusion and quality of life (not as an obligation), and sees the workplace as an arena for development of flexible forms of labour market attachment.

Whether the established tradition for dialogue and cooperation among the social parties in the Nordic countries represents drivers or barriers to the implementation of support-side approaches, as well as sufficient collaboration between the social parties on the company level, is yet to be seen. So far, such collaborative initiatives and formal agreements have favoured (or protected) those persons already employed, over vulnerable, jobless individuals. There are also other challenges associated with support-side approaches. We do not know whether the public employment and welfare services will manage to implement "place then train" approaches in any sustainable way. There is a risk that work inclusion based on "place then train" will be reduced to implementation of a set of evidence-based methods, "quick fix solutions" for motivated, "job ready" individuals, instead of job development, progression and retention for hard-to-place citizens with social, mental health and learning difficulties. We believe that a prerequisite for support-side approaches should be that practitioners in relevant professions are actively involved in vulnerable citizens' work inclusion processes.

Notes

1 *Intensjonsavtalen om et mer inkluderende arbeidsliv* (IA).
2 *Det rummelige arbeidsmarked* (DRAM).
3 The unemployment rate in Norway in 2015 was 3% according to NAV (2015).
4 LOV 2006-06-16 nr 20: Lov om arbeids- og velferdsforvaltningen.

References

Andreassen, T. A. (2009) Når politikken rettes mot arbeidslivet. Behov for kunnskap omfunksjonshemming i arbeidslivet [When Policy is Directed Towards the Labour Market], In: Tøssebro, J. (ed.) *Funksjonshemming: Politikk, hverdagsliv og arbeidsliv [Disability: Politics, Everyday Life and Worklife]*, Oslo: Universitetsforlaget.

Andreassen, T. A. & Aars, J. (2015) *Den store reformen. Da NAV ble til [The Great Reform. When NAV was Invented]*, Oslo: Universitetsforlaget. doi: org/10.18261/issn.1504–291x-2016–03–05.

Antonovsky, A. (1987) Unraveling the Mystery of Health: How People Manage Stress and Stay Well, Vol A., *Joint Publication in the Jossey-Bass Social and Behavioral Science Series and the Jossey-Bass Health Series*, San Francisco, CA: Jossey-Bass.

Anvik, C. H. & Gustavsen, A. (2012) *Ikke slipp meg! Unge, psykiske helseproblemer, utdanning og arbeid [Don't Let Me Go! Youth, Mental Challenges, Education and Employment]*, In: NF-report (Nordlandsforskning: online), Vol 13/2012, Bodø, Norway: Nordlandsforskning.

Bell, M. D., Lysaker, P. H. & Milstein, R. M. (1996) Clinical Benefits of Paid Work Activity in Schizophrenia, *Schizophrenia Bulletin*, 22(1): 51–67.

Berge, T. & Falkum, E. (2013) *Se mulighetene: arbeidsliv og psykisk helse [See the Possibilities: Worklife and Mental Health]*, Oslo: Gyldendal akademisk.

Bond, G. R., Becker, D. R., Drake, R. E., Rapp, C. A., Meisler, N., Lehman, A. F. & Blyler, C. R. (2001) Implementing Supported Employment as an Evidence-Based Practice, *Psychiatric Services*, 52(3): 313–322.

Bond, G. R., Drake, R. E. & Becker, D. R. (2008) An Update on Randomized Controlled Trials of Evidence-Based Supported Employment, *Psychiatric Rehabilitation Journal*, 31(4): 280–290.

Bonfils, I. S., Hansen, H., Dalum, H. S. & Eplov, L. F. (2017) Implementation of the Individual Placement and Support Approach: Facilitators and Barriers, *Scandinavian Journal of Disability Research*, 19(4): 318–333.

Bonvin, J.-M. & Galster, D. (2010) Making them Employable or Capable? Social Integration Policies at a Crossroads, In: Otto, H.-U. & Ziegler, H. (eds) *Education, Welfare and the Capabilities Approach. A European Perspective*, Opladen, Germany and Farmington Hills, MI: Barbara Budrich Publishers, 71–83.

Borg, M., Veseth, M., Binder, P.-E. & Topor, A. (2013) The Role of Work in Recovery from Bipolar Disorders, *Qualitative Social Work*, 12(3): 323–339.

Bredgaard, T. & Halkjær, J. L. (2016) Employers and the Implementation of Active Labor Market Policies, *Nordic Journal of Working Life Studies*, 6(1). doi: 10.19154/njwls.v6i1.4909.

Burns, T., Catty, J., Becker, T., Drake, R. E., Fioritti, A., Knapp, M. & Wiersma, D. (2007) The Effectiveness of Supported Employment for People with Severe Mental Illness: A Randomised Controlled Trial, *Lancet*, 370(9593): 1146–1152.

Cimera, R. E. (2011) Does Being in Sheltered Workshops Improve the Employment Outcomes of Supported Employees with Intellectual Disabilities?, *Journal of Vocational Rehabilitation*, 35(1): 21–27.

Cimera, R. E. (2012) The Economics of Supported Employment: What New Data Tell Us, *Journal of Vocational Rehabilitation*, 37: 109–117.

Corbière, M., Lecomte, T., Lesage, A., Villotti, P., Bond, G. R. & Goldner, E. M. (2014) Work Accomodation and Natural Supports for Maintaining Employment, *Psychiatric Rehabilitation Journal*, 37(2): 90–98.

Drake, R. E., Bond, G. R. & Becker, D. R. (2012) *Individual Placement and Support: An Evidence-Based Approach to Supported Employment*, New York: Oxford University Press.

Eichhorst, W., Kaufmann, O. & Konle-Seidl, R. (2008) *Bringing the Jobless into Work? Experiences with Activation Schemes in Europe and the US*, Berlin: Springer.

Ekspertgruppen (2015) *Et NAV med muligheter [A NAV with Opportunities], Report to the Ministry of Labour and Social Affairs, 9 April*, Oslo.

Esping-Andersen, G. (1990) *The Three Worlds of Welfare Capitalism*, Cambridge, UK: Polity Press.

European Commission (2011) *Supported Employment for People with Disabilities in the EU and EFTA-EEA*, Brussels: European Commission Directorate General Employment, Social Affairs and Equal Opportunities.

EUSE (2014) *European Union of Supported Employment Toolkit for Diversity*, www.euse-toolkit.eu/index.php/toolkit.

Falkum, E. (2012) *Risiko og inkludering: betingelser for funksjonshemmedes og eldres deltakelse i arbeidslivet [Risk and Inclusion: Conditions for Participation of the Disabled and the Elderly in Work]*, AFIs rapportserie, Vol 11/2012, Oslo: Arbeidsforskningsinstituttet. https://doi.org/10.7577/afi/rapport/2012:11.

Falkum, E., Schafft, A. & Spjelkavik, Ø. (2014) Arbeidsgivernes rolle i inkluderingen [Employers' Role in Work Inclusion], In: Frøyland, K. & Spjelkavik, O. (eds) *Inkluderingskompetanse. Ordinært arbeid som mål og middel [Inclusion Skills Competence. Ordinary Work as a Goal and as a Means]*, Oslo: Gyldendal Akademisk, 142–155.

Falkum, E. & Solberg, A. G. (2015) *Arbeidsgiveres inkluderingsevne [The Employers' Ability to Include]*, Notat Vol 5/2015, Oslo: Arbeidsforskningsinstituttet. https://doi.org/10.7577/afi/rapport/2015:5.

Folkenborg, K. (2014) Virksomhetenes sosiale ansvar [Corporate Social Responsibility], In: Frøyland, K. & Spjelkavik, Ø. (eds) *Inkluderingskompetanse. Ordinært arbeid som mål og middel [Inclusion Expertise. Ordinary Work as a Goal and Means]*, Oslo: Gyldendal Akademisk.

Frøyland, K. (2016) Applicability of IPS Principles to Job Inclusion of Vulnerable Youth, *Journal of Vocational Rehabilitation*, 45(3): 249–265.

Frøyland, K. (2018) Vital Tasks and Roles of Frontline Workers Facilitating Job Inclusion of Vulnerable Youth, *European Journal of Social Work*, 1–12. doi: 10.1080/13691457.2018.1423547.

Frøyland, K., Andreassen, T. A. & Innvær, S. (2018) Contrasting Supply-Side, Demand-Side and Combined Approaches to Labour Market Integration, *Journal of Social Policy*, 1–18. doi:10.1017/s0047279418000491.

Frøyland, K., & Kvåle, L. S. (2014) Utvikling av naturlig bistand på arbeidsplassen [Development of Natural Supports in the Workplace], In: Frøyland, K. & Spjelkavik, O. (eds) *Inkluderingskompetanse. Ordinært arbeid som mål og middel [Inclusion Skills Competence. Ordinary Work as a Goal and as a Means]*, Oslo: Gyldendal Akademisk, 366.

Frøyland, K. & Spjelkavik, Ø. (2014) *Inkluderingskompetanse. Ordinært arbeid som mål og middel [Inclusion Skills Competence]*, Oslo: Gyldendal Akademisk Forlag AS.

Frøyland, K. & Spjelkavik, Ø. (2017) *Effekt- og følgeevaluering av Lindesneslosen. Underveisrapport 2 [Evaluation of the Youth Project "Lindesneslosen". Second Report]*, Oslo: Arbeidsforskningsinstituttet.

Gilbride, D., Stensrud, R. & Vandergoot, D. (2003) Identification of the Characteristics of Work Environments and Employers Open to Hiring and Accommodating People with Disabilities, *Rehabilitation Counseling Bulletin*, 46(3): 130–137.

Goodwin-Smith, I. & Hutchinson, C. (2014) *Beyond Supply and Demand: Addressing the Complexities of Workforce Exclusion in Australia*, Report commissioned by Anglicare Australia, Adelaide: Flinders University.

Gustafsson, J., Peralta, J. P. & Danermark, B. (2013) The Employer's Perspective on Supported Employment for People with Disabilities: Successful Approaches of Supported Employment Organizations, *Journal of Vocational Rehabilitation*, 38(2): 99–111.

Halvorsen, R. & Hvinden, B. (2009) Nordisk politikk for funksjonshemmede møter internasjonal likebehandlingspolitikk [Nordic Policy for People with Disabilities Meets International Equal Treatment Policy], In: Tøssebro, J. (ed.) *Funksjonshemming: politikk, hverdagsliv og arbeidsliv [Disability: Politics, Everyday Life and Worklife]*, Oslo: Universitetsforlaget.

Hand, C. & Tryssenaar, J. (2006) Small Business Employers' Views on Hiring Individuals with Mental Illness, *Psychiatric Rehabilitation Journal*, 29(3): 166–173.

Hartnett, H. P., Stuart, H., Thurman, H., Loy, B. & Batiste, L. C. (2011) Employers' Perceptions of the Benefits of Workplace Accommodations: Reasons to Hire, Retain and Promote People with Disabilities, *Journal of Vocational Rehabilitation*, 34(1): 17–23.

Hauss, G. (2014) Generating Productive Citizens or Supporting the Weak? Ambivalences and Contradictions in Working with Young Welfare Recipients, *European Journal of Social Work*, 17(5): 656–671.

Holt, H., Jakobsen, V. & Jensen, S. (2013) *Virksomheders sociale engagement, Årbog 2013 [Corporate Social Responsibility, Yearbook 2013]*, Copenhagen: SFI – Det Nationale Forskningscenter for Velfærd.

Hvinden, B. (2008) Cultures of Activation: The Shifting Relationship between Income Maintenance and Employment Promotion in the Nordic Context, In: van

Oorschot, W., Opielka, M. & Pfau-Effinger, B. (eds) *Culture and Welfare State: Values and Social Policy in Comparative Perspective*, Cheltenham, UK: Edward Elgar Publishing.

Hyggen, C. (2017) Etterlater arbeidstrening arr hos unge ledige? Et vignett-eksperiment av arbeidsgiveres beslutninger ved ansettelser av unge i Norge [Does Work Training Leave Scars on the Faces of Young Unemployed?], *Søkelys på arbeidslivet*, 34(4): 236–251.

Ingebrigtsen, B. A. & Moe, A. (2015) *Evaluering av NAV Arbeidslivssenters bidrag til måloppnåelse innen delmål 2 og 3 i IA- avtalen [Evaluation of NAV Work Life Centres Contribution to Inclusive Worklife]*, Trondheim, Norway: NTNU Samfunnsforskning.

Ingold, J. & Stuart, M. (2015) The Demand-Side of Active Labour Market Policies: A Regional Study of Employer Engagement in the Work Programme, *Journal of Social Policy*, 44(3): 443–462.

Ingold, J. & Valizade, D. (2017) Employers' Recruitment of Disadvantaged Groups: Exploring the Effect of Active Labour Market Programme Agencies as Labour Market Intermediaries, *Human Resource Management Journal*, 27(4): 530–547.

Jakobsen, V., Larsen, M. & Jensen, S. (2015) *Virksomheders sociale engagement: Årbog 2015 [Corporate Social Responsibility: Yearbook 2015]*, Copenhagen: SFI – Det Nationale Forskningscenter for Velfærd.

Kinn, L. G., Holgersen, H., Borg, M. & Davidson, L. (2016) "Watch your Steps": Community Mental Health Professionals' Perspectives on the Vocational Rehabilitation of People with Severe Mental Illness, *Scandinavian Psychologist,* 3: 16. doi.org/10.15714/scandpsychol.3.e16.

Kirsh, B. (2000a) Work, Workers, and Workplaces: A Qualitative Analysis of Narratives of Mental Health Consumers, *Journal of Rehabilitation*, 66(4): 24–30.

Kirsh, B. (2000b) Organizational Culture, Climate and Person–Environment Fit: Relationships with Employment Outcomes for Mental Health Consumers, *Work*, 14(2): 109–122.

Klethagen, P. & Spjelkavik, Ø. (2018) Arbeidsinkludering og mentor *[Work Inclusion and Mentor]*, Oslo: Arbeidsforskningsinstituttet.

Lauveng, A. (2008) *Arbeidsmaur med gipset hjerte [Working with Plastered Heart]*, Oslo: Universitetsforlaget.

Lipsky, M. (2010) *Street-Level Bureaucracy: Dilemmas of the Individual in Public Services* (30th anniversary expanded ed.), New York: Russell Sage Foundation.

Luciano, A., Drake, R. E., Bond, G. R., Becker, D. R., Carpenter-Song, E., Lord, S., . . . & Swanson, S. J. (2014) Evidence-Based Supported Employment for People with Severe Mental Illness: Past, Current, and Future Research, *Journal of Vocational Rehabilitation*, 40(1): 1–13.

Martin, J. P. (2015) Activation and Active Labour Market Policies in OECD Countries: Stylised Facts and Evidence on their Effectiveness, *IZA Journal of Labor Policy*, 4(1): 4. doi: 10.1186/s40173-015-0032-y.

McQuaid, R. W. & Lindsay, C. (2002) The "Employability Gap": Long-Term Unemployment and Barriers to Work in Buoyant Labour Markets, *Environment and Planning C: Government and Policy*, 20(4): 613–628.

McQuaid, R. W. & Lindsay, C. (2005) The Concept of Employability, *Urban Studies*, 42(2): 197–219.

Ministry of Finance, Norway (2010) *Meld. St. 1 (2010–2011) National Budget 2011*, Oslo.

Ministry of Labour (2012) *NOU 2012:6 Arbeidsrettede tiltak [Work-Directed Measures]*, Oslo: Official Norwegian Report.

Ministry of Labour & Social Affairs, Norway (2017) *Meld. St. 40 (2016–2017) Eksport av norske velferdsytelser*, Oslo.

Murphy, A. A., Mullen, M. G. & Spagnolo, A. B. (2005) Enhancing Individual Placement and Support: Promoting Job Tenure by Integrating Natural Supports and Supported Education, *American Journal of Psychiatric Rehabilitation*, 8(1): 37–61.

NAV (2015) *Statistics 2015*, Oslo, Norwegian Labour and Welfare Administration, www.nav.no.

NAV (2017) *Statistics 2017*, Oslo. Norwegian Labour and Welfare Administration, www.nav.no.

Nøkleby, H., Blaasvær, N. & Berg, R. (2017) *Supported Employment for arbeidssøkere med bistandsbehov: en systematisk oversikt [Supported Employment for Job Seekers with Support Needs: A Systematic Review]*, Oslo: Folkehelseinstituttet.

OECD (2009) Sickness, Disability and Work, *Background Paper*, Paris: OECD.

Ose, S. O., Bjerkan, A. M., Pettersen, I., Hem, K.-G., Johnsen, A., Lippestad, J. & Saksvik, P. Ø. (2009) *Evaluering av IA-avtalen [Evaluation of the IA-Agreement]*, Trondheim, Norway: SINTEF.

Ose, S. O., Mandal, R. & Dyrstad, K. (2015) *Samarbeid og kommunikasjon rundt IA-avtalen og Jobbstrategien [Cooperation and Communication Around the IA-Agreement and Employment Strategy]*, Trondheim: SINTEF.

Peck, J. & Theodore, N. (2000) Beyond "employability", *Cambridge Journal of Economics*, 24(6): 729–749.

Ramvi, E., Skarpaas, L. S. & Løvereide, L. (2013) *Veien inn i arbeidslivet: lederes erfaring med inkludering av unge voksne med psykiske helseplager [The Way to Work: The Experience of Leaders with Youth with Mental Challenges]*, Stavanger, Norway: Universitetet i Stavanger.

Ray, K., Hoggart, L., Taylor, R., Vegeris, S. & Campbell-Barr, V. (2009) Rewarding Responsibility? Long-Term Unemployed Men and the Welfare-to-Work Agenda, *Environment and Planning C: Government and Policy*, 27(6): 975–990.

Reme, S. E., Monstad, K., Fyhn, T., Øverland, S., Ludvigsen, K., Sveinsdottir, V. & Lie, S. A. (2016) Effektevaluering av Individuell jobbstøtte (IPS) [Effect Evaluation of IPS], *Sluttrapport*, Bergen: Uni Research.

Riddell, S., Wilson, A. & Baron, S. (1999) Supported Employment in Scotland: Theory and Practice, *Journal of Vocational Rehabilitation*, 12(3): 181–194.

Rudstam, H., Hittleman, M., Pi, S. & Gower, W. S. (2013) Bridging the Knowing–Doing Gap: Researching a New Approach to Disability and Employment Programming, *Journal of Vocational Rehabilitation*, 39(1): 43–60.

Schafft, A. (2005) Praksislæring i arbeidslivet [Learning by Practice in Work Life], *Tidsskrift for psykisk helsearbeid*, 2(2): 186–188.

Schafft, A. (2014) Employer Guides: Improving Job Retention for People with Mental Health Issues. Experiences from a Norwegian Pilot Project, *Journal of Vocational Rehabilitation*, 41(1): 23–27.

Schafft, A. & Spjelkavik, Ø. (2014) Arbeidsgiveres erfaringer med inkludering [Employers' Experience with Inclusion], In: Frøyland, K. & Spjelkavik, Ø. (eds) *Inkluderingskompetanse. Ordinært arbeid som mål og middel [Inclusion Skills Competence. Ordinary Work as a Goal and as a Means]*, Oslo: Gyldendal Akademisk, 156–173.

Solovieva, T. I., Dowler, D. L. & Walls, R. T. (2011) Employer Benefits from Making Workplace Accommodations, *Disability and Health Journal*, 4(1): 39–45.
Spjelkavik, Ø. (2012) Supported Employment in Norway and in the Other Nordic Countries, *Journal of Vocational Rehabilitation*, 37(3): 163–172.
Spjelkavik, Ø. (2016) *Arbeidsrettet brukeroppfølging: "Place-train" ved NAV-kontoret [Work-Oriented User Follow-Up: "Place-Train" at the NAV Office]*, Oslo: Arbeidsforskningsinstituttet.
Spjelkavik, Ø., Hagen, B. & Härkäpää, K. (2011a) *Supported employment i Norden [Supported Employment in the Nordic Countries]*, Oslo: Arbeidsforskningsinstituttet. https://doi.org/10.7577/afi/rapport/2011:3.
Spjelkavik, Ø., Mamelund, S.-E. & Schafft, A. (2016) *Inkluderingskompetanse i NAV: evaluering av forsøket Kjerneoppgaver i NAV [Inclusion Skills Competence in NAV]*, Vol 2016:05, Oslo: Arbeidsforskningsinstituttet.
Spjelkavik, Ø., Schafft, A., Evans, M. & Weigelt, V. S. (2011b) *Supported Employment for People with Disabilities in the EU and EFTA-EEA: Good Practices and Recommendations in Support of a Flexicurity Approach*, European Commission Justice.
Spjelkavik, Ø. & Thingbø-Støldal, B. (2014) Jobbmatch og jobbutvikling [Job Match and Job Development], In: Frøyland, K. & Spjelkavik, Ø. (eds) *Inkluderingskompetanse. Ordinært arbeid som mål og middel [Inclusion Skills Competence. Ordinary Work as a Goal and as a Means]*, Oslo: Gyldendal Akademisk.
Stjernø, S. & Øverbye, E. (2012) *Arbeidslinja. Arbeidsmotivasjonen og velferdsstaten [Work First, Work Motivation and the Welfare State]*, Oslo: Universitetsforlaget.
Svalund, J. & Hansen, I. L. S. (2013) *Inkludering av personer med nedsatt funksjonsevne i arbeidslivet [Work Inclusion of Persons with Reduced Work Capacity]*, Oslo: Fafo.
Unger, D. D. (2002) Employers' Attitudes Toward Persons with Disabilities in the Workforce: Myths or Realities?, *Focus on Autism and Other Developmental Disabilities*, 17(1): 2–10.
Van Berkel, R., Caswell, D., Kupka, P. & Larsen, F. (2017a) *Frontline Delivery of Welfare-To-Work Policies in Europe: Activating the Unemployed*, New York: Routledge.
Van Berkel, R., Ingold, J., McGurk, P., Boselie, P. & Bredgaard, T. (2017b) Editorial Introduction: An Introduction to Employer Engagement in the Field of HRM. Blending Social Policy and HRM Research in Promoting Vulnerable Groups' Labour Market Participation, *Human Resource Management Journal*, 27(4): 503–513.
Vornholt, K., Uitdewilligen, S. & Nijhuis, F. J. N. (2013) Factors Affecting the Acceptance of People with Disabilities at Work: A Literature Review, *Journal of Occupational Rehabilitation*, 23(4): 463–475.
Waterhouse, P., Kimberley, H., Jonas, P., Glover, J. & National Centre for Vocational Education (2010) *What Would It Take? Employer Perspectives on Employing People with a Disability. A National Vocational Education and Training Research and Evaluation Program Report*, National Centre for Vocational Education Research (NCVER), Adelaide, Australia.
Wehman, P. (2012) Supported Employment: What Is It?, *Journal of Vocational Rehabilitation*, 37(3): 139–142.
Wulf-Andersen, T., Olsen, T. & Follesø, R. (2016) *Unge, udenforskap og social forandring Nordiske perspektiver [Youth, Exclusion and Social Change]*, Frederiksberg, Denmark: Frydenlund Academic.

Part IV

Nordic approaches to New Public Management

Professions in transition

Introduction

Annette Kamp, Agnete Meldgaard Hansen and Christin Thea Wathne

This section focuses on working life in the public sector and tells the story of the dramatic transformations that have taken place since the early 1980s.

The public sector in Norway and Denmark comprises a relatively large part of the total labour market. In both countries, around 30% of the labour force work in the public sector. Concomitant with the spread of neoliberal ideas, this sector has been subject to wide-reaching reforms inspired by New Public Management (NPM). As in most other Western countries, reforms have aimed at rationalization, marketization and retrenchment of the public sector. However, in the Nordic countries this development has been shaped in particular ways, influenced by the participation of organized labour, resulting in what we call a negotiated modernization of the public sector. The public sector has been and still is the most unionized sector in both Norway and Denmark.

Public sector workers in frontline jobs make up an important and large part of this sector in both numbers and salary expenses. Furthermore, they are also the groups most affected by NPM-inspired developments. These groups have experienced dramatic changes in the course of the prolonged modernization of the public sector; changes that aim at transforming their work and identities profoundly. NPM reforms focusing on marketization and standardization of public services have been criticized for leading to a loss of autonomy and discretion, and a higher workload and work intensification for public sector workers. In this respect, the Nordic countries resemble most other Western countries subject to NPM reforms. However, as part of this negotiated modernization, many public sector frontline workers have simultaneously acquired higher levels of formal education and have become what in the Nordic context are termed 'welfare professionals' (see elaboration of this concept in the following chapters). This development reflects the influence of trade union strategies of professionalization and strengthening of the professional status of groups in frontline jobs. In consequence, when addressing NPM and implications for working life in a Nordic context, processes of de-professionalization and professionalization are both involved.

Education, health and social care are major areas where welfare professions have been established and consolidated. However, the complex dynamics of negotiated modernization are also seen in e.g. the field of law enforcement. Teachers, kindergarten teachers, health care assistants, nurses, elderly care workers, social workers and police officers are thus among the large groups of public sector frontline workers for whom this project of professionalization plays an important role and whose working lives are at the same time profoundly transformed by NPM and later governance reforms. Welfare professionals are thus deeply entangled in the transformation of the welfare state, its goals and development. Firstly, they are part of the transformation, as their professional training and socialization form an integral part of current welfare state governance programmes, and, secondly, as well-organized, highly unionized actors, they pursue professional, ethical and political trajectories for the development of the welfare state. The three chapters in this section shed light on the complexities of this development from three different but complementary angles.

Chapter 11: Nordic New Public Management: the case of Denmark. By Annette Kamp and Agnete Meldgaard Hansen.

Each Nordic country has its own distinct 'reform profile', despite many similarities between them in the implementation of NPM. This chapter illuminates how NPM ideas entered the Danish welfare state through several waves of modernization and how they have influenced working life for welfare professionals. NPM reforms were, on the one hand, shaped in particular ways in Denmark, reflecting the influence of the Nordic approach. On the other hand, the Nordic approach, particularly industrial relations and the way they are played out at company level, was conversely also impacted by the introduction of NPM. Features like standardization, fragmentation and consumerism have affected working conditions; they have considerably changed meaning and identity at work and also opportunities for co-determination and consultation. However, these processes of creation and consolidation of groups of welfare professionals have simultaneously formed the basis of both local and national resistance, negotiation and translation of NPM reforms in relation to professional logics and ethics. The chapter concludes by considering the newer neoliberal trends, often dubbed New Public Governance (NPG), that have had a great impact on the public sector since the early 2000s. Under mantras such as co-production, citizen-centred services/care and empowerment of users, clients or patients, these reforms aim at reconfiguring the public sector in ways that support a redistribution of tasks and responsibilities between professionals and users. Currently we thus observe new challenges in welfare professionals' working lives that may imply new stress factors, but also new possibilities for boosting professionalism and meaningful work.

Chapter 12: Welfare professionals in transformation: the case of elderly care. By Agnete Meldgaard Hansen and Annette Kamp.

Elderly care is one of the largest and most costly areas of the Danish public sector and is the field where NPM has been most systematically implemented. The chapter illuminates how both shifts in the view of elderly people and their needs towards discourses of self-sufficiency and active ageing, as well as NPM and later NPG-inspired reforms play an important role in transforming working life. These shifts and reforms have influenced the development of core tasks, autonomy, care relations and professional identity in elderly care work profoundly. On the one hand, this development can be described as a movement away from holistic care ideals towards a narrower focus on provision of marketized, standardized care services, and towards reduced autonomy and discretion in work. On the other hand, Danish elderly care workers have also experienced a strengthening of professional and workplace communities, which supports collective action and care workers' exercise of responsible autonomy in everyday care interactions. Recent developments in the sector focusing on active ageing, rehabilitation and user involvement introduce new core tasks and represent new possibilities to develop the exercise of autonomy and professionalism in the sector.

Chapter 13: Welfare professionals in transformation: the case of police officers in Norway. By Christin Thea Wathne.

Similarly to Chapter 12 on elderly care, this chapter shows how the working lives of police officers have been transformed under the influence of both NPM-inspired reforms and broad shifts in the view of their core tasks and role in society. The chapter illuminates how institutional logics of police work in Norway are under transformation, moving from a humanist tradition focused on help and prevention of crime (community policing), towards a more militarist tradition focused on control and elimination of threats. This militarist tradition has proved to resonate well with NPM reforms, and in this complex dynamic, police work is transformed. Norwegian police officers have thus experienced an increased focus on efficiency and resource use, changes in the character of their interaction with the public, and centralization and increased distance to the public. Further changes include outsourcing of 'softer' police tasks to private security firms, stronger control and prioritization of tasks, standardization of frontline work and a shift in the professional knowledge base towards measurability and evidence-based approaches. As a result, the core tasks of the police have narrowed, and the space for professional autonomy and discretion has been reduced with the movement away from community policing based on situational assessments and professional discretion.

These latter two chapters make clear that NPM is not the only central influence on the working lives of welfare professionals. Both police officers and elderly care workers are affected by broader societal shifts in understandings of the object and focus of their work. We see changes in the understandings of crime and proper law enforcement, and of ageing and good care for elderly people. Attention to such shifts in broader societal discourses, and their entanglement with NPM and other governance reforms, is crucial when seeking to understand the transformation of welfare professionals' working lives.

Furthermore, the NPM hallmark of marketization has been influential for both welfare professions, and the dissemination of a logic of numbers and resource containment has had a considerable effect on working conditions. However, there are significant differences in both the timing and effects of these developments for the two professions. Where frontline elderly care work has been subject to extensive and pervasive standardization of tasks and work processes since the 1990s, frontline police work has only recently appeared to be moving in this direction. So far they seem to have maintained higher levels of professional autonomy and discretion in the execution of their daily tasks. Regarding outsourcing of tasks, police officers have experienced a loss of 'softer' tasks to private providers, underlining their movement towards a more controlling role and lowering the frequency of interaction with the public. In elderly care, mainly practical tasks have been outsourced to private providers, and public sector elderly care workers have largely retained the social and health care tasks that are most central to their professional identity and role perception. Attention to the timing, extent and character of marketization and standardization efforts thus appears crucial when assessing the effects of NPM on the working lives and identities of welfare professionals.

Moreover, both groups have experienced a transformation of their relationship with clients and the public. In both cases, we find a paradox with an emphasis on increased client/citizen-centredness in services, while professionals are also supposed to withdraw and have less contact with clients/the public. However, the character of this withdrawal from clients/the public differs and has different roots. Where elderly care workers are to withdraw from the lives of elderly clients to facilitate the clients' empowerment and increased self-sufficiency, the distancing of police work from the public seems to be more the result of an increasingly centralized organization of work and the shift from community policing towards a more militarist model. The paradox of simultaneous citizen-centredness and professional withdrawal may thus have quite different expressions in practice.

Against this background, the following three chapters may be read as attempts to open a window into the complex dynamics and transformations of working life and professionalism taking place in the Nordic welfare states in the wake of decades of NPM reforms.

Chapter 11

Nordic New Public Management

The case of Denmark

Annette Kamp and Agnete Meldgaard Hansen

Introduction

The establishment of universal welfare states is often seen as one of the most outstanding features of the Nordic societies. The existence of large and highly developed welfare states plays a key role in sustaining other important Nordic labour market characteristics such as gender equality and flexicurity. A large care sector providing care for children, the elderly and others in need has paved the way for a very high degree of labour market participation for both women and men. In the same vein, the security part of the flexicurity model implies the work of a large body of institutions and professional social workers. In this chapter, we focus our attention on the welfare state as a large employment sector with specific characteristics and implications for employees' working life.

We focus on the Danish public sector and the transformations of work and working conditions occasioned by the diverse NPM-inspired reforms introduced since the early 1980s. The reforms seen in the Danish public sector are in many cases similar to developments seen in the other Nordic countries, although variations and differences of course also appear (see e.g. Foss Hansen, 2011 for a comparative analysis). The insights presented can thus to a great extent be considered relevant to the other Nordic countries, but national variations and their specific implications for working life in the public sector are important to take into account.

Infused with neo-classical economic ideas of marketization, NPM (Hood, 1991) paved the way for new forms of management and governance in both the private and public sector, eventually spreading to most of the Western world. In Denmark, such NPM reforms have been discussed under the heading of 'public sector modernization' since 1983 (Danish Ministry of Finance, 1983). This chapter illuminates how these ideas entered the Danish welfare state through several waves of modernization, and how they have influenced working life in this sector.

Importantly, NPM reforms have been shaped in particular ways in the Danish context, reflecting the influence of the Nordic labour market model and the labour market parties. While NPM is often associated with trends towards de-professionalization (Dybbroe, 2008; Dalsgaard, 2013) and a challenge to public sector industrial relations (Pedersen, 1998), the Danish development has been characterized as a 'negotiated modernization' (Pedersen, 1998; Hjort, 2001). This negotiated modernization has not resulted in a dismantling of industrial relations, and public sector employees are still highly unionized. Furthermore, contrary to expectations of de-professionalization, it has actually promoted the rise and consolidation of a number of new 'welfare professions', meaning increasingly professionalized frontline workers in different areas of the welfare state (see later for a further explanation of the use of this concept in the Danish context). This is not to say that NPM reforms have not made their mark on public sector workplaces. Features like standardization, fragmentation and consumerism have considerably affected and changed the working conditions and working lives of public sector employees, and also opportunities for co-determination and consultation, which are important features of the Nordic model, as described in Part I of this volume. We argue that NPM reforms have indeed had consequences for working life in the public sector, but that these consequences are shaped by the particular Danish/Nordic context.

This chapter is thus based on the understanding that the Danish welfare state, and the welfare professionals working within it, mutually shape each other. In the course of continuous public sector reforms, these welfare professionals have experienced dramatic changes aiming to transform their work and identities profoundly. However, they are also deeply involved in the transformation of the welfare state, its goals and development. Firstly, they are part of the transformation, as their professional expertise, training and socialization form an integral part of welfare state governance (Johnson, 1995). Secondly, as well-organized and highly unionized actors, they pursue specific professional, ethical and political trajectories for the development of the welfare state.

Against this background, this chapter explores the following research question: How has NPM been adopted in the Danish public sector, and what have been the main impacts on the working life of welfare professionals?

Drawing on existing research, we will show how the period of NPM reforms since the early 1980s have, on the one hand, challenged and transformed working life in the public sector in terms of numerous standardization initiatives, introduced as a means of increasing managerial control over work performance, productivity, output and results. On the other hand, we will also describe instances of self-management, resistance and active individual and collective attempts by public sector professionals to shape their work in meaningful ways. These discussions revolve around the key themes of standardization, marketization, autonomy and trust.

The chapter is organized as follows. We first give an overview of the Danish public sector as a labour market. Then we describe how NPM developed in the Danish context and discuss the associated changes in the governance, management and organization of the welfare state. Thereafter, we present key research insights on how the reforms have impacted working life for groups of welfare professionals, and how these groups have collectively and individually resisted and negotiated them. We end the chapter with a concluding discussion.

The public sector as a labour market in Denmark

As a background to our further discussions, this section provides a brief overview of the Danish public sector as a labour market. At the end of 2017, 824,923 people were employed in the Danish public sector, compared to 1,837,755 in the private sector (Statistics Denmark, 2018b). Public sector workers thus comprise approximately 30% of the workforce; most of these (about 58%) are employed by one of Denmark's 98 local authorities, mainly in education and in health, social and care services. Most local authority employees hold so-called 'professional bachelor's degrees' (e.g. teachers, kindergarten teachers, nurses and social workers) or have a vocational education (e.g. in clerical or social and health-care work) (Local Government Denmark, 2016). However, the number of employees with a five-year academic degree has risen notably since 2010 (Christensen et al., 2017). The five Danish regions employ around 17% of public sector workers, mainly in hospitals and other secondary health-care services. About 24% are employed by the state e.g. in public administration and higher education (Statistics Denmark, 2018a).

The Danish labour market is highly gender-segregated, implying an uneven distribution of men and women in many sectors and occupations. About 70% of public sector workers are women, compared to 38% of private sector employees (Statistics Denmark, 2016). Public sector workers in Denmark are among the most well-organized in the world, with 80% of workers organized in trade unions and a 100% collective bargaining coverage (Høgedahl, 2017).

Like many other welfare states, the Danish welfare state went through a period of expansion from the 1950s onwards. However, since the 1980s there has been continuous political attention to limiting public sector growth and thereby also the number of public sector employees. A recent analysis shows that the number of public sector employees did in fact rise from the 1980s to around 2010 but has been stagnant since then. Furthermore, the number of public sector employees per citizen has decreased by 6.5% since 2010 and is now at its lowest since 1986 (Andersen, 2018).

Negotiated modernization: a soft Nordic variant of NPM

This chapter will show how NPM is translated in a Danish context, leading to what is often called a soft variant of NPM, in opposition to the hard variants that we see in e.g. the UK and New Zealand (Hjort, 2001; Dahl & Rasmussen, 2012). This section thus addresses the first part of our research question regarding the particular adoption of NPM in the Danish public sector.

Although market-based management of the public sector has been discussed in Denmark since the early 1980s, there has not been a straightforward development or a form of 'master plan' (Bovbjerg, 2011). Rather, it has been a question of taking over an international agenda in the form of a neoliberal vision of a transition from previous public and state governance towards a more market-based and competition-oriented governance model. This means that although the reform initiatives have been externally presented as comprehensive reform programmes, they appear to be more of a loose collection of reform ideas (Christensen & Laegreid, 2007).

The labour market parties and NPM

As indicated in the introduction to this chapter, NPM in Denmark has been characterized as a negotiated modernization. One element of this is that, in accordance with Danish labour market traditions, public sector unions have sought and obtained influence on the development and implementation of public sector reforms. This feature of Danish modernization efforts contradicts common assumptions that NPM reforms would almost automatically lead to an erosion of industrial relations and collective bargaining traditions in the public sector (Pedersen, 1998). According to Hjort, the public sector collective bargaining system at both central and local levels has:

> [s]lowly become geared to playing a crucial role in the continued modernization. Coupled with an ever stronger decentralization of the collective bargaining system, the parties have been obliged not only to increase flexibility in wage determination but also to pursue 'qualitative development goals': efficiency and reorganization, competence and quality development, staff training and organizational changes.
>
> (Hjort, 2001, p. 36)

In line with this, the NPM reforms in Denmark have been met with a professionalization strategy from many unions in the social, educational and health sectors. Many of the occupations involved are not professions in a traditional understanding of the concept, which assumes a long education and a monopoly in a well-defined area of practice (see e.g. Abbott, 2001), but the workers involved are what the Danes call 'welfare professionals'. The concept of 'welfare professionals' in Denmark covers the large groups of professionals, with varying educational levels, who work in frontline welfare state services, implying that their work involves interactions with users (clients, patients, pupils, citizens, consumers) in e.g. education, social and health care, social work, prisons, police work and others (Hjort, 2004; Järvinen & Mik-Meyer, 2012).

The professionalization strategies of these groups in relation to public sector reforms can be seen as attempts to expand their knowledge base and legitimacy in a period of change. For example, in the 1980s in the social and health sector, where many workers had few or no formal qualifications, one- and three-year courses were established. Workers in this field now gained formal qualifications in elementary nursing and gerontology, and could, if they wished, build on these qualifications to study for a full nursing degree (Dahl, 2000, 2005). The level of education for this type of work is comparably high, as most other European countries require no or very little vocational training to work in the sector (Genet et al., 2012).

Furthermore, the trade unions have entered into agreements on systematic and strategic competence development with the aim of ensuring flexibility through the softening of professional boundaries and creation of new job profiles, in return for more professional and personal development by employees (Hjort, 2004). Employees thus have access to continuing education, which is influenced by local management and trade union representatives.

The expanded knowledge base and increasingly formalized education of these groups brings them closer to the image of traditional professions. However, these developments have not resulted in actual monopolies of practice. Some groups (e.g. social and health-care assistants and nurses) obtain certifications and authorizations that secure their right to monopolize the practice of certain tasks. But generally, hiring policies and priorities, and divisions of labour between professional groups, are negotiated locally, and this can be a bone of contention between local management and employees as well as between professional groups. For example, professional social workers increasingly compete with non-social workers for jobs in social services (Fagbladet 3F, 2016), and the roles and divisions of labour between teachers and social educators in primary schools have since a 2013 school reform been the subject of extensive discussion and struggle (Kampmann, 2014).

The Danish version of negotiated modernization is therefore a modernization that involves local adaptations, where the labour market parties have sought and gained influence, especially in relation to the education and competence development of their members. The development-oriented version of human resource management (HRM) that is typical of the management aspect of NPM (see later) must therefore also be seen as a result of this dialogue and negotiation, which have continued from the 1980s until today.

Phases in the shaping of NPM

The development of NPM in Denmark started in the 1980s with marketization as its catchword (Greve & Ejersbo, 2014). It was based on criticism of the public sector of the 1960s, which was a hierarchical and bureaucratic system with direct top-down control (Bovbjerg, 2011).

The early NPM reforms (starting with the 1983 programme for public sector modernization) were motivated by an increasing demand for control of public budgets. Target and performance management was introduced; here, managers were to focus on policy goals and budgets, leaving implementation to administrative bodies (Bovbjerg, 2011; Greve & Ejersbo, 2014).

Furthermore, 'free' agencies were established in the ministries to create independence between politicians and those involved in implementation. This thinking was supported by the use of an increasing number of contracts as management tools, both interdepartmental contracts and individual performance contracts for public sector managers (Greve & Ejersbo, 2005). The contract approach also reflected a political ambition to 'rein in' the professions as groups which, based on their own interests, were thought to create public sector growth, and a comprehensive standardization process was thus introduced to enable this form of governance.

Later on in the development of NPM (from around 2001), market thinking was expanded to include users of public services by providing them with 'free choice' through 'quasi-market mechanisms', i.e. the establishment of market-like relationships between different institutions. Large sections of the public sector were transformed into state-owned companies that competed for public favour in the established 'free choice' market, based on the idea that users as customers should be able to choose between different institutions and use the one whose service suited their needs (Christensen & Laegreid, 2016).

At the same time, the free choice approach also implied the idea that competition between institutions would promote quality (Ahrenkiel et al., 2013). For example, a free choice arrangement in elderly care and the introduction of accrual accounting in 2007 have enabled calculation of all the costs of a particular public service in this area, in order to establish competition between public and private service producers (Bovbjerg, 2011; Kamp & Ryberg, 2016). This public facilitation of a private market for services represents a significant step away from the traditional Nordic welfare state model, where the state is the supplier of universal welfare services. Another example of this development is the establishment of autonomous and outcome-funded institutions, where financing is increasingly determined by their (measurable) performance in terms of e.g. the number of examinations or operations (Greve, 2008). The basic thinking has been to promote productivity through the establishment of a financial incentive structure.

The 2000s also heralded a development that focused on actual privatization of parts of the public sector by outsourcing welfare services to private companies. During this period, more extensive debate and criticism of NPM also gained momentum. The focus of the debate has been on the re-bureaucratization, fragmentation and standardization involved in the reforms (see e.g. Melander, 2008). A new 'Taylorization' of work, referring to the dull and meaningless work of Taylorism, has become a focal point of both academic and political discussions. We will return to these discussions later when we consider the implications of the NPM reforms for work in the public sector.

NPM and human resources

Alongside these new forms of governance, new forms of management, referred to as HRM, have also been introduced from the 'market'. This orientation towards particular forms of management must be understood as an integral part of NPM (Hood, 1991), but deserves a separate mention, partly because such ideas of leadership are formulated in distinctive ways in the Nordic context.

The message in these management approaches is that employees should be motivated by other than merely financial incentives. Where the market-oriented model requires the establishment of clear incentive structures with relatively 'tough' systems of reward and punishment, HRM theory operates with a wider range of instruments aiming to motivate employees with 'softer' forms of management such as support for *employees' involvement, responsibility development potential.* This is seen, for example, in value-based management, appreciative management and in work to create collaborative cultures. Culture and values, rather than rules and control, are the management tools. Training and development projects, including experiments with team-based working methods, also play an important role (Legge, 2005).

This focus on human resources may be seen as a contrast and reaction to the previous bureaucratic emphasis on rules and hierarchical control. In the Danish context, a soft, development-oriented HRM approach (Legge, 2005) has been practised. Where a tough human capital-oriented HRM in liberal economies such as the UK's has aimed to weaken trade unions and industrial relations-oriented organization (Godard & Delaney, 2000), in Denmark we see an approach grounded in industrial relations (Mathiesen & Hvenegaard, 1999; Navrbjerg, 1999).

However, it must be mentioned that although this management approach focuses on 'soft' forms of governance through employee involvement, it also breaks with the idea that the professions have a monopoly on deciding what is good treatment, service, education, etc. Professionals' independent judgement, based on their common set of knowledge, norms and values, has formed the very basis for managing complex issues in the public sector (Hjort, 2004). With new forms of management and a focus on leadership, we find that knowledge, norms and values are defined to a greater extent from above, which can put pressure on meaning, professionalism and identity at work. Finally, the increasing focus on leadership must be seen in connection with an interest in strategic management. This may mean that aspects of planning, assessment and evaluation are transferred upwards to those responsible for strategic management.

New neoliberal initiatives since the late 2000s

In the wake of the 2008 financial crisis, there have been widespread cuts in the Danish public sector. All public institutions must save 2% per annum. The education sector was initially excluded, but the requirement for cuts has applied to all sectors since 2015. As mentioned earlier, the number of public sector employees per citizen has decreased by 6.5% since 2010 and is now at its lowest level since 1986 (Andersen, 2018).

In the search for efficiency and rationalization, new ideas have gained a foothold. New Public Governance (NPG) is a collective term for these new trends; it involves a focus on creating new forms of collaboration and 'co-production' (Torfing & Triantafillou, 2013). Public–private partnerships are an important element in this development. These are primarily based on understandings of network regulation (Klijn & Koppenjan, 2000; Rhodes, 2007), rather than market-based competition. Another key element is user involvement, which implies that the self-reliant, responsible user is placed in the centre and is encouraged to perform parts of the work traditionally performed by professionals (Vrangbaek, 2015). At the same time, efforts are being directed towards enabling users to take responsibility for aspects of prevention, care and treatment. In this way, we see a redistribution of tasks and responsibilities, and changes in the roles of users and professionals and in the relationship between them (Holen, 2011; Barnes & Cotterell, 2012).

However, we cannot say that the basic NPM-inspired way of organizing and managing the public sector is disappearing. Researchers in public governance view the tendency towards new public governance as overlaying and co-existing with NPM rather than replacing it (Torfing & Triantafillou, 2013).

Limited success with wide-ranging consequences

Greve and Ejersbo (2014) argue that some of the most important results of the marketization ambitions of the NPM reforms have been achieved through privatization. Since 1988, when the first steps were taken to privatize Copenhagen Airport, there have been several privatizations of former state-owned companies, and a number of state-owned limited companies were also formed for subsequent privatization. Telecommunications, postal services, infrastructure and the energy sector are examples of this development. Privatization and marketization in the form of outsourcing in the major areas of welfare service (which is the focus of this chapter), such as the educational, social and health-care sectors, have so far had quite a limited impact. This may be partly due to great efforts by the trade union movement and some political parties to halt this tendency.

In one of the largest areas in economic and personnel terms, elderly care, the success of marketization has been limited, despite intense efforts to create more providers and free choice. From 2004 to 2012, the proportion of seniors using private care providers increased from 1.5% to 6%. Yet for practical aspects of this work, primarily cleaning, the percentage increased from 10% to 47% in the same period (Bertelsen & Rostgaard, 2013). However, repeated bankruptcies among private providers and constant problems in meeting contractual obligations indicate that the marketization and privatization strategy is not without its problems, even in a narrow economic perspective, and often requires unexpected additional work in the public sector as a backup when market solutions fail (see e.g. Ritzau, 2017; FOA, 2018).

In spite of this, efforts towards marketization and the establishment of quasi-markets using contract management in the public sector have led to a pervasive 'counting regime', extensive standardization and a focus on documentation. This form of micro-management from above, in combination with the new HRM-inspired forms of management described earlier, has changed the work of welfare professionals significantly. With this in mind, we now turn to the second part of our research question to consider the impact of NPM reforms on work in the public sector.

Working life and NPM

In this section, we will address the second part of our research question and consider some of the main discussions that have taken place in both research and practice regarding the implications of NPM for the working life of welfare professionals. It is important to note that modernization of the public sector is manifested in quite different ways in different fields (Bovbjerg, 2011). It is therefore difficult, if not impossible, to provide a general picture of the changes involved and their implications for the work of public employees. This section therefore presents important themes of working life research and pertinent studies that exemplify issues related to the themes. The issues are all linked in different ways to the comprehensive standardization and marketization efforts of the NPM reforms.

This presentation focuses on the welfare professions, not on e.g. employees in government administration. We include a number of quantitative and qualitative studies of the work of welfare professionals under NPM. The qualitative studies have been chosen to illustrate key dynamics in developments in working life under NPM in some of the major sectors of welfare work: elderly care, child care, health, education and social work. The quantitative studies provide a more general view of working conditions and working environment as perceived by public employees and members of the trade union federation FTF, which represents most welfare professions in Denmark. Against this background, we attempt to show how modernization has changed and challenged welfare work and become a burden for the professionals involved. We will also describe resistance and active attempts to shape the work both individually and collectively.

How standardization and marketization change and challenge working life

Many of the recent public sector reforms use standardization as their most important tool for controlling productivity, quality and economy (Foss Hansen, 2011). The establishment of entities that 'sell to' and 'buy from' each other requires standardization of services to enable the services exchanged to be counted and priced. This also applies to contract management i.e. central financial management of the entities involved through performance-based contracting and outsourcing of services to private suppliers. Here too, the services must be quantifiable and comparable. Similarly, quality management implies standardization, since its goal is to offer a 'uniform service level' which is determined by the quality standards that local authorities have to prepare on an annual basis.

Elderly care is one of the areas most pervasively subject to NPM-inspired reforms. Elderly care organizations have been criticized for implementing neo-Taylorist forms of work organization in the transition to marketized care. These forms of organization limit care worker autonomy by standardizing both tasks and time (Szebehely, 2006; Liebst and Monrad, 2008). A review of Nordic research (Szebehely, 2005) into elderly care was published in which one of the sections was concerned with employee working conditions (Trydegård, 2005), providing an overview of early Nordic research on the consequences of NPM. It shows that work under NPM is meaningful but also mentally and physically challenging. The pressure on professionals of having insufficient time to do the job in relation to their care orientation is a major problem, and all the more so when the work is based on market-oriented principles. Employees feel inadequate and frustrated because they cannot provide the help needed. This has been shown to be a significant stress factor in this work. Trydegård concludes her review as follows:

> Good quality in care work is a prerequisite for a good working environment and vice versa. This is my most enduring impression after taking part in 10 years of Nordic research on working conditions in elderly care in the Nordic countries.
>
> (Trydegård, 2005, p. 190)

A number of other areas of welfare work have revealed how the contrast between the professional logics and the NPM logic creates tension in the workplace. In social work, the neoliberal approach has meant that social policy has become increasingly subordinate to employment policy. It becomes a tool for bringing people into work, known as a transition from 'welfare to workfare' in the literature, combined with a 'work first' logic. The social work-based and resource-building perspectives that were previously the focus of the social work profession have given way to a unilateral policy of getting clients into (any) work as soon as possible (Torfing, 2004; Villadsen, 2007).

Furthermore, regulatory management and standardization have restricted professionals' scope for social work-based assessments. The move towards the work-first logic and an increasing burden of documentation has pressurized social workers. Researchers such as Caswell and Larsen (2015) have pointed out how the new forms of management and the work-first orientation that have been introduced since the late 2000s have significantly changed social work and led to an increasing sense of de-professionalization among social workers, as their professional autonomy and judgement have become marginalized.

Standardization basically means the creation of uniformity in a particular field. There are *terminological standards* that aim to provide exhaustive language to describe a field; such language creates a universe that allows for comparison and coordination across entities and institutions, but it also implies that certain aspects of work are described and evaluated, while other aspects are unquantifiable and ignored, and therefore disappear out of sight and consciousness (Timmermans & Epstein, 2010). When something is systematically monitored, something else is systematically overlooked.

This phenomenon whereby some aspects of professional work become visible and others invisible can be observed in day care for young children. Here NPM has manifested itself in new requirements for pedagogical professionalism in terms of children's learning and formulating precise goals and plans for activities. What we see is thus not standardization of the execution of the work, but a predominance of certain methods and a particular terminology. Several Danish qualitative studies have analysed the implications of the new requirements for professionalism in the wake of NPM. Ahrenkiel et al. (2013), using studies of the early childhood education sector as their basis, point out how new forms of governance, combined with an increased focus on learning rather than care, have an effect on the content and meaningfulness of the work and on professional identity. One of the main points of their review is that an increased focus on control, documentation and evaluation, and increasing expectations from the public (parents), have negative consequences for important aspects of professionalism because professionalism in this sector is characterized by what Ahrenkiel et al. call 'unnoticed professionalism'. This kind of professionalism is practical and largely based on routines and 'obvious' tasks. The result is greater time pressure, because professionals find that there must still be time for the 'unnoticed' work.

NPM in the health sector, in terms of standardization of knowledge and performance measurements, has had a substantial impact. Together with a greater focus on quality management, it has generally supported the increased medicalization of the field. Health-care professions themselves contribute to this, as the establishment of professional standards forms part of the continuous development of their professional knowledge base (Timmermans & Berg, 2003). This has important consequences for welfare professions such as nursing, where the knowledge base is heterogeneous, containing both humanistic and medical elements (Allen, 2014). Many studies have focused on the work and professional identity of nurses. For example, Ernst (2016), in an ethnographic study of work in a Danish emergency ward, shows how it is informed by two contradictory approaches to nursing: a humanistic and pluralist approach and an evidence-based medical approach. However, she also points out how the evidence-based approach wins the battle with the care approach. She emphasizes how evidence-based work creates new career opportunities and is embraced by some nurses with enthusiasm; while for other nurses, the new situation creates tension and stress.

In the same vein, a recent study (Kamp & Dybbroe, 2016) illustrates how the burden of documentation takes more and more time away from work with patients, resulting in time pressure and work intensification. For several years, psychiatric care has been subject to considerable rationalization, based on performance measurements and standardization of methods in the form of standardized treatment packages. Kamp and Dybbroe (2016), in their ethnographic study of diagnosis and treatment in an outpatient department, show how this development supports the medicalization of the field. Professionals with a humanistic orientation, such as nurses, teachers, psychologists and social workers, find their professional identity under pressure and interprofessional cooperation is threatened with fragmentation (Kamp & Dybbroe, 2016).

As mentioned in our previous section, standardization does not stand alone as a means of governance. Rather, standardization co-exists with strategic management based on principles of soft HRM, like trust, motivation and responsibilization. This phenomenon has until now received very little attention in Danish research. A few case studies in elderly care could however add some important points. Kamp and Ryberg (2016) point out how strategic management has acquired a prominent status in debates on the future of elderly care. A quote from a debate report written in cooperation between the labour market parties Local Government Denmark and FOA may illustrate this:

> Leaders should be able to manage trustful and inclusive processes, to promote employees' well-being and feeling of involvement and responsibility. At the same time, we need leaders who can manage change and create meaning, motivation and security in everyday working life, where change and new demands are the norm.
>
> (Local Government Denmark & FOA, 2012, p. 3)

Kamp and Ryberg show how this increased emphasis on management may imply that professionals must negotiate different rationales of governance e.g. when increased control and documentation practices co-exist with employee involvement processes. This may widen the scope for autonomy but often in contradictory ways. A study (Rasmussen, 2012) on middle managers in elderly care underlines how these contradictory management rationales also impact this group. She illustrates how middle managers may follow different strategies in order to meet contradictory demands, but also how they often experience stressful working conditions.

A representative survey among Danish employees, the APL-III survey from 2015 (Caraker et al., 2015), suggests that the experiences described here cannot be seen as isolated cases confined to individual qualitative studies or particular fields of work. The survey reveals that 75% of public sector employees find that more documentation requirements have been introduced into their work and that 79% experience an increased workload without any increase in the number of staff in their workplace. Some 57% of FTF members state that their work causes mental stress and that they often have to work under severe time pressure. In addition, 60% of public employees want more influence on the organization of their daily work. A 2018 study of the working environment as reported by over 9,000 FTF members similarly concluded: 'FTF members have a heavy workload. 36% have a heavy or very heavy workload, and 22% have a high & very high pace of work. This is significantly higher than among wage earners in general' (Anker & Grundtvig, 2018, p. 9). Furthermore, 22% of FTF members reported being always or often stressed, and only 49% (as compared to 63% of wage earners in general) found that their opportunity to deliver quality in work was high or very high (Anker & Grundtvig, 2018).

These studies and examples from different kinds of welfare work point to a number of challenges for welfare professions related to the increased standardization and market orientation of their work. With the NPM reforms, new management logics, expressed differently in different areas, gain a foothold in the work and often put pressure on welfare professionals' care orientation, ethics and professional logics. In addition, the research indicates widespread experiences of work stress and intensification, greater time pressure, increased documentation and control, decreased autonomy, and invisibility and devaluation of certain aspects of professional work.

Resistance, trust and responsible autonomy

The problems raised by the studies discussed here clearly demonstrate trends seen not only in the Nordic countries but also internationally. However, we would argue that the distinctive Danish tendency to professionalize welfare work has also played and still plays a part. Many of the above-mentioned welfare professions have, as previously described, in parallel and partly in interaction with NPM, been subject to a professionalization trend. This implies that these groups subscribe to certain common professional ideals and ethics, and act collectively in debates and struggles concerning developments in the public sector. Further, many studies point out how professionals actively attempt to maintain professional ideals in the public sector, and despite marketization, fragmentation and cuts, make an effort to create a coherent and well-functioning sector.

One example of welfare professionals' collective resistance to the consequences of NPM is the series of strikes that arose in the context of public sector collective bargaining in 2008. Large numbers of employees in care, health and education went on strike. Important slogans for the unions were 'time for care' and 'more warm hands', which referred to the fact that documentation took time and attention from meaningful work in contact with patients, clients and citizens. Several researchers have pointed out how these strikes were not only oriented towards the ongoing wage negotiations but were also part of a greater social struggle for the quality of the work of these professions and for recognition of their work and professional skills over and above the NPM reforms (Dahl, 2010; Gleerup, 2010). Dahl (2010), in a study in the health and social care sector, points out that welfare professionals' experience of standardization and devaluation of their work under NPM is particularly frustrating and taken as a clear lack of respect, because the government at the same time was supporting professionalization of the field (cf. negotiated modernization). In Dahl's words, the state is Janus-faced in simultaneously supporting the professionalization and de-professionalization of work.

When the Danish government later implemented the so-called 'trust reform' (Danish Government et al., 2013), it was also a reaction to the many protests that, then and later, arose from professionals and unions due to the difficulty of using their professional skills and judgement, and the sense of distrust and bureaucracy created by this regime. Former experts on ministerial governance also warned about the new proliferation of bureaucracy that took time away from actual work with clients (Gjørup & Hjortdal, 2007). The trust reform followed the Nordic labour market model in being based on a tripartite agreement between the (then centre-left) government and public employers and employees. It had the official title: 'Principles for Collaboration on Modernization between the Parties in the Public Sector'. The text of the agreement emphasized concepts such as dialogue, openness, meaningful work and professional scope for action, and stated: 'Leadership and governance should be based on trust and responsibility' (Danish Government et al., 2013), thus meeting much of the criticism that welfare professionals and their organizations had raised over the years. At the same time, however, key NPM principles regarding goal and performance management and documentation were also maintained, and the agreement was accompanied by a goal to improve efficiency in the public sector by 2020 and cut costs by EUR1.6 billion (DKK12 billion) (Møller, 2013). The trust reform has subsequently had little influence, except in some local and regional projects (see e.g. Middelboe, 2016), and the right-wing government that came to power in 2015 has not picked up the threads. Recent research has also shown that the changes resulting from NPM are quite stable (Torfing & Triantafillou, 2013; Greve & Ejersbo, 2014). Thus, the trust reform does not appear to have fundamentally addressed the criticism of the consequences of NPM for the work of welfare professionals.

The critiques of working conditions in the public sector have also led to action in the field of working environment interventions. The psychosocial working environment in the public sector has become an object of concern and joint action among the labour market parties. For example, in 2007 a tripartite agreement between the government, local authorities and the central trade union federations instituted obligatory job satisfaction measurements every third year in all public sector workplaces (Danish Government et al., 2007). Furthermore, collective agreements in the public sector have in recent years included funding of different forms of expert support for cooperative projects between employers and employees in local workplaces to improve the psychosocial working environment (see e.g. Local Government Denmark and The Danish Association of Local Government Employees Organisations, 2015).

One thing is nationwide resistance and collective interventions from welfare professionals and their organizations, but quite another is welfare professionals' active attempts to transform and translate governance measures into professionally meaningful practice in everyday work. A key example of such processes of local transformation can be found in the education sector. There have been a variety of primary school reforms. Standardized tests and standardized plans for pupils were among the NPM-inspired measures introduced into Danish schools in the 2000s. Studies of how such requirements have been transformed into practice by teachers (Limborg et al., 2012) show how the pupil plans to a very great extent have been translated and adapted to enable them to be seen as a useful and constructive tool to support teaching.

Numerous studies of elderly care also demonstrate the breadth of this phenomenon. Firstly, the everyday practice of home care work is regularly reorganized to enable adaptation of care to the changing needs of individual clients and to reach the large number of clients. Everyday practice differs significantly from the highly scheduled, standardized services that form the basis for the work plan (Kamp et al., 2013). Tufte (2013) also shows how time is subject to negotiation and reorganization. She demonstrates how professionals expand and redistribute their time to allow for the necessary quality time in the many everyday situations to be dealt with. As mentioned earlier, standardization implies that certain aspects of work become invisible or even illegitimate. This is very clearly seen in the standardization of home care. However, several studies (Kamp, 2012; Kirchhoff and Karlsson, 2013) show that what the latter authors call 'secret services' are provided. Social aspects of the work that are no longer considered as part of home care are nevertheless performed, and these help to maintain the social relationships that are necessary in everyday care work.

A further example of welfare professionals' active adaptation of NPM-inspired requirements in their everyday work can be found in nursing. Despite many years of attempts to increase coordination between public institutions, the NPM reforms have led to an extensive fragmentation of the public sector (Greve & Ejersbo, 2014), which welfare professionals must attempt to deal with in order to perform meaningful work. In a recent study of community nurses' use of a telemedicine system for wound treatment, Kamp and Hansen (2019) show how, contrary to the cost-saving intention of the system, nurses use it to enhance treatment quality by gaining increased access for their patients to specialized health care and resources elsewhere in the health-care system. Similarly, they innovatively use the system to ensure better coordination and progress for their patients, which Allen (2014) calls 'trajectory mobilization', thus linking different parts of the health-care system and compensating for the fragmentation.

In light of this, we can refer to a form of responsible autonomy, an expression with a long history in working life studies and the Nordic socio-technical tradition (Trist & Bamforth, 1951; Friedman, 1977; Hvid, 2014). This is a kind of autonomy that welfare professionals adopt to help them perform their work in a meaningful way in practice. In this way, they can, at least to some extent, maintain a sense of professional pride. As new institutionalism-inspired studies show, in many areas involving different and competing logics we find that professionals translate and edit these logics to fit specific contexts in everyday practice (Blomgren & Waks, 2015). However, many of the above-mentioned studies of welfare professionals' work indicate that this is not without repercussions; it often involves significant emotional work and can also lead to what may be called 'moral stress' i.e. stress due to limited possibilities to perform work perceived as professional and ethical (Sørensen, 2015).

Concluding discussion

In this chapter, we have shown how NPM has been adopted in the Danish public sector and the main impacts it has on working life for welfare professionals. The Danish case can be considered similar to the other Nordic countries, but attention must of course be given to national variations in reform history and adaptation when considering the consequences of NPM for working life in the public sector.

Drawing on existing research, we have shown how NPM reforms in Denmark have taken shape as a negotiated modernization of the public sector in which welfare professions and their organizations have played an active role. The public sector collective bargaining system has undergone changes, including becoming more decentralized and allowing for more flexibility in wage determination. But industrial relations and collective bargaining traditions have not been eroded with NPM as expected by some scholars (Pedersen, 1998). Furthermore, many unions in the health, social and educational sectors have pursued professionalization strategies in relation to NPM reforms, emphasizing education and competence development of their members in correspondence with the HRM dimension of NPM.

The Nordic tradition of social dialogue and negotiation with the labour market parties has thus had an influence on the adaptation of NPM reforms in Denmark. However, this does not mean that NPM reforms have not had significant impacts on the working lives of welfare professionals. Standardization and marketization efforts have transformed their work and put pressure on welfare professionals' care orientations, ethics and professional logics. In relation to this, the cited research shows widespread experiences of work stress and intensification, greater time pressure, increased documentation and control, decreased autonomy, and invisibility and devaluation of certain aspects of professional work. Similar experiences are reported in the international literature on the working life of welfare professionals under NPM, though of course with different national and context-specific characteristics (see e.g. Cooke, 2006; Evetts, 2009; Leicht et al., 2009; Gale, 2012; Bolton & Wibberley, 2014; Cohen et al., 2018). These international similarities in impacts on working life indicate that the Nordic model does not represent an unchallenged safeguard against neoliberal governance and management trends, and their consequences for working life in the public sector.

However, the professionalization of welfare work is an important trait of developments in Denmark that are not seen to the same extent in many other Western countries influenced by NPM. We have argued that this professionalization plays a role in shaping the impacts of NPM on working life, as the public sector is consequently populated by well-organized groups of workers who subscribe to certain common professional ideals, ethics and logics. Welfare professionals work to adapt and translate NPM reform initiatives in accordance with these in their daily work, and despite marketization, fragmentation and cuts, make an effort to create a coherent and well-functioning sector. Furthermore, they intervene collectively in debates and struggles concerning the development of public sector work. Public criticism, protests and industrial action by welfare professionals have thus started protracted and widespread debates on the quality of services and work and the working environment in the sector, and on recognition and trust of welfare professionals. While these debates have resulted in some initiatives to improve the psychosocial work environment in public sector workplaces, they have so far not materialized in significant changes or actual breaks with NPM principles of governance in the public sector.

As was briefly touched upon earlier, the NPG trend that currently co-exists with NPM principles of governance presents new and interesting changes to the work of welfare professionals. The increasing prevalence of the concepts of user involvement and empowerment challenges traditional roles and relationships between welfare professionals and clients. Only a few studies of the implications of this trend for professionals' working lives have so far been conducted (Järvinen, 2012; Matthiessen and Rostgaard, 2016; Hansen and Kamp, 2018; Kamp and Holen, 2018). These studies point towards new challenges related to the emotional labour of welfare work and to how NPG trends may be perceived as both a challenge and a boost for professionalism and the experience of meaning in work (see also Chapter 12 in this volume). These and other new governance trends call for further research on the development of working life for welfare professionals in the Nordic countries.

References

Abbott, A. (2001) Sociology of Professions, In: *International Encyclopedia of the Social & Behavioral Sciences*, Oxford, UK: Pergamon, 12166–12169.

Ahrenkiel, A., Schmidt, C., Nielsen, B. S., Sommer, F. & Warring, N. (2013) Unnoticed Professional Competence in Day Care Work, *Nordic Journal of Working Life Studies*, 3(2): 79. http://dx.doi.org/10.19154/njwls.v3i2.2551.

Allen, D. (2014) Re-Conceptualising Holism in the Contemporary Nursing Mandate: From Individual to Organisational Relationships, *Social Science & Medicine*, Pergamon, 119: 131–138.

Andersen, S. H. (2018) *Laveste antal offentligt ansatte pr. borger siden 1980'erne [The Lowest Number of Public Employees Per Citizen Since the 1980s]*, Copenhagen: The Economic Council of the Labour Movement.

Anker, N. & Grundtvig, G. (2018) *FTF-dokumentation: FTF'ernes psykiske arbejdsmiljø – arbejdspres, stress og mulighed for at levere kvalitet i arbejdet [FTF-Documentation: FTF-Members' Psychosocial Work Environment– Workload, Stress and Possibilities for Delivering Quality in Work]*, Copenhagen.

Barnes, M. & Cotterell, P. (2012) *Critical Perspectives on User Involvement*, Bristol, UK: Policy.

Bertelsen, T. M. & Rostgaard, T. (2013) Marketisation in Eldercare in Denmark: Free Choice and the Quest for Quality and Efficiency, In: Meagher, G. & Szebehely, M. (eds) *Marketisation in Nordic Eldercare: A Research Report on Legislation, Oversight, Extent and Consequences*, Stockholm: Stockholm University, 127–161.

Blomgren, M. & Waks, C. (2015) Coping with Contradictions: Hybrid Professionals Managing Institutional Complexity, *Journal of Professions and Organization*, Oxford University Press, 2(1): 78. http://dx.doi.org/10.1093/jpo/jou010.

Bolton, S. C. & Wibberley, G. (2014) Domiciliary Care: The Formal and Informal Labour Process, *Sociology*, 48(4): 682–697.

Bovbjerg, K. M. (ed.) (2011) *Motivation og mismod [Motivation and Despondency]*, Aarhus, Denmark: Aarhus Universitetsforlag.

Caraker, E. et al. (2015) *Fællesskabet før forskellene: hovedrapport fra APL III-projektet om nye lønmodtagerværdier og interesser [Solidarity over Differences: Main Report From the APL III Project About New Wage Earner Values and Interests]*, Copenhagen: LO & FTF.

Caswell, D. & Larsen, F. (2015) Frontlinjearbejdet i leveringen af aktiv beskæftigelse-spolitik: hvordan faglige, organisatoriske og styringsmæssige kontekster påvirker dette [Frontline Work in the Delivery of an Active Employment Policy: How Professional, Organizational and Governmental Contexts Affect This], *Tidsskrift for Arbejdsliv*, 17(1): 9–27.

Christensen, P. S., Drescher, M. & Holm, M. L. (2017) *Markant flere offentligt ansatte med lang videregående uddannelse [Significantly More Public Employees with a Master's Degree]*, Copenhagen: DST Analyse.

Christensen, T. & Laegreid, P. (2007) *Transcending New Public Management: The Transformation of Public Sector Reforms*, Abingdon, UK: Ashgate.

Christensen, T. & Laegreid, P. (2016) *The Routledge Handbook to Accountability and Welfare State Reforms in Europe*, Oxford, UK: Taylor and Francis.

Cohen, L., Duberley, J. & Smith, P. (2018) Losing the Faith: Public Sector Work and the Erosion of Career Calling, *Work, Employment and Society*, http://dx.doi.org/10.1177/0950017017746906.

Cooke, H. (2006) Seagull Management and the Control of Nursing Work, *Work, Employment & Society*, 20(2): 223–243.

Dahl, H. M. (2000) *Fra kitler til eget tøj: Diskurser om professionalisme, omsorg og køn [From Smocks to Private Clothes: Discourses on Professionalism, Care and Gender]*, Aarhus, Denmark: Institut for Statskundskab, Aarhus Universitet.

Dahl, H. M. (2005) Re-Imagining the (Welfare) Professional as a Specialized Generalist, *Knowledge, Work and Society*, 3(2): 21–39.

Dahl, H. M. (2010) Nye styringsformer og anerkendelseskamp: den vrede hjemmehjælper? [New Forms of Government and Struggle for Recognition: The Angry Home Helper?], *Kvinder, Køn & Forskning*, 4: 19–29.

Dahl, H. M. & Rasmussen, B. (2012) Paradoxes in Elderly Care: The Nordic Model, In: Kamp, A. & Hvid, H. (eds) *Elderly Care in Transition: Management, Meaning and Identity at Work. A Scandinavian Perspective*, Frederiksberg, Denmark: Copenhagen Business School Press, 29–49.

Dalsgaard, L. (2013) Fagprofessionelle i nyere forvaltningslitteratur [Professionals in Recent Public Administration Literature], *Nordisk Administrativt Tidsskrift*, 1(90): 40–57.

Danish Government, AC, Danish Regions, FTF, LGDK & OAO (2013) *Principper for samarbejde mellem parter på det offentlige arbejdsmarked om modernisering [Principles for Cooperation between the Public Sector Labour Market Parties Concerning Modernization]*, Copenhagen.

Danish Government, Local Government Denmark, Danish Regions (2007) *Aftale mellem regeringen, KL, Danske Regioner, LO og AC [Agreement between the Government, LGDK, Danish Regions, LO and AC]*, Copenhagen.

Danish Ministry of Finance (1983) *Redegørelse til folketinget om regeringens program for modernisering af den offentlige sektor [Report to Parliament on the Government's Programme for Modernization of the Public Sector]*, Copenhagen.

Dybbroe, B. (2008) Crisis of Care in a Learning Perspective: Introduction to the Danish Section, In: Wrede, Henriksson, Johansson, Høst & Dybbroe (eds) *Care Work in Crisis: Reclaiming the Nordic Ethos of Care*, Lund, Denmark: Studentlitteratur.

Ernst, J. (2016) Evidence-based Nursing in the IED: From Caring to Curing?, *Nordic Journal of Working Life Studies*, 6(1): 47. http://dx.doi.org/10.19154/njwls.v6i1.4885.

Evetts, J. (2009) New Professionalism and New Public Management: Changes, Continuities and Consequences, *Comparative Sociology*, 8(2): 247–266.

Fagbladet 3F (2016) Socialrådgivere i mindretal på jobcentre [Social Workers Outnumbered in Job Centres], *Fagbladet 3F*, 13 June.

FOA (2018) Konkurs nummer 50 i privat ældrepleje [Bankruptcy Number 50 in Private Elderly Care] (Press Release 19.01.18), Copenhagen: FOA- Fag og Arbejde.

Foss Hansen, H. (2011) NPM in Scandinavia, In: Christensen, T. & Lægreid, P. (eds) *The Ashgate Research Companion to New Public Management*, Abingdon, UK: Ashgate Publishing Ltd, 113–129.

Friedman, A. (1977) Responsible Autonomy Versus Direct Control Over the Labour Process, *Capital & Class*, 1(1): 43–57.

Gale, J. (2012) Government Reforms, Performance Management and the Labour Process: The Case of Officers in the UK Probation Service, *Work, Employment and Society*, 26(5): 822–838.

Genet, N., Boerma, W., Kroneman, M., Hutchinson, A. & Saltman, R. B. (2012) *Home Care across Europe: Current Structure and Future Challenges*, Copenhagen: European Observatory on Health Systems and Policies (WHO).

Gjørup, J. & Hjortdal, H. (2007) *Tilgiv os: vi vidste ikke hvad vi gjorde [Forgive Us: We Didn't Know What We Were Doing]*, Copenhagen: Politiken.

Gleerup, J. (2010) På vej mod nye infrastrukturer for ligelønskampen? en anerkendelsesteoretisk analyse af forløbet omkring ok08 [Towards New Infrastructures in the Fight for Equal Pay? A Theory of Recognition-Based Analysis of the Collective Bargaining Process 08], *Tidsskrift for Arbejdsliv*, 12(4): 29–45.

Godard, J. & Delaney, J. T. (2000) Reflections on the 'High Performance' Paradigm's Implications for Industrial Relations as a Field, *ILR Review*, 53(3): 482–502.

Greve, C. (2008) *Contracting for Public Services*, Oxford, UK: Routledge.

Greve, C. & Ejersbo, N. (2005) *Contracts as Reinvented Institutions in the Public Sector: A Cross-Cultural Comparison*, Westport, CT: Praeger.

Greve, C. & Ejersbo, N. (2014) *Moderniseringen af den offentlige sektor [The Modernization of the Public Sector]*, third edition, Copenhagen: Akademisk Forlag.

Hansen, A. M. & Kamp, A. (2018) From Carers to Trainers: Professional Identity and Body Work in Rehabilitative Eldercare, *Gender, Work and Organization*, 25(1): 63–76.

Hjort, K. (2001) *Moderniseringen af den offentlige sektor [The Modernization of the Public Sector]*, Roskilde, Denmark: Roskilde Universitetsforlag.

Hjort, K. (2004) *De professionelle, forskning i professioner og professionsuddannelser [The Professionals, Research on Professions and Professional Education]*, Roskilde, Denmark: Roskilde Universitetsforlag.

Høgedahl, L. (2017) *Offentlige overenskomstforhandlinger og konfliktløsning -Danmark i et nordisk perspektiv [Public Sector Collective Agreements and Conflict Resolution: Denmark in a Nordic Perspective]*, Aalborg, Denmark: Aalborg University.

Holen, M. (2011) *Medinddragelse og lighed: en god idé? En analyse af patienttilblivelser i det moderne hospital [Involvement and Equality: A Good Idea? An Analysis of Patient Becomings in the Modern Hospital]*, Roskilde, Denmark: Roskilde University.

Hood, C. (1991) A Public Management for All Seasons?, *Public Administration*, 69(1): 3–19.

Hvid, H. (2014) Socioteknik som samfundsforandring [Socio Technics as Social Change], *Tidsskrift for Arbejdsliv*, 16(2): 126–133.

Järvinen, M. (2012) Fra afhængighed til autonomi: At arbejde med stofbrugere [From Dependence to Autonomy: Working with Drug Users], In: Järvinen, M. and Mik-Meyer, N. (eds) *At Skabe En Professionel: Ansvar Og Autonomi I Velfærdsstaten [Creating a Professional: Responsibility and Autonomy in the Welfare State]*, Copenhagen: Hans Reitzel, 29–51.

Järvinen, M. & Mik-Meyer, N. (eds) (2012) *At skabe en professional: Ansvar Og Autonomi I Velfærdsstaten [Creating a Professional: Responsibility and Autonomy in the Welfare State]*, Copenhagen: Hans Reitzels Forlag.

Johnson, T. (1995) Governmentality and the Institutionalization of Expertise, In: Johnson, T., Larkin, G. & Saks, M. (eds) *Health Professions and the State in Europe*, Oxford, UK: Routledge, 7–24.

Kamp, A. (2012) Meaning of Work in Elderly Care in Denmark: Fragile Reconstructions, In: Kamp, A. & Hvid, H. (eds) *Elderly Care in Transition: Management, Meaning and Identity at Work, A Scandinavian Perspective*, Frederiksberg, Denmark: Copenhagen Business School Press, 107–132.

Kamp, A. & Dybbroe, B. (2016) Struggles of Professionalism and Emotional Labour in Standardized Mental Health Care, *Nordic Journal of Working Life Studies*, 6(February): 67–86.

Kamp, A. & Hansen, A. M. (2019, forthcoming) Negotiating Professional Knowledge and Responsibility in Cross-Sectoral Telemedicine, *Nordic Journal of Working Life Studies*.

Kamp, A., Hohnen, P., Hvid, H. & Scheller, V. K. (2013) *New Public Management: konsekvenser for arbejdsmiljø og produktivitet [New Public Management: Consequences for Working Environment and Productivity]*, Roskilde, Denmark: Roskilde University.

Kamp, A. & Holen, M. (2018) *Brugerinddragelse: ny professionalisme og nye omsorgsrum? [User Involvement: New Professionalism and New Care Spaces]*, Nordisk Välfärdsforskning. Universitetsforlaget. doi: 10.18261/issn.2464-4161-2018-01-05.

Kamp, A. & Ryberg, M. (2016) New Public Management: ledelse, arbejde og faglighed i forandring [New Public Management: Management, Work and Professionalism under Transformation], In: Glasdam, S. & Jørgensen, J. W. (eds) *Det nære sundhedsvæsen: perspektiver på samfundsudvikling og møder mellem mennesker [Primary health care: perspectives on social development and social relations]*, Copenhagen: Munksgaard, 46–56.

Kampmann, N. E. S. (2014) Lærer-pædagogsamarbejde: en politisk konstruktion og ledelsesudfordring [Teacher–Social Educator Cooperation: A Political Construction and Management Challenge], *Tidsskrift for Arbejdsliv*, 16(1): 25–38.

Kirchhoff, J. W. & Karlsson, J. C. (2013) Expansion of Output: Organizational Misbehaviour in Public Enterprises, *Economic and Industrial Democracy*, 34(1): 107–122.

Klijn, E. H. & Koppenjan, J. F. M. (2000) Public Management and Policy Networks, *Public Management: An International Journal of Research and Theory*, 2(2): 135–158.

Legge, K. (2005) *Human Resource Management. Rhetorics and Realities*, New York: Macmillan International Higher Education.

Leicht, K. T., Walter, T., Sainsaulieu, I. & Davies, S. (2009) New Public Management and New Professionalism across Nations and Contexts, *Current Sociology*, 57(4): 581–605.

Liebst, L. S. & Monrad, M. (2008) Imellem empati og depersonalisering: En følelsessociologisk analyse af tayloriseringens konsekvenser for hjemmeplejere [Between Empathy and Depersonalization: A Sociology of Feelings-Based Analysis of the Consequences of Taylorization for Home Care Workers], *Tidsskrift for arbejdsliv*, 10(1): 56–71.

Limborg, H. J., Albertsen, K. & Flensborg Jensen, M. (2012) Dokumentationskrav i folkeskolen: tidspres, kraenkelse eller faglig udfordring? [Documentation Requirements in Primary School: Time Pressure, Offence or Professional Challenge?], *Tidsskrift for Arbejdsliv*, 14(4): 10–29.

Local Government Denmark (2016) *Det Kommunale Arbejdsmarked i tal [The Local Authority Labour Market in Numbers]*, Copenhagen.

Local Government Denmark and FOA (2012) *Fremtidens ledelse på ældreområdet [Future Management of the Elderly Care Sector]*, Copenhagen.

Local Government Denmark and The Danish Association of Local Government Employees Organisations (2015) *Samarbejde om Psykisk Arbejdsmiljø i Kommunerne (SPARK) [Cooperation on the Psychosocial Working Environment in Local Authorities]*. http://vpt.dk/spark.

Mathiesen, K. & Hvenegaard, H. (1999) Nye samarbejdsformer mellem ledelse og medarbejdere i staten [New Forms of Cooperation between Management and Employees in the State], *Tidsskrift for Arbejdsliv*, 3: 31–46.

Matthiessen, M. U. & Rostgaard, T. (2016) *At arbejde rehabiliterende i hjemmeplejen gør arbejdet meningsfuldt [Working with Rehabilitation in Home Care Makes Work Meaningful]*, Copenhagen: KORA.

Melander, P. (ed.) (2008) *Det fortrængte offentlige lederskab, offentlig ledelse efter New Public Management [Suppressed Public Leadership, Public Management After New Public Management]*, Copenhagen: Jurist- og Økonomforbundet.

Middelboe, R. (2016) 3 ud af 4 har ikke hørt om tillidsreformen [3 out of 4 Have Not Heard of the Trust Reform], *Nyt fra HK*, November.

Møller, B. (2013) Den vigtige tillidsreform [The Important Trust Reform], *Mandag Morgen*, June.

Navrbjerg, S. (1999) *Nye arbejdsorganiseringer, fleksibilitet og decentralisering [New Work Organisations, Flexibility and Decentralization]*, Copenhagen: DJØF forlaget.

Pedersen, D. (1998) Mod forhandlet ledelse: resultatet af en dansk moderniseringsstrategi [Towards Negotiated Management: The Result of a Danish Modernization Strategy], In: *Arbejdspladser og medarbejdere i amter og kommuner: en antologi om kvalifikationer og kompetencer [Workplaces and Employees in Regions and Local Authorities: An Anthology on Qualifications and Competences]*, Copenhagen: Det Personalepolitiske Forum.

Rasmussen, B. (2012) New Public Management: Constructing a New Management Identity in Care for the Elderly, In: Kamp, A. & Hvid, H. (eds) *Elderly Care in Transition: Management, Meaning and Identity at Work. A Scandinavian Perspective*, Frederiksberg, Denmark: Copenhagen Business School Press, 165–187.

Rhodes, R. A. W. (2007) Understanding Governance: Ten Years On, *Organization Studies*, 28(8): 1243–1264.

Ritzau (2017) Kommuner har ingen plan når private plejefirmaer går konkurs [Local Authorities Have No Plan When Private Care Companies Go Bankrupt], *dr.dk*, 2 September.

Sørensen, P. K. (2015) *Moralsk stress: En arbejdslivsanalyse af psykisk arbejdsmiljø, deltagelse og retfærdiggørelsesprocesser blandt højtuddannede vidensarbejdere i Danmark [Moral Stress: A Working Life Analysis of Psychosocial Working Environment, Participation and Justification Processes among Highly Educated Knowledge Workers in Denmark]*, Roskilde, Denmark: Roskilde Universitet.

Statistics Denmark (2016) *Beskæftigede lønmodtagere (ultimo november 2016) efter tid, køn, sektor og arbejdstidens omfang [Employed Wage Earners (to November 2016) by Time, Gender, Sector and Working Hours]*, Statistikbanken, Danmarks Statistik.

Statistics Denmark (2018a) *Den offentlige beskæftigelse steg i fjerde kvartal [Public Employment Rose in the Fourth Quarter]*, Copenhagen: Danmarks Statistik.

Statistics Denmark (2018b) *Størst stigning i antal lønmodtagere i København [Biggest Rise in the Number of Wage Earners in Copenhagen]*, Copenhagen: Danmarks Statistik.

Szebehely, M. (2005) *Äldreomsorgsforskning i Norden. En kunnskapsöversikt. [Elderly Care Research in the Nordic Countries. A Review]*, Copenhagen: Nordisk Ministerråd.

Szebehely, M. (2006) Omsorgsvardag under skiftande villkor: en jämförande studie av den nordiska hemtjänsten [The Everyday Life of Care under Changing Conditions: A Comparative Study of Nordic Home Care], *Tidsskrift for arbejdsliv*, 8(1): 49–66.

Timmermans, S. & Berg, M. (2003) *The Gold Standard: The Challenge of Evidence-Based Medicine and Standardization in Health Care*, Philadelphia, PA: Temple University Press.

Timmermans, S. & Epstein, S. (2010) A World of Standards But Not a Standard World: Toward a Sociology of Standards & Standardization, *Annual Review of Sociology*, edited by K. S. M. Cook, 36: 69–89.

Torfing, J. (2004) *Det stille sporskifte i velfærdsstaten: en diskursteoretisk beslutningsprocesanalyse [Quiet Transformation in the Welfare State: A Discursive Decision Process Analysis]*, Aarhus, Denmark: Aarhus Universitetsforlag.

Torfing, J. & Triantafillou, P. (2013) What's in a Name? Grasping New Public Governance as a Political-Administrative System, *International Review of Public Administration*, 18(2): 9–25.

Trist, E. L. & Bamforth, K. W. (1951) Some Social and Psychological Consequences of the Longwall Method of Coal-Getting, *Human Relations*, 4(1): 3–38.

Trydegård, G.-B. (2005) Äldreomsorgspersonalens arbetsvillkor i Norden: En forskningsöversikt [Working Conditions for Elderly Care Personnel in the Nordic Countries: A Review], In: Szebehely, M. (ed.) *Äldreomsorgsforskning i Norden. En kunnskapsöversikt [Elderly Care Research in the Nordic Countries. A Review]*, Copenhagen: Nordisk Ministerråd, 143–196.

Tufte, P. (2013) Is There Time Enough? Temporal Resources and Service Performance in the Danish Home Care Sector, *Nordic Journal of Working Life Studies*, 3(2): 97–112.

Villadsen, K. (2007) *Det sociale arbejdes genealogi [The Geneaology of Social Work]*, Copenhagen: Hans Reitzels Forlag.

Vrangbaek, K. (2015) Patient Involvement in Danish Health Care, *Journal of Health Organization and Management*, 29(5): 611–624.

Chapter 12

Welfare professionals in transformation

The case of elderly care

Agnete Meldgaard Hansen and Annette Kamp

Introduction

With marketization and consumerism as its main principles, New Public Management (NPM) is often described as an approach that implies an attack on professionals' position in society (Freidson, 2001; see e.g. Dahl, 2005b) and a process towards de-professionalization (Dybbroe, 2008; Dalsgaard, 2013). Professions are generally characterized by their specific and demarcated knowledge domain, their wide autonomy in performance of their professional tasks and their adherence to a common code of professional ethics (Abbott, 1988). In principle, NPM implies that professions are confronted with market-based or utilitarian ethics, and aims at centralizing knowledge so that it rests with management, for example through standardization and contracting. In that respect, this development somewhat resembles Taylorist principles of work organization aiming to secure management control.

Indeed, mistrust of professionals and their altruism was one of the core arguments for NPM. With reference to new institutional economics and principal-agent theory, bringing governance back to the 'principals' by introducing means of controlling the professionals has been central (Hood, 1991). Therefore, although other arguments e.g. ensuring citizens' rights to equal services were also stressed, NPM was strongly associated with taming professionals' autonomy and identity (Dahl & Rasmussen, 2012).

A key question here is to what extent this aim has actually been accomplished. First, the negotiated character of these changes must be taken into account. As we have shown in Chapter 11, recent studies show that, at least in a Nordic context, different forms of new professionalization are taking place which transform professional identities and autonomy, as well as roles and relationships between professionals and citizens/clients (Hansen, 2015; Wathne, 2015; Hansen & Kamp, 2018). Second, NPM must, as explained in the previous chapter, be seen as a miscellany of different forms of governance rather than a monolith where the forms will vary between different empirical fields. Other discourses than that of marketization may play an important role in shaping the understanding of professionalism in specific fields e.g. discourses on old age and ageing in elderly care, on childhood and pedagogy in daycare work, and on the criminal subject and crime in police work. Thus, we see public sector professionalism not simply as under threat from NPM but as something achieved through historical processes and struggles, as well as under continuous transformation, and sometimes challenge, in close connection with developments in public sector governance and policy ideals. In some ways, NPM has contributed to weakening professionalization, but in other ways, NPM has actually been a vehicle of professionalization for some groups, such as elderly care workers and kindergarten teachers (Dahl, 2005c; Hjort, 2005).

Against this background, we would argue that there may be great differences in the way modernization and NPM have affected work in different sectors. Thus, when answering questions as to how NPM and other forms of public governance affect working life, we have to be sensitive to the specific contexts.

The focus for this chapter is elderly care. This is an area that has been emblematic for the development of NPM in the Danish public sector. As this is one of the largest and most costly parts of the public sector, it was the field where NPM-inspired reforms were most intensely and systematically implemented. Moreover, the reforms have had a significant impact on working conditions in elderly care, with the result that this field has played a prominent role in critical debates on NPM (Kamp & Hvid, 2012a).

In terms of its characteristics, elderly care is also a sector which is very 'Nordic': it is based on universalistic principles regarding the coverage of its services, and in fact it covers a quite large percentage of elderly Danish people. Further, care workers in this sector have since the 1990s been professionalized, with their own vocational education qualifications. However, they are, as explained in Chapter 11, not professionals in a classical sense; they are welfare professionals, frontline workers in welfare state services, whose work involves interactions with users (Hjort, 2004; Järvinen & Mik-Meyer, 2012). They are thus examples of the professionalization that has accompanied the introduction of NPM. At the same time, contemporary conceptions of ageing and the implied discourses of active ageing (Katz, 2000; Walker, 2009) play an important role in changing care work and professionalism in this field. This development has also had a great impact on the way new forms of governance, in terms of citizen-centred care and co-production, are designed.

The aim of this chapter is to explore the transformation of professionals' working life that has resulted from the introduction of NPM and newer forms of public governance, often dubbed New Public Governance (NPG), in a specific field: Danish elderly care. More specifically, we ask *how professional autonomy, meaning and identity at work have been transformed during the period of modernization since the early 1980s.*

In order to illuminate this development, our starting point is our over ten years of research in this field. We also include contributions from other Danish and Nordic researchers belonging to the rich tradition of Nordic care research (see e.g. Dahl & Eriksen, 2005; Szebehely, 2005). This chapter thus takes the form of a compilation of different contributions, primarily qualitative studies and often involving extensive fieldwork.

First, we give an overview of the context, i.e. elderly care in Denmark, and describe the main features of NPM and NPG reforms since the early 1980s. We then present our analysis of developments in work and professionalism under three headings: *transformation of the core task*, *autonomy under pressure* and *new care relationships and professional identities*. Finally, in the discussion and conclusion section, we discuss the implications of these developments for working life in elderly care and their possible future directions.

The context: elderly care and elderly care workers in Denmark

Elderly care work in Denmark is characterized by a quite significant overrepresentation of female workers; about 92% of the workers in elderly care services are women (KRL, 2017). The elderly care profession has gendered roots as 'women's work' as it is related to traditionally femininely connoted reproductive work in the home (e.g. cooking, cleaning, and physical as well as psychological care for family members). The profession originates in so-called 'housewife substitution' programmes instituted in the 1940s by the welfare state, aiming to aid frail elderly clients and others with necessary housework (Dahl, 2000; Petersen, 2008).

The Danish elderly care sector expanded quite significantly over the latter half of the 20th century. The field of homecare services in particular was expanded. This expansion was due to welfare state de-institutionalization policies, emphasizing that clients should remain 'as long as possible in their own homes' to avoid the more expensive care services provided in nursing homes. This was welcomed by many clients, who preferred the more individualized and flexible care provided in their own homes (Petersen, 2008; Dahl & Rasmussen, 2012). The expansion of the sector continues to this day. While austerity in general has been at the top of the political agenda since 2008, healthcare policies in Denmark pursue a general strategy of decentralization. More and more healthcare tasks and responsibilities are pushed downwards in the healthcare system from expensive, specialized hospitals to the primary healthcare sector and to patients'/clients' homes. This increases both the amount and complexity of tasks in homecare (LGDK et al., 2017). This development implies a large, stable labour market for public sector homecare. Danish local authorities employ about 78,000 people in homecare (KRL, 2017).

Elderly care work was originally considered unskilled work appropriate for housewives working part-time and thus requiring no formal education (Wærness, 1984; Dahl, 2000; Petersen, 2008). Today, however, educational levels of elderly care workers providing healthcare services are higher in Denmark than in most other European countries (Genet et al., 2012). In Denmark, the majority of elderly care workers have a vocational qualification as 'social and healthcare helpers' or 'social and healthcare assistants'; these courses take two years and two months, and three years and ten months, respectively.

NPM in elderly care

Elderly care, being one of the most costly areas of public service, is the field where NPM-inspired reforms have been most intensely and systematically implemented, and the reforms have had a significant impact on Danish elderly care work. The most important change was the implementation of the so-called purchaser–provider model, which was enforced by legislation in 2001 but was already being used in the 1990s (Eskelinen et al., 2006). This model, inspired by the NPM principle of marketization, entails a split between the purchaser and provider of care, where the purchaser (the local authority) orders specific care services from either public or private care providers. The purchaser–provider model requires care tasks to be explicitly defined, described and priced, in order to be exchangeable on the created care market. It thus involves a standardization of care tasks. With these reforms, care tasks are transformed into standardized care *services* that can be given a price and a fixed time, and be exchanged on a market. In this way, elderly care has been reorganized according to rationales of increased marketization, economic efficiency and standardization (Vabø, 2005; Szebehely, 2006; Kamp & Hvid, 2012b; Kamp et al., 2013), and the recipients of care have been reframed as *consumers* choosing between *services* (Højlund, 2006; Rostgaard, 2011). NPM principles for public sector care work continue to have significant influence despite widespread criticism (see Chapter 11 and later in this chapter). This widespread criticism has led to some 'softening' of the model and to elements of flexibility being implemented (see e.g. La Cour & Højlund, 2001), but the model continues to be the basic organizing principle of elderly care provision in Denmark.

NPG and citizen-centred care

However, the NPM story is not the only one to be told, and in later years these reforms were supplemented with a wave of reforms focusing on active ageing and self-sufficiency in care for elderly clients (Hansen, 2015, 2016a). A fairly new development in the Danish elderly care field (starting in the late 2000s), is a 're-birth' of a help-for-self-help and activation agenda, related to broader policy developments focusing on promotion of 'active', 'healthy' and 'successful' ageing (Katz, 2000; Minkler & Fadem, 2002; Walker, 2009). This focus on enabling client self-care has existed as a professional principle in the sector for many years but has been seen by many elderly care workers as difficult to realize within the standardized time and task regime of NPM (Swane, 2003). In the current resurfacing of these aims in elderly care, a move to link them with the field of rehabilitation has taken place. A wave of so-called 'everyday rehabilitation' programmes has been implemented in Danish public sector elderly care services (Månsson, 2007; Kjellberg et al., 2013; Christensen et al., 2015). The central need for elderly clients articulated in relation to these programmes is a need for freedom, self-sufficiency and independence from (publicly provided) help. Furthermore, telecare and a number of other new technologies have recently been introduced in care work as means of accomplishing better and more efficient care (Hansen & Grosen, 2019; Kamp & Hansen, 2019). These technologies are generally part of the movement towards empowerment and responsibilization of the client. Thus, changing relations and identities of clients and professionals are on the agenda. In the following section, we will discuss the impact of these diverse reforms and reorganizations on the core task, autonomy and professional identities of elderly care workers.

Transformation of the core task: from housework and social contact to rehabilitation and activation

The core task in elderly care work i.e. the provision of care in clients' homes or apartments in elderly care centres, is not as simple to define as it may first appear. The tasks of elderly care workers have changed over time and have been under continuous negotiation in relation to changing ideals of care and governance in Denmark. While NPM leads to redefinition and fragmentation of tasks, new articulations of the elderly as active and resourceful people have also played a role. Further, the continuous effort to professionalize and 'defeminize' the work is important. Like other care professionals, care workers in elderly care struggle for recognition of their work as based on qualifications, not just something that anyone (any woman) can do (Skeggs, 2005).

Following Hanne Marlene Dahl's work on homecare (Dahl, 2000), elderly care work must be understood in relation to how the needs of care recipients are articulated. With this understanding, care recipients' needs are not considered objective and easily identifiable entities but as politically contested and negotiated in the context of welfare state policies and practices (see also Fraser, 1989). How needs are articulated will affect how the tasks and the identity of the care worker are defined.

In the early days of Danish elderly care services, the main tasks performed were housework (Lewinther, 1997), though as Dahl (2000) shows, tasks such as providing 'understanding' and 'social contact' were also part of the work. Dahl observes a historical development away from negative articulations of the care needs of fragile elderly people that characterized the early days of elderly care provision, towards more positive and pleasant articulations (from the late 1960s onwards), such as 'creating wellbeing', 'creating growth' and 'enabling life-realization' (Dahl, 2005a). In line with this development, elderly care work in Denmark has since the 1980s been influenced by an ideal of activation and 'help-for-self-help', where the task of the elderly care worker, rather than performing tasks for clients, instead is to enable them to care for themselves (Swane, 2003).

Another important development in the articulation of care needs and care tasks is that the social, cognitive and emotional aspects of care work, such as the relief of loneliness and the provision of social contact to elderly clients, have disappeared from politico-administrative discourses on publicly provided elderly care. These tasks are instead seen as belonging to 'civil society' or 'the community' (Dahl, 2005a). These tasks and needs were written out of official documents on elderly care as early as the 1960s, which must also be seen as part of an effort towards professionalization, emphasizing unique qualifications and distancing from care dispositions that are assumed to be a basic human (or female) quality (Dahl, 2000). However, the question of whether or not social contact should be a central task and aspect of elderly care work is still highly contested in the Danish elderly care field (Kamp, 2012; Hansen, 2015). The tasks of elderly care work and the needs to be met have thus changed and been delimited over time.

The delimitation of tasks was formalized and extended with NPM and the implementation of the purchaser–provider model in elderly care. This development for example implied a separation of 'practical tasks' and 'care tasks', a separation that paved the way for marketization of the practical part of the job, such as shopping, cleaning, cooking, etc. where nearly 50% is now provided by private firms (Kamp, 2013). But it also implied a fragmentation of work into small tasks that could be distributed in different ways to optimize work organization and efficiency (Szebehely, 1995). In this way, classic ideals of holistic care became increasingly difficult to practise (Dybbroe, 2008).

However, the new paradigm of rehabilitation has changed the field and was initially received with enthusiasm by care workers (Rostgaard & Matthiessen, 2016). Physical training and motivation for self-development and independence from help are central aspects of these programmes and have thus become new tasks for elderly care workers. Basically, they are now tasked with training clients, physically and mentally, to take care of themselves. In most local authorities, rehabilitation takes place in close cooperation with a physiotherapist or occupational therapist, who establishes an action plan, stating the aims of the clients and the milestones to be achieved. The division of labour between therapists and care workers may be subject to negotiation; however, the care workers often remain with the task to execute the plan (Flensborg Jensen, 2017). This implies that new pedagogical and motivational tasks are becoming part of care work (Hansen & Kamp, 2018)

This development is accompanied by an increasing use of new technologies (in the Danish context labelled 'welfare technologies'), which are to enhance the client's independence from help. However, welfare technologies also imply other tasks, often termed articulation and inclusion work (Star & Strauss, 1999; Oudshoorn, 2008). Care workers are involved in developing the use of the technologies, determining which clients are eligible to use them and making them work in practice by adjusting them to the individual client (see e.g. IDA & LGDK, 2008; Nickelsen, 2013; Kamp & Ballegaard, 2018; Hansen and Grosen, 2019).

To sum up, the ideals of care, the professional orientation and the tasks of elderly care have changed dramatically over time. Exclusion of tasks has constricted the field, whereas the fragmentation of tasks introduced by NPM has narrowed the scope for holistic care. The turn towards rehabilitation seems to have brought some new areas for development. However, it is important to note that the ideals and practices involved do not simply replace each other. What we find in this field is a complex co-existence of different ideals and practices, which are often hierarchized, as illustrated by e.g. Kamp (2012) and Hansen (2015).

Professional autonomy under pressure and development

Accounts of the early days (from the 1940s to the 1980s) of elderly care provision describe a flexible day-to-day adjustment and negotiation of care tasks between care workers and care recipients (Pedersen & Andersen, 2016). This flexibility reflected a view that 'care needs are complex and shifting and should be responded to in a flexible manner' (Vabø, 2009, p. 350). The concrete tasks of care work were thus negotiated in the day-to-day care encounter and not originally subject to much external regulation. However, homecare workers in particular worked alone, and development in work through discussions with colleagues or training was almost non-existent (Pedersen & Andersen, 2016).

This situation changed with the increasing concern for growing welfare state budgets that gained ground from the 1970s onwards. The implementation of NPM profoundly changed the opportunities for autonomy and discretion. As described earlier, a split between provider and purchaser was established. Consequently, the assessment of the needs of the elderly was no longer part of care workers' work; care workers were simply to execute the tasks allotted to each user by the specialized department of care assessors. In addition, the intricate regime of management now introduced meant a standardization of tasks. The execution of tasks was then recorded by care workers using a small personal computer, the palm pilot, which enabled management to aggregate information electronically. Ideally, this would allow management to control and monitor the care work accomplished by care workers in every home (Scales, 2013; Kamp & Ryberg, 2016). Obviously, this regime resulted in intensive control and narrowed the scope for discretion in elderly care work.

Empirical studies have pointed out how this has resulted in a lack of discretion and recognition for care workers. Christiansen (2002), who conducted an extensive survey among care workers on the consequences of NPM, points out how NPM implied a lack of influence at work, lack of information and lack of possibilities for development and innovation. Moreover, a large majority of the respondents experienced greater workload and time pressure. Qualitative interviews that were also part of this study showed how the new temporal order tended to fragment work; this hampered the establishment of trustful relationships with elderly people, which are crucial for the meaning of the work and for creating a good workflow in practice. This development led to an overall experience of deskilling among care workers (Dybbroe, 2008) and a crisis of recognition, which surfaced most clearly in the large strike by care workers in 2008 (Dahl, 2009; Gleerup, 2010).

This development has often been called neo-Taylorism, and following this line of thought, an instrumentalist approach to work might have been expected to ensue. However, several studies point out that this is far from the case. They show how care workers develop different strategies in order to maintain a quality of care that lives up to their own ethical standards, implying that extra work is done, standards are creatively reinterpreted or work is informally reorganized, in order to take the shifting needs of elderly people into account (Liebst & Monrad, 2008; Dahl, 2009; Tufte, 2013). In this way, we see that care workers exercise what is often termed responsible autonomy (Friedman, 1977), implying that autonomy in work does not perish but lives on. It should be noted that responsible autonomy is a collective phenomenon, and while NPM caused fragmentation and standardization of tasks, large public workplaces with communities of well-organized professionals were retained in Denmark, allowing for the development of such strategies. This is in stark contrast to more individualized working conditions existing in e.g. the UK (Hayes & Moore, 2017). The practice of responsible autonomy is, however, not without costs. For example, Liebst and Monrad (2008) highlight the emotional strain involved, while others such as Tufte (2013) reveal the self-intensification at play. These tendencies are echoed in Norwegian research into elderly care (Rasmussen, 2004; Kirchhoff & Karlsson, 2013).

New trends in elderly care focusing on active ageing and self-sufficiency may, however, pave the way for a revitalization of autonomy (Kamp, 2013; Hansen, 2015). As mentioned in the section above, new tasks like physical training and motivation for self-development have been introduced. This does not mean that the standardization and time scheduling of work introduced as part of NPM have been abandoned. However, making rehabilitation happen implies adjusting activities to the individual person. In the study by Hansen and Kamp (2018) care workers describe how rehabilitative care implies that they have become more observant, analytical and able to see the physical and mental potentials of clients to develop and participate in care and practical tasks, as illustrated by the following quote:

> I think you see a bigger picture. Before, you would come and clean – fine . . . Now, you see other possibilities and think: . . . 'you [the client] could maybe take the duster?' In that way – get people involved, right? Where I might have been more inclined to do more things before, without questioning.
>
> (Laura, home trainer; Hansen & Kamp, 2018)

In this way, care workers' knowledge of elderly clients' lifestyle, problems, resources and potentialities come into play, encouraging the development of creative ways of training. Hence, rehabilitative elderly care is generally viewed by care workers as upgrading their work (Hansen, 2015; Rostgaard & Matthiessen, 2016).

To sum up, the detrimental effects of NPM on autonomy and discretion seem well-documented. The division between assessment and execution severely restricted care workers' use of their knowledge and qualifications. However, at the same time, new forms of organization that resulted from NPM have encouraged the establishment of elderly care workers as a professional and workplace community, which acts as a resource for different forms of responsible autonomy or organizational misbehaviour, implying that (some) autonomy was maintained. New trends in elderly care also encourage the use of broader assessments of clients' resources and life situation.

New care relationships and professional identities

The personal relationships and attachments established between care workers and care recipients have been the subject of much of the literature on elderly care work in the Nordic countries (Wærness, 1984; Szebehely, 1995; Lewinther, 1997; Astvik, 2003; Christensen, 2005). Intimately related to the constitution of care relationships is also the question of professional identities for care workers. Care relationships and the professional identities of care workers have been and are the target of both NPM and more recent reform efforts. These have at their core a transformation of the identities and relationships of care workers and care recipients.

Authors emphasizing empathy, reciprocity, personal knowledge, continuity and attachment as vital elements in good care relationships have argued that these elements have become more difficult to achieve after the NPM reforms and their fragmentation of time and space described earlier (Wærness, 1984; Lewinther, 1997; Liebst & Monrad, 2008; Wrede et al., 2008). Other authors, like Dahl (2017), go one step further, questioning whether continuity and attachment actually exist today. She suggests that we should rather talk about accidental 'meetings between known and unknown', resulting from the complex organization, the many actors involved and the discontinuity of care.

In addition, efforts to achieve professionalization have affected the development of relationships and identities. These efforts entail a 'defeminization' of elderly care work. Care workers are encouraged to distance themselves from traditional female 'caring dispositions' and experience-based approaches to care work, and instead adhere to formal, specialized knowledge and methods in order to become reflexive, 'real professionals' and increase their status (Dahl, 2005c; Fejes, 2012; Hansen & Kamp, 2018).

Another significant development for care relationships and identities has been the NPM-inspired articulation of clients as consumers and care workers as providers of care services. Clients are positioned as rational market actors in charge of their own care provision, with the power to choose between the services on offer by different providers, and thus as empowered to exit a care relationship if it is not satisfactory (Eskelinen et al., 2006; Rostgaard, 2006). However, studies have shown that clients are reluctant to become the envisioned freely choosing care consumer, giving continuity in the care relationship higher priority than the free choice of care provider (Rostgaard, 2011). As a counterpart to this (not fully realized) care customer, care workers are positioned as providers of standardized services and given a low degree of professional discretion and influence on services. On the one hand, as Eskelinen et al. (2006) have pointed out, this development stands in stark contrast to attempts to professionalize elderly care work, creating a contradictory position for care workers. On the other hand, as described earlier, the standardization and marketization of tasks involved an outsourcing of many of the practical care tasks, such as cooking, shopping and cleaning. These tasks are often devalued and not considered central to professional identity in the elderly care profession, and care workers thus do not tend to see their outsourcing as a threat to their professionalism (Kamp, 2012). Standardization and marketization thus not only offer a challenge to professional autonomy but also an opportunity to strengthen professional identity as tasks that are considered non-professional are toned down.

Later developments have introduced other articulations of the care relationship, adding to its complexity and to the complexity of care worker and client identities. With the described activation and rehabilitation efforts that have become widespread in the Danish elderly care sector, the care relationship is by some care workers described as becoming more equal and cooperative, allowing them to exit the service role articulated in marketized care relationships. As a care worker in a study of homecare rehabilitation efforts commented:

> It becomes less like 'masters and servants', you see? . . . Previously, you rushed in and did all kinds of things . . . and now it's just become more equal, I think. So we help each other out, or: 'so you can do that, and then I'll do this'.
>
> (Rita, social and healthcare assistant, Hansen, 2015)

With rehabilitation and activation efforts, clients are given a more active role and are encouraged and trained to perform as many care tasks as possible themselves. Care workers disassociate themselves from the image of 'the maid' and take on an identity as coaches, sometimes helping out, but primarily motivating and training clients to care for themselves (Hansen, 2015; Hansen & Kamp, 2018). The care relationship in this manner becomes a joint project to achieve goals of self-sufficiency and independence from help for clients.

However, the care relationship as a 'joint project' between equal partners seems to be an ideal not always attainable in practice. The care worker's professional identity as a motivating coach and partner is dependent on the client assuming an identity as a person in training for independence. In cases where clients for different reasons do not cooperate with the project of rehabilitation, the care relationship and care worker identities can become paternalistic and responsibilizing; activity and independence are then not merely encouraged but demanded of clients and seen as a duty (Mendes, 2013; Hansen, 2016a, 2016b).

Another aspect of the new rehabilitative care relationship is an element of withdrawal and distance on the part of the care worker. The goal of rehabilitation and activation is 'to set clients free' from the need for publicly provided elderly care, and thus care relationships are seen as needing to be phased out or reduced as much as possible so that public sector intervention in the private sphere of the client is minimized. Dahl (2005a) has described this development as a different form of welfare state retrenchment from the retrenchment efforts associated with NPM. This withdrawal from the client's private sphere is realized in a number of ways. In the study of rehabilitation efforts mentioned earlier, care workers started to work 'with their hands behind their backs' i.e. they withdrew physically from the care relationship, leaving clients to do practical and physical tasks themselves and gradually phasing out the care relationship (Hansen, 2016a).

Furthermore, welfare technologies are in many situations used to support care worker withdrawal. For example, telecare technologies are employed to provide so-called 'virtual homecare', where homecare visits take place through video conversations. Clients may for example no longer receive a physical visit to help them take their medicine, but instead receive a video call from a care worker. Care worker presence in the client's home is thus minimized in accordance with the ideal of setting clients free (Kamp & Ballegaard, 2016). Other technologies support the withdrawal of the care worker intervention from clients' intimate bodily sphere. For example, automatic wash-and-dry toilets are employed to enable disabled and elderly clients to handle post-toilet hygiene without the help of a care worker, thus avoiding the transgression of normal boundaries of bodily autonomy (Hansen & Grosen, 2019).

To sum up, competing images of the care worker as an empathic carer, a service worker, a reflexive knowledgeable professional, a distanced and motivating coach, an equal partner, a paternalistic professional, and a flexible and responsive monitor of needs exist alongside each other. Developments in the elderly care sector have led to a landscape of multiple and sometimes contradictory identities for care workers, who interact with clients in multifaceted and complex care relationships.

Concluding discussion

This chapter has focused on the specific field of elderly care in order to provide a nuanced picture of how NPM and later reforms have influenced the working lives of welfare professionals. We argue that NPM, at least in a Nordic version, does not simply lead to de-professionalization and loss of autonomy.

Danish elderly care has actually been subject to quite classical NPM reforms (Hood, 1991), creating internal markets through contractualization and leading to standardization and fragmentation of work. However, it has remained a largely public area of employment, employing well-organized welfare professionals.

As we point out, much research in the area does indeed show how NPM has implied fragmentation of tasks, loss of autonomy, recognition and professionalism, which are the effects usually associated with NPM reforms. But as we also show, this is not the whole story. Various tasks have been included in and excluded from elderly care over a long period of time, reflecting shifting discourses that frame the conception of the needs of elderly people, but no doubt also in intimate interaction with reforms aiming at rationalization and retrenchment in the sector. Also involved are the continuous efforts to enhance professionalization.

At the same time, although autonomy has been attacked by reforms, we point out how the large and well-organized communities of workers in elderly care have also been a site for resistance, misbehaviour and responsible autonomy, implying that although work has formally been standardized, it is seldom carried out by the book. Many studies included in our chapter underline how standardized work routines often fall short when addressing the shifting needs and tasks in work with frail elderly people. We also demonstrate how new conceptions of ageing and elderly people have paved the way for other forms of care based on principles of rehabilitation. These forms of care offer more autonomy and have formed a basis for a renewal of professionalism. That is also true of the influx of new so-called welfare technologies that aim to sustain the process of rehabilitation. New tasks and new possibilities for increasing discretion in care work seem to be the result, and these possibilities are embraced by welfare professionals.

We can thus observe how the process of professionalization is ongoing. There are times where autonomy is weakened and the core tasks shift over time, but there are also times when the profession can be reshaped and transformed. This may be seen as characteristic of this type of profession. As a form of historically achieved institutionalization, elderly care functions as a site for shaping and influencing the different types of reforms introduced, thus reflecting Nordic negotiated modernization.

However, welfare professions are not as strong and independent institutions as classical professions. Rather, they resemble occupations and are much more dependent on and interconnected with the state with its shifting demands on the profession and the policy trends that evolve. So they must as institutions be more flexible in adapting and renegotiating knowledge domains and professional identities (Jørgensen, 2009).

As we have underlined, professional identities are not simply shifted over the course of time; different orientations co-exist in the field which may lead to tensions and conflicts among professionals. Here, the plural and shifting role of the client poses a major challenge. Care relations are traditionally conceived as central to professional identity, but developments in the field of elderly care in many ways challenge the classical conception of care relations based on empathy and continuous contact. While NPM introduced marketized relations in the form of consumerism, NPG encourages the self-reliant and empowered partner. Researchers in the field agree that these policy goals are not easily accomplished, as all clients do not necessarily take on the new roles. However, we show how this development implies that welfare professionals must negotiate possibly contradictory relations.

In our introduction to this chapter, we raised the broader question of how public sector modernization in the Nordic countries has evolved and its implications for welfare professions. Taking elderly care as a case, we would argue that Nordic NPM may provide possibilities to retain autonomy and professionalism, but we also show that it may not be without costs in terms of struggles, emotional strain and self-intensification. New reforms aiming at changing roles and relations between professionals and clients may, however, more radically change the scene and possibly provide new opportunities for building autonomy and professionalism.

References

Abbott, A. D. (1988) *The System of Professions: An Essay on the Division of Expert Labor*, Chicago, IL: University of Chicago Press.

Astvik, W. (2003) *Relationer som arbete. Förutsättningar för omsorgsfulla möten i hemtjänsten [Relationships as Work. Preconditions for Caring Encounters in Homecare]*, Stockholm: Department of Psychology, Stockholm University.

Christensen, K. (2005) The Modernization of Power in Norwegian Home Care Services, In: Eriksen, T. R. & Dahl, H. M. (eds) *Dilemmas of Care in the Nordic Welfare State: Continuity and Change*, Aldershot, UK: Ashgate, 33–46.

Christensen, U., Malling, G. M. & Christensen, B. (2015) *Hverdagsrehabilitering: Rapport fra en kvalitativ undersøgelse [Everyday Rehabilitation: Report from a Qualitative Study]*, University of Copenhagen and Copenhagen Municipality.

Christiansen, J. M. (2002) *Hjemmeplejen i en omstillingstid. Personalets syn på deres arbejde, på omstillingerne og på fremtiden: belyst ud fra en spørgeskemaundersøgelse [Homecare in a Time of Transition. Employees' Views on their Work, on Transitions and on the Future: Illuminated through a Survey]*, Copenhagen: CASA.

Dahl, H. M. (2000) *Fra kitler til eget tøj: Diskurser om professionalisme, omsorg og køn [From Smocks to Private Clothes: Discourses on Professionalism, Care and Gender]*, Aarhus, Denmark: Department of Political Science, Aarhus University.

Dahl, H. M. (2005a) A Changing Ideal of Care in Denmark: A Different Form of Retrenchment?, In: Dahl, H. M. & Eriksen, T. R. (eds) *Dilemmas of Care in the Nordic Welfare State: Continuity and Change*, Aldershot, UK: Ashgate, 47–61.

Dahl, H. M. (2005b) Fra en klassisk til en (post?)moderne opfattelse af professioner? [From a Classical to a (Post?)Modern View on Professions?], In: Eriksen, T. R. & Jørgensen, A. M. (eds) *Proffesionsidentitet i forandring [Professional Identity under Transformation]*, Copenhagen: Akademisk Forlag.

Dahl, H. M. (2005c) Re-imagining the (Welfare) Professional as a Specialized Generalist, *Knowledge, Work and Society*, 3(2): 21–39.

Dahl, H. M. (2009) New Public Management, Care and Struggles about Recognition, *Critical Social Policy*, 29(4): 634–654.

Dahl, H. M. (2017) *Struggles in (Elderly) Care: A Feminist View*, New York: Palgrave Macmillan.

Dahl, H. M. & Eriksen, T. R. (eds) (2005) *Dilemmas of Care in the Nordic Welfare State*, London: Routledge.

Dahl, H. M. & Rasmussen, B. (2012) Paradoxes in Elderly Care: The Nordic Model, In: Kamp, A. & Hvid, H. (eds) *Elderly Care in Transition: Management, Meaning and Identity at Work. A Scandinavian Perspective*, Frederiksberg, Denmark: Copenhagen Business School Press, 29–49.

Dalsgaard, L. (2013) Fagprofessionelle i nyere forvaltningslitteratur [Professionals in Recent Public Administration Literature], *Nordisk Administrativt Tidsskrift*, 1(90): 40–57.

Dybbroe, B. (2008) Crisis of Care in a Learning Perspective: Introduction to the Danish Section, In: Wrede et al. (eds) *Care Work in Crisis: Reclaiming the Nordic Ethos of Care*, Lund, Sweden: Studentlitteratur.

Eskelinen, L., Hansen, E. B. & Frederiksen, M. (2006) Fra omsorg til service: nyorientering i hjemmeplejen via frit valg? [From Care to Service: New Orientation of Homecare through Free Choice], *Socialvetenskaplig Tidskrift*, 1: 19–34.

Fejes, A. (2012) Knowledge at Play: Positioning Care Workers as Professionals through Scientific Rationality and Caring Dispositions, In: Kamp, A. & Hvid, H. (eds) *Elderly Care in Transition: Management, Meaning and Identity at Work. A Scandinavian Perspective*, Frederiksberg, Denmark: Copenhagen Business School Press, 83–105.

Flensborg Jensen, M. C. (2017) Gender Stereotypes and the Reshaping of Stigma in Rehabilitative Eldercare, *Gender, Work & Organization*, 24(6): 656–674.

Fraser, N. (1989) Talking about Needs: Interpretive Contests as Political Conflicts in Welfare State Societies, *Ethics*, 99(2): 291–313.

Freidson, E. (2001) *Professionalism: The Third Logic*, Cambridge, UK: Polity Press.

Friedman, A. (1977) Responsible Autonomy Versus Direct Control Over the Labour Process, *Capital & Class*, 1(1): 43–57.

Genet, N., Boerma, W., Kroneman, M., Hutchinson, A. & Saltman, R. (2012) *Home Care across Europe: Current Structure and Future Challenges*, Copenhagen: European Observatory on Health Systems and Policies (WHO).

Gleerup, J. (2010) På vej mod nye infrastrukturer for ligelønskampen? en anerkendelsesteoretisk analyse af forløbet omkring ok 08 [Towards New Infrastructures in the Fight for Equal Pay? A Theory of Recognition-Based Analysis of the Collective Bargaining Process 08], *Tidsskrift for Arbejdsliv*, 12(4): 29–45.

Hansen, A. M. (2015) Rehabilitating Elderly Bodies and Selves: New Forms of Care Work, Professional Identity and Status in Rehabilitative Home Care, PhD thesis, Roskilde, Denmark: Roskilde University.

Hansen, A. M. (2016a) Rehabilitative Bodywork: Cleaning Up the Dirty Work of Homecare, *Sociology of Health & Illness*, 38(7): 1092–1105.

Hansen, A. M. (2016b) Rehabiliterende kropsarbejde i hjemmeplejen [Rehabilitative Bodywork in Homecare], *Tidsskrift for Arbejdsliv*, 18(2): 26–40.

Hansen, A. M. & Grosen, S. L. (2019, forthcoming) Transforming Bodywork in Eldercare with Wash-and-Dry Toilets, *Nordic Journal of Working Life Studies*.

Hansen, A. M. & Kamp, A. (2018) From Carers to Trainers: Professional Identity and Body Work in Rehabilitative Eldercare, *Gender, Work and Organization*, 25(1): 63–76.

Hayes, L. J. B. & Moore, S. (2017) Care in a Time of Austerity: The Electronic Monitoring of Homecare Workers' Time, *Gender, Work and Organization*, 24(4): 329–344.

Hjort, K. (2004) *De professionelle, forskning i professioner og professionsuddannelser [The Professionals, Research on Professions and Professional Education]*, Frederiksberg, Denmark: Roskilde Universitetsforlag.

Hjort, K. (2005) *Professionaliseringen i den offentlige sektor [Professionalization in the Public Sector]*, Frederiksberg, Denmark: Roskilde Universitetsforlag.

Højlund, H. (2006) Den frit vælgende ældre [The Freely Choosing Elderly Person], *Dansk Sociologi*, 17(1): 41–65.

Hood, C. (1991) A Public Management for All Seasons?, *Public Administration*, 69(1): 3–19.

IDA & LGDK (2008) *Debatoplæg om teknologi i velfærden [Discussion Paper on Technology in Welfare]*, Copenhagen.

Järvinen, M. & Mik-Meyer, N. (eds) (2012) *At skabe en professionel: Ansvar Og Autonomi I Velfærdsstaten [Creating a Professional: Responsibility and Autonomy in the Welfare State]*, Copenhagen: Hans Reitzels Forlag.

Jørgensen, C. H. (2009) Fag mellem arbejds organisation og uddannelse. Har fagene en fremtid bag sig? [Occupations between Work Organization and Education. Do the Occupations Have a Future Behind Them?], *Tidsskrift for Arbejdsliv*, 3: 13–32.

Kamp, A. (2012) Meaning of Work in Elderly Care in Denmark: Fragile Reconstructions, In: Kamp, A. & Hvid, H. (eds) *Elderly Care in Transition: Management, Meaning and Identity at Work. A Scandinavian Perspective*, Frederiksberg, Denmark: Copenhagen Business School Press, 107–132.

Kamp, A. (2013) Rehabilitering i hjemmeplejen - begejstring, krydspres og paradokser [Rehabilitation in Homecare: Excitement, Cross-Pressure and Paradoxes], *Gerontologi*, 29(2): 16–21.

Kamp, A. & Ballegaard, S. A. (2016) Virtual Care: Practising Care in Times of Citizen Empowerment and Retrenchment, *Nordic Working Life Conference 2016*, Tampere, Finland.

Kamp, A. & Ballegaard, S. A. (2018) *Skærmopkald i hjemme og sygepleje: Videosamtalers betydning for pleje – og omsorgsarbejde [Videocalls in Homecare and Homenursing: The Significance of Videoconversations for Care Work]*, Roskilde, Denmark: Roskilde University and VIVE.

Kamp, A. & Hansen, A. M. (2019, forthcoming) Negotiating Professional Knowledge and Responsibility in Cross-Sectoral Telemedicine, *Nordic Journal of Working Life Studies*.

Kamp, A., Hohnen, P., Hvid, H. & Scheller, V. K. (2013) *New Public Management: konsekvenser for arbejdsmiljø og produktivitet [New Public Management: Consequences for Working Environment and Productivity]*, Roskilde, Denmark: Roskilde University.

Kamp, A. & Hvid, H. (eds) (2012a) *Elderly Care in Transition. Management, Meaning and Identity at Work. A Scandinavian Perspective*, Frederiksberg, Denmark: Copenhagen Business School Press.

Kamp, A. & Hvid, H. (2012b) Introduction: Elderly Care in Transition, In: Kamp, A. & Hvid, H. (eds) *Elderly Care in Transition: Management, Meaning and Identity at Work. A Scandinavian Perspective*, Frederiksberg, Denmark: Copenhagen Business School Press, 13–28.

Kamp, A. & Ryberg, M. (2016) New Public Management: ledelse, arbejde og faglighed i forandring [New Public Management: Management, Work and Professionalism under Transformation], In: Glasdam, S. & Jørgensen, J. W. (eds) *Det nære sundhedsvæsen: perspektiver på samfundsudvikling og møder mellem mennesker [The Local Healthcare*

System: Perspectives on Societal Development and Meetings between People], Copenhagen: Munksgaard, 46–56.

Katz, S. (2000) Busy Bodies: Activity, Aging, and the Management of Everyday Life, *Journal of Aging Studies*, 14(2): 135–152.

Kirchhoff, J. W. & Karlsson, J. C. (2013) Expansion of Output: Organizational Misbehaviour in Public Enterprises, *Economic and Industrial Democracy*, 34(1): 107–122.

Kjellberg, P. K., Hauge-Helgestad, A., Madsen, M. H. & Rasmussen, S. R. (2013) *Kortlægning af kommunernes erfaringer med rehabilitering på ældreområdet [Mapping of Local Authorities' Experiences with Rehabilitation in the Eldercare Sector]*, Odense, Denmark: Socialstyrelsen.

KRL (2017) *Antal ansatte: det kommunale område fordelt på kontonummer og køn [Number of Employees: Local Authorities, by Account Number and Gender]*, Copenhagen: Kommunerne og Regionernes Løndatakontor.

La Cour, A. & Højlund, H. (2001) Den fleksible hjemmehjælper [The Flexible Home Helper], *Social kritik*, 76: 6–18.

Lewinther, M. (1997) Hjemmehjælp og Hjemmehjælper i Forandringens Arena [Homehelp and Homehelper in the Arena of Change], *Kvinder, Køn & Forskning*, 6(2): 66–77.

LGDK, Danish Regions and The State (2017) *Afrapportering: Udvalg om det nære og sammenhængende sundhedsvæsen [Report: Committee for the Near, Local and Integrated Healthcare System]*, LGDK, Danish Regions and the State.

Liebst, L. S. & Monrad, M. (2008) Imellem empati og depersonalisering: En følelsessociologisk analyse af tayloriseringens konsekvenser for hjemmeplejere [Between Empathy and Depersonalization: A Sociology of Feelings-Based Analysis of the Consequences of Taylorization for Home Care Workers], *Tidsskrift for arbejdsliv*, 10(1): 56–71.

Månsson, M. (2007) *Hemrehabilitering: vad, hur och för vem? [Home-Rehabilitation: What, How and For Whom?]*, Solna, Sweden: Fortbildning AB/Tidningen Äldreomsorg.

Mendes, F. R. (2013) Active Ageing: A Right or a Duty?, *Health Sociology Review*, 22(2): 174–185.

Minkler, M. & Fadem, P. (2002) 'Successful Aging': A Disability Perspective, *Journal of Disability Policy Studies*, 12(4): 229–235.

Nickelsen, N. C. M. (2013) Criteria of Implementing Feeding Assistance Robots in Disability Care: A Sociomaterial Perspective, *Journal of Comparative Social Work*, 8(2): 1–29.

Oudshoorn, N. (2008) Diagnosis at a Distance: The Invisible Work of Patients and Healthcare Professionals in Cardiac Telemonitoring Technology, *Sociology of Health & Illness*, 30(2): 272–288.

Pedersen, D. & Andersen, I. (2016) *Ældreplejen gennem to generationer [Elderly Care through Two Generations]*, Copenhagen: Munksgaard.

Petersen, J. H. (2008) *Hjemmehjælpens historie: Idéer, holdninger og handlinger [The History of Homecare: Ideas, Opinions and Actions]*, Odense, Denmark: Syddansk Universitetsforlag.

Rasmussen, B. (2004) Between Endless Needs and Limited Resources: The Gendered Construction of a Greedy Organization, *Gender, Work and Organization*, 11(5): 506–525.

Rostgaard, T. (2006) Constructing the Care Consumer: Free Choice of Home Care for the Elderly in Denmark, *European Societies*, 8(3): 443–463.

Rostgaard, T. (2011) Care As You Like It: The Construction of a Consumer Approach in Home Care in Denmark, *Nordic Journal of Social Research*, (Special Issue): 1–16.

Rostgaard, T. & Matthiessen, M. U. (2016) *At arbejde rehabiliterende i hjemmeplejen gør arbejdet meningsfuldt [Working with Rehabilitation in Home Care Makes Work Meaningful]*, Copenhagen: KORA.

Scales, K. (2013) Book review: Kamp, A. & Hvid, H. (eds) *Elderly Care in Transition: Management, Meaning and Identity at Work. A Scandinavian Perspective, Work, Employment & Society*, 27(5): 902–903.

Skeggs, B. (2005) The Making of Class and Gender through Visualizing Moral Subject Formation, *Sociology*, 39(5): 965–982.

Star, S. L. & Strauss, A. (1999) Layers of Silence, Arenas of Voice: The Ecology of Visible and Invisible Work, *Computer Supported Cooperative Work*, 8: 9–30.

Swane, C. E. (2003) 'Hjälp till självhjälp' som strategi i hemtjänsten ['Help for Self-Help' as a Strategy in Homecare], In: Szebehely, M. (ed.) *Hemhjälp i Norden: illustrationer och reflektioner [Home Care in the Nordic Countries: Illustrations and Reflections]*, Lund, Sweden: Studentlitteratur, 211–239.

Szebehely, M. (1995) *Vardagens Organisering: Om vårdbiträden och gamla i hemtjänsten. [The Organization of Everyday Life: About Care Workers and Elderly People in Homecare]*, Lund, Sweden: Arkiv förlag.

Szebehely, M. (2005) *Äldreomsorgsforskning i Norden. En kunnskapsöversikt. [Elderly Care Research in the Nordic Countries. A Review]*, Copenhagen: Nordisk Ministerråd.

Szebehely, M. (2006) Omsorgsvardag under skiftande villkor: en jämförande studie av den nordiska hemtjänsten [The Everyday Life of Care under Changing Conditions: A Comparative Study of Nordic Home Care], *Tidsskrift for arbejdsliv*, 8(1): 49–66.

Tufte, P. (2013) Is There Time Enough? Temporal Resources and Service Performance in the Danish Home Care Sector, *Nordic Journal of Working Life Studies*, 3(2): 97–112.

Vabø, M. (2005) New Public Management i nordisk eldreomsorg: hva forskes det på? [New Public Management in Nordic Elderly Care: What Is Being Researched?], In: Szebehely, M. (ed.) *Äldreomsorgsforskning i Norden: en kunskapsöversikt [Elderly Care Research in the Nordic Countries. A Review]*, Copenhagen: Nordisk Ministerråd, 73–112.

Vabø, M. (2009) Home Care in Transition: The Complex Dynamic of Competing Drivers of Change in Norway, *Journal of Health Organization and Management*, 23(3): 346–358.

Wærness, K. (1984) The Rationality of Caring, *Economic and Industrial Democracy*, 185–211. http://dx.doi.org/10.1177/0143831X8452003.

Walker, A. (2009) Commentary: The Emergence and Application of Active Aging in Europe, *Journal of Aging & Social Policy*, 21(1): 75–93.

Wathne, C. T. (2015) Som å bli fremmed i eget hus: Politiets opplevelse av mening og motivasjon i lys av nye styringssystemer [Becoming a Stranger in One's Own House: Police Officers' Experiences of Meaning and Motivation in Light of New Management Systems], PhD thesis, Oslo University.

Wrede, S., Henriksson, L., Hôst, H. & Johansson, S. (2008) Introduction: Care Work and the Competing Rationalities of Public Policy, In: Wrede, S. et al. (eds) *Care Work in Crisis: Reclaiming the Nordic Ethos of Care*, Lund, Sweden: Studentlitteratur, 15–37.

Chapter 13

Welfare professionals in transformation

The case of police officers in Norway

Christin Thea Wathne

Introduction

The Norwegian Ministry of Justice and Public Security and the National Police Directorate constitute the central leadership of the Norwegian Police Service (Politi- og lensmannsetaten), which is one of the oldest government agencies in Norway. The police districts are divided into police station districts and rural police station districts. Each police district is led by a chief of police, who is responsible for all police services, the budget and the results. The Norwegian Police Service currently has approximately 13,000 employees. When women were given the equal right to enter the police force in 1958, the police force had a masculine air about it, and the police corps consisted almost entirely of men. Today, 46% of all employees in the police force are women, while 31% of those trained as police officers are women. In total, 32% of the managerial positions are held by women (Politiet, 2018a).

The Norwegian Police has been a national police force since 1937. In addition to performing the usual police tasks in rural areas, the Norwegian rural chief of police has had a number of public and civil tasks that have helped give the police a civil image (Støkken, 1981, p. 36). Although the government established and ran a three-month police academy in 1919, there were no formal educational requirements for being employed as a police officer in Norway until far into the 1950s. Before 1920, any training in upholding public order was largely carried out in the day-to-day police work. After the war, a two-year educational programme was established at the Norwegian Police Academy, and from 1992 it was changed to a three-year degree-level programme. This development contrasts sharply with that in Denmark, where the police are still to this day trained in a two-year police academy for its national police, called Politiskolen (Politiskolen, 2018). Since 2004, the Norwegian police education programme has been accredited as a Bachelor's degree (Hove, 2012). Today, the Norwegian Police University College offers two Master's programmes (The Norwegian Police University College, 2018). In other words, the Norwegian Police University College safeguards the professional standards of the Norwegian police by developing and communicating the knowledge, skills and attitudes that the police need to have in order to ensure security, law and order. Knowledge from the legal courses and investigation classes have held a dominant position in the training programme all the way up to the present day. It was only from the 1980s onwards that the focus on broad, knowledge-based maintenance of public order and a service directed at the public was formally included in the programme. With the university college project (Høgskoleprosjektet), this became even more prevalent (Hove, 2012). In the 1990s, the idea was that this study programme would qualify the candidates for a broader police role, which is expressed in the emphasis on prevention and the social sciences. The programme was now geared at the generalist and would provide a broad qualification for operative police work, investigation and preventative work, alongside certain administrative tasks (Hove, 2012). In sum, it can be said that this modern police has been more public, more specialized and more professional than the pre-modern police forces were (Bayley, 1985).

The Norwegian police's ideological roots in the Scandinavian welfare model

There are several similarities between the structural conditions for police work in Denmark and Norway. In both countries, the police have their ideological roots in the Scandinavian welfare model, where the public sector is responsible for ensuring that all citizens have access to basic financial, social and cultural goods and services: "In order to secure a reasonable standard of living for all individuals independent of family background, welfare payments and public services are relatively generous. This model is oriented toward the objective of securing equality" (Høigård, 2011, p. 273). The function of the police in maintaining public order has remained a core function for the past 350 years, even though parts of the content of this function have changed in line with the development of society (Ellefsen & Larsson, 2014, p. 30). While the way problems are solved depends on the degree to which the various situations demand help or control, the emphasis on control and help also depends on how the police employee reads the situation and shapes his or her own role. The norms for how to define various situations may depend on the individual, or they may develop differently at different police units. However, the norms for how to understand and define society and various situations are also influenced by various institutional logics. By institutional logics we mean: "the socially constructed, historical patterns of cultural symbols and material practices, including assumptions, values, and beliefs, by which individuals and organizations provide meaning to their daily activity, organize time and reproduce their lives and experiences" (Thornton & Ocasios, 2008, here in Thornton et al., 2013, p. 2). In general, it can be said that the dominant institutional logics in the police are to various degrees geared at controlling citizens rather than serving them (Ministry of Justice and Public Security, 2009). Different institutional logics are reflected in two different police traditions, which can roughly be divided into two historical lines: a tradition of restraint and a militaristic tradition (NOU, 2017, p. 28). The tradition of restraint is characterized by the view that the police shall be restrained in their use of force, be focused on regulation by law and aim to avoid shooting or killing people. In this tradition, political and practical discretion in the day-to-day police work are both emphasized, and it is to this tradition that the Norwegian police belongs. By contrast, the militaristic tradition is characterized by secrecy, hierarchic lines of command, risk management and military solutions that involve weapons and uncompromising tactics. The goal is to eliminate threats, and there is little emphasis on practical discretion in the day-to-day work. This tradition has its roots in the continental parts of Europe and other parts of the world (NOU, 2017, p. 28). With its strong emphasis on efficiency and quantifiable results, the instrumental logic of the NPM reforms can be seen to have helped to change the societal view of crime and what the police's tasks are and how to solve them. In this way, the reforms have also opened up a possibility for the Norwegian police tradition to move in a more militaristic direction.

To create a clearer context for this line of thinking, we shall look at society's understanding of the core tasks of the police from a perspective of historical reform.

The core tasks of the police in a historical reform perspective

Historically, the core tasks of the police have been defined in the tension between control tasks and help/preventive tasks. As mentioned earlier, the definition of core tasks is related to the institutional logics that have characterized the social mandate of the police at any given time. After World War II, police tasks were about control and fighting crime. Both at the police academy of the day and in professional practice there was more emphasis on control than on assistance and help to the public. Using physical force to solve tasks was regarded as a more expedient tool than communication. The focus on problems with law and order and crime reduction in the 1950s and up until the 1970s leads us to describe the police organization in this period as "the force and control model" (Wathne, 2016). In the 1960s and 1970s, the police force gradually changed in a more humanistic direction, in line with the general development of public institutions in Norway at the time.

The work methods of the police were characterized more by communication, and the agency moved towards a "community policing model". The community policing model was introduced in Norway in 1978–79 (Holmberg, 2005, p. 207), framed in ten basic principles for the police (Ministry of Justice and the Police, 1981) and entailed decentralization of police work where the police increasingly emphasized prevention and greater public safety (Balvig & Holmberg, 2004, p. 11). The model reached its zenith in the 1980s, when police professionalism meant a more self-regulated police that was less affected by bureaucratic management structures (Sklansky, 2014). The humanistic logic of the community policing model states that police should be generalists and act in cooperation with the public (Ministry of Justice and the Police, 1981, p. 35). The fact that it was only in the 1990s that police education started to emphasize prevention and social sciences demonstrates how slowly the police education adapted to this model. The humanistic professional logic was in line with official police documents about how the police should work. However, during the 1990s this humanistic professional logic was challenged by the tougher tone of justice policy and the stronger orientation towards the situation of victims rather than towards the marginalized groups in the streets (Ministry of Justice and Public Security, 2009, p. 249). At the same time, a number of NPM-inspired reforms in Europe caused a movement away from the traditional Weberian bureaucratic model in the public sector (Meyer et al., 2014).

The reforms were rooted in a criticism that the welfare state project had turned local authorities into unresponsive bureaucratic organizations (Hansen, 2013, p. 120). One consequence of this criticism is that confidence in the professions has been weakened and that the professions have become more vulnerable to market, profitability and bureaucracy management (Freidson, 2001, here in Døving et al., 2015, p. 33). The professions have also reduced the use of discretion in their work (Døving et al., 2015).

Since the turn of the millennium, we find clear signs in society at large of a pendulum movement away from decentralized management towards centralized management with an emphasis on management by objectives (Røvik, 2009). Since it is difficult to quantify the effects of broad, preventive police work, the idea that humanistic good intentions were sufficient for guiding allocation of police resources was headed for a fall in Norway as well (Larsson, 2012). The traditional broad prevention methods lost their legitimacy in favour of more targeted and quantifiable approaches (Hough, 2010; Reiner, 2013). The changes must be seen in light of the introduction of management by objectives and results as a general principle for organizing tasks in the government since 1991. The focus on reporting goal achievement implied that the concept of "responsibility" changed its meaning from being about controlling the power of the police over citizens and protecting their legal rights to being accountable for how the police spend their resources[1] (Walker, 2005). Whereas community policing emerged as society in general became more humanistic, NPM logic also came through the door along with NPM reforms and management by objectives. This may be one of the reasons that several police studies show that policy culture mobilizes resistance to organizational changes inspired by NPM reforms (Finstad, 2000; Holgersson, 2005; Gundhus, 2006; Andersson & Tengblad, 2009).

NPM reforms have a clear ideological-political dimension where the logic of economism, its concepts and approaches dominate (Røvik, 2009, p. 34). Traces of how NPM trickled into the police can be found in the rhetoric of police management; whereas the police in the 1990s *discovered* crimes and solved them, today they "produce" cases. These changes must be seen in light of how language can reinforce logics that rub off on cultural values and the way employees think (Ferraro et al., 2005, p. 20). Founded on a view of knowledge that is based on tracking effects using statistics as a tool, this management by objectives promotes an evidence-oriented understanding of knowledge-based police work, which has an effect on the police profession as a whole. Although neither "evidence" nor "what works" (which are key terms of the evidence movement) play any role in NPM (Johansson et al., 2015, p. 71), both NPM and the evidence movement are connected to the same institutional logic. In this context, the opportunity of the police employees to choose what tasks to perform and how to perform them is diminished. In other words, the profession-based freedom to exercise discretion is changing. In practice, the introduction of management by objectives meant a new structural instrument for political and administrative leadership (Christensen & Lægreid, 2006, p. 155). In line with new ideals about how organizations should be put together, the NPM reforms can also be seen to contribute to changing management roles in the direction of business managers (Røvik, 2009, p. 161). I will come back to this issue at the end of my chapter dealing with change in social identity.

The legitimacy of the NPM principles is based on the fact that these methods work well in the private sector, that they are supported by economic research (Ferraro et al., 2005) and that the evidence wave is being driven by the public sector (Skaftnesmo, 2012, p. 351). The strong support for management by objectives in public administration can be seen in the context of the stricter requirements for professional practice set by governments in Western countries and that the professions respond by providing documentation of "what works" (Ekeland, 2012). However, this evidence-based tradition can also be driven by the professions themselves and may affect the organization in various ways. For instance, part of the motivation for the Danish police federations to fight for a general qualification for police training was that the federations were not politically recognized and did not have a right to be consulted or represented (Christensen, 2012, p. 99). One reason that everyone wants to be part of the evidence wave may be linked to the fact that the evidence-oriented understanding of knowledge reigns supreme in the knowledge hierarchy (Lumsden & Goode, 2016). It is then easy to forget that evidence-based knowledge work is also shaped by the data obtained and how these are understood, and that even empirical bases must be established and assessed with contextual insight (Skaftnesmo, 2012, p. 350).

Reformative changes from the turn of the millennium

It was only at the turn of the millennium that the NPM reforms really started to make an impact in the police. In line with the strong emphasis in the NPM reforms on resource utilization and effects, the reasoning behind Police Reform

2000 (Politidirektoratet, 2006) was that new criminal policy challenges and the increasing public demand for public service provision required an organizational shift to make more effective use of the available resources (Report No 22 to the Storting, 2000–2001). This reform involved centralization, whereby the number of police districts was reduced from 54 to 27 in 2002. The final evaluation of Police Reform 2000 showed a positive effect with regard to fighting serious crime; however, it also revealed that one of the main challenges of the police service going forward was to be accessible and oriented towards the general public (Sæveraas & Alexandersen, 2006).

The police reform adopted in 2015, the so-called "Community Policing Reform" (Nærpolitireformen), can be seen as a continuation of Police Reform 2000. The main objective of this most recent reform was to build a community police that is operative, visible and accessible, and that has the capacity and expertise to prevent, investigate and prosecute crimes as well as ensure the safety of residents. The reasoning for this is that the police are under significant pressure to change, and that organized crime is challenging the Norwegian policing model and setting new requirements for what constitutes a good police service (NOU, 2013, p. 9).

Here we see how society's view of crime affects the structure of the police organization as well as its focus and methodology. In line with the emphasis on serious crime, the police's core tasks are redefined as tasks which directly help to prevent and fight crime and preserve the safety and security of citizens, and in which the police is the only agency with the authority and means to carry out these tasks. This means that the core tasks of the police are narrowed to concern events and tasks in which the police has the right and duty to exercise power. In other words, the pendulum is swinging from assistive tasks towards controlling tasks. Considering that the police have traditionally spent most of their time on events not related to crime, and that cases in which the police on patrol only take action at the scene are found to make up over 80% of cases (Finstad, 2000, p. 170), this redefinition represents a clear shift. An important difference is that while the key element of the original community policing model was proximity between the police and the public *before* anything happened, the key element of this ongoing community policing reform is that new technology and mobility are giving us a police force that is present when we need it i.e. after something has happened.

The Community Policing Reform also implies a relatively strong centralization with a reduction in the number of police districts, police stations and rural police station districts, and thus falls in line with how the Scandinavian nations are reforming their police forces into more centralized units. The purpose of this centralization was also to reduce the size of management and achieve good management and leadership of the police (NOU, 2013, pp. 9, 30). Here we see a reflection of the control-oriented NPM reform element borrowed from various types of recent institutional economic theory in which one seeks to "make the manager manage" (Christensen et al., 2012, p. 216).

Reform elements from management theory modelled on the private sector in which decentralization and delegation are important have not been used as much in Norway. Based on the chosen reform measures, it is a paradox that the reform is actually named the "Community Policing Reform". The reform builds on an analysis of the police in which the phrase "community policing" is not even mentioned and which argues substantially against this model of policing (NOU, 2013, p. 9). Thus, we see that the concept of community policing is given a new content, something that can contribute to a reconstruction of reality – the physical world, social relations, social identities (Fairclough, 1992, p. 87). In an evaluation of the reform, it emerges that the entire concept of community policing seems to have gained a bad name and that several of the police employees interviewed joke that the reform should instead be called "the 'remote' policing reform" (Bakli et al., 2017, pp. 45, 47). The evaluation finds that the concept is not descriptive of the content of the reform and that both external actors and the police itself see what is happening as a centralization process.

In the following section, we shall move away from the core tasks of the police in a perspective of historical reform and examine their core tasks at an operational level.

Transformations of core tasks

The police is one of the professions with the broadest mandate in society (Larsson et al., 2014). The role of the Norwegian police is outlined in the Norwegian Police Act and the police instructions regulating the behaviour of those given police authority (Ministry of Justice and the Police, 2007, ch. 1, section 1–1; Botheim et al., 2013, p. 5). The overall objective of the police is "through preventive and helping activities contribute to society's overall effort to promote and consolidate the citizens' security under the law, safety and welfare in general" (The Norwegian Police Act, 1995, ch. 1, section 1). In line with the Police Act and policing instructions, important police tasks include maintenance of public order as well as assistance in connection with criminal offences or difficult situations of a non-criminal nature. The specific core tasks of the police have traditionally consisted of a variety of both assistive and control tasks, such as "catching thieves", helping the victims of and investigating burglary, maintaining public order in the streets by patrolling on foot, on horseback or in cars etc. As mentioned, the police have traditionally spent most of their time on events not relating to crime. Finstad exemplifies this as calling an ambulance or locksmith, removing prostitution clients, helping drunk people asleep in a gateway, checking up on people who attract police attention, de-licensing cars with unpaid road tax and insurance etc. (Finstad, 2000, pp. 170–171). Police work has a strong element of individual discretion in the way it is carried out and involves both emotional and relational aspects in that the way in which the police handle their situations is part of what they deliver (Hochschild, 1983). This has also been part of the Norwegian welfare state's services in a broader perspective.

In Britain, a combination of NPM reforms and emphasis on law and order have omitted certain aspects of policing, and the emphasis on quantifiable police tasks has been at the expense of work on minor public order issues (Hough, 2010, pp. 71, 75). Additionally, the police's handling of terrorism and terrorist threats have changed their firearms policy and practice (Finstad, 2015, p. 241) and can collectively be understood to have formed the basis for a development in a more militaristic direction.

Like the Norwegian police, the British police have belonged to the tradition of restraint marked by limited use of power and by cooperation with the public (Finstad, 2015). Finstad believes that "the great cooperation project" between the police and the public (including the criminal public) can be explained by noting that the public in various ways recognize the presence and actions of the police (Finstad, 2000, p. 178). This cooperation is founded on the community policing logic in which the entire population shall regard the police as "theirs", regardless of political divisions in society. Unlike encounters with other bureaucratic organizations, the first encounter that members of the public have with the police is often verbal and in person (Støkken, 1981). However, redefining the core tasks in the direction of focusing on serious crime and terrorism, centralizing the police and new technological solutions imply that the police's professional practice may not necessarily be taken for granted in the future. In the following section, we will examine how resource prioritization and outsourcing of certain tasks have laid the foundation for narrowing the core tasks of the police.

Emphasis on finances and changes in public contact

Research shows that the emphasis on demands for efficiency and resource utilization in the NPM-inspired reforms has created certain challenges for the link between professional management and financial management (Tranøy & Østerud 2009, p. 17; Christensen et al., 2012, p. 215). In line with this, the general experience of police employees is that financial conditions take precedence over fulfilling their tasks in the optimal way according to professional standards, and this perception is most widespread among employees engaged in tasks related to maintaining public order (Wathne, 2015). The fact that it is generally the managers who to the greatest extent see the financial conditions as taking precedence must be seen in the context of the fact that it is these very managers who are held accountable for the financial results in this performance management system. These findings must be seen in light of the fact that the police in recent years have taken on numerous new and more complex tasks, as well as a greater number of cases. This has contributed to the current situation of less visible police despite increased funding. Fewer visible police employees, combined with population growth, may have led to the increased workload for uniformed police when it comes to responding to the more direct enquiries from the public. A majority of the police employees feel that a lack of resources causes them to not be able to carry out their work tasks in the way they would like to, and nearly as many managers (90%) as non-managers (87%) are of this opinion (Wathne, 2015). It is the uniformed police (92%) who experienced having inadequate resources to fulfil their tasks in the way they would like to the greatest degree – 80% of these have a reduced feeling of mastery due to lack of resources. This must be seen in light of the fact that it is the police specialists who have benefitted most from the increased budgets in terms of number of full-time equivalents (FTEs) (Gjørv, 2012, p. 312; Botheim et al., 2013, p. 11). In other words, an increased prioritization of the more specialized police force, which is not as directly visible to the public, has been occurring over time. However, the traditional distribution in which the uniformed police are largely out on the streets while the investigators work inside an office is undergoing rapid change. Today, investigators also work "outdoors", and uniformed police carry out investigations as the first police patrol on site. This new way of organizing the work must be seen in the context of the development of new concepts such as "police work at site" (*politiarbeid på stedet*, PAS). In PAS, the patrol that responds to an event takes the first investigative steps at the scene. By taking photographs with their phones and recording interrogations, they secure documentation and evidence far more quickly (Gundhus et al., forthcoming, 2018). Such hybrid police tasks are emerging as a result of reforms and affect the degree and manner of each police employee's contact with the public.

Outsourcing of softer police tasks changes the image of the police

De-prioritizing of front-line assistive tasks is a developmental feature exemplifying that the process of redefining the core tasks of the police in the direction of serious crime started long before it was explicitly stated in strategic documents. Another factor pulling in the same direction is that many of the "softer" police tasks have been outsourced to private companies, primarily to security guards. The police themselves say they must cooperate with this sector in order to meet public demand for increased security (National Police Directorate, 2012, p. 52). In 2018, the National Police Directorate and the Confederation of Norwegian Enterprize (NHO) signed an agreement that the police and the security industry would cooperate more closely to prevent crime and maintain public order (Politiet, 2018b). This cooperation involves everything from day-to-day sharing of information to joint drills, crisis and public security work. This agreement makes Norway the first European country to formalize this type of cooperation (Norwegian Federation of Service Industries and Retail Trade, 2018). Today, private businesses have taken on the role of maintaining order at shopping centres, subways and other "semi-public" spaces. It is also common to meet a security guard at the reception desk when arriving for a meeting with a police employee at the police districts, and in this way the public face of the police is somewhat altered. This development can be seen as a market-inspired NPM measure borrowed from the private sector, in which parts of business operations are outsourced (Allvin et al., 2006). This measure has become increasingly common following a more liberalistic working life and labour market, and has also spread from the private to the public sector.

Furthermore, civilian employees are now responsible for a large part of the police's interaction with the public. The police also purchase a number of other private services that may not be easy to distinguish from ordinary police work, for instance offices, custody facilities and prisoner transport services (Larsson & Gundhus, 2007, p. 23). Not only do these changes narrow the role of the police towards control tasks but they may also contribute to making the role of the police less clear in the eyes of the general public. This development may further accelerate through measures incorporated in the ongoing police reform in which the police will cooperate even more with other parties, at the same time as the needs of more users will be met through digital services to the public such as online police reports etc. The idea is to facilitate "back-stage" the experience of a better police service among the public, though this does not always involve more face-to-face encounters with the public (Gundhus et al., forthcoming, 2018).

In the following section we shall examine how the centralization measures of the NPM reforms, along with new technological solutions, form the basis of a stronger management of patrols and less freedom of action for general work with the public.

Stronger management through prioritization of tasks

The tightening of the police employees' freedom of action and discretion concerning which tasks to carry out is grounded in familiar NPM rhetoric, which is all about better utilitization of resources and increased capacity. In this context, the role of central operations is key. In an overall sense, the central operation's task is to manage the operative units and the ongoing, prioritized operations in the district, as well as to prioritize in accordance with the allotted resources and priority directives (Hellesø-Knutsen, 2003). Even though it is ultimately the individual police officer who is responsible for how an assignment is carried out, it is the operator or operational manager who makes the final decision in the event of any disagreement on how to carry out tasks. The operators implement measures, lead and support the execution of assignments and communicate with police patrols via the police radio and telephone (Hellesø-Knutsen, 2003, pp. 9–10). The regulation of central operations can thus be said to intervene in the large scope for individual discretion that police officers normally have within the framework of laws, rules, instructions, procedures and priorities. In the ongoing police reform, central operations have received a more prominent role in controlling resources, and the centralization has given them a greater geographic area to manage. A qualitative study shows that when police patrols are to a greater extent controlled from central operations rather than deciding for themselves what to do, many police employees report having to decline public-initiated tasks which they previously would have carried out (Gundhus et al., forthcoming, 2018). This may well be tasks that do not involve serious crime but which nonetheless are valuable services to the public. The police's assignments from the public have in part consisted of norms for good practice and have constituted a police role which can be linked to the traditional community policing logic. In major cities and in some police districts, enquiries from the public go directly to central operations, which must then prioritize where to direct efforts. In this way, central operations carry out a relatively large part of the rejections of requests from the public. A study carried out in 2013 shows that while 62% of all police employees experienced having to reject members of the public asking for help every week or more frequently, even though they would have liked to help, the equivalent figure for employees in central operations was 71% (Wathne, 2015).

Because the role of central operations to prioritize gives it partial control of the police service's freedom of action, this prioritization may function as a source of both stress and coping for the patrols on duty. When asked to what degree they found it difficult that decisions on what to do were to be made at central operations, slightly more than 40% replied that they found it difficult to a great or to some extent, while 10% did not find it difficult at all. There were no statistically significant differences in age when it came to the perceived difficulty of having decisions made by the central operations (Wathne, 2015). Some may find the transfer of responsibility to the central operations to be negative, because parts of the control and freedom of action are in fact taken away from the police employees who are actually in the situation and given to a unit that is largely protected against visual scrutiny etc. In addition, the task of central operations is to prioritize according to allotted resources and priority directives, but this may also lead to the central operations implementing solutions that are effective in terms of resource considerations but which may run counter to considerations for proper and considerate policing (Dahl & Myhrer, 2009, p. 24). On the other hand, the central operations' decision concerning what is to be done as a situation unfolds may be seen by some police employees as positive guidance, and for some perhaps a relief, as part of the responsibility for finding a solution to potentially tricky situations is largely removed from the individual police officer. However, while this reduction of control is taking place, the police officers who are actually present in the situation experience the same demands for action from the public with whom they also interact face to face and from whom they receive immediate reactions.

Studies have shown that inner motivation, or the motivation to help others, can change to become a source of frustration if the work situation does not make it possible to help (Andersen & Pedersen, 2014, p. 68). A study of the police shows that having to say no to members of the public felt more difficult than experiencing threats and violence: while 58% found having to say no to people who asked for help difficult, 53% found experiencing violence equally difficult (Wathne, 2015). More employees in the rural police service than other police employees reported finding it difficult to say no to members of the public; this indicates that the relational proximity here may make it more difficult to reject requests for help even if they are not in line with the overall priorities. In the same way, the public in more rural areas are also seen by the police more as individuals rather than one large mass. The public's demand to understand or reverse a rejection from the police may require time and patience from the police employee.

Standardization of front-line work

Freidson believes that due to NPM reforms, many professions have been put under financial pressure to reduce costs by running the risk of standardizing and minimizing the services they provide as well as the quality of those services (Freidson, 2004). In the police, we see that although the police reforms have contributed to strengthening control of the police's prioritization of tasks, a stronger standardized control of *how* the police is to carry out its tasks has not been implemented to the same extent. For example, a study of the Norwegian police from 2013 shows that front-line police employees experience a relatively low degree of standardization in their work (Wathne, 2015). The reason for this may be that it has been difficult to standardize front-line work due to the high degree of individual discretionary judgement they use in carrying out their work tasks (Lipsky, 1980; Freidson, 2004). However, it looks as though the wave of digitalization that is upon us is helping to penetrate the wall that the strong degree of discretion involved in the work has built around the autonomy of the professions. A study of the 2018 police reform shows that the technological measures of the reform are helping to provide new ways of carrying out the tasks, which in part involves standardizing front-line work as well (Gundhus et al., forthcoming, 2019). For example, the police's freedom of action is standardized to a greater degree through so-called action cards that describe procedures and give guidelines for action. The design of the ICT systems helps to standardize what information the police employee is to collect and what information the managers and employees shall receive, and in what form. Furthermore, the nature of the reform involves more police work being done behind the scenes through artificial intelligence, either from a police patrol with a tablet or mobile phone or inside an office. New methods for obtaining information shall be in line with "The Police's Intelligence Doctrine", which is intended to contribute to developing intelligence as a key element in knowledge-based management. The reform thus challenges the established front-line work tools, which have traditionally had a strong element of individual discretionary judgement and in which relationships and relational work have been central (Gundhus et al., forthcoming, 2018).

The arguments presented in favour of standardized policing methods and work processes are that having a better knowledge base will enable the police to carry out their tasks more efficiently and that standardizing how to carry out the tasks will also make it easier to measure results and make comparisons (NOU 2013:9, 2013, p. 44). This enthusiasm for standardization must be seen in relation to the fact that comparing results to the targets set is an important purpose of the NPM reforms' management by objectives. Further management by objectives in policing is clearly stated in the ideals and operationalizing of effect targets in the ongoing community policing reform (Gundhus et al., forthcoming, 2018). Another purpose is to compare the results of the units to other units' results to find out which is best run. Use of benchmarking is dependent on quantifiable data (indicators) which provide information on the results for each unit (SSØ, 2010, p. 31). The arguments for a stronger standardization of police work are also about securing uniform police services to the public no matter where they live in the country. Standardization of police cars and new IT are intended to help to manage resources more efficiently where needed. The idea is that when all employees have access to the same information through various IT solutions, this will help to make police employees more easily replaceable, so that they can be allocated where they are needed, much like pieces in a game. In this way, a mobile police corps can be created which will utilize its resources and be present where they are needed (Gundhus et al., forthcoming, 2018).

Centralization distances the police from the public

A consequence of the centralization measures in the NPM reforms in which rural police offices and police districts are closed down and the police is gathered in larger units, is that police employees must cover a larger geographic area. Previously, police employees were integrated in their local community through work and housing, and thus built relationships with the locals. In larger cities, the police employees had more delineated geographic areas to serve. Here, the police employees have carefully built up trust over time between the police and the youth gangs in the local areas. With centralization, going on assignments to unfamiliar areas in practice means that police employees are stripped of one of their most important tools in community policing logic, namely their relationships with and knowledge of their public. When reorganization removes the police from the public by breaking up close relationships, a number of police employees feel distanced from the public they serve (Gundhus et al., forthcoming, 2018). While close contact with the public gives a contextual and "thicker" knowledge base, the information obtained behind the scenes gives a more purposive knowledge base on which to act. The purposive knowledge base has legitimacy in an NPM logic because it can show more easily how resources can be linked to quantifiable results. At a more general level, centralization is pulling the police in the direction of a more urban style of policing whereby stronger methods need to be used when approaching groups, because they do not know the involved parties and lack contextual information and knowledge of the groups (Gundhus et al., forthcoming, 2018). By redefining issues related to local youth gangs that need to be helped onto a different track to be about eliminating organized crime (Gundhus et al., forthcoming, 2019), the NPM logic can be seen to pull the Norwegian police in a more militaristic direction. From a discursive perspective, such a shifting of traditions involves redefining the challenges that society and the police face and the way in which these challenges are conceptualized. This development means that the entire Norwegian policing tradition is undergoing a change and may eventually lead to the Norwegian police also being permanently armed. It is also immediately easy to see how this military-like logic fits with the NPM logic at play in the Norwegian police: strong emphasis on hierarchy, rules and procedures, risk management and little focus on discretionary practice. By contrast, there is a fundamental and principal discrepancy between the humanistic professional logic of the police and the NPM logic, because the humanistic logic assumes that the performance of police tasks also requires professional discretion and contextual judgements. This affects how structural and organizational changes may influence the development of individual and collective constructions of meaning and brings us to the significance of the knowledge base.

A changing knowledge base

In an overall sense, stronger control and new methods for police work shall contribute to a more objective and scientific knowledge base and ensure that the police work in a knowledge-based way (Gundhus et al., forthcoming, 2018). In this context, the Police's Intelligence Doctrine (Politiets etterretningsdoktrine), which is heavily inspired by the Armed Forces' intelligence doctrine (Gundhus et al., forthcoming, 2019), is central. The intelligence doctrine is intended to give the police service, and managers in particular, decision-making support in the form of sound knowledge on problems and dangers which threaten the values they are to protect and thus help them to carry out their tasks. Intelligence is focused on decision-making bases concerning individuals, groups or phenomena which create or may create crime, as well as undesirable or extraordinary occurrences (National Police Directorate, 2014). The target group for the doctrine is all police employees. The doctrine and the new policing methods have a profound effect on the police's knowledge base as well as the police role. Digitalization and standardization enable the logic behind the strategic evidence-based knowledge base, which is firmly based in the NPM logic, to move from the police service's corporate governance by objectives down to the operative level. The front-line's freedom of action is reduced when it comes to choice of tasks to carry out and how to do so. The role of the front-line is largely reduced to gathering data which is then analysed and used in decision-making support at a higher level in the organization (Gundhus et al., forthcoming, 2019).

While the knowledge base previously was rooted in experience-based professional judgement, today it is more about quantifiable factors and evidence. In other words, today's hegemonic knowledge base is more scientific, quantifiable and less contextual. Even though this is not the case at the police academy, the police organization introduces procedures and objectives that are geared more towards control rather than assistance and help to the public.

For the police, "knowledge-based police work" is promoted as the legitimate base both in central police documents and in the discourse on the development of the police. Knowledge-based police work is a common category for new models for management by objectives, problem-based police work and crime investigation (Gundhus, 2006, p. 12), and it contrasts with more random and individual experience-based police work. Knowledge-based police work is evidence-based and emphasizes observable or quantifiable effects as valid grounds for action. Observable and quantifiable effects are almost the only objectives seen as a valid knowledge base for operation, management and resource allocation. Just as a strict evidence-based approach completely dominates society's knowledge hierarchy (Lumsden & Goode, 2016), evidence-oriented knowledge work has also attained a hegemonic position in the police. When effects that can be measured directly constitute the dominant knowledge base, a demarcation line is created against more discretionary professional police work, which loses its legitimacy.

When the police management base their management system on a management by objectives that is based on an evidence-oriented understanding of knowledge, as well as on procedures and standardization at an operative level, this represents a challenge not only in relation to ethical aspects of professional practice but also the interaction between colleagues in which the police profession develops standards for its work (Wathne, 2015). Because each incident is both general and unique, a sound professional policing effort requires insight based on the unique context, professional discretion, experience and instrumental knowledge. Therefore, it is difficult to standardize policing work through fixed, detailed procedures. Replacing insight with procedure works as long as thing go as expected, but it is inadequate when one has to act in a unique moment or according to what the specific situation requires (Skaftnesmo, 2012, p. 356). However, though much of the police work is difficult to standardize because it is context-dependent and requires discretion, it is fully possible to evidence-base and standardize the more technical arrest methods etc.

In sum, the focus of the NPM reforms on cost-effectiveness and verifiable results, along with stricter control, centralization and standardization, have pushed policing in the direction of control tasks which are increasingly based on instrumental analyses. In the following section, I will discuss how these changes affect the police's social identity.

Transformations of professional identity of the police

As mentioned in the introduction, the core tasks of the police have historically been defined along the tension between control tasks and help/preventive tasks. Traditionally, police identity has been based on the humanistic professional logic where the police are generalists, integrated in the local community and acting in cooperation with the public. In this context, the front-line police made discretionary decisions to a great extent, and accountability meant controlling the power of the police over citizens and protecting their legal rights. NPM-inspired reforms have caused a shift leading to changes in the institutional logics of public agencies and creating new positions of power and knowledge that represent a first step towards a new social construction of reality (Berger & Luckmann, 2000; Meyer et al., 2014). In Norway, we see how the community policing model is being abandoned in favour of a specialist model which to a greater extent considers quantifiable factors as plausible markers for good police work. These circumstances fundamentally affect identity.

As an analytical concept, social identity enables us to understand reproduction and changes in institutions because it highlights how the actor's perceptions and actions spring from this membership in a social group (Meyer et al., 2014, p. 3). Organizational identity consists of those attributes that members feel are fundamental to and uniquely descriptive of the organization and that persist within the organization over time (Pratt & Foreman, 2000, p. 20). In the police, organizational identity must at any given time be seen in connection with the knowledge base that constitutes valid platforms for action. Changes in the knowledge base can function as a catalyst for the development of a new police identity, and vice versa. This point must be seen in relation to the fact that to this day, the police management still assert that the ten basic principles of professional humanistic logic apply (Ministry of Justice and the Police, 1981), while at the same time we see quantifiable knowledge being emphasized as the way forward.

In line with how social context can help shape social identities, individual preferences and frames of reference (Friedland & Alford, 1991, p. 232; Meyer et al., 2014, p. 1), front-line police officers and police management can develop different professional identities. Empirical studies have shown that the management's professional identity to a certain extent follows the formal role displacement of the NPM reforms towards that of a business manager who is mainly concerned with financial results and "production". For example, the findings of the Auditor General showed that 21 out of 25 police districts lacked incentives to cooperate across district boundaries in investigations that crossed district lines, because the cooperation was not rewarded financially or shown in target and reporting systems in the management dialogue (Office of the Auditor General of Norway, 2010). This indicates that NPM logic and management by objectives can teach employees to think in a different way and to change cultural norms and values (Christensen & Lægreid, 1997, p. 392) and that NPM reforms can contribute to moving the manager's role in the direction of a business manager (Røvik, 2009, p. 161).

In line with this, a Norwegian study has found that police managers adopt elements from management logic to a greater degree compared to non-managers. Police managers are motivated more by management by objectives than non-managers, which can be partly explained by the fact that managers tend to think that management by objectives better captures the most important aspects of police work than do the front-line employees (Wathne, 2015). Increasingly, non-managers feel that management by objectives does not capture important aspects of the police work.

The facts that police managers are recruited from the ranks of ordinary policemen and that well over 90% of all police employees are motivated by a desire to make a difference for others, strengthens the hypothesis that the managers' hierarchical position pushes the motivation towards external incentives, rather than the assumption that externally motivated managers seek or are recruited to management positions (Wathne, 2015). When managers are measured by results in the management by objectives system, and to a lesser degree provide services directly to the public, the instrumental logic that governs the management system gets stronger motivational force, and the police manager's motivation shifts outwards. This is a paradox in light of a study that shows that the motivation of police employees for their work is in line with "public service motivation" (Wathne, 2015), where individuals are motivated by tasks in the public sector because they have internalized values that are embodied in these organizations (Perry & Wise, 1990, p. 372; Vandenabeele, 2011, p. 90). In this way, the erroneous assumption from the field of economics that man is an economic actor can become self-fulfilling (Ferraro et al., 2005). Measures that aim to increase internal competition and reward employees who act in accordance with set goals can over time lead to an organization that consists of employees who pursue their own interests rather than the best interests of the organization (Ferraro et al., 2005).[2] In other words, the professional social identity changes when the logic of the management system rubs off on the cultural values and the employees' thinking. In this way, NPM reforms can function as an identity project where new professional roles and social identities emerge: "from a servant of the state, its interests and its people to a manager of organizations and scarce resources" (Meyer & Hammerschmid, 2006, pp. 1001, 1011). Even if specific groups of employees can be associated with a specific institutional logic, one cannot assume that all members of the group will always relate to the same logic: "They may be influenced by the nature of the issues at hand – how they characterize it, or how important they think it is" (Pollitt, 2013, p. 348). This means that even if these logics may have contributed to developing different ideas of what constitutes good practices among managers and non-managers, it is not necessarily the case that managers and front-line officers have two distinctly separate professional identities. When police employees relate to competing institutional logics, they can construct new and hybrid identities that draw on several types of logic by mixing new orientations with old ideas (Meyer & Hammerschmid, 2006, p. 1013). It is reasonable to assume that the new police identity does not emerge as a clear transition from one identity to another, but as the development of a hybrid identity.

Conclusion

As I have shown in this chapter, NPM is transforming the Norwegian police in several ways. The NPM reforms' focus on efficiency and quantifiable policing tasks has, along with the construction of a more dystopic risk assessment, narrowed the police's core tasks towards control tasks. This narrowing of tasks is reinforced by the standardization made possible and assisted by digitalization and transports the logic behind the evidence-based knowledge basis of management by objectives from management level to the operational level. In practical terms, this means a weakening of the close, dialogue-based policing represented by the community policing model and the university college project (Høgskoleprosjektet). Standardization must be seen in relation to the fact that the professions were from the 1970s subjected to criticism about their privileges and powers, which diminished trust and contributed to an emphasis on more control (Døving et al., 2015, p. 33). Previous studies have shown that the front-line has exhibited strong resistance to the changes brought by reforms and to stronger control, a resistance which has strengthened traditional assumptions and work practices rather than challenging the police officers' objective and identity (Gundhus, 2006; Chan, 2007; Andersson & Tengblad 2009). However, the technological measures in the police reform contribute to a partial standardization of front-line work by reducing the freedom of choice of tasks and solution methods. This is a significant difference which also makes it more challenging to mobilize resistance to the changes. In this way, NPM, together with the digitization wave, has weakened the police profession in new ways. What will happen to police identity and public relations over time remains to be seen.

Notes

1 At the end of the 1980s, the concept of "audits" became increasingly common and more and more entities were required to provide detailed accounts of their activities (Walker, 2005, p. 3).

2 This does not mean that police employees who follow the NPM logic are necessarily more concerned with their own careers than the organization's interests. It may be a question of loyalty based on the belief that a police employee, as part of that state's political power, must conform loyally to the demands which management puts on them.

References

Allvin, M., Aronsson, G., Hagström, T., Johansson, G. & Lundberg, U. (2006) *Gränslöst arbete: socialpsykologiska perspektiv på det nya arbetslivet [Boundless Work: Social Psychological Perspective on the New Working Life]*, Malmo, Sweden: Liber.

Andersen, L. B. & Pedersen, L. H. (2014) *Styring og motivasjon i den offentlige sektor [Governance and Motivation in the Public Sector]*, Copenhagen: Jurist og økonomiforbundets forlag.

Andersson, T. & Tengblad, S. (2009) When Complexity Meets Culture: New Public Management and the Swedish Police, *Qualitative Research in Accounting & Management*, 6(1/2): 41–56.

Bakli, O., Botheim, I. & Lassen, V. (2017) Evaluering av nærpolitireformen [Evaluation of the Community Policing Reform], *Statusrapport 2016*, DIFI rapport 2017:2.

Balvig, F. & Holmberg, L. (2004) *Politi og tryghed: Forsøg med nærpoliti i Danmark [Police and Security: Experiments with Community Policing in Denmark]*, Copenhagen: Djøf/Jurist-og Økonomforbundet.

Bayley, D. (1985) *Patterns of Policing: A Comparative International Analysis*, New Brunswick, NJ: Rutgers University Press.

Berger, P. L. & Luckmann, T. (2000) *The Social Construction of Reality: A Treatise in the Sociology of Knowledge*, Harmondsworth, UK: Penguin Social Sciences.

Botheim, I., Søvik, S., Strøm, M. & Bakli, O. (2013) Evaluering av politidirektoratet [Evaluation of the Police Directorate], *DIFI rapport* 2013:3. www.difi.no/sites/difino/files/difi-rapport-2013–3-evaluering-av-politidirektoratet.pdf.

Chan, J. (2007) Making Sense of Police Reforms, *Theoretical Criminology*, 11(3): 323–345.

Christensen, M. J. (2012) *Fra det evige politi til projektpolitiet. En kamp om position og ideologi [From the Eternal Police to the Project Police. A Struggle for Position and Ideology]*, Copenhagen: Jurist og økonomforbundets forlag.

Christensen, T., Egeberg, M., Larsen, H. O., Lægreid, P. & Roness, P. G. (2012) *Forvaltning og politikk [Management and Policy]*, third edition, Oslo: Universitetsforlaget.

Christensen, T. & Lægreid, P. (1997) Forvaltningspolitikk: mot New Public management? [Management Policy: Towards New Public Management], In: Christensen, T. & Egeberg, M. (eds) *Forvaltningskunnskap*, Otta, Norway: Tano Aschehoug, 367–404.

Christensen, T. & Lægreid, P. (2006) *Reformer og lederskap [Reforms and Leadership]*, Oslo: Universitetsforlaget.

Dahl, S. & Myhrer, T. G. (2009) *Å kunne vurdere, forklare og beklage. Seminar with Placement Supervisors on Power and Ethics in 2008 and 2009: Outline, Insights and Suggestions*, Oslo: Politihøgskolen.

Døving, E., Elstad, B. & Storvik, Aa. (2015) Profesjon, ledelse og organisasjon: perspektiver og begreper [Profession, Leadership and Organization: Perspectives and Concepts], In: Døving, E., Elstad, B. & Storvik, A. (eds) *Profesjon og ledelse [Profession and Leadership]*, Oslo: Fagbokforlaget.

Ekeland, T.-J. (2012) Sjelens ingeniørkunst. Om psykologien og psykologens selvforståelse [Soul Engineering. About Psychology and Psychology Self-Understanding], *Journal of Norwegian Psychology Association 2012*, 49(8): 747–752.

Ellefsen, B. & Larsson, P. (2014) Skandinavisk politihistorie [Scandinavian Police History], In: Larsson, P., Gundhus, H. O. I. & Granér, R. (eds) *Innføring i politivitenskap [Introduction to Police Science]*, Oslo: Cappelen Damm, 29–52.

Fairclough, N. (1992) *Discourse and Social Change*, Cambridge, UK: Polity Press.
Ferraro, F., Pfeffer, J. & Sutton, R. I. (2005) Economics Language and Assumptions: How Theories Can Become Self-Fulfilling, *Academy of Management Review*, 30(1): 8–24.
Finstad, L. (2000) *Politiblikket [Police Gaze]*, Oslo: Pax.
Finstad, L. (2015) Det enkleste er ikke pistol. [The Simplest is Not a Gun], In: Korsell, L., Larsson, P. & Christophersen, J. G. (eds) *Ekstraordinære tider: Festskrift til Per Ole Johansen [Extraordinary Times: Festschrift for Per Ole Johansen]*, Oslo: Novus Forlag, 225–247.
Freidson, E. (2001) *Professional Powers: A Study of The Institutionalization of Formal Knowledge*, Chicago, IL: University of Chicago Press.
Freidson, E. (2004) *Professionalism: The Third Logic*, Cambridge, UK: Polity Press.
Friedland, R. & Alford, R. R. (1991) Bringing Society Back In: Symbols, Practices, and Institutional Contradictions, In: DiMaggio, P. J. & Powell, W. W. (eds) *The New Institutionalism in Organizational Analysis*, Chicago, IL: University of Chicago Press.
Gjørv, A. B. (2012) *Report from the 22 July Commission*, NOU 2012:14. www.regjeringen.no/contentassets/bb3dc76229c64735b4f6eb4dbfcdbfe8/no/pdfs/nou2012201200140000dddpdfs.pdf.
Gundhus, H. I. (2006) "For sikkerhets skyld": IKT, yrkeskulturer og kunnskapsarbeid i politiet ["Just in case": Information Technology, Occupational Cultures and Knowledge Work in the Police], PhD dissertation, University of Oslo.
Gundhus, H. O. I., Talberg, N. & Wathne, C. T. (forthcoming, 2018) In: Sørli, V.L. & Larsson, P. (eds) *Politireformer: Idealer, realiteter, retorikk og praksis [Police Reforms: Ideals, Realities, Rhetorics and Practise]*, Oslo: Cappelen Damm Akademisk.
Gundhus, H. O. I., Talberg, N. & Wathne, C. T. (forthcoming, 2019) In: Sunde, I.M, & Sunde, N. (eds).
Hansen, H. F. (2013) NPM in Scandinavia, In: Christensen, T. & Lægreid, P. (eds) *The Ashgate Research Companion to New Public Management*, Abingdon, UK: Ashgate.
Hellesø-Knutsen, K. (2003) Belastninger og opplevd stress ved Operasjonssentralen [Loads and Experienced Stress at the Operations Centre], Oslo politidistrikt (Hovedfag thesis), Norwegian University of Science and Technology, Trondheim, Norway.
Hochschild, A. R. (1983) *The Managed Heart: Commercialization of Human Feeling*, Berkeley, CA: University of California Press.
Høigård, C. (2011) Policing the North, In: Tonry, M. & Lappi-Seppälä, T. (eds) *Crime and Justice in Scandinavia*, 40, Chicago, IL: The University of Chicago Press, 265–348.
Holgersson, S. (2005) Yrke: polis: yrkeskunskap, motivation, IT-system och andra förutsättingar för polisarbete [Occupation: Police: Professional Knowledge, Motivation, IT Systems and Other Prerequisites for Police Work], PhD dissertation, Linköping University, Sweden.
Holmberg, L. (2005) Policing and the Feeling of Safety: The Rise (and Fall?) of Community Policing in the Nordic Countries, *Journal of Scandinavian Studies in Criminology and Crime Prevention*, 5(2): 205–219.
Hough, M. (2010) Policing, New Public Management and Legitimacy, In: Brookes, S. & Grint, K. (eds) *The New Public Leadership Challenge*, Basingstoke, UK: Palgrave Macmillan, 70–84. https://doi.org/10.1057/9780230277953_5.

Hove, K. (2012) *Politiutdanning i Norge: fra konstabelkurs til bachelorutdanning [Police Education in Norway: From Constable Course to Bachelor Education]*, Oslo: Politihøgskolen. https://brage.bibsys.no/xmlui/handle/11250/175009.

Johansson, K., Denvall, V. & Vedung, E. (2015) After the NPM Wave: Evidence-Based Practice and the Vanishing Client. Offentlig Förvaltning, *Scandinavian Journal of Public Administration*, 19(2): 69–88.

Larsson, P. (2012) Ideology as a Cover Up: Community Policing in Norway, *European Journal of Policing Studies* (ISSN: 2034-760X) Volume 1.

Larsson, P. & Gundhus, H. O. I. (2007) Policing i et norsk perspektiv [Policing in a Norwegian Perspective], In: Gundhus, H. I., Larsson, P. & Myhrer, T.-G. (eds) *Polisiær virksomhet: hva er det – hvem gjør det? [Police Business: What Is It – Who Does It?]*, Forskningskonferansen 2007, PHS forskning 2007:7, Oslo: Politihøgskolen, 11–30.

Larsson, P., Gundhus, H. O. I. & Granér, R. (eds) (2014) *Innføring i politivitenskap [Introduction to Police Science]*, Oslo: Cappelen Damm Akademisk, 29–52.

Lipsky, M. (1980) *Street-Level Bureaucracy: Dilemmas of the Individual in Public Services*, New York: Russell Sage Foundation.

Lumsden, K. & Goode, J. (2016) Policing Research and the Rise of the "Evidence-Base": Police Officer and Staff Understandings of Research, Its Implementation and "What Works", *Sociology*. doi: 0038038516664684.

Meyer, R. E., Egger-Peitler, I., Höllerer, M. A. & Hammerschmid, G. (2014) Of Bureaucrats and Passionate Public Managers: Institutional Logics, Executive Identities, and Public Service Motivation, In: *Public Administration*, 92(4). https://doi.org/10.1111/j.1467–9299.2012.02105.x.

Meyer, R. E. & Hammerschmid, G. (2006) Changing Institutional Logics and Executive Identities: A Managerial Challenge to Public Administration in Austria, *American Behavioral Scientist*, 49(7): 1000–1014.

Ministry of Justice and the Police (1981) *Politiets rolle i samfunnet: delutredning [The Role of the Police in Society: Partial Investigation]*, NOU 1981:35, Oslo: Universitetsforlaget.

Ministry of Justice and the Police (2007) *Alminnelig tjenesteinstruks for politiet [General Service Instructions for the Police]*, (politiinstruksen) from 1990 (in force from 1 July 2006), Oslo: Cappelen Akademisk forlag.

Ministry of Justice and Public Security (2009) *Et ansvarlig politi: Åpenhet, kontroll og læring [A Responsible Police: Openness, Control and Learning]*, NOU 2009:12. www.regjeringen.no/nb/dokumenter/nou-2009–12/id560793/.

National Police Directorate (Politidirektoratet) (2012) Politiets omverdensanalyse [Analysis of Societal Context by the Police], *POD Publication*, No 2012/10. www.politi.no/vedlegg/rapport/Vedlegg_1900.pdf.

National Police Directorate (Politidirektoratet) (2014) *Etterretningsdoktrine for politiet [Intelligence Doctrine for the Police]*, Versjon 1.0.

Norwegian Federation of Service Industries and Retail Trade (2018) *Police and Security Officers Formalize Cooperation*. www.nhosh.no/bransjer/sikkerhet-og-beredskap/nyheter-sikkerhet/2018/Politi-og-vekter/.

NOU 2013:9 (2013) Justis- og beredskapsdepartementet. Ministry of Justice and Public Security, Ett politi: rustet til å møte fremtidens utfordringer – Politianalysen [Police: Equipped to Meet the Challenges of the Future – Police Analysis]. www.regjeringen.no/nb/dokumenter/nou-2013–9/id730815/.

NOU 2017:9 (2017) *Politi og bevæpning. Legalitet, nødvendighet, forholdsmessighet og ansvarlighet [Police and Armed Forces. Legality, Necessity, Proportionality and Accountability]*. https://www.regjeringen.no/no/dokumenter/nou-2017-9/id2545750/.

Office of the Auditor General of Norway (2010) *Riksrevisjonens undersøkelse av politiets innsats mot organisert kriminalitet [Investigation of Police Efforts Against Organized Crime by the Committee on Scrutiny and Constitutional Affairs]*, Dokument 3:10 (2009–2010). www.riksrevisjonen.no/SiteCollectionDocuments/Dokumentbasen/Dokument3/2009–2010/Dokumentbase_Dok_3_10_2009_2010.pdf.

Perry, J. L. & Wise, L. R. (1990) The Motivational Bases of Public Service, *Public Administration Review*, 50(3): 367–373.

Politidirektoratet (2006) *Sluttevaluering Politireform 2000*. Sandvika: Agenda. http://evalueringsportalen.no/evaluering/sluttevaluering-politireform-2000/Politireform%20 2000%20–20hovedrapport2006endeligversjon.pdf/@@inline.

Politiet (2018a) *Vil ha flere kvinnelige ledere [Want More Female Executives]*. www.politiet.no/aktuelt-tall-og-fakta/aktuelt/nyheter/2018/03/08/vil-ha-flere-kvinnelige-ledere/.

Politiet (2018b) *Formelt samarbeid mellom politiet og sikkerhetsbransjen [Formal Cooperation between the Police and the Security Industry]*. www.politiet.no/en/aktuelt-tall-og-fakta/aktuelt/nyheter/2018/01/formelt-samarbeid-mellom-politiet-og-sikkerhetsbransjen.

Politiskolen (2018) *Om politiskolen [About the Police Academy]*. http://politiskolen.dk/om-politiskolen.

Pollitt, C. (2013) The Logics of Performance Management, *Evaluation*, 19(4): 346–363.

Pratt, M. & Foreman, P. O. (2000) Classifying Managerial Responses to Multiple Organizational Identities, *Academy of Management Review*, 25(1): 18–42.

Reiner, R. (2013) Who Governs? Democracy, Plutocracy, Science and Prophecy in Policing, *Criminal Justice*, 13(2): 161–180.

Report No 22 to the Storting (2000–2001) *Politireform 2000: Et tryggere samfunn [Political Reform 2000: A Safer Society]*. www.regjeringen.no/no/dokumenter/stmeld-nr-22–2000–2001-/id431872/.

Røvik, K. A. (2009) *Trender og translasjoner. Ideer som former det 21. århundrets organisasjon [Trends and Translations. Ideas that Shape the 21st Century Organization]*, Oslo: Universitetsforlaget.

Sæveraas, R. & Alexandersen, G. (2006) *Sluttevaluering. Politireform 2000 [Final Evaluation. Police Reform 2000]*, Sandivka, Norway: Agenda utredning og utvikling AS.

Skaftnesmo, T. (2012) Evidensbasering: Den nye eminensen [Evidence Base: The New Eminence], *Norsk pedagogisk tidsskrift*, 96(5): 348–360.

Sklansky, D. A. (2014) The Promise and the Perils of Police Professionalism, In: Brown, J. M. (ed.) *The Future of Policing*, New York: Routledge, 343–353.

SSØ (2010) *Resultatmåling. Mål- og resultatstyring i staten [Performance Measurement. Target and Performance Management in the State], Veileder 12/2010*, Oslo: Senter for statlig økonomistyring.

Støkken, A. M. (1981) *Politiet i det norske samfunn [Police in Norwegian Society]*, Oslo: Universitetsforlaget.

The Norwegian Police Act (1995) LOV-1995-08-04-53. https://lovdata.no/dokument/NL/lov/1995-08-04-53.

The Norwegian Police University College (2018) (Politihøgskolen) Master's Degree Programmes. www.phs.no/studietilbud/master/.

Thornton, P. H. & Ocasios, H. (2008) Institutional Logics, In: Greenwood, R., Oliver,. C., Sahlin-Andersson, K. & Syddaby, R. (eds) *The SAGE Handbook of Organizational Institutionalism*, Thousand Oaks, CA: Sage, 99–129.

Thornton, P. H., Ocasio, W. & Lounsbury, M. (2013) *The Institutional Logics Perspective: A New Approach to Culture, Structure, and Process*, New York: Oxford University Press.

Tranøy, B. S. & Østerud, Ø. (eds) (2009) *Den fragmenterte staten. Reformer, makt og styring [The Fragmented State. Reforms, Power and Governance]*, Oslo: Gyldendal Akademisk.

Vandenabeele, W. (2011) Who Wants to Deliver Public Service? Do Institutional Antecedents of Public Service Motivation Provide an Answer?, *Review of Public Personnel Administration*, 31(1): 87–107.

Walker, S. (2005) *The New World of Police Accountability*, Thousand Oaks, CA: Sage.

Wathne, C. T. (2015) Som å bli fremmed i eget hus: Politiets opplevelse av mening og motivasjon i lys av nye styringssystemer [Like Being a Stranger in One's Own House: Police Experience of Meaning and Motivation in Light of New Management Systems], PhD dissertation at Department of Criminology and Sociology of Law, University of Oslo.

Wathne, C. T. (2016) Kvinners plass i politiet i lys av arbeidsmetoder [Women's Place in the Police in Light of Working Methods], *Tidsskrift for kjønnsforskning*, 39(1): 3–23.

Part V

Terms of employment

Precarious work in a Nordic setting

Introduction

Helge Hvid and Eivind Falkum

The spread of precarious work is considered by many observers to be the greatest threat to the established security structures in the labour market. In many countries, the established social policy and employment relations do not offer much protection to people with insecure and unpredictable employment relationships. Therefore, they must find other approaches to creating a dignified life.

Also in the Nordics, work seems to be becoming increasingly precarious. This creates challenges for the Nordic approach, and different approaches are being sought to meet these.

Chapter 14: Precarity in Nordic working life? By Mari Holm Ingelsrud, Niels Warring, Janne Gleerup, Per Bonde Hansen, Anders Jakobsen, Anders Underthun and Søren Salling Weber.

In this chapter, the phenomenon of 'precarity' in the Nordic context is presented and discussed, based on a literature study. The prevalence of precarious work is investigated and the question of whether the Nordic communities are resilient to precarization is raised. The answer is 'yes, so far'. However, the answer is also that precarization poses major challenges to the Nordic tradition.

Chapter 15: Experiences of precarious work among graduates in the Danish labour market. By Janne Gleerup, Anders Jakobsen and Niels Warring.

When flexibly employed academics in Denmark feel insecure about their job situation, it is not just an expression of their individual choices about what work they want to do. It also reveals a broader trend where public employees, who have traditionally had highly secure employment in the Nordic countries, find their job and income security to be fading. The dynamic interplay between societal developments and subjective experiences of quality and conflicts in working life is examined.

Chapter 16: The formation and destabilization of the standard employment relationship in Norway: the contested politics and regulation of temporary work agencies. By Per Bonde Hansen and Anders Underthun.

Here temporary work agencies are studied in a historical perspective. Both employers and trade unions have been heavily involved in the regulation of temporary work agencies. Norway has a relatively strong version of standard employment. The regulation of temporary work agencies contributed to the creation of this strong version.

Chapter 17: Working life on Nordic labour platforms. By Søren Salling Weber.

This chapter explores how the platform economy and the sharing economy affect those who are working there. Digital platforms are created to organize labour more effectively. However, they also change the way work is organized for employees and places them in relatively vulnerable positions. Initiatives to include the platform economy in the Nordic approach are highlighted.

Chapter 14

Precarity in Nordic working life?

Mari Holm Ingelsrud, Niels Warring, Janne Gleerup, Per Bonde Hansen, Anders Jakobsen, Anders Underthun and Søren Salling Weber

Introduction

Precarious work, understood as work conditioned by a lack of security and predictability (Standing, 2014), is not a new phenomenon in the history of capitalism. However, according to Isabell Lorey (2015 [2012]), our experience of precarity is relative, always mediated by the social and political institutions shaping societal life. Lorey argues that contemporary precarious work is characterized by new and specific dynamics following the rapid globalization of the world economy since the 1980s. Kalleberg (2009, p. 1) emphasizes that "uncertain and unpredictable work contrasts with the relative security that characterized the three decades following World War II", while Beck (2000) describes a "new political economy of insecurity". With reference to Karl Polanyi's classic work from 1944, *The Great Transformation*, we also see signs of a new "big transformation" of society suggesting that precarization mirrors new forms of crises in global developments in capitalism. Processes of flexibilization, polarization and degradation of work have all been associated with precarious work (Kalleberg, 2003; Sennett, 2006; Munck, 2013; Paret, 2016).

Despite critical voices warning against the transition to an age of insecurity and social instability at the turn of the millennium (Sennett, 1998; Beck, 2000), the norm of the standard employment relationship (SER), understood as full-time, continuous employment with one employer (Vosko, 2009, p. 396) still dominates Nordic working life. Is then precarization in the Nordic countries a relevant theme for research?

Two main questions guide this chapter: (1) "How is the precarization of employment expressed in Norway and Denmark?" and (2) "Is the Nordic model resilient to precarization?" We start by analysing the relationship between flexibilization and precarization in a brief literature review. Here, we pay particular attention to how processes of flexibilization, polarization and work degradation are related to precarization and insecurity. We then give a short account of how Norway and Denmark fare on some measures associated with precarity. The challenge of measuring precarization with standardized quantitative instruments is a point that we will touch upon, also considering relevant results from qualitative studies.

To answer the second question, we will describe how legal, normative and economic boundaries govern the employment relationship in Norway and Denmark. We also discuss how standard employment is challenged by processes of flexibilization, increasing polarization and decreasing union density. We conclude the chapter by summing up the discussions and relating them to issues dealt with in the three following chapters in this Part of the book.

Precarious work: what are we talking about?

Attempting to grasp the complexity of precarization, Vosko (2010) defines precarious employment as employment relationships characterized by insecurity, low income and limited social rights. She argues that precarious employment is shaped by the relationship between employment status (whether paid worker or self-employed), forms of employment (temporary versus permanent or part-time versus full-time), the social context (occupation, industry, geographic location), the social location of the worker (gender, race, citizenship) and dimensions of labour market security.

The deregulation of capital markets, elimination of price controls and trade barriers, privatization of state enterprises, tight economic policies, limitation of state aid schemes and security systems, and weakening of trade unions' influence are all held to be drivers of a growing international precarity (Harvey, 2005; Boas & Gans-Morse, 2009). Kalleberg (2012) asserts that two trends are particularly apparent: the first is an increasing inequality in job quality, skills and wages through polarization processes that particularly undermine middle-class jobs. Secondly, Kalleberg asserts that precarity is a more persuasive phenomenon that affects all workers through increased insecurity. As such, Kalleberg argues that discussions about the precarization of work must take both trends into account. Increasing polarization leads to growing differences in job quality and job security between workers at the high and low ends of the labour market. Kalleberg's argument dovetails Sennett's (2006) observation that this new work organizational tendency in contemporary capitalism influences jobs at all levels (Sennett, 2006).

Among theorists concentrating on the polarization trend, Robert Castel (2002) links precarity to a division of society into different integration zones. The fully integrated are represented by those who are (still) in a standard employment relationship of full-time fixed employment with regulated contractual relations. At the other end of the scale, we find the disconnected, a category that also includes the unemployed. The precariat, Castel argues, can be regarded as being in a transition zone between the integrated and the disconnected. Here, increasing precarity represents a dis-integration of society, a coming-apart that might have other societal and social consequences (Castel, 2002). Arguing that "the precariat" is a "new dangerous class" in the making, Guy Standing (2014) describes how members of the precariat experience similar types of insecurity without sharing a common vision of what sort of good society they would like to create. The precariat is a floating labour supply moving in and out of jobs and is characterized by a lack of occupational identity around which their lives can be generatively structured. The precariat often enjoy fewer rights than full citizens and sometimes lose rights along the way. Standing has defined seven forms of labour insecurity that are related to precarity as a phenomenon: labour market insecurity, employment insecurity, job insecurity, work insecurity, skill reproduction insecurity, income insecurity and representation insecurity. According to Standing, it is the breakdown of security into one or more of these dimensions that constitutes precarity. Labour insecurity in one or more forms also leads to a more heterogeneous labour force. Perhaps most importantly, class divisions have been supplemented by (im)migrant divisions and hierarchies (McDowell et al., 2009).

Sennett (2006) argues that organizational changes in firms at the cutting edge of the economy have a cultural influence on broad aspects of life, from the valuation of skills to consumption and politics. The economic logic of the stock market favours short-term thinking, creating volatile businesses run by consultants who are in it for quick gains. The ability of businesses to adapt rapidly is seen as a prerequisite for success. The ethos of flexibility is increasingly guiding working life, changing how we are valued as workers, how we work and how we live. For employees, flexibility is linked to increased risk and insecurity in work through the shift towards more precarious employment (Allen & Henry, 1997). Also taking the standpoint of the workers, Kalleberg (2009) defines precarious work as "employment that is uncertain, unpredictable and risky from the point of view of the worker" (Kalleberg, 2009, p. 2).

Different forms of labour flexibility have expanded and become core elements in the development of post-Fordist and neoliberal labour market (de)regulations and state policies (Castel & Dörre, 2009). A recent review (Spreitzer et al., 2017) identifies three dimensions of flexibility that underlie research on alternative work arrangements: the employment relationship, the scheduling of work and where work is done. Flexibility on these dimensions offers possibilities for both employers and employees, albeit sometimes in conflicting ways. Flexible employment relationships include direct non-standard employment (on-call work, part-time work and seasonal employees), agency work and contract work. Flexibility in the employment relationship is positive from the vantage point of the firm, minimizing risks involved in hiring. Standing (2014) states that numerical flexibility related to growth in temporary and part-time jobs and outsourcing is an important rationale for precarization. He also points to increased wage flexibility in moving from fixed to flexible pay and how what he calls "social income" (the sum of income needed) is becoming more insecure. Finally, functional flexibility is related to management control over work and the ability to shift employees between tasks, positions and workplaces. It involves potential de-professionalization and reduction of the influence of occupations and professions and their unions, thus resulting in growing insecurity and individualization.

The individualization of risk through increased flexibility does not have the same consequences for all employees. For some groups of high-skilled workers, increasing flexibility offers the possibility of tailoring one's working life according to one's own preferences. Contract work for this category of workers might represent great possibilities, while the perceived risk and insecurity remain low. At the other end of the labour market, low-skilled workers who are easily replaceable might find themselves struggling to find a job that offers continuity of employment and adequate payment (Spreitzer et al., 2017). For these workers, flexibility is synonymous with unpredictability and insecurity. As such, the flexibilization of employment contributes to the polarization of work as discussed earlier.

Precarity has previously been associated with the deterioration of work and employment relationships among unskilled and skilled workers in the private sector (Kalleberg, 2009; McKay et al., 2012). However, there is an increasing awareness of how precarity is spreading to public employees and highly educated workers. According to Isabell Lorey (2015 [2012]), the increasing focus on precarity reflects the fact that we are currently undergoing a change towards "governmental precarization". She separates the common existential condition of precariousness from the historically specific feelings of precarity that result from institutional attempts to mediate precariousness. What constitutes the current neoliberal governmentalization is the increasing individualization of the processing of precariousness and the creation of security. Through flexibilization, economic risks are shifted from employers to employees.

Other scholars, however, challenge the widespread idea that precarious work is exclusively linked to recent processes of neoliberal politics and flexibilization. According to Betti (2016), a gendered historical approach shows that women and migrants experienced a "significant level of precariousness" even during the period regarded as the heyday of the standard employment relationship and the "golden age" of capitalism (Hobsbawm, 1994), i.e. the first three decades or so after World War II. In this perspective, precariousness is not a new phenomenon, rather it is embedded in industrial capitalism. Thus, it is not the existence of precarious work in itself, but the level of precariousness and how precariousness spreads across the work force that have changed.

The theories reviewed in this section cover various aspects of precarization: polarization, flexibilization and work degradation. The next section investigates how precarization is expressed in Norway and Denmark, specifically with respect to increasing polarization through flexibilization and increasing job insecurity. We also argue that the most used statistical measures of precarity might conceal significant developments in Nordic working life that only appear when we focus on specific sectors.

Precarity in the Nordic countries?

Compared to the situation in many other countries, precarious work is spreading slowly in the Nordics. Some statistics even suggest that the period since the late 2000s has hardly shown any increase in different types of "atypical" work. The term atypical work simply describes deviations from what is regarded as typical, i.e. the standard employment relationship. Hence, it is not identical to precarious work. As Vosko (2010, p. 2) has pointed out, there is clearly a relationship between the two concepts, but some non-standard or atypical employment can be relatively secure, and precariousness may apply to all kinds of work for remuneration. In this chapter, however, we find it relevant to base our discussion on statistics on atypical work, as we consider the scope of atypical work as a marker and prerequisite for the existence of precarious work.

The part-time employment rate is high in Norway (24% of total employment in 2015), while in Denmark it is closer to the level of the rest of the EU28 (21% and 19%, respectively). Figures from Eurostat show an increase in the part-time employment rate in Denmark and EU28 (from 18% and 17% in 2005) and a small decrease in Norway (from 26% in 2005). They show a stable temporary employment rate at around 11% in EU28, and 7% in Denmark and Norway. There is a small increase in the long-term unemployment rate in all countries, from 1.1% in 2005 to 1.7% in 2015 in Denmark and from 0.8% to 1% in Norway. These figures are lower than those of EU28 at 4% in 2005 and 4.5% in 2015.[1] However, the prevalence of precarious jobs is likely to be underestimated in surveys such as the Labour Force Survey. For instance, those workers holding the most precarious positions, such as immigrant workers, are unlikely to be invited to answer the questionnaires.

The Nordic countries are, like the rest of the Western world, witnessing increasing economic polarization (OECD, 2017). Research specifically on migrant labour suggests that migrants tend to end up in non-standard employment arrangements to a greater extent than native citizens (Ødegaard, 2014; Neergaard, 2015; Raess & Burgoon, 2015; Broughton et al., 2016, p. 50). Migrant workers are often overrepresented in the temporary work agency (TWA) industry, reflecting the TWA industry both as an entry point to the labour market and the role the industry plays in terms of facilitating cross-border mobility (Coe et al., 2009, 2010; Friberg, 2016).

For Norway, this both applies to short-term, circular migration and more long-term migration (Nergaard et al., 2011). Approximately 40% of registered employees in the staffing industry in Norway were non-Norwegian citizens in 2016 (Ellingsen et al., 2018) compared to approximately 25% just six years earlier (Nergaard et al., 2011). Migrants are often in a less regulated space as posted workers and are put under pressure from (foreign) employers that operate in Norway to work for sub-standard wages and conditions, even though this is deemed illegal by the Work Environment Act. Eldring and Schulten (2016) point out that labour market regulations have little effect if not enforced or monitored closely. However, studies show that working conditions for Eastern European EU nationals in 2010 had improved from levels in the first years following the 2004 EU enlargement. For instance, Alsos and Eldring (2014) find that the strengthened regulation on wages through the general applicability of the collective agreement had some positive effects. However, 38% of posted Polish workers in Norway still received below the stipulated minimum wage in 2010. Haakestad and Friberg (2017) conclude that large-scale migration has had a degrading and deskilling effect on skilled work in the Norwegian construction industry.

In addition, with reference to Denmark and Sweden, Refslund and Thörnquist (2016) point out that migrants are often constrained to take on jobs in comparatively unorganized sectors and therefore become "low-wage" competitors. Refslund (2016) finds that labour migrants in certain industries such as cleaning and agriculture are constrained by not knowing how to claim their rights in the Danish agreement-based model of industrial relations. Hansen and Hansen (2009) find that for instance very few East European construction workers are organized, and attribute this to high wages and different cultures in their home countries. Andersen and Felbo-Kolding (2013) show how migrant workers are perceived as more willing to accept flexible jobs and are presented with worse working conditions by employers. However, it is not only a lack of knowledge of the capacity to enforce their rights that makes it difficult for many migrants to decline temporary or flexible employment. It is also due to a continuous decline in social security for migrants (Bredgaard et al., 2009; Mailand & Larsen, 2011). As Rasmussen et al. (2016) point out, this results in more regulation gaps, which means for migrants that: "The boundaries between forced labour and very exploitive conditions tend also to be blurred" (Rasmussen et al., 2016, p. 82). In a comparison between Denmark and Norway, Friberg et al. (2014) find that differences in institutional configurations between the countries result in different outcomes for Polish migrant workers. Due to higher levels of union organization, the majority of Polish migrants in Denmark earn wages much closer to those of Danish workers than Polish migrants in Norway.

At the other end of the labour market, surveys among highly educated workers in Denmark show higher figures for temporary employment than the labour force surveys, and the numbers have increased significantly in recent years (Pedersen & Ribe, 2013; Scheuer, 2017). There are other uncertainties connected to a precise quantification of precarious work. One example is the attempt to measure the amount of involuntary part-time work, where what is considered involuntary is debated. There is also the often confusing and mixed use of the notions of atypical, contingent and precarious work. Atypical work can be anything but precarious work, if one asks successful freelancers or independent professionals. On the other hand, workers in standard employment relationships may hold severely stressful jobs, be affected by insecurity and have experienced periods of unemployment.

If we define precarity in line with Kalleberg (2012) and others, we have to look beyond mere changes in the prevalence of atypical forms of employment relationships and take several factors into account that identify changes in both work and society at large. The societal and economic developments pointed out earlier increase pressure on employees. Several surveys have attempted to measure perceived job insecurity and general feelings of insecurity. Data collected by the Norwegian Work Research Institute in collaboration with the union YS in an annual survey representative of the working population since 2009, shows a slight increase in how worried employees are over the risk of losing their job (Steen et al., 2017). A Danish survey on general feelings of insecurity (including job insecurity) shows that numbers have more than doubled over since the late 2000s (Andersen, 2014). Numbers are highest among the lower classes (based on income, education, etc.), but the relatively highest increase is among the upper and middle classes. Differences in results from surveys can probably to some degree be explained by national differences in labour market conditions, but they might also mirror difficulties in producing detailed and valid figures on such a complex matter as perceived insecurity. Since precarity is so strongly related to subjective experiences and general life situations, it is relevant to approach the phenomena in different methodological ways. A growing number of research projects based on qualitative data have emerged. Qualitative data can inform about broader consequences of precarious work that will not normally be visible in statistics. These can for example be considerations of whether to have children or not (Chan & Tweedie, 2015) or processes of marginalization among youth (Nielsen et al., 2017).

There is a need for a continuous broadening of perspectives and knowledge of tendencies towards precarity in the Nordic countries. As a relational phenomenon, it is also appropriate to discuss precarization in context, much in the same way as when discussing relative poverty. This includes the subjective experiences of having fewer opportunities than are considered part of a "normal" life lived by the majority. In the Nordic countries, post-Fordist (de)regulations and neoliberal policies have gradually affected institutional arrangements and labour market dynamics (Gleerup et al., 2018). In the following section, we discuss some of the characteristics of the Norwegian and Danish policies and regulations.

Industrial relations and the regulation of work arrangements

To answer the second question posed in the introduction, "Is the Nordic model resilient to precarization?", this section gives an overview of the regulation of work arrangements in Norway and Denmark. We focus on regulation of the employment relationship and employment protection, including the Danish flexicurity model. To assess the resilience of the Nordic model, we examine recent changes in the regulation and the impact of EU legislation, with a particular focus on the EU directive on temporary agency work.

There are some marked differences in the Norwegian and Danish regulation of work, particularly in employment protection and temporary employment. Working arrangements in Norway are regulated through a combination of legislation and collective agreements, whereas in Denmark employment protection and the employment relationship are regulated in collective agreements. According to Gooderham et al. (2015), the emergence of *flexicurity* challenges the notion of one Nordic model of industrial relations.

Union density is high in the Nordic countries compared to other European countries. In Denmark, around 70% are union members, while in Norway the density is at around 50%. One important reason for the difference is that in Denmark unemployment benefits were for a long time covered by the unions, whereas in Norway the state offers such benefits. However, both countries are witnessing a fall in the degree of unionization (Nergaard, 2016).

The Norwegian Working Environment Act: do recent changes point towards increased precarization?

The Norwegian Working Environment Act,[2] with some exceptions, applies to all undertakings that engage employees. It explicitly states that the general rule for employment (as defined in §14–9) is that "the employee shall be employed permanently", but that an agreement on *temporary* employment, or employment which has a defined start and end date, can be made in the following cases:

1. When the work is of a temporary nature
2. Temporary substitution (i.e. during sick leave for the permanent employee)
3. Internship/apprenticeship
4. As part of work training (sponsored by the state)
5. For athletes, coaches, referees and others in organized sports
6. For a period up to 12 months, including up to 15 percent of the employees in the organization.

This shows that the standard employment relationship retains its strong position. However, point 6 was included in 2015 as part of a liberalization of temporary employment. Temporary positions and the hiring of agency workers are to be exceptions. There are quite strict laws governing the use of temporary employees or agency workers, mainly allowing this when the work itself is temporary, as replacements for permanent employees on leave of absence or in the case of trainees. The Working Environment Act, granting employees both the possibility to influence work and the duty to participate, also covers industrial relations. Collective agreements may include exemptions to the Working Environment Act to the extent that is covered by the act. For instance, while the law states that normal working hours are 40 hours per week, unions with more than 10,000 members may agree with employers or employers' organizations on working hours for their members that exceed these limitations. There is no minimum wage in Norway. However, some sectors subject to increased labour migration after the expansion of the EU in 2004 introduced a general application of collective wage agreements to counteract wage dumping (Eldring & Alsos, 2012).

The EU Directive on Temporary Agency Work (EC, 2008) aims to ensure satisfactory working conditions for temporary agency workers and to develop the sector as a flexible solution for employers.[3] The Directive was not implemented in Norway until 1 January 2013 and was met with massive opposition from the labour unions, viewing this as a further liberalization of temporary agency work and a threat to the rule of bilateral permanent employment. Since only the first aim of the directive, that of ensuring that agency workers' working conditions are equal to those of the permanent staff, was implemented, some have argued that there have been no changes in the law regarding the right to engage temporary agency workers in Norway (Eriksen & Nesheim, 2016). By contrast, Bergene (2016; Bergene & Ewing, 2015) argues that the Directive's recognition of temporary agencies as employers represents a qualitative shift in the view of labour as a commodity in Norwegian working life.

The Norwegian employee unions also contested the expansion in the right of employers to hire temporary workers that came into effect from January 2015. After negotiations, the right to hire at least one temporary employee for any reason for a duration of up to 12 months was implemented, but with several restrictions. Among the most important was the restriction on work tasks, where employers cannot hire another temporary employee to do the same types of tasks performed by the initial temporary worker in the first year after the first temporary engagement. Furthermore, a temporary employee who had been employed for more than four years by the same employer gained the right to a permanent position with that employer. The 2015 changes in the legislation reduced the necessary duration of temporary employment to three years. Although it is too soon to evaluate the full consequences of the regulatory changes, the intention of the changes is to liberalize the use of temporary labour while also offering greater rights for temporary employees. The recognition of temporary employment as a functional alternative to the standard employment relationship serves to normalize non-standard employment relationships (Bergene et al., 2015).

These recent changes envision a new phase in the history of the standard employment relationship. Historically speaking, a long period of movement towards increased government control of employment arrangements halted in the early 1980s. The regulations, such as protection from unfair dismissals and restrictions on the use of temporary work agencies, were maintained in most sectors during the 1980s and 1990s. In 2000 the ban on temporary work agencies and private intermediation of labour was lifted. Even though the important legislation that governs the standard employment relationship in Norway is still mostly intact, the above-mentioned changes in the Working Environment Act represent a break with the regulations of the past and a step in the direction of a less extensive standard employment relationship (Hansen, 2018).

The Danish flexicurity model: a structural barrier to precarious work?

The growth of different forms of flexibility is related to the development of precarious work, as argued earlier. In Denmark, the system of flexicurity has developed through collective agreements over several decades. In the comparative literature on policy development, the "flexicurity model" is touted as an ideal for ensuring employment, skill development and income security in a highly flexible and thus competitive labour market (Auer & Cazes, 2002, p. 16; Broughton et al., 2016, pp. 28, 46). The logic behind the model is that these labour market policies shorten periods of unemployment. In effect, it implies that employers have been awarded greater flexibility in the right to hire and terminate employment relationships. In return, employees have been granted security in the form of relatively generous unemployment benefits and training provision. There is extensive welfare and high unemployment benefits related to short-term unemployment. From a working life perspective, the "flexicurity" system means that the uncertainties inherent in flexible forms of employment are often outweighed by other forms of security in the labour market, and the work is thus not experienced as precarious by workers. However, since the late 1990s, the model has gradually been changed and the security part of the labour market model has been weakened.

Retaining the level of security needed to achieve real "flexicurity" relies on both continued political support for welfare subsidies, the strength of unions and innovative institutional development to meet the demands of new forms of precarious employment (Rasmussen et al., 2016). In the wake of the economic crisis, the Danish model seemed able to "normalise atypical work" (Bredgaard et al., 2009, p. 17), which meant that collective agreements and unemployment benefits generally covered all workers, including those in irregular employment. However, the broad national comparisons risk masking relative differences *within* the Danish labour market. There are differences in the contractual arrangements between sectors and between employees in Denmark.

Although marginal part-time work and temporary work is less common than permanent employment in the Danish labour market, workers holding these positions are more exposed. Employees in the private sector and manual workers generally have the lowest protection. The "white-collar act" (Funktionærloven) grants salaried employees a longer period of notice before termination.[4] EU legislation has been adopted as a minimum regulation. But since working conditions are regulated through collective agreements, the implementation of EU law has had limited effects (Andersen & Mailand, 2005). The regulation with collective agreements entails that "sector institutions may be just, if not more important, than national IR-settings, when exploring the incidence of precarious employment and contingent work" (Rasmussen et al., 2016, p. 102). The degree of security offered to workers is highly differentiated across the labour market. In sectors with a lower degree of unionization and relatively more labour migration, employees do not profit from the rights and benefits associated with employee participation in the labour market.

Close to a third of the Danish workforce is employed in "atypical" work, and although a fair amount of these workers are well-established and not relevant to include in the precariat, being outside the formal agreements of the normal full-time, permanent jobs that are the norms for regulation can have many consequences. It can be difficult to obtain certain social benefits like unemployment pay, occupational pension schemes, private health care insurance schemes and paid maternity, paternity and parental leave (Mailand & Larsen, 2011, p. 27). Also, formal rights to further training and education are difficult to obtain for workers outside the standard employment relationship. Broader societal consequences include difficulty in getting a home loan or establishing a family. Although the flexicurity model builds on mutual agreements on providing security to employees, it primarily offers security to those in normal full-time, permanent jobs. Workers outside the labour market or with contingent work might only experience the flexibility part of "flexicurity", which makes the model a barrier to creating a decent life. On a broader societal level, this is also the result of a movement from welfare to workfare (Peck, 2001) where social benefits are dependent on stable labour market affiliation. The transformation of the state to a "competition state" (Pedersen, 2013) with its focus on securing the best opportunities for companies to compete in a global market is part of this development.

Although we have argued that the flexicurity model is not necessarily a strong barrier to the spread of precarity, flexicurity can in principle be developed to deal with tendencies to more precarious work for a growing number of groups in the labour market. The main question, however, is whether the challenges imbedded in the capitalist economy, and not least the political responses, are too substantial for flexicurity-related models to deal with. The objective pressure on capital accumulation and probable continuous financial crises will create pressure on collective agreements challenging the scope of security offered to employees. Furthermore, the flexicurity model only exists as long as there is strong support for unions, not least regarding the number of potential members they are able to attract. Although membership is not declining dramatically, it is argued that if membership rates drop just slightly more, employers will not automatically negotiate as enthusiastically with unions. Finally, the policies of the unions are also an important factor to take into account. Until recently unions have not paid much attention to issues of precarity. However, they are now beginning to realize the necessity of developing responses to precarity; it is necessary to ensure their support and participation in finding both short-term and long-term solutions to deal with precarity.

Conclusion

Perspectives on the "precarization" of work have emerged as an important approach to describe and explain structural changes in the labour market, the institutionalization of employment, the organization of work and the quality of working life. In this chapter, we have outlined key contributions that highlight how precarization involves higher job insecurity and how this is related to the use of flexible employment models, skill and wage polarization, and discussed how these tendencies lead to a more general degradation of work quality. In some respects, the situation in the Nordic countries stands in contrast to this literature with a relatively high degree of employment security and education levels and a lower wage polarization. Yet the Nordic countries do not operate in isolation and are clearly marked by pressures of liberalization through flexibilization, increasing polarization and insecurity.

We have discussed how this pressure is expressed in Norway and Denmark in this chapter. First, we presented trends of polarization in labour markets, which occur both between and within sectors of employment. Enclaves of low or unskilled migrant workers in comparatively under-regulated spaces represent precarious working conditions in the low end of the job quality spectrum. The extensive flexibilization of employment, even within some areas of highly qualified work, increasingly splits off employees into a precarious employment periphery where work is experienced as insecure. It is thus important to recognize relative differences *within* the Nordic labour markets. We then showed how higher general job insecurity results from increasing individualization of risk through increased flexibility, as an ongoing structural change for employees in parts of the Nordic working life previously judged as stable. In this respect, it is important to recognize the dynamic character of the labour market institutions in the Nordic countries. As shown by the examples of regulation of temporary employment, temporary agency work and the Danish flexicurity model, collective agreements and legislation are not only differentiated but also continually renegotiated.

The answer to our second question of whether the Nordic model is resilient to precarization might therefore be: "so far". Even though they are among the most egalitarian countries in the world, the Nordic countries are witnessing increasing inequality and polarization, which creates more insecure working conditions within vulnerable sectors of work. Decreasing union density, increasing individualization of working arrangements and the globalization of finance and labour are forces shifting the power balance in favour of capital. Developments in these areas pose challenges to the underlying premises of high job quality in the Nordic countries. The structural developments described not only express but also demand continuous reconfigurations of labour market institutions.

Nordic working life research can contribute by paying attention to and analysing the problems of precarious work and working with the actors involved to ameliorate the situation. In the following chapters, the authors will present various perspectives on precarization in the Norwegian and Danish labour markets. Both the empirical basis and the focus in the chapters vary by emphasizing, respectively, the level of regulation, work organization and the subjective experience of precarious work. However, by being centred on the concept of precarity, the chapters are not only united in their empirical interest in atypical and flexible forms of employment but also in their critical analytical interest.

In continuation of this, it is important not to take the fall of the standard employment relationship for granted, but rather to take its status as an expression of a particular and context-dependent balance of social forces. Separating necessary structural developments from strategically imposed ones remains an important critical impulse for Nordic working life research.

It might be tempting to see precarization as an irrelevant research field in the comparatively well-functioning Nordic labour markets. However, the critical, structurally oriented interest in the experience of insecurities in working life expressed in the concept of precarity constitutes an exciting opportunity for Nordic working life research to contribute to social change. The reality of global commerce and regulation means that Nordic working life research must take global development tendencies into account when understanding localized working life problems. All in all, research into precarity highlights and aims to understand how the liberalization and flexibilization of work seems to be an economically functional trend that can create new challenges in working life. These are challenges that we must engage with, understand, give voice to and amend through historical perspectives and critical analysis.

Notes

1 Tables can be found here: Part-time work: http://ec.europa.eu/eurostat/tgm/table.do?tab=table&init=1&plugin=1&language=en&pcode=tesem100; Temporary employment: http://ec.europa.eu/eurostat/tgm/table.do?tab=table&init=1&plugin=1&language=en&pcode=tesem110; Long-term unemployment: http://ec.europa.eu/eurostat/tgm/table.do?tab=table&init=1&plugin=1&language=en&pcode=tesem130.

2 www.arbeidstilsynet.no/contentassets/e54635c3d2e54157 85a4f23f5b852849/working-environment-act-october-web-2017.pdf.

3 http://ec.europa.eu/social/main.jsp?catId=706&langId=en&intPageId=207.

4 www.eurofound.europa.eu/observatories/eurwork/comparative-information/national-contributions/denmark/denmark-flexicurity-and-industrial-relations.

References

Allen, J. & Henry, N. (1997) Ulrich Beck's Risk Society at Work: Labour and Employment in the Contract Service Industries, *Transactions of the Institute of British Geographers*, 22(2): 180–196.

Alsos, K. & Eldring, L. (2014) Lovfestet minstelønn i Norge? [Statutory Minimum Wage in Norway?], *Søkelys på arbeidslivet*, 31: 249–266.

Andersen, J. G. (2014) *Sociale klasser og utryghed. En tabelsamling [Social Classes and Insecurity. Tables]*, Notat, Aalborg Universitet: CCWS.

Andersen, S. K. & Felbo-Kolding, J. (2013) *Danske virksomheders brug af østeuropæisk arbejdskraft [Danish Companies' Use of Eastern European Labour]*, Copenhagen: FAOS.

Andersen, S. K. & Mailand, M. (2005) *The Danish Flexicurity Model: The Role of the Collective Bargaining System*, Report from FAOS, Department of Sociology, University of Copenhagen, September 2005, Copenhagen: FAOS.

Auer, P. & Cazes, S. (2002) *Employment Stability in an Age of Flexibility*, Geneva: International Labour Office. doi: 10.1177/102425890401000215.

Beck, U. (2000) *The Brave New World of Work*, Cambridge, UK: Polity Press.

Bergene, A. C. (2016) Trollet som sprakk eller et møte med den trojanske hest? Svar til Torstein Nesheim og Birthe Eriksen: Vikarbyrådirektivet – Trollet som sprakk [The Troll That Exploded or a Meeting with the Trojan Horse? Reply to Torstein Nesheim and Birthe Eriksen], *Søkelys på arbeidslivet*, 33(1–2): 171–181.

Bergene, A. C., Egeland, C., Hansen, P. B. & Wathne, C. T. (2015) *Når unntaket blir en del av regelen. En kunnskapsoversikt over forskningen på midlertidige ansettelser* [When the Exception Becomes Part of the Rule. Summary of Research on Temporary Employment], *AFI-rapport 1/2015*, Oslo: Arbeidsforskningsinstituttet. https://doi.org/10.7577/afi/rapport/2015:1.

Bergene, A. C. & Ewing, K. (2015) Vikarbyrådirektivet: Liberalisering eller likebehandling? [The Directive of Temporary Employment Agencies: Liberalization or Equal terms?], *Søkelys på arbeidslivet*, 32(1–2): 137–157.

Betti, E. (2016) Gender and Precarious Labor in a Historical Perspective: Italian Women and Precarious Work between Fordism and Post-Fordism, *International Labor and Working-Class History*, 89: 64–83.

Boas, T. & Gans-Morse, J. (2009) Neoliberalism: From New Liberal Philosophy to Anti-Liberal Slogan, *Studies in Comparative International Development*, 44: 137–161.

Bredgaard, T., Larsen, F., Kongshøj Madsen, P. & Rasmussen, S. (2009) *Flexicurity and Atypical Employment in Denmark*, CARMA Research Paper, 1: 1–21.

Broughton, A., Green, M., Rickard, C., Swift, S., Eichhorst, W., Tobsch, V., . . . & Tros, F. H. (2016) *Precarious Employment in Europe*, European Parliament, Directorate-General for Internal Policies, Policy Department A: Economic and Scientific Policy, Brussels.

Castel, R. (2002) *From Manual Workers to Wage Laborers: Transformation of the Social Question*, Piscataway, NJ: Transaction Publishers.

Castel, R. & Dörre, K. (eds) (2009) *Prekartiät, Abstieg, Ausgrenzung: Die soziale Frage am Beginn des 21. Jahrhunderts [Precarity, Decline, Exclusion: The Social Issue at the Beginning of the 21st Century]*, Frankfurt am Main, Germany: Campus.

Chan, S. & Tweedie, D. (2015) Precarious Work and Reproductive Insecurity, *Social Alternatives*, 34(4): 5–13.

Coe, N. M., Johns, J. & Ward, K. (2009) Managed Flexibility: Labour Regulation, Corporate Strategies and Market Dynamics in the Swedish Temporary Staffing Industry, *European Urban and Regional Studies*, 16: 65–85.

Coe, N. M., Jones, K. & Ward, K. (2010) The Business of Temporary Staffing: A Developing Research Agenda, *Geography Compass*, 4: 1055–1068.

EC (2008) Directive 2008/104/EC of the European Parliament and of the Council. *Of* 19 November 2008 on Temporary Agency Work. http://eur-lex.europa.eu/legal-content/EN/TXT/HTML/?uri=CELEX:32008L0104&from=EN.

Eldring, L. & Alsos, K. (2012) European Minimum Wage: A Nordic Outlook, *Fafo-report 2012:16*, Oslo: Fafo.

Eldring, L. & Schulten, T. (2016) Migrant Workers and Wage-Setting Institutions: Experiences from Germany, Norway, Switzerland and the United Kingdom,

In: Galgoczi, B., Leschke, J. & Watt, A. (eds) *Labour Migration in Troubled Times*, Farnham, UK: Ashgate, 235–260.

Ellingsen, D., Underthun, A., Wathne, C. T., & Ingelsrud, M. H. (2018) Arbeid gjennom bemanningsbyrå i Norge: En mangfoldig typologi av arbeidstakere [Diversity of Motivations and Positions: A Typology of Staffing Industry Employees in Norway], *Søkelys på arbeidslivet*, 35(1–2): 56–76.

Eriksen, B. & Nesheim, T. (2016) Vikarbyrådirektivet: Trollet som sprakk. Kommentar til Bergene, A. C. & Ewing, K. (2015) "Vikarbyrådirektivet: liberalisering eller likebehandling?" [Comment on Bergene, A. C. & Ewing, K. (2015)], *Søkelys på arbeidslivet*, 33(1–2): 162–170.

Friberg, J. H. (2016) The Rise and Implications of Temporary Staffing as a "Migration Industry" in Norway, *Nordic Journal of Migration Research*, 6(2): 81–91.

Friberg, J. H., Arnholtz, J., Eldring, L., Hansen, N. W. & Thorarins, F. (2014) Nordic Labour Market Institutions and New Migrant Workers: Polish Migrants in Oslo, Copenhagen and Reykjavik, *European Journal of Industrial Relations*, 20: 37–53.

Gleerup, J., Nielsen, B., Olsén, P. & Warring, N. (2018) *Prekarisering: og akademisk arbejde [Precarization and Academic Work]*, Copenhagen: Frydenlund.

Gooderham, P., Navrbjerg, S., Olsen, K. & Steen, C. R. (2015) The Labor Market Regimes of Denmark and Norway: One Nordic Model?, *Journal of Industrial Relations*, 57(2): 166–186.

Haakestad, H. & Friberg, J. H. (2017) Deskilling Revisited: Labour Migration, Neo-Taylorism and the Degradation of Craft Work in the Norwegian Construction Industry, *Economic and Industrial Democracy*. https://doi.org/10.1177/0143831x17735671.

Hansen, J. A. & Hansen, N. W. (2009) Polakker på det danske arbejdsmarked-frie fugle eller ny randgruppe? Et kvantitativt studie af polske arbejdsmigranters løn-og arbejdsvilkår i Storkøbenhavn [A Quantitative Study of Polish Work Immigrants' Terms of Wage and Work in the Copenhagen Area], *Tidsskrift for arbejdsliv*, 11(2): 24–40.

Hansen, P. B. (2018) The Growth and Decline of the Standard Employment Relationship? The Authorities, Trade Unions and Employers and Their Response to Temporary Work Agencies in the Engineering Industry and Attitudes Towards Temporary and Permanent Employment in Norway 1947–2000, PhD thesis, University of Oslo.

Harvey, D. (2005) *A Brief History of Neoliberalism*, Oxford, UK: Oxford University Press.

Hobsbawm, E. (1994) *The Age of Extremes: A History of the World, 1914–1991*, New York: Pantheon Books.

Kalleberg, A. L. (2003) Flexible Firms and Labor Market Segmentations: Effects of Workplace Restructuring on Jobs and Workers, *Work and Occupations*, 30: 154–175.

Kalleberg, A. L. (2009) Precarious Work, Insecure Workers: Employment Relations in Transition, *American Sociological Review*, 74(1): 1–22.

Kalleberg, A. L. (2012) Job Quality and Precarious Work: Clarifications, Controversies, and Challenges, *Work and Occupations*, 39(4): 427–448.

Lorey, I. (2015 [2012]) *State of Insecurity. Government of the Precarious*, London and New York: Verso.

Mailand, M. & Larsen, T. P. (2011) *Trade Unions and Precarious Work: Danish Country Report to the BARSORI-Project*, FAOS Research paper, 121, Copenhagen: FAOS.

McDowell, L., Batnitzky, A. & Dyer, S. (2009) Precarious Work and Economic Migration: Emerging Immigrant Divisions of Labour in Greater London's Service Sector, *International Journal of Urban and Regional Research*, 33(1): 3–25.

McKay, S., Jefferys, S., Paraksevopoulou, A. & Keles, J. (2012) *Study on Precarious Work and Social Rights* (Report for the European Commission (VT/2010/084)), London: Working Lives Research Institute, London Metropolitan University.

Munck, R. (2013) The Precariat: A View From the South, *Third World Quarterly*, 34(5): 747–762.

Neergaard, A. (2015) Migration, Racialization and Forms of Unfree Labour, In: Schierup, C-U., Munck, R., Likic-Brboric, B. & Neergaard, A. (eds) *Migration, Precarity & Global Governance*, New York: Oxford University Press, 139–159.

Nergaard, K. (2016) *Organisasjonsgrader, tariffavtaledekning og arbeidskonflikter 2014 [Union Coverage, Collective Agreements and Industrial Conflicts 2014]*, Oslo: FAFO.

Nergaard, K., Nesheim, T., Alsos, K., Berge, Ø. M., Trygstad, S. & Ødegaard, A. (2011) *Utleie av arbeidskraft 2011 [Labour Hire in 2011]*. www.fafo.no.

Nielsen, M., Gørlich, A., Grytnes, R. & Dyreborg, J. (2017) Uden sikkerhedsnet. Prekarisering blandt unge på kanten af arbejdslivet [No Safety Net. Precarization amongst Youth in the Periphery of the Labour Market], *Tidsskrift for Arbejdsliv*, 19(1): 29–45.

Ødegaard, A. M. (2014) Arbeidsinnvandring og fleksible bemanningsstrategier i fire bransjer [Work Immigration and Flexible Employment Strategies in Four Industries], *Søkelys på arbeidslivet*, 31: 100–117.

OECD (2017) *Understanding the Socio-Economic Divide in Europe: Background Report*. OECD Centre for Opportunity and Equality. www.oecd.org/els/soc/cope-divide-europe-2017-background-report.pdf.

Paret, M. (2016) Politics of Solidarity and Agency in an Age of Precarity, *Global Labour Journal*, 7(2): 174–188.

Peck, J. (2001) *Workfare States*, New York: Guilford Press.

Pedersen, M. S. & Ribe, M. Ø. (2013) Akademikerprekariatet. *Rapport om akademikernes arbejdsmarked 2002–2010* [The Academic Precariat. *Report on Academics' Labour Market 2002–2010*], Copenhagen, "Analyse og tal", September.

Pedersen, O. K. (2013) Political Globalization and the Competition State, In: Brincker, B. (ed.) *Introduction to Political Sociology*, Copenhagen: Hans Reitzel, 281–298.

Polanyi, K. (2001 [1944, 1957]) *The Great Transformation. The Political and Economic Origins of Our Time*, Boston, MA: Beacon Press.

Raess, D. & Burgoon, B. (2015) Flexible Work and Immigration in Europe, *British Journal of Industrial Relations*, 53(1): 94–111.

Rasmussen, S., Refslund, B., Sørensen, O. H., Larsen, T., Sørensen, O. H. & Larsen, T. P. (2016) *Reducing Precarious Work in Europe through Social Dialogue: The Case of Denmark (Final National Report)*. www.research.mbs.ac.uk/ewerc/Our-research/Current.

Refslund, B. (2016) Intra-European Labour Migration and Deteriorating Employment Relations in Danish Cleaning and Agriculture: Industrial Relations under Pressure from EU8/2 Labour Inflows?, *Economic and Industrial Democracy*, 37: 597–621. https://doi.org/10.1177/0143831x14550421.

Refslund, B. & Thörnquist, A. (2016) Intra-European Labour Migration and Low-Wage Competition: Comparing the Danish and Swedish Experiences across Three Sectors, *Industrial Relations Journal*, 47(1): 62–78.

Scheuer, S. (2017) *Atypisk beskæftigelse i Danmark Om deltidsansattes, midlertidigt ansattes og soloselvstændiges vilkår [Atypical Employment in Denmark. On Part Time Employees', Temporary Employees' and Self-Employeds' Employment Conditions]*, LO-dokumentation No 1/2017.

Sennett, R. (1998) *The Corrosion of Character. The Personal Consequences of Work in the New Capitalism*, New York: Norton.
Sennett, R. (2006) *The Culture of the New Capitalism*, New Haven, CT: Yale University Press.
Spreitzer, G. M., Cameron, L. & Garrett, L. (2017) Alternative Work Arrangements: Two Images of the New World of Work, In: Morgeson, F. P. (ed.) *Annual Review of Organizational Psychology and Organizational Behavior*, 4: 473–499.
Standing, G. (2014) *The Precariat. The New Dangerous Class*, second edition, London: Bloomsbury.
Steen, A., Ellingsen, D. & Nygaard, M. (2017) *Norsk arbeidsliv 2017. Bransjer i søkelyset. [Norwegian Working Life. A Closer Look at Eight Industries]*, Oslo: YS/AFI.
Vosko, L. F. (2009) Less Than Adequate: Regulating Temporary Agency Work in the EU in the Face of an Internal Market in Services, *Cambridge Journal of Regions, Economy and Society*, 2(3): 395–411.
Vosko, L. F. (2010) *Managing the Margins: Gender, Citizenship, and the International Regulation of Precarious Employment*, Oxford, UK: Oxford University Press.

Chapter 15

Experiences of precarious work among graduates in the Danish labour market

Janne Gleerup, Anders Jakobsen and Niels Warring

Introduction

The Nordic labour market systems are strongly regulated by collective agreements and influential labour market organizations. This is also true of Denmark, where the model is often described as the flexicurity model, combining a high level of flexibility with a high level of social security. However, during recent decades, the balance between flexibility and security has tipped in favour of flexibility, and it is becoming increasingly difficult to access social benefits during periods of unemployment (Ibsen, 2011; Madsen, 2011). In this context, the debate on the spread of precarious work has recently taken off and received increasing attention in current analyses of labour market changes in Denmark (Larsen, 2011; Mailand & Larsen, 2011; Rasmussen et al., 2017). The case of graduates in Denmark illustrates how the problem of precarious work is emerging everywhere, not just among marginal groups in less developed welfare regimes. Earlier, the term "precarious work" was primarily associated with increasingly insecure wage and work conditions for unskilled or low-skilled workers, vulnerable groups and migrant workers (Kalleberg, 2009). Problems in these parts of the labour market are still unsolved and tend to increase. However, now it seems that highly skilled, well-educated groups in the labour market are also experiencing changes towards more precarious work in terms of more temporary work contracts and generally more insecure work and wage conditions. A university degree is no longer a guarantee of security; you cannot educate yourself out of the risk zone any more.

Based on results from two related research projects, this chapter presents empirical examples of how precarious work is experienced and dealt with by graduates in the Danish labour market. The data consists of a series of semi-structured qualitative interviews with a broad focus on the interviewees' life situation and experiences with precarious work. This chapter starts out by elaborating briefly on the specific forms and consequences of precarity in Denmark. We reflect on the concept of precarious work, explaining how and why we define it as we do. We argue that the complexity of the phenomenon calls for an interdisciplinary approach, viewing subjective experiences in the light of current changes in the labour market interwoven with globalization and the transformation of the Nordic welfare state model. We then briefly describe key components of the contemporary tendencies towards increased precarious work among graduates, along with the overall critical theoretical framework that inspired us in the interpretation of precarity as a subjective experience. Secondly, we introduce the two empirical research projects that we draw upon, before presenting theme-based analytical findings that show how precarious work affects the (working) lives of graduates. We sum up by suggesting how the qualitative insights on precarity may elucidate modern Nordic working life, and how these findings may indicate more fundamental transitions in the labour market and the Danish welfare model in general. Finally, we engage in a prospective discussion on how qualitative working life studies on precarity may inform discussions and decision-making processes in the face of these new tendencies. As an example, we discuss whether the labour movement, as a uniquely influential actor in the Danish labour market system, may play a new role by addressing precarity proactively, based on dialogue with affected members and in cooperation with employer organizations and the government.

Is the spread of precarious work a relevant research topic in Denmark?

When viewing the problems of precarious work in an international comparative perspective, it is fair to question the urgency of the problems of precarity in Denmark. Denmark does not really have working poor in a global context, but even here more and more people are becoming "combiners" of several low paid jobs to make a living. So far, these conditions affect only a minority in Denmark, yet still represent a worldwide tendency. A current Danish debate about precarious work concerns the question of whether the spread of precarious work is just a marginal phenomenon or whether the tendency expresses a general societal trend that will eventually reach the core of society and potentially affect a majority of employees and organizations. Researchers in Denmark disagree on the answer, but if we view labour market changes in an international perspective, there seem to be strong structural and political drivers towards more precarious work (Altvater & Mahnkopf, 2002; Dörre, 2009; Kalleberg, 2009; Harvey, 2010; Standing, 2016). It is unlikely that Denmark, as a small open market economy and member of the European Union, will or can develop in completely the opposite direction to the rest of the world. Hence, research on precarization is justified in its own right, but it may also serve as a perspective on the analysis of other labour market changes shaping Nordic working life, which are discussed in other chapters of this book. Firstly, precarization could clearly lead to more inequality in society. This might be in the form of increased economic inequality produced by new divisions between insiders and outsiders in the labour market, if not the rise of a whole new and dangerous class, "the precariat", as Standing (2011) argues. In continuation of this, it is fair to expect that some groups will be more affected than others, revealing differences among professions as well as divisions based on ethnicity, gender and age. Secondly, technology may play a part in the process towards precarization, with the rise of the platform economy (Rasmussen & Madsen, 2017). Thirdly, the spread of precarization is inextricably linked to processes of globalization (Harvey, 2004, 2010) that affect structural conditions that will shape Nordic working lives in the future. Finally, research on precarization sheds light on changes related to the Nordic traditions of strong trade unions operating at the institutional level in cooperation with employer organizations. Can trade unions address the problem of precarious work in ways that maintain their relevance in the Nordic model?

Precarity among graduates

Historically, educational politics changed in Denmark after World War II. The "university of the masses" was born and this led to a huge growth of people gaining a university degree. Today 12% of the workforce consists of graduates who find jobs in all kinds of (emerging) areas, and every third new job is taken by a graduate (Blankholm, 2016). However, statistics also show that somewhere between 20 and 30% of graduates are affected by precarity, depending on how precarity is measured (Pedersen & Ribe, 2013; Ejlertsen, 2017). Other statistics indicate slightly lower figures (Scheuer, 2017), suggesting only a small growth in precarious work. However, researchers all agree that precarity is present among graduates and seems to be spreading in various highly skilled fields. More and more graduates are employed on temporary contracts, and full-time permanent jobs are gradually being transformed into temporary, project-based or part-time jobs (Mortensen & Damholt, 2017). Tendencies differ depending on fields of work, but e.g. in public administration we can identify a quite significant shift away from permanent to temporary employment. About 20% of the graduates working in the public sector now work on temporary contracts, and this development is part of a larger transformation of the public sector, to some extent related to budget cuts and destabilized budget structures (project economy), hindering long-term planning and encouraging more shortsighted planning logics in public institutions. Tendencies pulling towards temporary work are becoming "the new normal".

Some may ask whether well-educated groups are at all vulnerable to the spread of temporary contracts in the labour market. Compared to precarity among blue-collar workers in the industries, the well-educated are in many ways better off. Their high level of education enhances their employment opportunities, and they earn up to 80% more throughout their working lives than skilled manual workers (Udvalg om bedre universitetsuddannelser, 2018). In other words, is the spread of precarious work among people with higher education a broad societal problem, or does it only concern a small part of an otherwise privileged social group? Even though society educates and needs people with higher education, and even though unemployment rates for graduates are declining, we would argue that graduates are vulnerable in several ways. Changes in conditions for employment undermine not only income security but also the quality of work conditions among knowledge workers is threatened by precarity. As we will show, these professionals also find that this affects the quality of work in itself.

The notion of precarity

The history of precarious work is as long as the history of work in general, and problems of precarity have throughout the centuries been constituted by shifting power relations, basically related to the interplay between capital and work. The specific term precarity originates from France and turns up in writings as early as at the beginning of the 19th century. Marx and Engels later described precarity as an integral dimension of the capitalist mode of production, and after a short historical period of Fordist regulation in the European labour market models in the 20th century, the debate on precarious work returned in the early 1980s as a consequence of neoliberal deregulation alongside other labour market reforms that provoked insecure work and pay conditions (Gleerup et al., 2018). Further, the Nordic welfare state model is influenced by the neoliberal turn. In a Danish context, the *universal welfare model* built throughout the 20th century is now challenged by the ideals of a *workfare model* that reduces the level of state-guaranteed security and unemployment benefits (Esping-Andersen, 2000; Mckay et al., 2012). After the millennium, the state ideal has moved towards the *competitive state*, infused by ideas of the project society/project economy (Hirsch, 1998; Hardt & Negri, 2000; Pedersen, 2011). The notion of precarity must be determined in the light of such societal changes that involve various structural and political drivers changing working lives in Denmark in general, but particularly among precarious workers.

Whereas classical questions about work and pay conditions have been subject to extensive research and public debate in Denmark, the focus on precarious work and the discussion of its content and extent is relatively new. Precarious work can be defined and analysed in many ways depending on the dimensions of the phenomenon to be explored (Campbell & Price, 2016). Guy Standing (2011) has suggested that precarity should be understood as the absence of different forms of labour security. Relating precarity not only to forms of employment but also to the question of (in)security, the notion allows for a broader understanding of precarious work, where security is a relative and relational phenomenon based on both objective criteria and subjective experiences. Following this, we suggest the terms *potential* and *actual precarity* to underline how precarization can be understood as a continuum between poles that contains many individual differences and shifting in and out of precarious work. Potential precarity also affects the not-yet precarious individuals, as a "horizon" influencing their choices and experiences of security and insecurity.

By using the terms potential and actual precarity, we gain access to an understanding of the processes that form the growth in precarious work as related to broader societal and labour market transformations. In this way, it is also possible to depict how precarity is spreading into the world of full-time employment. In particular, the expansion of different forms of labour flexibility that have become core elements in the development of post-Fordist and neoliberal labour market regulations and state policies show us that precarity must be seen in a continuum rather than as an "either-or" (Lambert & Herod, 2016). When we explore the phenomenon of precarity in a broader historical societal perspective, we find that the process reflects a gradual erosion of the full-time permanent employment norm developed throughout the era of Fordism (Castel & Dörre, 2009).

As working life researchers, we aim to explore the subjective dimension of precarity. The focus on changed welfare systems and labour market regulations must therefore be supplemented by interpretations of changes in worker subjectivity. The classical image of the worker as a wage earner has been undergoing transformations flavoured by new ideals of employees as bearers of an "entrepreneurial mindset" with strong imperatives to the worker to be passionately engaged in work as a means for self-realization or even emancipation (Ekman, 2013). Understanding modern precarious worker subjectivity calls for viewing precarious work as not only affecting people's work but also their entire lifeworld. It has strong effects on family life, feelings of exclusion from core elements of society, guilt and shame, etc. Of course, precarity is a phenomenon that affects people through their labour market participation (or lack of it), but if we distinguish rigidly between labour market work and leisure time, we may risk overlooking important dimensions of precarious working life subjectivity. Living in precarity requires a lot of unpaid work since those affected are constantly forced to spend time and effort on finding the next job and thereby maintain their income and professional identity as highly educated employees.

All these influential drivers of change make it impossible to operate with a strict generic or decontextualized concept of precarity. Rather, we stress the importance of defining precarity in the light of (and with sensitivity towards) these trends, thus viewing precarity in an everyday life perspective.

Qualitative research on precarious work among graduates

Until now, the vast majority of research on precarious work has focused quantitatively on important issues of who is affected by precarious work, where and how. However, qualitative research has also been conducted (Birch & Strandvad, 2005; Bourguignon, 2012; Fersch, 2014). Some projects have specifically dealt with people with higher education This includes Sander's large study that includes the construction of four different typologies that categorize ways graduates experience and handle precarity (Sander, 2012). Sander's results show major differences in how the challenges are met and how far precarity affects the ability to act upon one's own work and life situation. Others have analysed how the prospect of a precarious working life can influence how young graduates plan family life (*reproductive insecurity*, Chan and Tweedie, 2015), while Armano and Murgia (2013) discuss how knowledge workers' strong identification with their work can lead to self-exploitation. As we will see, some of these findings are also reflected in our Danish material.

The empirical findings that we present in the following section derive from two related current Danish research projects exploring how precarious work conditions are beginning to emerge in the highly skilled part of the labour market. The projects deal with the overall question of how precarious work is experienced and raise questions as to how precarity affects professional identities and the meaning of work: how do those affected interpret and respond to their situation and how do they cope with the growing insecurity and unpredictability of their working life?

The first research project we draw on in this chapter is the PhD project "Precarity and Professional Identity", conducted by Anders Jakobsen (as yet unpublished). The research focuses on the relationship between precarity and meaning in work and contains a series of qualitative interviews with graduates exploring how they interpret precarious work as both an opportunity and a constraint to experiencing meaning in work. The second research project "Precarity: Of Academic Work" is being conducted by Gleerup and colleagues (2018) and funded by the Danish Association of Masters and PhDs (Dansk Magisterforening). The research focuses on the socio-historical background to precarious work as a basis for a qualitative study including over 40 interviews exploring how precarity is experienced and dealt with by graduates in various highly skilled fields of work in the public and private sectors. The participants are cultural workers, freelancers, university teachers and employees in public administration.

The overall theoretical framework and research design of both projects are inspired by the tradition of critical theory, combining an analysis of societal, political and economic structures with a psychosocial analysis of subjective dynamics and orientations. When linking societal and subjective issues through critical theory, we try to avoid approaches that understand subjective experience as a mirror of objective conditions. Subjective experience is always more than that, and the patterns in the dialectic connection between micro and macro levels are difficult to grasp making use of a single level of perspective.

In our research as a whole, we draw on a variety of theoretical sources of inspiration. In this chapter, we highlight the work of Regina Becker-Schmidt, which we find relevant to the study of precarious work among graduates

(Becker-Schmidt, 1982; Jakobsen, 2018). Her central concept is that of ambivalence. According to Becker-Schmidt, all (wage) labour is not just an expression of instrumental orientations within the worker. Furthermore, it is neither just an expression of identification nor a source of individual gratification. Instead, work is experienced ambivalently, and these ambivalences stem from unsolved conflicts on the societal level, but also from conflicts in the private life and biography of the individual (Becker-Schmidt, 1982). Subjective experiences of precarious work are thus clearly ambivalent: precarious work may on the one hand be experienced as an opportunity for meaning in work by working in one's professional field, which may not be possible otherwise. On the other, precarious work is often a source of negative feelings, due to lack of recognition, lack of interaction with peers and lack of security in terms of income and pension.

The analysis of our empirical data also draws on what we define as an everyday life perspective, theoretically inspired by the French researcher Henri Lefebvre (Lefebvre, 1991) and his critical approach to everyday life with core notions of (and focus on) space and rhythms as important components in the shaping of our everyday lives. Against this background, we aim to show how tendencies towards precarious work are experienced and dealt with by affected graduates in a lifeworld perspective. Although the subjective experiences of precarious work are in focus in the interviews, our aim has been to understand precarity as affecting a person's whole life situation, which explains our use of everyday life theory.

In the following presentation of selected empirical findings, we focus on these three themes: meaning of work, participation in the workplace and precarity in a life perspective. The findings illuminate precarious work as a subjective phenomenon in these three important, albeit far from exhaustive, dimensions.

Experiences of meaning and meaninglessness

In highly skilled work, as in all other work, the experience of meaning, or the absence of it, is an important factor for the subjective experience of work quality (Ravn, 2008; Kamp, 2011). With a rising proportion of graduates working under precarious conditions in Denmark, the question arises not only of the structural consequences of precarious work among graduates but also of the subjective experience of quality and meaning in work. A closer look reveals that the relationship between precarious work in different forms and the subjective experience of meaning in work is not obvious. Thus, on the one hand, Standing describes how precarious work leads to loss of a work-based or professional identity, because the flexible character and instrumental orientation of (and in) precarious work leads to a loss of a feeling of community and ethical standards and norms, reducing work to "careerless jobs" without "social memory", reciprocity or fraternity (Standing, 2011, pp. 12, 23).

On the other hand, freelance highly skilled work at least in some forms seems to be associated with high commitment and identification, and thus presumably high degrees of subjective meaning (Ekman, 2013). Due to the very different professional fields and somewhat different degrees of work security among the graduate precariat, differences in the relationship between precarious work and the experience of meaning in work must be expected.

Meaning is in our understanding rooted in a critical perspective, where work is viewed as both socially constituted and as an important form of human expression: a life activity. As such, work becomes on the one hand an important potential source of meaning, but on the other, work may also be a source of experiences of alienation and meaninglessness if instrumental or rigid (wage) labour orientations gain the upper hand (Kamp, 2011; Gleerup et al., 2018). In continuation of the critical perspective, the central research interest becomes how these experiences may serve as a conserving or transformative potential for the critique and development of precarious academic work.

In the above-mentioned study by Jakobsen, the majority of the participants experience precarious work as both a possibility and a barrier to experiencing meaning in work. On the one hand, precarious employment is experienced by the participants as an opportunity for working within what they understand as their professional field and which is not accessible to them (for reasons of competition or otherwise) under normal full-time permanent employment conditions. On the other, many participants emphasize the harsh price to pay in terms of the unpredictable and insecure working conditions involved. The majority of the experiences are thus to some degree ambivalent. The participants have to balance the two goals of income security and the opportunity to do meaningful work. This implies yet another balancing and negotiation as to whether a job opportunity is actually professionally meaningful enough. Many participants find this constant balancing and negotiation of identity to be a strain. All wage labour involves such compromises, but these participants point out that it is the permanent state of these inner negotiations that they find wearing.

However, the participants differ. One participant underlines how precarious work allows her to work within what she understands as her professional field, which would not be accessible to her otherwise. For her, precarious work becomes a possibility for experiencing meaning in work:

> Yes, I think I would call myself self-employed, and for instance not an entrepreneur, in other words self-employed in the sense that I myself find the work I want to do. Yes, like I decide myself which work I find attractive and which things I want to do, and if something comes along which I think would be nice, then of course I say yes.
>
> (Woman, humanities, in her thirties, currently self-employed)

She continued as follows:

> Yes, I chose to be self-employed because I thought it was the only way I could work with or talk about my professionalism all the time.

This participant has apparently succeeded in establishing herself as a self-employed professional, basing her work on her educational background and experiencing meaning in work by employing her professional skills in different assignments. Other participants underline how precarious working conditions are a heavy price to pay for working within, or even just on the fringe of, their professional field. As one participant states:

> But there are also just some things which the whole time make it a bit negative, also where you can feel that the more years you have been in it, the more it wears you down. We also don't get a pension so in a way you really cannot put it aside.
>
> (Woman, natural sciences, in her forties, currently in a temporary position)

This participant has for many years been working in temporary teaching positions at a university. She has been quite content with this, but is now increasingly worried about her prospects, pointing out how the goal of professional meaningfulness may lead to one staying "too long" in precarious working conditions. At the other extreme, one participant underlines how lack of meaning in precarious work has led him to quit a job:

> Professionally, I wasn't very happy with it. Because even though it was interesting to work with these people, it wasn't very interesting professionally to me and didn't have much to do with my professional identity, I thought, so I quit the job.
>
> (Male, humanities, in his thirties, currently unemployed)

The participants thus experience precarious work very differently, in some cases as an opportunity and in others as a barrier to experiencing meaning in work.

Participation in the workplace

In the project by Gleerup et al. (2018) we find that an important aspect of precarious work life revolves around the conditions for participation at the workplace level. Many of our participants experience a variety of unfair differences and illegitimate inequality between the permanent and temporary staff. Besides the inequalities in formal employment conditions and pay between temporary and permanent staff, many stress the difficulties of *social* and *professional* integration at work. Hence, many of the participants working on temporary contracts have trouble "finding their place" as a member of the workplace community. From a social perspective, some point out that temporary workers are rarely invited to annual summer seminars, Christmas dinners or other social activities. From a professional point of view, some stress how it hurts when temporary workers are not invited to take part in meetings about how to organize, conduct or develop the work. Some find that permanent staff tend to overlook the contributions by temporary staff, while others reason that the permanent staff are unaware of who the temporary workers are, let alone their unequal pay and working conditions. Some feel almost invisible or taken for granted by permanent staff. As one puts it:

> It's the sense of not. . . You're just not important. It shows in so many ways, we're expected to do all sorts of things, but we don't get paid for it.

At small well-functioning workplaces, employment differences seem to play a minor role, since the need for close cooperation supports group solidarity and shared interests. At large workplaces like a university, differences tend to exclude the temporary staff from important professional parts of the workplace community. As one university teacher puts it:

> I'd very much like to join a research group, but I know perfectly well that when it comes to money and funding of new projects, I'm not included.

These examples show how the lack of social and professional recognition from colleagues matters a great deal to the participants. When talking about the inequality, many participants try to balance their analysis, often stressing that permanent staff can be very friendly, and some participants even blame themselves, reasoning that they should have been more outreaching or explicit in showing their qualifications and eagerness to invest in the workplace. Others state pragmatically that they do not expect to be treated as equals with permanent staff, as long as temporary staff are not ignored and their position as co-producers is recognized at the workplace level. As we shall see, these problems are also interwoven with the participant's relationship with management.

The difficult relationship with management

Temporary staff are vulnerable in the interplay with management. Many of them describe their temporary position as "a permanent trial", meaning that they feel continuously tested, sometimes without really knowing what criteria they are being judged by. Consequently, many participants over-perform. They take on more responsibility than their contract stipulates, and they accept an unfair distribution of the workload in order to show their dedication and willingness to work hard. Furthermore, participants tell how they are constantly looking for signs indicating that they might get a permanent position or at least another time-limited contract when their current contract finishes. As one participant explains:

> You're constantly interpreting all kinds of signs that might reveal if management is ready to prolong your employment for a couple of months extra.

Some argue that as a temporary worker it is impossible to report sick at work. The risk of negative consequences is simply too high. These examples show that temporary workers suffer from unclear performance expectations, making them very worried about how to navigate in clever ways in order to maintain and improve their employment relationship.

The empirical findings as a whole clearly show that at the organizational level the tendency towards more precarious work leads to changes affecting both the work environment and the quality of work. Increasingly unequal work and learning conditions emerge, formal and informal privileges become more and more differentiated and, in several cases, the temporary workers find that the workload is unfairly distributed. In addition, management and colleagues may overlook qualifications among the temporary staff that could improve work quality. It is evident that the situation affects not only temporary employees but also permanent staff, either directly or indirectly. This is partly because continuity is lost when large turnover becomes "the new normal", partly because the quality of the social climate erodes within this fragmented atmosphere. At some large workplaces, extensive use of temporary contracts results in competitiveness among several temporary employees all striving for a permanent position. Hence, not only the work environment but also the quality of work are affected. Professional standards can be undermined by a poorly functioning work environment if inequality and competition rather than cooperation and mutual learning define the atmosphere and set unsatisfactory conditions for performing highly skilled work. The participants find that management rarely supports their aspirations to perform serious and meaningful work, and their wish to be included in professional communities at work is often overlooked.

Professional identity and responsibility

The empirical findings show that the possibilities of maintaining and developing a professional identity matter a great deal to the participants. In some fields of work, graduates are recruited for specialized tasks, and they experience good opportunities for using their professional skills, even if only for six months or less. Examples cited are cultural workers such as specialized archaeologists recruited for exciting excavations. However, others find little opportunity to make use of their skills. Some of the participants have chosen to supplement their income from precarious highly skilled work with part-time unskilled jobs. Some work in the care sector, others have cleaning jobs in the evenings. In this way, they hold onto their profession, even though their basic income derives from unskilled work. Combining suitable work for graduates with unskilled work often gives rise to doubts and ambivalence about strategy: "Shall I give up on my professional identity or keep trying to get a full-time job suitable for a graduate?" Participants tend to hold onto their professional identity by striving for employment within their professional field. However, conditions for professional development in their fields tend to weaken and become differentiated, leaving the temporary employees with little or no access to further education. Management invests educational effort in permanent staff, and interesting development work is given to them, rather than to the temporary staff. Long-term strategies of workplace development do not include the temporary staff, and their individual qualifications are often not recognized as potentially useful in future planning. In the end, these factors may lead to de-qualification of temporary graduates.

Most temporary workers experience ambivalence related to their sense of professional responsibility. They want to engage and take responsibility for the quality of work, but their time-limited contracts and lack of inclusion in the professional community at work stand in the way. The interview data show different strategies to deal with such circumstances. Some engage even harder when contracts are soon to run out. Others tend to let go of professional standards in order to protect themselves from disillusionment because their involvement goes unacknowledged. Some tell us that this is a very ambiguous situation to be in, since they do not want to downgrade their involvement, but they are forced by circumstances to let go of responsibility. Sometimes reasons are practical: they need to spend increasingly more time and effort on finding a new job when their contract is almost over. It can be an ambivalent challenge, leaving unfinished business behind, when a contract runs out:

> I was kept on illegally for four months. They don't feel bad about it, and I wanted to be kept on. Then they gave me the work nobody else wants. . . But I write everything down in manuals for the next temporary employee. It's only fair to do that, when you know you'll be out of here soon. But I'm thinking: good luck! Being a temporary worker, you have to protect yourself a little bit. You can't get too emotionally involved, wondering how they're going to manage when I'm gone.

As the quote shows, it is an ambivalent matter to maintain a sense of moral and professional responsibility, and often the participants are struggling to find a balance between engagement and self-protection. They also show that considerable knowledge is lost due to the large turnover in staff, and sometimes initiatives or projects must start all over again or end before time because it is impossible to establish continuity. As one explains about an important development project that fell apart:

> It leaves a ruin of unfinished work. I was allowed to take up a project left behind, but I had to give up on it. It was work started by temporary staff

who aren't here any more – perspectives on the project have vanished with them. What a waste, it could have been so great, doing the project. 90% of all the work never done relates to the fact that there's no structure, people have just left.

Precarity in a life perspective

The spread of precarious work also influences the private lives of the participants. Especially among the young graduates, planning problems matter: can we afford to have children if both parents are loosely attached to the labour market? Can we afford to buy the bigger flat we need when we'll both be out of a job in a few months? Should we move to another part of the country because one of us has got a time-limited job offer there? What are the long-term consequences of jobs without pension benefits? Will I suffer from poverty in my old age? Such questions make it difficult for the participants to keep faith in the future, and many of them anticipate that social security in the welfare system will erode before they retire.

Even though some participants emphasize that they do not see full permanent employment as the solution to all their problems, and despite some being able to find their way by combining different jobs or making a living as freelancers and self-employed professionals, it is evident from the data from both projects that the majority find precarious work to be stressful. Temporality and unpredictability are defining factors in their everyday life. This makes it difficult to plan the future, and many experience a gradual loss of control over their own lives. The sense of not belonging anywhere means that the mechanisms of individualization strike harder, as does the sense of insecurity, the lack of recognition, the loss of professional integrity and the sense of disappointment. All of these are severe negative companions to the emerging precarity.

Although the participants point to structural or organizational factors as the reason for precarity, there is also a strong undercurrent of feelings of guilt and shame. Shame is a well-known effect of processes of exclusion and marginalization and affect the whole life situation of staff in precarious employment. The companion to shame, guilt, also appears as a theme for some of the participants. They struggle with doubts like: maybe it's also my own fault, I could have done this or that better to improve my career opportunities. Probably this theme is especially significant among graduates due to high levels of professional expectations underlined by an individualized responsibility for maintaining and developing professional competencies. In a life perspective, feelings of shame and guilt spread to all spheres of everyday life and can dramatically affect and dismantle opportunities to be proactive.

Among the younger graduates, we sometimes trace a more pragmatic or hopeful attitude than among the experienced. The young graduates still have hopes for a permanent job in the future, and some identify positive aspects of trying out different kinds of temporary jobs while waiting for the right permanent job to show up. They take the opportunities to improve their qualifications and CVs through a series of time-limited jobs. However, most of them also fear that this is not just an initial phase but may instead reflect an emerging structural change in the labour market whose full consequences they as graduates are the first to experience. As one of the participants puts it:

> Both my parents are graduates with full-time permanent jobs. I've got good marks and I suppose I thought I could be like them. Now I've had temporary work for more than five years. Maybe this is how things actually are! I hope not!

Other young participants argue that they have been cheated by "the educational promise". They were advised to choose higher education and had counted on this providing maximum security. Now they find that they apply for jobs they cannot get, because they are overqualified as graduates.

Wishes for change

Finally, we asked the participants what thoughts they had about how their life situation could be changed for the better and how precarity should be dealt with on a societal level. Some would like the public to know more about precarious work and pay conditions spreading among graduates. Others ask for networks and trade union support to negotiate better conditions in temporary contracts. Some suggest, in complete contrast, that trade unions should make efforts to abandon temporary work contracts completely. This strategy, however, can also backfire on precarious workers. One university teacher explains how she sometimes feels caught in ambivalence between principles and reality:

> I'm so much against all the time-limited job offers – we're being exploited, it should be forbidden! Still, every time I get a new offer, I agree. Sometimes I even ask my trade union to help me out on a formal level, so that my contract can be extended once again.

This last quote provokes the question: are the precarious workers well supported by their trade union, or does the trade union fail to grasp their specific needs and interests? Some participants do not believe that the trade union really cares about them, while others argue that organizing precarious employment is the most important current trade union challenge and provide practical ideas and suggestions on how to improve work conditions through trade union initiatives.

Summing up the empirical findings

Throughout this chapter, we have aimed to show that precarity exists within the field of highly skilled work. Summing up the empirical themes, we find that ambivalence characterizes individual strategies in various ways. Participants find it difficult to achieve and maintain professional identity and meaning in work when subjected to a series of temporary work contracts and highly uncertain career prospects. Many struggle to find ways in which they can combine a fair level of income security with a meaningful job content corresponding to their high level of education.

In relation to workplace participation, precarious graduates also experience a variety of difficulties. Workplace integration is hard to achieve, and interplay with colleagues and management is vulnerable. Different kinds of inequality exist, and the graduates find their professional identity and sense of responsibility undermined by the temporality, unpredictability and shortsightedness that accompany the precarious work conditions.

Finally, when viewing precarity in an everyday life perspective, we find that graduates are affected in many regards. Some feel deceived by "the educational promise", realizing that a university degree cannot protect them from a precarious working life. Young graduates in particular fear the future, anticipating scenarios of permanent precarity or old age in poverty. To some extent, they turn their analysis inward and hence struggle with feelings of shame and guilt. Others, however, turn their analysis outwards, arguing that precarity problems must not be individualized, since they are rather products of negative societal developments that must be counteracted. These graduates call upon their trade unions to hear their voice and renew their policies.

The results of our research projects indicate that it is important to continue to make use of both sociological and humanistic approaches to identify the variety of consequences of precarity. This is in order to interpret how the spread of precarious work affects individuals, families, workplace communities and the quality of work itself – and thereby clearly also society at large. Such analytical work may inform and enhance discussions and decision-making processes at several levels.

Perspectives of action for change

It is not easy to predict the consequences of precarity in the future, and the complexity of the phenomenon indicates that overcoming problems should not be left to the labour market parties to solve alone, since the problem is rooted in developments in capitalism and heavily interwoven with political aims to reorganize systems of social security in the welfare state. However, the Nordic labour market models are characterized by unique traditions of strong cooperation between the social parties and the government, and the vast majority of Danish workers are still members of trade unions. In light of this, it is relevant to ask whether trade unions could engage in dialogue with members affected by precarity and develop new policy strategies in cooperation with them, developing more explicit and well-founded alliances between precarious and non-precarious members. Collecting and exploring the experiences of precarity in a shared learning environment could pave the way for politicizing insights and translate them into new demands within (and beyond) the labour market negotiation system. Individualization and feelings of guilt and shame are not only experienced by precarious workers. More and more people in permanent jobs suffer from stress and work-related depression and take sick leave as a result of unsustainable labour market developments. The tendency towards increasing uncertainty regarding the future welfare state model is shared by permanent and temporary staff alike, and this may constitute a potential for unions to gather and build on experiences across members' specific employment conditions. Unions have the opportunity to bridge the seemingly opposing interests of secure and precarious workers.

Finally, sustainable working conditions are not only important from an employee perspective. Also at the political level, it is gradually recognized that knowledge work will play an important role in the future, and if the labour market involves more and more precarious work, the quality of work may be at risk. Hence, politicians at national level could renew the Nordic tradition of close cooperation with the social parties and develop Nordic alternatives to the spread of precarity.

References

Altvater, E. & Mahnkopf, B. (2002) *Globalisierung der Unsicherheit: Arbeit im Schatten, schmutziges Geld und informelle Politik [Globalization of Insecurity: Work in the Shadows, Dirty Money and Informal Politics]*, Münster, Germany: Westfälishces Dampfboot.

Armano, E. & Murgia, A. (2013) The Precariousness of Young Knowledge Workers: A Subject-Oriented Approach, *Global Discourse*, 3(3–4): 486–501.

Becker-Schmidt, R. (1982) Modsætningsfyldt realitet og ambivalens: kvinders arbejdserfaringer i fabrik og familie [Conflictual Reality and Ambivalence: Women's Work Experiences in Factory and Family], *Udkast*, 10(2): 164–198.

Birch, S., & Strandvad, S. (2005) Frihed og ufrihed i det kreative arbejde: en undersøgelse af unge danske filminstruktører i et Foucault perspektiv [Freedom and Bondage in Creative Work: A Study of Young Danish Movie Directors in a Foucault Perspective], PhD thesis, Copenhagen: Institute of Sociology, University of Copenhagen.

Blankholm, U. O. (2016) *Jobindex*, 2016–08–01.

Bourguignon, A. (2012) A Psycho-Sociological View on Precarity: The French Case, In: Hepp, R.-D. (ed.) *Prekarisierung und Flexibilisierung*, Münster, Germany: Westfälisches Dampfboot, 340–368.

Campbell, L. & Price, R. (2016) Precarious Work and Precarious Workers: Towards an Improved Conceptualization, *The Economic and Labour Relations Review*, 27(3): 314–332.

Castel, R. & Dörre, K. (eds) (2009) *Prekariat, Abstieg, Ausgrenzung: Die soziale Frage am Beginn des 21. Jahrhunderts [Precariat, Decline, Exclusion: The Social Question at the Beginning of the 21st Century]*, Frankfurt am Main, Germany: Campus.

Chan, S. & Tweedie, D. (2015) Precarious Work and Reproductive Insecurity, *Social Alternatives*, 34(4): 5–13.

Dörre, K. (2009) Prekarität im Finanzmarkt-Kapitalismus [Precarity in Financial Market Capitalism], In: Castel, R. & Dörre, K. (eds) *Prekariat, Abstieg, Ausgrenzung: Die soziale Frage am Beginn des 21. Jahrhunderts [Precariat, Decline, Exclusion: The Social Question at the Beginning of the 21st Century]*, Frankfurt am Main, Germany: Campus: 35–64.

Ejlertsen, M. (2017) Hver femte akademiker er midlertidigt ansat [Every Fifth Graduate is Temporarily Employed], *Magisterbladet.dk*, 6.10.2017, http://magisterbladet.dk/magisterbladet/2017/092017/092017_p44.

Ekman, S. (2013) Fantasies about Work as Limitless Potential: How Managers and Employees Seduce Each Other through Dynamics of Mutual Recognition, *Human Relations*, 66(9): 1159–1181.

Esping-Andersen, G. (2000) *The Three Worlds of Welfare Capitalism*, Cambridge, UK: Polity Press.

Fersch, B. (2014) Det truede arbejdsliv: hvad er prekært arbejde? [The Threatened Working Life: What is Precarious Work?], *Kritisk Debat*, 79. http://kritiskdebat.dk/articles.php?article_id=1383.

Gleerup, J., Nielsen, B. S., Olsén, P. & Warring, N. (2018) *Prekarisering: af akademisk arbejde [Precarity: Of Academic Work]*, Frederiksberg, Denmark: Frydenlund.

Hardt, M. & Negri, A. (2000) *Empire*, Cambridge, MA: Harvard University Press.

Harvey, D. (2004) The "New" Imperialism: Accumulation by Dispossession, *Socialist Register*, 40: 63–87.

Harvey, D. (2010) *The Enigma of Capital and the Crises of Capitalism*, Oxford, UK: Oxford University Press.

Hirsch, J. (1998) *Vom Sichersstaat zum nationalen Wettbewerbsstaat* [*From Security-State to National Competition State*], Berlin: I. D. Verlag.

Ibsen, C. L. (2011) Strained Compromises? Danish Flexicurity During Crisis, *Nordic Journal of Working Life Studies*, 1(1): 45–65.

Jakobsen, A. (2018) Faglighed, mening og ambivalens i prekært akademisk arbejde [Professionalism, Meaning and Ambivalence in Precarious Academic Work], *Tidsskruft for Arbejdsliv*, 20(1): 30–46.

Kalleberg, A. (2009) Precarious Work, Insecure Workers: Employment Relations in Transition, *American Sociological Review*, 74(1): 1–22.

Kamp, A. (2011) Mening i arbejdet: for lidt, for meget, til forhandling? [Meaning in Work: Too Much, Too Little, Up For Negotiation?], *Tidsskrift for Arbejdsliv*, 13(2): 8–27.

Lambert, R. & Herod, A. (eds) (2016) *Neoliberal Capitalism and Precarious Work: Ethnographies of Accommodation and Resistance*, Cheltenham, UK: Edward Elgar.

Larsen, T. (2011) *Insidere og outsider: den danske models rækkevidde [Insiders and Outsiders: The Reach of the Danish Model]*, Copenhagen: Jurist- og Økonomforbundets Forlag.

Lefebvre, H. (1991) *The Production of Space*, N. Donaldson-Smith trans., Oxford, UK: Basil Blackwell.

Madsen, P. K. (2011) Flexicurity i modvind: en analyse af den danske flexicurity-model [Flexicuiry in a Head Wind: An Analysis of the Danish Flexicurity Model], *Tidsskrift for Arbejdsliv*, 13(4): 8–21.

Mailand, M. & Larsen, T. P. (2011) *Trade Unions and Precarious Work: Danish Country Report to the BARSORI-Project*, Copenhagen: FAOS Forskningsnotat, No 121.

Mckay, S., Jefferys, S., Paraksevopoulou, A. & Keles, J. (2012) *Study on Precarious Work and Social Rights* (Report for the European Commission (VT/2010/084)), London: Working Lives Research Institute, London Metropolitan University.

Mortensen, M. V. & Damholt, C. (2017) *Tidsbegrænsede ansættelser i Danmark [Temporary Employment in Denmark]*, Copenhagen: Dansk Magisterforening.

Pedersen, M. S. & Ribe, M. Ø. (2013) *Akademikerprekariatet. Rapport om akademikernes arbejdsmarked 2002–2010 [The Academic Precariat. Report on the Graduate Labour Market 2002–2010]*, Copenhagen: Analyse og tal.

Pedersen, O. K. (2011) *Konkurrencestaten [The Competition State]*, Copenhagen: Hans Reitzels Forlag.

Rasmussen, S., Larsen, T. P. & Andersen, P. T. (2017) Det prekære arbejdsliv: en indledning [The Precarious Working Life: An Introduction], *Tiddskrift for Arbejdsliv*, 20(1): 5–9.

Rasmussen, S. & Madsen, P. K. (2017) Platformsøkonomien og prekariatet [The Platform Economy and the Precariat], *Tidsskrift for Arbejdsliv*, 20(1): 46–62.

Ravn, I. (2008) Mening i arbejdlivet: definition og konceptualisering [Meaning in Working Life: Definition and Conceptualization], *Tidsskrift for Arbejdsliv*, 10(4): 59–75.

Sander, N. (2012) *Das akademische Prekariat: Leben zwischen Frist und Plan [The Academic Precariat: Life between Time Limit and Plan]*, Konstanz, Germany: UVK Verlagsgesellschaft.

Scheuer, S. (2017) *Atypisk beskæftigelse i Danmark [Atypical Employment in the Danish Labour Market]*, LO-dokumentation Nr. 1/2017, Copenhagen: LO.

Standing, G. (2011) *The Precariat: The New Dangerous Class*, London/New York: Bloomsbury Academic.

Standing, G. (2016) *The Corruption of Capitalism*, London: Biteback Publishing.

Udvalg om bedre universitetsuddannelser (2018) *Universitetsuddannelser til fremtiden [University Education for the Future]*, Copenhagen: Udvalg om bedre universitetsuddannelser – Uddannelses- og Forskningsministeriet, https://ufm.dk/publikationer/2018/filer/rapport-universitetsuddannelser-til-fremtiden.pdf.

Chapter 16

The formation and destabilization of the standard employment relationship in Norway

The contested politics and regulation of temporary work agencies

Per Bonde Hansen and Anders Underthun

Introduction

The flexibilization of post-Fordist production, neoliberal governance and the precarization of employment relations have typically been held as important processes for shifting power structures in Western welfare states in recent decades (Allen & Henry, 1997). For instance, Peck and Tickell (2002) argue that an emerging neoliberal order has put considerable pressure on the political and economic functions of the state, while Jessop (2002) argues that Western welfare states to various degrees have undergone a shift from the Keynesian, redistributive welfare state to a neoliberal competition state.

One of the key organizing principles of the state in political-economic terms is the regulation and status of *employment relations*, or more specifically: What is the status of different forms of employment? The *standard employment relationship* (SER), understood as permanent, open-ended, full-time employment in a bilateral employment relationship (Vosko, 2008), has been one of the hallmarks of Western welfare states. However, the imperative of *flexibility* (e.g. Atkinson, 1987) in a post-Fordist economic order has challenged the dominant position of the SER. In complete contrast, precarious employment (Standing, 2011) is characterized by insecurity, low income, often fixed-term contractual employment and inferior social and statutory entitlements (Vosko, 2009). Often cited as a symbol of precarious employment, temporary work agencies (TWA) rest their operations on mediating mostly fixed-term labour to provide flexible, on-demand man-hours to a client organization (Vosko, 2009). The idea of labour as a *commodity* has been highly controversial, in particular by labour interests which have highlighted the precarious nature of such work arrangements. In a historical context, TWA work has also been controversial for employers, as the SER supported capital interests that were dependent on growing and predictable labour services.

The contested nature of the TWA industry has implied strict regulation across Europe, in particular in welfare states where the SER has retained a high status, such as the Nordic countries (Vosko, 2009; Thelen, 2012). In this chapter, we ask how the economic, legal and normative foundation of the SER in comparison with temporary agency work has been debated, contested and regulated in Norway from 1945 to 2018.

We argue that the concrete contestation of TWA employment has been vital in shaping and reshaping the strong Norwegian version of the SER. The norms for "standard" and "non-standard" employment relationships were for a long time unspecified and have repeatedly been subject to change. However, the research in this field largely relates to the changes in the regulation of temporary work from the 1990s onwards,[1] and in this way failed to recognize the historical and dialectic process of co-constitution between the *standard* and *non-standard* in employment relations. In our argument, we also emphasize that it is important not to take the gradual fall of the SER for granted, but rather to consider its more fluctuating status as an expression of a particular and context-dependent balance of social forces. A further aim of this chapter is to pay special attention to the role of employers as an organized class. Historical research in this field has mainly focused on trade unions and workers, while research on employers and their historical role has tended to focus on employers as individual actors.[2]

Based on written sources from various archives and more recent documents and academic publications, this chapter will discuss this topic from a historical perspective. We will also reflect upon the current status of the SER in relation to temporary agency work. We organize the chapter in the following manner. First, we provide a theoretical background to the status of the SER in Western welfare states. Second, we present four, relatively distinct, periods of Norwegian employment history with a focus on how the *economic*, *normative* and *legal* foundations of the SER both influenced and were influenced by the contested negotiation of TWAs. We conclude by discussing the current debate on temporary and precarious work in a Norwegian context, marked by the remarkable lingering strength of the SER affected by the considerable changes to how Western welfare states are organized and have been affected by a global, neoliberal economic order.

The standard employment relationship

Historical-dialectic perspectives on the relationship between capital and the state in post-World War II Western welfare states reflect a focus on the interplay between forms of capitalist accumulation and the institutional "fixes" (Peck & Tickell, 1994) that have changed throughout the course of history. For instance, the shift from Fordist mass production and Keynesian-oriented welfare provision and employment stimulation to a post-Fordist flexible accumulation and innovation-oriented "Schumpeterian competition state" (Jessop, 2002, p. 95) is a typical way of seeing the historical and functional connection between the state and capitalist organization (Cerny, 1997; Amin, 1994; Brenner, 2004).

Even though these institutional changes or fixes have had different expressions in different national contexts (Esping-Andersen, 1999; Hall & Soskice, 2001), the parameters for economic activity have changed quite dramatically following processes such as economic globalization and supranational deregulation. In this way, the struggle over the economic, normative and legal foundation of the SER is very different today (2018) than it was in 1945.

The SER became the typical employment relationship in Western capitalist economies after World War II, both in quantitative terms and as a political and legal norm. According to Vosko (2010), the SER rests on three pillars: (1) a bilateral employment relationship between an employer and a worker, where the worker performs work under the direct supervision of the employer; (2) a full-time position; and (3) continuous employment. The SER thus involved a relatively high degree of job security for workers.

In a historical perspective, the pillars of the SER have repeatedly been subject to change and struggle. Thus, an analysis of the content and status of the SER as an organizing principle of Norwegian working life must treat employment norms as dynamic and dependent on changing historical circumstances and a changing institutional, political and normative context. In this chapter, we argue that the pillars of the SER are founded historically on legal, normative and economic conditions or what we coin *foundations* (Hansen, 2018a). We argue that the strength of these foundations constitutes and is constituted by the changing balance of social forces and the varying opinions and interests of the actors in the historical periods we cover.[3] We concentrate our analysis of the foundations of the SER on the pillars of continuous employment and the bilateral employment relationship. The pillar of continuous employment serves as an example.

The legal foundation concerns permanent employment as a status that is interwoven into a cluster of rights providing social protection based on the asymmetric relationship between labour and capital. A central element is the protection against unfair dismissal. The right to permanent employment can be traced back to the late 19th century and the emergence of trade unions. Unions challenged the management prerogative, which was practised in line with the somewhat paradoxical slogan "freedom of work". This implied that decisions regarding hiring or firing workers were solely a matter for the employer (Seierstad, 1986; Bjørnson, 2007). Through trade union mobilization, the employment relationship changed from being an agreement entered into in the name of "freedom of contract", to a position with associated rights. In other words, the employment contract was given a more formalized form or status (Jacoby, 2004; Freedland, 2013).

The normative foundation concerns the extent to which permanent employment is considered the ideal employment relationship. The concept of "job ownership" is highly relevant for both the normative and legal foundations of the SER. According to Selig Perlman (1928), unions have fought for the right to, so to speak, own their positions in a company. In other words, unions have opposed the view that the company and the job to be done solely belong to the capitalist, as the owner of the means of production. Expressions of such "job ownership" imply formal and informal arrangements such as protection against dismissals, seniority systems and occupational regulations (cf. Seierstad, 1982, 1986).

The economic foundation concerns the demand for labour, often with certain skills. The growth of the SER was not only the result of regulations and norms. Permanent employment was mostly achieved in the period known as the golden age of capitalism, the three decades of economic boom after World War II, characterized by a great demand for labour and a policy of full employment (Hobsbawm, 1995), contrasting with the imperative for flexible labour (Kalleberg et al., 2003).

Increased numbers of employees in a permanent, bilateral employment relationship not only implied job security for workers and a certain stability for employers. Permanent employment was also important for the establishment of a system of industrial relations. Unions built their strongholds among the so-called core proletariat i.e. the relatively secure and well-paid part of the working class. Union density reached its peak in many countries when such workers accounted for the largest share of the workforce (Hyman, 1999, p. 100).

The dominant role of certain groups of workers leads to another important element of the SER. To whom was it accessible? As Leah Vosko (2010) has argued, the SER must be seen in the light of its *exclusions*. Another important characteristic of the SER is, in other words, its exclusivity. Two important exclusion criteria are gender and citizenship.

First, the SER is based on what Vosko calls a "gender contract", a division of labour between female "caregivers" and male "breadwinners". Second, the SER was based on citizenship boundaries and intimately connected with the nation state (Vosko, 2010, pp. 3–5). However, in a Norwegian context, the exclusions from the SER have not only been gender and citizenship. For example, until 1975, workers under the age of 21 and those who had held a job for under two years were not entitled to protection against dismissal. In addition, many people employed in seasonal work and in the construction industry had virtually no rights to continuous employment. Thus, we argue that the Norwegian variant of the SER primarily rested on a division between a "core" and "periphery" of workers, where the normative basis was that the core was not accessible for everyone. In other words, the fundamental "contract" to which the state, trade unions and employers in Norway have adhered has involved certain types of employees being more loosely tied to the labour market (Hansen, 2018a, pp. 34–35). In this perspective, precariousness can be seen as embedded in the constitution of the SER.

The SER and the regulation of temporary agency work 1945–2018

Based on this framework, the changes in the SER in Norway from 1945 to 2018 can be divided into four periods. As we aim to illustrate, the status and scope of the SER has been dependent on norms, legal regulations and economic factors. However, the content of each of these and the balance between them have changed considerably. The SER has rested with varying strength at different times on these three foundations. In the first period, from 1945 to 1970, the legal foundation of the SER was relatively weak. This changed dramatically in the 1970s, when the SER became enshrined in law. In the third period (1980–1998), the strong normative support for an extensive SER lost ground as the economy became more unpredictable compared to the decades preceding the mid-1970s. In the fourth period (2000 onwards), the legal foundation of the SER was formally weakened through the liberalization of temporary agency work. That said, the legal foundation has also had a fluctuating tendency following trade union initiatives to extend the statutory status of collective agreements in the mid-2000s, the implementation of the EU Directive on Temporary Agency Work in 2013, new provisions on temporary work in 2015, and consultations and propositions related to stricter regulation of the TWA industry in 2017–2018.

In our historical account, we focus on the engineering industry and on how employers and trade unions responded to the TWAs in this sector. From the third period, we extend our focus to the national level and the legal regulations and strategies of the Confederation of Norwegian Enterprise (NHO) and the Norwegian Confederation of Trade Unions (LO). The main reason for this is that the SER prior to the 1970s was largely a product of sector-level negotiations. In that respect, the engineering industry is a case study of how the Norwegian variant of the SER was shaped in a specific historical context of labour shortage and economic growth in a specific sector where the position of the SER was stronger than in most other sectors. Nevertheless, the norms for typical and atypical employment had not been determined even in the engineering industry. Further, this sector played a leading role in general developments in Norwegian working life. The shift of focus from the sectoral to the national level in the 1980s was primarily due to the increased involvement of national level actors, as the SER was enshrined in law during the 1970s (Hansen, 2018a).

The SER: a normative and economically dependent phenomenon (1945–1970)[4]

During the first phase, from 1945 to 1970, the legal foundations of the SER were weak. TWAs were unregulated, as was temporary employment in general. Protection against dismissal was severely restricted. This implied that the pillars of the SER rested on the economic foundation. Almost three decades of economic boom in the "golden age of capitalism" kept the demand for labour at a high level and implied a decline in precarious employment. However, the response of trade unions and employers to the TWAs in the engineering industry shows that the pillars also rested on a quite strong normative foundation in this sector. The confederation of employers in the engineering industry (Mekaniske Verksteders Landsforening) and the Norwegian Iron and Metal Workers Union (Norsk Jern- og Metallarbeiderforbund) organized a broad initiative to control and limit the TWA industry.

The response of the employers must be seen in relation to the period of economic boom and a policy of full employment, with high levels of demand for labour, which allowed for extensive turnover initiated by employees. According to the employers, TWAs had a negative impact on this situation (Hansen, 2018b). Employers also reacted to the fact that turnover increased the wages of the workers, the so-called wage drift (Holden, 1998). The following quote illustrates how temporary work agencies could provoke strong reactions among employers. According to Rein Henriksen, director general of a large Norwegian company, Borregaard, and also a member of the Central Board of the Norwegian Employers' Confederation, an "obvious reason" for the wage drift was:

> [t]he case that firms that are doing human trafficking – to put it that way – are able to operate, regardless of all guidelines, and I would like to ask whether a proper campaign can be initiated to put a stop to this traffic . . . Is it not possible to put an end to the piracy going on everywhere? Cannot firms and organizations on both sides get together to exclude these firms completely?[5]

Some employers probably opposed the TWAs not only for economic reasons but also because they regarded permanent employment as the ideal employment relationship. As we shall see, employers in the engineering industry tried to boycott the TWAs. According to one of the firms, the purpose was to "bring the workers, who are now like vagabonds in the TWAs, back to their home towns and back to their old firms".[6] The resistance may have been based on a perception that the employees belonged to the employers. Unlike the permanent employees, the agency workers were regarded as agents of instability, atypical or even suspicious.

The employers in the engineering industry aimed at strengthening the bilateral employment relationship in order to maintain a permanent core of skilled employees in each company. The ultimate motive was to gain control of the labour force. How did the employers attempt to recover the permanent, bilateral employment relationship? First, employers attempted to mobilize through moralism, as shown in this example from a letter in 1956: "We have discovered a new incidence of distasteful hijacking of people that causes great harm to us". In the letter, a firm was complaining about the loss of some employees who started to work for a TWA. Second, employers attempted to define the phenomenon and in that way discover a way to relate to it collectively. More specifically, the employers tried to agree on the content of the concept of temporary work agencies. The aim was to define the concept in such a way that it would not include activities which were related but still desirable.[7] However, the employers also adopted actions that were more forceful.

In 1955, the employers in the engineering industry decided to boycott the agencies. In the beginning, the boycott was carried out silently and only by a few members of the confederation. Later, the boycott extended to formal agreements between larger groups of cooperating employers. In 1970, 37 firms with a total of 20,000 employees signed an agreement that in general banned the use of TWAs but at the same time accepted a strictly limited use of TWAs for certain work assignments. An important provision in the agreement stipulated that workers who resigned from one of the cooperating firms to join a TWA were given six months' suspension from working for a TWA if the TWA was working for one of the cooperating firms (Hansen, 2018b).

The Iron and Metal Workers Union pursued a similar approach, but the trade unions were not, it seems, as militant as the employers. The unions rejected the agencies but accepted the agency workers as members. According to the Iron and Metal Workers Union, the TWAs caused problems in different ways, some of which may be illustrated by the following quote by a local union representative in the Norwegian Iron and Metal Workers Union in 1965:

> These firms are typical of what we call private employment bureaus. Their activities to a large extent involve supply of labour to firms . . . Union density is terrible; about 80 to 90% are not organized. We view the activities of these firms as very unfavourable in industrial development. They weaken our fight to improve wages and working conditions. They pay their employees randomly and they work overtime as long as they want.[8]

The criticism raised by local unions rested on two principles that both concerned the question of solidarity: first, the unions promoted the need for equality between workers. According to several union representatives, temporary agency workers earned more than permanent workers. The union representatives also claimed that the temporary agency workers did not adhere to working time regulations and worked longer hours. Second, local unions promoted the need for stability among the workforce. The mobile character of the TWAs made it difficult for trade unions to control their activities and to include the agency workers in the union (Hansen, 2018a, chapter 3).

In their attempt to exclude the TWAs from the labour market, leading unions and employers in the engineering industry pursued complementary strategies to cope with them. The reasons for controlling the TWAs varied, but the complementary strategies led to a common approach which implied that the SER was maintained as the standard. The response of both trade unions and employers in the engineering industry to the TWAs made it reasonable to argue that exceptions to the SER should be strictly limited in this sector. The resistance to the TWAs and the demand for labour were core ingredients of a strong normative and economic foundation at a time when the legal foundation of the SER was weak (Hansen, 2018a, pp. 344–346). Above all, both employers and employees were interested in retaining control. In the period of strong economic growth after World War II, it was believed that a lack of control would increase wage drift and turnover between firms, industries and parts of the country (Bull, 1981). The TWAs were in this perspective an "employer" out of control, as were the workers who engaged in these enterprises.

The legal foundation is strengthened: the SER is enshrined in law (1971–1980)

The year 1971 marked the beginning of a new phase in the history of the SER in Norway. From 1971 to 1980, the SER also became strongly institutionalized in legal terms and was extended to include more workers than previously. Admittedly, the legal regulations that constituted the SER had a longer history. Protection against unfair dismissals was introduced in 1936, and private mediation of labour was prohibited in 1947. In other words, the bilateral employment relationship and permanent employment were legally protected, but during the 1970s, the legal foundation of these pillars was significantly strengthened.

An important legal change that strengthened the SER was the prohibition of the hiring out of labour in 1971. This was banned in the Employment Promotion Act, but exceptions could be granted. The ban was primarily motivated by the "problems in the engineering industry", in particular relating to the lack of control from the employers' point of view. The TWAs were believed to contribute to "wage drift" and labour shortages. In other words, the main argument of the ban was to protect employers from the TWAs and the agency workers.[9] The potentially precarious position of agency workers, protection of workers in general and the maintenance of the SER played a minor and more implicit role in the preparatory work by the government. Yet the effect of the ban was that the bilateral employment relationship was legally established as the model employment relationship. At the same time, protection against dismissals was strengthened, and temporary work was, for the first time by law, strictly limited through the Working Environment Act of 1977. In a 1980 revision of the Employment Promotion Act, the *hiring in* of labour was also banned, thus limiting both the supply and demand side of temporary agency work. Thus, it is reasonable to argue that it was not until this decade that the SER became enshrined in law (Hansen, 2018a, pp. 131–133, 148).

The 1970s was the highlight of an extended period towards enhanced government control of access to labour for employers and access to employment for employees. However, the effect of the legal regulations remained limited. The ban on the hiring out of labour did not work as intended. Many TWAs continued their activities. One reason was the lack of means to enforce the law. Another was that labour shortages more or less "forced" employers to use TWAs as tools for additional labour (Hansen, 2018b). At the individual company level, it was not always easy to subscribe to the collective interest of excluding TWAs.

However, the continued use of TWAs can hardly be seen as an expression of changed attitudes towards them among trade unions or members of the confederation of employers in the engineering industry in general. The normative foundation of the permanent, bilateral employment relationship remained intact during most of the 1970s. An important expression of this was an agreement between the confederation of employers in the engineering industry and the Iron and Metal Workers Union, which was signed in 1975. The purpose of the agreement was to make the ban on the hiring out of labour work as intended. According to the agreement, contracting and exceptional use of TWAs had to be discussed and approved by union representatives. An important reason for the employers to accept the involvement of trade unions was the imminent threat of industrial action related to the use of TWAs. In other words, the resistance of the employers, and thus the normative foundation of the SER, seemed dependent on the ability of trade unions to mobilize workers at their workplaces (Hansen, 2018a, pp. 187–198).

Cracks form in the normative and economic foundations (1981–1998)

The early 1980s heralded a new phase, as the SER ceased to strengthen and expand. In the following years, the unambiguous trend towards increased government control of access to labour and employment came to an end. This trend had included the introduction of protection against unfair dismissals in 1936, the prohibition of private intermediation of labour in 1947, the expansion of protection against dismissals in 1956, the universalization of protection against dismissals in 1975, the Working Environment Act of 1977 and the bans on hiring out and hiring in labour, in 1971 and 1980 respectively. However, the legal foundation of the SER was not dismantled. As a legal phenomenon, the SER survived during the 1980s and 1990s in most sectors (Hansen, 2018a, pp. 264ff, 337), despite significant political changes in Norway that stemmed from pressures of liberalization (cf. Peck & Tickell, 1994). Before liberalization struck labour institutions, other sectors of the economy, such as housing and credit markets, were subject to deregulation during the 1980s (Furre, 2000; Sørvoll, 2014).

However, the SER eventually also became subject to the same pressures. One reason was rising unemployment from the late 1980s, and there were also normative changes regarding the recognition of temporary employment as an acceptable, or even necessary, supplement to the SER. The first steps in this direction were cautious. Yet they were important, as they were taken in the engineering industry i.e. the sector that had played a leading role in the strict regulation of TWAs and, thus, in the making of the SER.

In 1980, the Iron and Metal Workers Union and the confederation of employers in the engineering industry made a joint proposal regarding the legal regulation of TWAs. According to the two organizations, it was necessary to "strike a better balance between the need for stability in the labour market, on the one hand, and the need for mobility, on the other" in the engineering industry.[10] In short, the need for stability would be met by regulations that would keep the TWAs under control. The solution to the need for mobility was to allow general exceptions to the rules on hiring in labour for both TWAs and regular firms. The joint proposal must be seen in the light of a more insecure situation due to structural changes in the engineering industry, as well as normative changes regarding the need for mobility in the labour market (Hansen, 2018a, pp. 220–230).

Later, the Confederation of Norwegian Enterprise put the question of flexibility high on the agenda. It was, according to the CEO in 1988, necessary to "slaughter some sacred cows". The CEO invited the members of the central board to critically evaluate the existing restrictions on TWAs and the protection against dismissals.[11]

During the first half of the 1990s, employers mobilized for increased access to temporary employment. An important contextual factor was the crisis in the Norwegian economy that intensified at the beginning of the decade. The Confederation of Norwegian Enterprise advised its members to use the opportunities that existed in legislation to achieve the required flexibility. Among the advice was to consider the use of zero-hour contracts, implying permanent employment without specifying the number of working hours.[12]

To what extent did this call for flexible labour represent a weakening of normative support for the existing SER? On the one hand, the advice was a response to a number of legislative changes. In 1990, layoffs became less favourable for employers as they became obliged to pay wages for a given number of days after the dismissal. In 1994, it was decided that work that was part of the core activities of a firm should only be performed by employees in permanent positions. On the other hand, the mobilization for flexibilization in the 1990s was a definite break with the past and significantly weakened the normative foundation of the SER. The decision in 1994, which made it illegal to hire temporary workers to carry out the core work of the firm, was an attempt to bring the use of temporary workers in line with the intentions of the existing legislation. More than a legal tightening of the access to use temporary workers, the decision confirmed that temporary employment as a general rule should be limited to temporary work. As a legal principle, it was established in the Working Environment Act of 1977, but it was at that point already established as practice and norm. At least in the engineering industry there was a common understanding, shared by both trade unions and employers, that the majority of employees should have permanent jobs, but not *too* many. Certain types of employees should be more loosely tied to the labour market, and the borderline between the core of permanent workers and the periphery of temporary workers was largely decided by the "nature" of the work. Permanent work assignments should imply permanent employment.

The employers' demand for temporary employment in the 1990s went beyond this enduring organizational principle. Thus, the demand represented a weakening of the normative support for the SER, compared to the period prior to the 1990s (Hansen, 2018a, pp. 276ff).

Internal discussions in LO show that the mobilization for flexibilization went hand in hand with a change in the balance of the two sides of the labour market and the creation of a new normative standard for the use of temporary employment. One expression of this was the design of a strategy to cope with what were called "new developments in the labour market" in the early 1990s.[13] The LO's possible strategy to defend standards of working life in Norway was to accept some unfavourable changes in order to gain the necessary strength to counteract the deterioration of these standards in general. More specifically, the LO agreed to accept some increase in the use of TWAs if certain conditions were met (Hansen, 2018a, pp. 288ff).

The response of the LO, which may be called a way of strategic and conditional resignation, was a clear sign that the relative balance had changed but still not dissolved. If the employers were on the back foot when they accepted the protection against unfair dismissal during the preliminary negotiations over the Working Environment Act of 1977, the tables had turned in the early 1990s. The consequence was that the normative foundation of the SER was weakened, paving the way for a liberalization of temporary agency work.

The SER undermined or still going strong? (2000–2018)

In 2000, the general ban on temporary agency work was lifted. But did the legal foundation of the SER begin to crumble? In many respects it did. When the formal legal boundary to labour hire was lifted, this challenged the distinction between work and other economic commodities. Labour as a *commodity* became subject to trade on a larger scale as the lifting of the general prohibition against labour hire made the service universally available. However, even though it is fair to state that the legal foundation of the SER was weakened, many restrictions were retained in Norwegian labour law. The most important provision following the liberalization in 2000 was that labour hire was to be permitted as a response to a *temporary need*. As such, national legislation still gave considerable privilege to the SER. However, the conditional provisions under the Norwegian Labour Act were not accompanied by a strong enforcement mechanism, as the Norwegian Labour Inspection Authority (Arbeidstilsynet) no longer had universal authority to prohibit the use of illegal labour hire. Instead, the regulations on illegal labour hire were to be enforced through the legal system.

What were the immediate effects of liberalization on Norwegian working life? In the period 2000–2008, labour hire expanded rapidly in absolute and relative numbers (Jordhus-Lier et al., 2015), peaking at around 1.5% of total employment in Norway in 2008. During this period, the deregulation of labour hire coincided with the EU expansion of 2004, and a large part of the influx of workers from Eastern Europe consisted of hired workers through various forms of TWAs. A majority of these workers operated in industries that would have prohibited labour hire prior to the year 2000, including segments such as construction, hospitality, transport and health services. Many of these workers were not covered by collective agreements. Because there was no minimum wage in Norway, many workers were paid well below negotiated wage levels in Norway (Dølvik et al., 2006). It was therefore not only the legal foundation of the SER that was threatened in the aftermath of the liberalization. The *normative* foundation of the SER also came to the fore in debates about the many cases of social dumping associated with hiring Eastern European agency workers in Norway. Moreover, the low wages of posted workers threatened the competitive position of firms that did pay negotiated wages and offer permanent employment, and this challenged workers in SERs. It thus seemed impossible to reconcile the liberalization of labour hire with the liberal space of labour migration.

The potential for wage dumping associated with the posting of workers within the EU/EEA area had been recognized by the Norwegian government even before Norway joined the EEA in 1994 (Alsos & Eldring, 2008). In September 1993, Norway adopted an act on the general applicability of collective agreements but with very limited extensions (Norwegian Law Data, 2006). EEA membership did not imply a major influx of European workers for the first decade but became highly relevant when a large number of Eastern European workers entered the Norwegian labour market from 2004 onwards.

LO made a request in 2003 that the act on the general applicability of collective agreements should include statutory extension of collective agreements for construction and metal workers. Through the tripartite advisory board on wage matters (Tariffnemda), Norway established that the act was to be extended to construction workers, metal workers and electricians from 2005 onwards. For the construction industry, this implied regional provisions from 2005 and national provisions from 2007. Other industries followed suit, such as mechanical engineering and shipyards (2008), agriculture (2010) and cleaning (2011). From 2017, transport services, hospitality services, fisheries and electricians were also covered by the extension act at the national level.

In one way, the extension of collective agreements to a de facto minimum wage legislation can be interpreted as an SER-centred reaction because it decreased the wage gap between workers in an SER and those outside, thus protecting the SER as well as improving the working conditions of those in a non-standard employment relationship. Alsos and Eldring (2008) point out that the purpose of extending the scope of the act varied somewhat between Norway and other European countries. In Europe, the most important reason for wanting extension acts was to ensure the diffusion of collective agreements, because labour migration was seen as undermining organized labour.

In Norway, Alsos and Eldring argue that it was more to do with ensuring wage levels and working conditions similar to Norwegian levels, given that foreign workers' wages and working conditions were inferior. In this way, the struggle for statutory extensions of collective agreements and thus the strengthening of the legal foundation of the SER was firmly based on the particularly strong normative foundation of the SER in Norway.

The disparity between workers in an SER and hired workers was not only a matter of concern in Norway. The issue was raised by many EU countries after the 2004 EU expansion, and in 2008 the EU launched its directive on temporary agency work (Vosko, 2009). One of the most important provisions in the directive was to ensure the *equal treatment* of temporary agency workers with workers recruited directly to the client company (Countouris & Horton, 2009), which was prompted by a concern about a growing core and periphery among European workers. The directive therefore included provisions related to equal pay for the equivalent position that the agency worker was replacing, equal working conditions and equal access to workplace amenities. The directive has nevertheless been implemented differently across Europe, reflecting the variation of labour regulation in national contexts and the controversy of labour hire as a challenge to the SER (Thelen, 2001; Bergene & Ewing, 2015). In Norway, the directive came into force on 1 January 2013, when new provisions on the equal treatment of temporary agency workers and permanent staff entered the Norwegian Working Environment Act (The Norwegian Government, 2012; The Norwegian Working Environment Act, 2015). In addition to these provisions, the implementation implied that the client or hiring company was seen as responsible for discussing the extent and operation of hiring practices with union representatives. The client company is also responsible for ensuring that the principle of equal treatment is respected by the de facto employer of hired workers i.e. the TWA. However, as Eriksen and Nesheim (2016) point out, the implementation of this regulation through legislative provisions does not guarantee that actual hiring practices adhere to the principles outlined here.

In some respects, the EU directive mirrored SER-centrism (Vosko, 2008) because of the principle of equal treatment between agency workers and the workers they were meant to (temporarily) replace. Combined with the statutory extension of collective agreements in selected client industries, the directive and its implementation through amendments to the Norwegian Labour Act (Lovdata, 2012) would, in theory, minimize the gap in wages and working conditions between workers in and outside an SER.

However, the directive also signalled a legitimization and strengthening of the status of temporary agency work across the EU. The directive was partly put in place to *liberalize* the TWA industry in terms of removing regulations that prevented their operation in national contexts (Bergene & Ewing, 2015). Although the normative foundation of the SER seems important in these policy developments, the legal and economic status of the SER may in fact have been weakened through the implementation of the EU Directive on Temporary Agency Work. After all, another intention of the directive was to improve general access to labour hire.

Although the statutory extension of collective agreements was put in place to combat social dumping more than a decade ago, there are still reports of considerable wage dumping and inferior working conditions among hired workers operating in Norway. A major difference from the period just after the EU expansion is that growing segments of the TWA industry are reported to be involved in illegal labour hire or operating with wages well below those of the general collective agreement. While the organized part of the TWA industry has seen less growth since the financial crisis of 2008–2009, these more unorganized segments of the industry are reported to have become more important, particularly within the construction industry. In a report commissioned by the Norwegian union *Fellesforbundet* (Elstad, 2017), findings in the Oslo area show that the share of labour hire in construction work grew from 17% in 2013 to 36% in 2017, and according to investigations on building sites in Oslo, about 85% of the labour hire can be considered to be illegal. The reports led to mobilization across the political spectrum and across industrial interests to regain *control* of "fragmented industries". Even the Federation of Norwegian Construction Industries (*Byggenæringens Landsforening*) has been critical to recent developments and highlights fragmentation and loss of control as detrimental to the industry, both in terms of work quality and how inferior working conditions hamper future recruitment to construction-related professions (cf. Haakestad & Friberg, 2017). Interestingly, this reported loss of control of labour hire undermines the intended growing status of labour intermediation as a functional answer to the declining importance of the *economic* foundation of the SER. The question is whether the reaction from the organized class of employers in construction can spark a recapitalization of the *normative* foundation of the SER as an organizing and *ordering* principle that serves capital interests as well as worker interests. This is an interesting historical parallel to the situation in the engineering industry in the 1950s, 1960s and 1970s. In this period, individual firms in the engineering industry could profit from engaging TWAs, due to the labour shortage and the need to hire workers on a temporary basis. At the same time, the use of TWAs intensified staff turnover and more or less forced employers to outbid each other in a game situation reminiscent of a "tragedy of the commons". The situation for construction firms today is similar, yet with the important distinction that the precarization of (particularly immigrant) labour is a more pronounced part of the tragedy than the loss of control by employers. Nevertheless, the situation has prompted action across the political spectrum, culminating in a parliamentary majority in May 2018 to permit labour hire only in client workplaces where collective agreements apply (The Norwegian Parliament, 2018). Interestingly, the parliamentary majority also intends to enhance the legal foundation of the SER *within* the TWAs, as employment through an agency in principle will be expected to conform to many aspects of permanent, full-time and open-ended contracts.

Concluding remarks

This chapter has discussed historical changes in the status of the SER in Norway with a focus on the controversies surrounding the use of TWAs. In a period of serious labour shortages in the 1950s and 1960s, the emergence of TWAs was seen as a threat to labour stability by both employers and unions in the engineering industry. As a result of joint campaigns, the mediation of workers by third parties such as TWAs was prohibited by law in 1971 and was seen as an alien phenomenon during the heyday of the SER in the 1970s. The prohibition of TWAs was grounded in a strong coalition that influenced the making of the Norwegian variant of the SER. In simple terms, the need for job security coincided with the need for control of the labour force. As a result, the economic, normative and legal foundations of the SER were strengthened during the first three decades or so after World War II. However, the SER was never extended to include *all* workers, and the boundaries between permanent and temporary employment were never removed. Due to pressure to allow more flexibility in an economy marked by the crisis of Fordist production and a more fluctuating demand for labour, the prohibition was contested in the 1980s and 1990s and finally lifted in 2000. In this way, organized employers mobilized to reduce their share of the risk associated with operating in an unpredictable market economy.

Lifting the ban was controversial at the time and became even more controversial with the EU expansion in 2004. This sparked a debate about the rapid precarization of the Norwegian and European labour markets, where the TWA industry was a central part of the discussions as it was instrumental in opening up European labour flows with limited regulation. Even after the EU Directive on Temporary Agency Work was implemented as an attempt to alleviate the polarizing effects (wages, working conditions) of labour hire and labour externalization, the debate in Norway lingers to this day, particularly due to the the fragmentation and precarization of the construction industry. Prior to the 2017 general election, the opposition parties and the major labour union confederation called for a new prohibition, and in 2018 a parliamentary majority voted for stricter regulation of the right to hire in labour and for obliging TWAs to adhere to the SER principles of permanent, full-time and open-ended contracts.

The period since 2000 may be interpreted as a transformative phase in the history of the SER. Attempts have been made to reconcile employers with their access to and control of labour with renewed control of employment by the labour movement in a new regime or "institutional fix" (Peck & Tickell, 1994), where TWAs have been legalized. However, the political developments since 2016 suggest that the normative strength of the SER has demonstrated its magnitude in parliamentary processes, and that the contestation of TWA employment continues to play a vital role in shaping and reshaping the Norwegian version of the SER.

Notes

1 This is especially the case for Norway, with some exceptions. For example, Seierstad (1982, 1986); Bull (1986). Internationally the situation is different. Some recent contributions focus on precarious labour and the standard employment relationship in a historical perspective. Examples include: Vosko (2010); Van Der Linden (2014); Betti (2016); De Vito (2016).
2 This is particularly evident in the Norwegian context but is also debated in international contributions such as Stone (1974) and Jacoby (2004).
3 The following paragraphs are based on Hansen (2018a, pp. 31–33).
4 The periods 1, 2 and 3 are based on Hansen (2018a). In this chapter, we only refer to a small selection of relevant documents.
5 National Archives of Norway, PA-0886 Norwegian Confederation of Employers, series Fdc. Box 47. Minutes from meeting, Central Board of the Norwegian Confederation of Employers, 1.4.1970, pp. 62–63. Our translation.
6 National Archives of Norway, PA-1700 Federation of Norwegian Manufacturing Industries, Series Dci (hereafter TBL). Box 6. Letter from Drammen Slip & Verksted to the Confederation of Employers in the Engineering Industry, 9 September 1955. Our translation.
7 TBL. Box 6. Transcript of circular letter from the Confederation of Employers in the Engineering Industry to its members, 3.9.1955.
8 The Norwegian Labor Movement Archives and Library, ARK-1659, Norwegian Iron and Metal Workers Union (NJ&MF), case archive, 1955–1988, File 50-44, 1965. Letter from NJ&MF, Branch 34 Sandefjord to NJ&MF, 12. januar 1965 (sic).
9 Ot. prp. nr. 53. (1970–71); Innstilling om arbeidsutleiefirmaenes virksomhet, vedlegg til Ot. prp. nr. 53 (1970–71); Innst. O. nr. 61 (1970–71).
10 National Archives of Norway, PA-1700 Federation of Norwegian Manufacturing Industries. Series F – Case Archive X. Box 512. Letter from NJ&MF og M.V.L. to Kommunal- og arbeidsdepartementet, dated 15. oktober 1980. Our translation.
11 Minutes from meeting, Central Board of the Norwegian Confederation of Employers, 26 October 1988, transcript of recording tape. Our translation.
12 Confederation of Norwegian Enterprise (NHO), case archive 1994–1999. File 261.0 Working Environment Act 1994. Circular letter from NHO to county and national associations, dated 22 December 1994.
13 Norwegian Confederation of Trade Unions, case archive 1988–2000, archive code. 414. Memo from Department for social policy (Samfunnspolitisk avdeling), Ny trend i arbeidsmarkedet i regulerte former i LOs strategi, dated 25 January 1993.

References

Allen, J. & Henry, N. (1997) Ulrich Beck's Risk Society at Work: Labour and Employment in the Contract Service Industries, *Transactions of the Institute of British Geographers*, 22(2): 180–196.

Alsos, K. & Eldring, L. (2008) Labour Mobility and Wage Dumping: The Case of Norway, *European Journal of Industrial Relations*, 14(4): 441–459.

Amin, A. (ed.) (1994) *Post-Fordism: A Reader*, Boston, MA: Blackwell.

Atkinson, J. (1987) Flexibility or Fragmentation? The United Kingdom Labour Market in the Eighties, *Labour and Society*, 12: 87–105.

Bergene, A. C. & Ewing, K. D. (2015) Vikarbyrådirektivet: liberalisering eller likebehandling? [Temporary Agency Work Directive: Liberalization or Equal Treatment?], *Søkelys på arbeidslivet*, 32(1–2): 137–157.

Betti, E. (2016) Gender and Precarious Labor in a Historical Perspective: Italian Women and Precarious Work between Fordism and Post-Fordism, *International Labor and Working-Class History*, 89: 64–83.

Bjørnson, Ø. (2007) En annen arbeiderbevegelse [A Different Labour Movement], *Arbeiderhistorie 2007*, Årbok forarbeiderbevegelsens historie, Oslo: LO Media.

Brenner, N. (2004) *New State Spaces: Urban Governance and the Rescaling of Statehood*, Oxford, UK: Oxford University Press.

Bull d.y., E. (1981) *Retten til en fortid [The Right to a Past]*, Oslo: Universitetsforlaget.

Bull d.y., E. (1986) Frihet og retten til arbeid på 1800-tallet [Freedom and the right to work in the 19th century], *Tidsskrift for arbeiderbevegelsenshistorie*, 1: 109–124.

Cerny, P. (1997) Paradoxes of the Competition State: The Dynamics of Political Globalization, *Goverment and Opposition*, 32(2): 251–274.

Countouris, N. & Horton, R. (2009) The Temporary Agency Work Directive: Another Broken Promise?, *Industrial Law Journal*, 38(3): 329–338.

De Vito, C. D. (2016) Labor Flexibility and Labor Precariousness as Conceptual Tools for the Historical Study of the Interactions among Labor Relations, In: Roth, K. H. (ed.) *On the Road to Global Labor History*, Leiden, the Netherlands and Boston, MA: Brill.

Dølvik, J. E., Eldring, L., Friberg, J. H., Kvinge, T., Aslesen, S. & Ødegård, A. M. (2006) Grenseløst arbeidsliv? Endringer i bedrifters arbeidskraftsstrategier etter EU-utvidelsen [Work Life Without Borders? Changes in Manpower Strategies in Firms After the EU Enlargement], *Fafo-rapport 58*, Oslo: Fafo.

Elstad, L. (2017) Ulovlig innleie i byggebransjen i hovedstadsområdet [Illegal Labour Hire in the Construction Industry in Oslo Metropolitan Area]. https://elogit.no/sites/elogit/files/arkiv/rapport.pdf.

Eriksen, B. & Nesheim, T. (2016) Vikarbyrådirektivet: Trollet som sprakk – Kommentar til Bergene [Temporary Agency Work Directive: The Troll That Exploded – A Comment to Bergene], *Søkelys på arbeidslivet*, 33(1–2): 162–170.

Esping-Andersen, G. (1999) *Social Foundations of Postindustrial Economies*, Oxford, UK: Oxford University Press. https://doi.org/10.1093/0198742002.001.0001.

Freedland, M. (2013) Burying Caesar: What was the Standard Employment Contract?, In: Stone, K. V. W. & Arthurs, H. (eds) *Rethinking Workplace Regulation Beyond the Standard Contract of Employment*, New York: Russell Sage Foundation.

Furre, B. (2000) *Norsk Historie 1914–2000*, Gjøvik, Norway: Samlaget.

Haakestad, H. & Friberg, J. H. (2017) Deskilling Revisited: Labour Migration, Neo-Taylorism and the Degradation of Craft Work in the Norwegian Construction Industry, *Economic and Industrial Democracy*. doi:10.1177/0143831x17735671.

Hall, P. A. & Soskice, D. W. (2001) *Varieties of Capitalism*, Oxford, UK: Oxford University Press.

Hansen, P. B. (2018a) Standardarbeidsforholdets vekst og fall? Fagbevegelsens, arbeidsgiveres og myndigheters respons på bemanningsbyråer i verkstedsindustrien og holdninger til fast og midlertid arbeid i Norge 1947–2000 [The Rise and Fall of the Standard Employment Relationship? The Responses of Trade Unions, Private Capital and the Government to the Temporary Work Agencies and Attitudes to Permanent and Temporary Work in Norway 1947–2000], PhD thesis, University of Oslo.

Hansen, P. B. (2018b) En smak av uorganisert kapitalisme. Arbeidsgivere i verkstedindustrien i møte med bemanningsbyråene 1955–71 [A Taste of Disorganized Capitalism. Employers in the Engineering Industry in the Face of the Temporary Work Agencies in 1955–71], In: Sørvoll, J., Helle, I. & Korsvik, T. R. (eds) *Kollektive bestrebelser. En bok til Knut Kjeldstadli på 70-års-dagen [Collective Endeavours. A Book to Knut Kjeldstadli on the 70th Anniversary]*, Oslo: NOVUS forlag.

Hobsbawm, E. (1995) *The Age of Extremes: A History of the World, 1914–1991*, London: Abacus.

Holden, S. (1998) Wage Drift and the Relevance of Centralised Wage Setting, *The Scandinavian Journal of Economics*, 100(4): 711–731.

Hyman, R. (1999) Imagined Solidarities: Can Trade Unions Resist Globalization?, In: Leisink, P. (ed.) *Globalization and Labour Relations*, Cheltenham, UK: Edward Elgar, 94–116.

Jacoby, S. M. (2004) *Employing Bureaucracy Managers, Unions, and the Transformation of Work in the 20th Century*, Abingdon, UK: Taylor & Francis.

Jessop, B. (2002) *The Future of the Capitalist State*, Cambridge, UK: Polity Press.

Jordhus-Lier, D. C., Coe, N. M. & Bråten, S. T. (2015) Contested Growth: The Development of Norway's Temporary Staffing Industry, *Geografiska Annaler. Series B. Human Geography*, 97(1): 113–130.

Kalleberg, A. L., Reynolds, J. & Marsden, P. V. (2003) Externalizing Employment: Flexible Staffing Arrangements in US Organizations, *Social Science Research*, 32: 525–552.

Lovdata (2012) *Lov om arbeidsmiljø, arbeidstid og stillingsvern mv.* [The Working Environment Act]. https://lovdata.no/dokument/NL/lov/2005-06-17-62/KAPITTEL_14#§14-9.

Norwegian Law Data (2006) Law About the Statutory Extension of Collective Agreements [Almenngjøringsloven]. https://lovdata.no/dokument/NL/lov/1993-06-04-58.

Peck, J. & Tickell, A. (1994) Searching For a New Institutional Fix, In: Amin, A. (ed.) *Post-Fordism: A Reader*, Boston, MA: Blackwell, 280–315.

Peck, J. & Tickell, A. (2002) Neoliberalizing Space, *Antipode*, 34(3): 380–404.

Perlman, S. (1928) *A Theory of the Labor Movement*, New York: Macmillan.

Seierstad, S. (1982) *Hvordan fagbevegelsen formet arbeidslivet. Perspektiver på den historiske utviklinga av arbeidslivet i Norge [How the Trade Union Movement Shaped the Working Life. Perspectives on the Historical Development of Working Life in Norway]*, Oslo: Pax Forlag A/S.

Seierstad, S. (1986) Arbeid som rettighetsgivende status i et kapitalistisk arbeidsliv [Employment as a Right Providing Status in a Capitalist Working Life], *Tidsskrift for arbeiderbevegelsens historie*, 1: 127–145.

Sørvoll, J. (2014) The Politics of Cooperative Housing in Norway and Sweden 1960–1990 (1945–2013), The Swedish Deregulation of 1968 and the Norwegian Liberalization of the1980s, PhD thesis, University of Oslo.

Standing, G. (2011) *The Precariat: The New Dangerous Class*, London: Bloomsbury.

Stone, K. (1974) The Origins of Job Structures in the Steel Industry, *Review of Radical Political Economics*, 6(2): 113–173.

Thelen, K. (2001) Varieties of Labour Politics in the Developed Democracies, In: Hall, P. A. & Soskice, D. W. (eds) *Varieties of Capitalism*, Oxford, UK: Oxford University Press.

Thelen, K. (2012) Varieties of Capitalism: Trajectories of Liberalization and the New Politics of Social Solidarity, *Annual Review of Political Science*, 15(1): 137–159.

The Norwegian Government (2012) The EU Directive on Temporary Agency Work: Implementation in Norwegian Law from 1 January 2013. Press release on 18 December 2012. www.regjeringen.no/en/topics/labor/the-working-environment-and-safety/innsikt/vikarbyradirektivet/the-eu-directive-on-temporary-agency-wor/id709611/.

The Norwegian Parliament (2018) *Changes in the Working Environment Act (Permanent and Temporary Employment and Labour Hire from Temporary Work Agencies)*. www.stortinget.no/no/Saker-og-publikasjoner/Publikasjoner/Innstillinger/Stortinget/2017-2018/inns-201718-355l/?all=true.

The Norwegian Working Environment Act (2015) *Act Relating to Working Environment, Working Hours and Employment Protection etc.* www.arbeidstilsynet.no/binfil/download2.php?tid=92156.

Van Der Linden, M. (2014) San Precario: A New Inspiration for Labor Historians, *Labor: Studies in Working-Class of the Americas*, 11: 9–21.

Vosko, L. (2008) Temporary Work in Transnational Labor Regulation: SER-Centrism and the Risk of Exacerbating Gendered Precariousness, *Social Indicators Research*, 88: 131–145.

Vosko, L. (2009) Less than Adequate: Regulating Temporary Agency Work in the EU in the Face of an Internal Market in Services, *Cambridge Journal of Regions, Economy and Society*, 2(3): 395–411.

Vosko, L. (2010) *Managing the Margins. Gender, Citizenship, and the International Regulation of Precarious Employment*, Oxford, UK: Oxford University Press.

Chapter 17

Working life on Nordic labour platforms

Søren Salling Weber

The emergence of the platform economy

This chapter engages with a set of phenomena that have been subject to increasing public scrutiny in the Nordic states in recent years, collectively known as the 'platform economy'. The platform economy denotes a class of business models utilizing internet-based digital infrastructure for private parties' decentralized, marketized organization of short-term work. Perhaps *the* most debated case in a Nordic context has been the taxi platform Uber, but the Airbnb platform is also commonly known, and several Nordic platforms arranging everything from household labour to specialized translation work are now in use (Dølvik & Jesnes, 2017; Rasmussen et al., 2017). There is disagreement on how to conceptualize and thus delineate the use of digital, internet-based platforms to organize societal interaction. The term platform economy is a critical term adopted by unions, politicians and researchers to describe working life implications of what has frequently been called the sharing economy. The debates about the Uber platform, both in the Nordic countries and in the rest of Europe, have been crucial in this change of terminology. Uber claimed to be a 'sharing platform' by utilizing existing private goods in the form of cars and phones to 'create use value'. But the platform developers rely on the drivers' wage labour to ensure the functionality and profit of their platform. As such, the new platform companies are not just characterized by their use of digital, internet-based technologies to utilize idle resources through free work but by their reorganization of *labour*. If successful with their business models, the operators of the platforms become mediators and thus impose a reorganization of the labour in the affected sectors of work. At the same time, they bypass the institutionalized employment relationship and thus their responsibility as employers. They create growth in 'jobless' wage labour where it is unclear who has responsibility both for the work itself and the wages, organization and working time. However, the consequences for working life are still somewhat unclear in a Nordic context.

This chapter aims to introduce, illustrate and examine the development trajectory and working life issues of Nordic labour platforms. Firstly, the controversies surrounding the use of internet-based platforms for the organization of work are introduced, which forms a basis for the interest in the development in the Nordic countries. Next, a case study of the relation between the development of a labour platform and workers' lives in the Nordic welfare regimes is presented. The platform is studied in three interrelated analytical dimensions: the technological development of the platform as a production system, the organization of work on the platform and the workers' attempts to manage the work and their working lives. Following this, it is argued that the working life problems depicted in the case study can be understood as an interplay between the development of the labour platforms as a production system and the workers' relatively precarious positions in the Nordic labour markets. Finally, the structural constraints and/or possibilities to address the presented problems in the development trajectory of Nordic labour platforms are discussed.

Sharing, collaborative or platform economy? Some conceptual remarks

The international research on digital platforms to organize interaction is growing but diverse in scope and interest. In short, these platforms replace the conventional employment relationship with a three-party interaction between customer, platform and worker. Some, such as Rifkin (2015), envision a complete dissolution of wage labour as the dominant institutionalization of work in contemporary capitalism. The convergence of consumer and producer roles in the relations on the platforms poses potentials for a freer organization of work but also a loss of clearly defined career prospects and security (Antonio, 2015; Ritzer, 2015; Sundararajan, 2016). These uncertainties about the developments are reflected in the literature.

On the one hand, considerable attention has been given to the platforms under the labels of the 'sharing' or 'collaborative' economy. These terms highlight the potential for technologies to create and support the autonomous organization of work, freed from the rigid boundaries and restraints of wage labour. They imply an interest in the social qualities and normative functionality of the new technologies (for excellent conceptual overviews, see Dredge & Gyimóthy, 2015; Cheng, 2016). For instance, it has been shown that the development of technologies can strengthen alternative 'moral landscapes', which transcend the market as the dominant principle of interaction (Molz, 2013). Even when new technologies are developed by companies exclusively for profit, strong communities can utilize them to increase their scope of action to pursue their values and goals (Barta & Neff, 2016). Values can thus be embedded in the use of technologies in unforeseeable ways. There has therefore been discussion of the potentials for enhanced utilization of resources (Botsman & Rogers, 2010) and the building and use of platforms as capital for a new cooperative movement (Scholz & Schneider, 2016). Taken together, the literature on the sharing and collaborative economy highlights the potential to use the technologies to humanize work and further sustainability by ensuring autonomy and control *in* the work and the quality *of* the work.

On the other hand, much empirical research highlights the abundant contradictions between the ideals and practices connected to the use of the technologies. As Dianne Dredge and Szilvia Gyimóthy succinctly note about the 'collaborative economy', the development of platforms is often strongly embedded in the competition of a market economy: 'Exchange is most often monetized, systematized in a business model and facilitated by technology' (Dredge & Gyimóthy, 2015, p. 292). In continuation, many authors point out how the developers of the platforms leverage the positive associations of the sharing economy to legitimize competitive advantages (e.g. Hill, 2015; Rogers, 2016; Scholz, 2016). Some authors have suggested the adoption of the term platform *capitalism* to highlight the fact that although the employment relationship disappears, the capital aspect of the labour market remains. New forms of exploitation are made possible through an erosion of the standard employment relationship (Srnicek, 2017). In continuation, a growing body of international literature points out the risk that the platforms will shift the balance of forces in the labour market by accumulating capital to enforce a customer-oriented profit extraction with highly precarious conditions for labour: low wages, extremely flexibly organized one-off tasks and a lack of social benefits and union representation (Huws et al., 2016; Standing, 2016; Schor et al., 2017).

The conceptual contrast between platform capitalism and sharing highlights how the promising technologies can lead to a crisis in the labour market by discontinuing the existing institutionalized separation of labour and work. Overall, these findings provoke scepticism of the concept of sharing as a designation of the business models without an analytical differentiation between various *forms* and *functions* of the technology-mediated interaction (Belk, 2013; Dredge & Gyimóthy, 2015, 2017). Richardson (2015, p. 122) argues that the technologies in the sharing economy are inherently paradoxical in that its new positive performances are concurrently 'masking new forms of inequality and polarisations of ownership'. She argues that a continued critical engagement is in fact necessary to support the potentials for alternative economies (Richardson, 2015).

In the Nordic countries, research on labour platforms mostly provides an overview through descriptive categorizations of the developing platforms, whereas engagement with subjective experiences of work on the platforms is sparse. One important finding about work on the platforms is that economically motivated, practical service labour might not provide the same work identity and sociocultural gratification as knowledge-intensive work in the tourism industry: there is a big difference between the 'social lifestyle entrepreneurs' establishing local businesses and Airbnb's individualized 'micro-competitive platform capitalism' (Meged & Christensen, 2017). But the conceptual field is still open. The current controversies in the international literature can perhaps be summarized in an ideal-typical conceptual contrast to categorize the use of platforms in the Nordic countries (see Table 17.1).

Table 17.1 Ideal-typical continua for use of platforms (author's product)

Ideal-typical comparison	*Platform capitalism*	*Sharing*
Regulating idea	The market	The commons
Goal of development	Profit (extraction: 'rent' for use of platform)	Use value (local development)
Ownership of technology	Patented	Open source
Organization	Centrally controlled, homogenous	Decentralized, differentiated
Object	Labour	Goods (physical/digital)
Asset transaction	Money	Reputation ('trust')
Interaction	Asymmetrical: defined by demand	Reciprocal: 'prosumers'
Function for involved workers	Livelihood	Pastime
Access to technology	Restricted	Unrestricted
Platform responsibility for quality of work	Yes	No
Worker control over working time	No	Yes
Character of work	Instrumental: *tasks* as labour	Meaningful: work as work
Embedded in local communities	No	Yes

Both platform capitalism and the sharing economy challenge the institutionalized class compromise in the form of the employment relationship in the Nordic countries. But the development of the platforms will most likely be both exploitative and altruistic, and the conceptual contrast serves both as an indication of the complexities of the development and a delimitation of the following discussion of a case study (Yin, 2003) of Nordic platform capitalism. The case study was conducted to explore and understand the working life ramifications of the digitized organization of labour without an employment relationship in a Nordic context.

A case study of working life on a Nordic labour platform

The case presented in the following section is a patented, closed-off website and app developed to create and extract profit from transactions in a niche labour market. The case study combines an analysis of the 'standards' for the labour with theoretically themed semi-structured interviews with five workers, the director and operations manager on the platform (Weber, 2017). I present it here in order to engage with the experience of working life in Nordic labour platforms.

Given the limited empirical material, the case does not provide conclusive answers to the questions raised here, but it offers a useful empirical starting point to illustrate and discuss the development trajectory of platforms in the Nordic countries. It also serves as a useful delimitation of the following discussion to platforms utilized for the organization of wage labour, as it is an example of the ideal-typical criteria for platform capitalism presented in Table 17.1. It appears to be typical when compared to the developing platforms in the Nordic countries. Most platforms organize service labour, provide a minimum wage, attempt to standardize the work and do not recognize an employment relationship (Dølvik & Jesnes, 2017; Rasmussen et al., 2017).

Workers on the case platform register on the platform to take on standardized service tasks, mostly 'regular' or 'extensive' cleaning but also 'handyman' work or gardening. Spatio-temporally, the tasks are organized to meet customers' demands. Tasks typically take two to five hours, but in principle can take up to eight hours and might be repeated if necessary. Prices are fixed, and workers receive a minimum hourly wage of DKK120. Some workers have obtained a higher salary due to their consistently good customer reviews. The platform provides conflict mediation and security for the transaction. It also protects workers from obvious discrimination by customers. As competing platforms are not willing to provide transparency, and statistics are sparse, it is difficult to tell whether the platform is a market leader. But the company has undergone rapid growth in use, technological development, geographic coverage and financial investments, establishing itself in both Denmark and Sweden. The development of the platform began in 2015 and the organization of work in early 2016. At the time of the study (Weber, 2017), the platform offered exclusively cleaning and handyman work for private persons, but today it also provides cleaning to companies. In early autumn 2016, around 125 workers were active on the platform, and the number had almost doubled by December 2016. By May 2017, the platform claimed to have registered around 3,000 workers. This indicates both the rapid growth and temporary engagement of the workers.

Technological acceleration: the rule of constant change

According to the developers of the case platform, such platforms are a rationalization of the societal organization of labour. The director refers to the rapid growth of platforms such as Uber to illustrate how platforms make new societal connections possible and thereby 'create value'. The 'value proposition' (Gyimóthy, 2017, p. 34) seems to be to utilize the space–time compression of modern communication technologies to design or *create* a market where people can effectively delegate small tasks, whether cleaning, buying groceries, getting help for elderly family members or practical handyman work. By providing the necessary infrastructure, the platform creates the conditions for an efficient exchange. The platform developers charge 20% of the cost of each task arranged on the platform to extract value. According to the developers, the low entry barriers optimize the use of time and will therefore prevail as a more rational and efficient mode of organization of labour. This reflects a cultural understanding that the institutional restrictions of the employment relationship will inevitably be bypassed if they act as a barrier to acceleration (Rosa, 2013, p. 192). Or, as expressed by the operations manager on the platform: 'wouldn't you like to spend your time on something else?'

Their strategy is to rationalize the distribution and organization of labour by accumulating capital in a digital tool with automated management of the tasks. To do so, they attempt to realize a second value proposition: the platform manages tasks automatically instead of through direct (human) supervision, replacing management with an IT system.

> The more manual processes we can bypass, the better it is . . . So we spend a lot of time developing, planning, designing and . . . testing. Testing, testing, testing.
>
> So, we constantly measure our efficiency in . . . everything.
>
> (Operations manager)

This dynamic can be conceptualized as an expression of technological acceleration.

> The most evident and consequential shape that modern acceleration takes is the intentional, technical, and above all technological (i.e. machine-based) acceleration of goal-directed processes.
>
> (Rosa, 2013, p. 71)

Technological acceleration furthers productivity but must continuously be reinvented due to the 'economic motor of competition', which creates the preconditions for continued change in the organization of both labour and working life (Rosa & Scheuerman, 2009, p. 189; Rosa, 2013, pp. 161–163). This creates constant changes in the production system of the platform, even for the 'core' workers employed to manage the platform:

> So now another investment is coming in the new year. And that investment is going to be somewhat bigger, because in the meantime the company has already increased in value. So the next investment will be used to develop even more, you see? And again, Uber is constantly developing [their platform]. Airbnb is too. So, you could say . . . I don't ever think – and God forbid we might even say! – that we'll make it to a point where you think: 'Oh, now everything's working the way it's supposed to'. That's not how it works, because if you sit down and think: 'Oh, well then, that's fine', then you'll be overtaken on the inside, really.
>
> (Operations manager)

This quote illustrates how the 'economic motor of competition' drives investments in the development of the patented platforms. The developers plan to establish an efficient monopoly, but they are constantly forced to attract capital to develop their platform. The production system is referred to as their 'core output'. There is a built-in aspiration for monopoly which is not unique to, but is particularly pronounced in, the development of the 'lean platforms' (Srnicek, 2017). The developed technology is decisive for the functionality and competitive position of the platform, which makes it possible to take on entire markets by mobilizing *external*, 'idle' resources or users (Demary, 2014; Standing, 2016, pp. 61, 216–217; Gyimóthy, 2017, p. 34). This pushes the developers into continued investment in their digital tools and changes in the organization of labour.

> This is the way in which we, anyone, starts up a new company today: You throw yourself off the edge of a cliff.
>
> (Operations manager)

However, the automation of the organization and management of the labour necessitates continued (financial) investment in technological development. A worker describes the platform development:

> This stage goes on and on. It is never ending. Technology changes day by day, so if you want to exist in a market, you must change. As a rule, you could say.
>
> (Worker)

The competitive relationship to other platforms and the possibilities of investment foster continued attempts to maximize the functionality and productivity of the platform.

The organization of tasks: automated, standardized and individualizing

As indicated, the development of an efficient market for tasks between interchangeable parties employed in the development of the platform reorganizes the work. The developers strategically chose 'these few areas' of cleaning and service labour typical of emerging platforms. This enables the platform developers to reinforce an already highly customer-oriented and fragmented organization of undeclared labour to accommodate the rationality of continued acceleration.

The developers must necessarily develop organizational capacity for this *separation* of work into smaller *tasks* arranged among strangers. Apart from the incentives of customers' rating of work, the developers' strategy for 'establishing trust' or 'matching expectations' is a new Taylorization: labour is pre-defined as tasks organized by an IT system. Workers are allocated a certain amount of time to go through certain pre-defined steps, which are described for them on a digital learning platform. The developers standardize the labour to make this transaction work, to 'ensure that the suppliers [workers] appreciate the standard we want to give' (Operations manager).

The standards for the work are highlighted as 'easy' by the developers, but the idea of automated interchangeability clashes with the quality achieved with continuity in and contextualization of the labour: 'It's not any standard job. People don't have standard expectations' (Worker). Whereas the ability to meet the demands of the customers is a source of positive affirmation for one of the workers, the transient relation to the customers is a source of uncertainty for others:

> You know . . . I didn't have any feedback . . . And one of my clients, the company, the person who I'm in contact with, told me that that person didn't want it any more. I don't know if I did something wrong, or he didn't want the system at all. Or he didn't want, you know. I don't know. But maybe I did something badly. I'm not sure.
>
> (Worker)

This reflects that it is difficult to ensure the quality of the work without embedding the labour into a relationship which permits an intersubjective validation. The director notes that this might even be the reason that they have the most success organizing cleaning, relative to other work: compared to other forms of 'gig work', it favours 'trust' in the relation between customer and worker. Paradoxically, the developers must undermine the embedding of the labour into a continuous relationship between customers and workers to maintain their monopoly to arrange the tasks. This entails a lack of control and changes the organization of the work, not only for the workers but also for the company:

> For me, no, it's not possible. And for these systems, it's also difficult for the company to change.
>
> (Worker)

The 'trust' of recurring tasks in continuous relationships is difficult to embed in the automated matches between customers and workers on the platform.

The spatio-temporal flexibilization of work

The fragmentation of work into tasks is not only substantial and relational but also spatio-temporal (Rosa, 2013, pp. 110, 168, 172). The platform creates a 'technical standard' (cf. Rosa, 2013, p. 235) of immediate engagement with the organization of tasks on the platform. This 'annihilation of space' is a central mechanism in social acceleration and points towards a form of disembedded market on the platform (cf. Rosa, 2013, pp. 40, 216). The workers must take on various tasks for various customers at various places and times. But in contrast with fully digitized 'crowd labour', the physical services of the gig economy remain geographically bound (Ilsøe & Madsen, 2017, p. 44). This creates an everyday working life problem for the engaged workers to 'stack' the tasks into a closely knit, coherent and efficient schedule, using the platform's coordination mechanisms. One of the interviewees manages to do this, creating an intensification of her everyday life, where she takes on more activities with fewer breaks. For the others, the unpaid planning and coordination becomes an everyday working life problem.

> It's not . . . completely . . . you know, programmable. I cannot make a plan because there are some jobs I have to choose between, so my options are not . . . unlimited.
>
> (Worker)

For the two workers who rely solely on labour on the platform, they must engage immediately when they appear on the platform.

Worker:	*Maybe sometimes you didn't see the phone, and two hours passed . . .*
Interviewer:	*. . . and it's gone?*
Worker:	*It's gone.*

The technical standard of immediate engagement with the 'just-in-time' organization of tasks in the gig economy leaves workers in a reactive state (De Stefano, 2016). The awareness of the possibility of obtaining tasks potentially replaces the stable rhythm of repetitive actions over time by the anxious, but enduring and profound indeterminacy (Holt et al., 2013, p. 64; Rosa, 2015, p. 80).

Labour platforms as social acceleration?

The greatest problem for workers was the lack of control over their time with the concurrent individualized competition for the extremely flexibly organized tasks on the platform. This was experienced as a problem for the workers, even though they managed it very differently in their working lives. These problems cannot be understood without considering the specificities of platforms as production systems. Employers are replaced by a digital system. The workers find that: 'it's somehow impossible to have co-workers' (Worker). Their relationship with customers is the only, fragile, source of an intersubjective validation of their work. This creates uncertainty in their work experience and in the planning of their everyday life. The following quote from a worker summarizes the most difficult aspects of life with labour on the platforms:

'Travelling time, filling up your time and feedback. And the money is not too much' (Worker).

When workers take on tasks on the platforms, they establish a fragile common interest with the platform developers around the emerging technologies: that of making the transaction work. But the case illustrates the risk that this ideal of an efficient market for tasks between interchangeable parties employed in the development of the platform, creates a new standard to meet an extreme IT-mediated flexibility in the organization of everyday life. This tendency can be contrasted with a normative ideal of the organization of work founded in Nordic working life research: that the work must help to build sustainable rhythms in the workers' working lives (Hvid, 2006; Kamp et al., 2011). The extremely flexible spatio-temporal organization of what is nevertheless extremely standardized labour is a management-controlled new Taylorization which undermines control of the work and disrupts the formation of working life rhythms (Hvid, 2006, p. 146). Despite their best intentions, the platform developers cannot realize the accelerative effects of the technical innovation in a competitive market without compromising the sustainability of the organization of work for the involved workers.

Workers' experiences of the poor quality of working time on the platforms can thus be understood as an extreme case of broader societal development trends towards changed temporality and heightened flexibility in the use of modern technologies for the organization of work (Rosa & Scheuerman, 2009; Rosa, 2013, 2015; Rosa et al., 2017). In the workers' working lives, it creates a 'desynchronization' of the rhythmic coordination between labour and other spheres of activity in working life (Rosa, 2013, p. 186). This latently leads to a loss of anticipatory power, a proliferation of time conflicts and introduces a 'situational logic', both in everyday life and over a lifetime (Rosa, 2013, pp. 76, 113, 231ff). Following Standing (2014) and Rosa (2013, pp. 144ff), it seems pertinent to question whether this has consequences for the development of one's coherent work identity embedded in one's long-term life aspirations.

Nordic labour platforms: a case of precarity?

The working life problems clustered in the interviewed workers' experiences with work on the platform can be interpreted as expressions of precarity (cf. Standing, 2014; see also the introduction to precarity, Chapter 14). The cause of the problems expressed by the interviewees is probably that those engaging in the interviews of the case study are those experiencing dependency on and problems with the labour on the platforms. All the interviewees took on the tasks to make money, but they *all* perceived it as supplementary or transitory, even if the tasks were indeed their primary source of income at the time of the interviews. Two workers combined the tasks with part-time employment, and one was supporting his studies. Two relied solely on income from the platform but considered it unsustainable. Four of the five workers felt overqualified, knew no others engaged on the platform and were subjectively unsatisfied with the quality of the work. The interviews seem to demonstrate the situation for workers in relatively precarious positions on the Danish labour market for whom the offer of fragmented, unreliable labour is better than none.

At the same time, when compared with secondary information, the differences in the working lives of the interviewed workers seem to illustrate a broader pattern of differentiation among the workers, both on the case platform and on the Nordic labour platforms generally. Firstly, according to the operations manager of the case platform, the 'middle-aged unemployed' are 'indisputably the largest group' active on the platform, followed by students. Secondly, two of the five were migrant workers who did not expect to stay long term in the country, and at the time of the case study, approximately one-fifth of the workers on the platform were foreigners, indicated by language. Thirdly, the workers did not rely on social security, and the platform developers criticized the fact that the lack of an employment relationship means that work on platforms is not institutionally recognized. If work on the platform is not recognized as active participation in the labour market, it might lead to a loss of state-financed social benefits in the Nordic countries (Mailand & Larsen, 2011, p. 27; Dølvik & Jesnes, 2017, pp. 36–37). The case presented thus fuels the suspicion presented elsewhere that some workers engaged on labour platforms in Denmark do not rely on welfare benefits and are not part of the welfare system (Meged & Christensen, 2017). When compared with a recent quantitative examination of Danish labour platforms, the group seems exemplary: along with immigrants and students, unemployed are the most prevalent category of people in the 42,000 that are estimated to have earned money through websites or apps in Denmark (Ilsøe & Madsen, 2017, p. 40). As such, there is probably a differentiation of the workers on the platform, where the interviewees as migrants and unemployed are among the more vulnerable workers.

Furthermore, the transient relationship between platform developers, customers and workers fragments the logical basis for the development of worker collectives and associative power resources for unions. As expressed by a union representative: 'Nobody sees each other, nobody talks to each other . . . So where do we . . . What is our role?' (Union representative). The platforms form a transient, individualizing and de-personalizing basis for improvement of their situation. This might undermine the recognition of common problems with work on the platform. More generally, the platforms' side-stepping of established industrial relations risks removing one pillar of work regulation: the employment relationship. The platforms can be argued to have the character of what has been called 'bogus self-employment' (Rasmussen & Kongshøj Madsen, 2017). Especially in Denmark, 'social partners' position is key in explaining incidences of precarious employment' (Rasmussen et al., 2016, p. 102). In general, the labour market parties find the platforms drive 'unfair competition', and employers are thus sympathetic, although not actively contributing, towards attempts to standardize the conditions (interview with representative of sector organization). This gives parties in the labour market some common ground on the issue of unfair competition. But they have not yet developed common strategies for action, especially not in Denmark (Rasmussen et al., 2016; Dølvik & Jesnes, 2017; Ilsøe, 2017). As such, the platforms are effectively bypassing the collective bargaining system and the associated forms of regulation.

Overall then, the experience of the transient organization of tasks on the platform seems a case of precarious labour (Standing, 2016, pp. 219–221, 229). The depicted economic dependency on work on the platforms and the low 'social income' seems decisive for the experience of precarity on the platforms in the international literature (Berg, 2016; Huws et al., 2016, p. 15; Ravenelle, 2017; Schor et al., 2017). Guy Standing (2014, p. 121) calls the *necessary* but unpaid work to coordinate and organize labour in everyday life a precarious 'work-for-labour'. Although the *hourly* wage on the platforms is decent, and the income is indicated as 'supplemental' in quantitative surveys, the workers, 'may take on several jobs at the same time, partly because wages are falling, partly for insurance or risk management' (Standing, 2014, p. 119). Rosa highlights how the institutions that ensure sustainable coordination of different spheres of activity are increasingly challenged by the norm of acceleration which creates increasing flexibilization and precarity of employment (Rosa, 2013, pp. 112, 220). The job, labour and income insecurity are expressed as the individualized experience of lack of rhythm, validation and control in the organization of labour in the gig economy. This might in turn reinforce a transient, insecure or indeed precarious working life. As Rosa highlights:

> *For the less privileged*, temporary work, precarious forms of employment and fixed-term labour contracts both indicate and enforce this accommodation to performance criteria and thus to permanent competition and existential uncertainty.
>
> (Rosa, 2015, p. 87, my italics)

For the workers who are in precarious positions in the Nordic labour markets, the platforms lower the barriers of entry to labour but also change the conditions for coordinating labour with working life. It therefore seems pertinent to consider institutional resources that could create a divergent development trajectory of Nordic labour platforms relative to the gloomy picture depicted in the international literature and illustrated in the case study.

The development trajectory of Nordic labour platforms?

A number of mechanisms might restrict or indeed reshape the platforms in the Nordic countries. While the relative precarity of the engaged workers can perhaps in part explain their engagement with the platforms, it also suggests a differentiated impact of the platforms rather than the sweeping 'disruption' of many already well-organized sectors of employment. An extrapolation from the case study suggests that the societal division of labour will constrain the platforms to impose a reorganization of labour in vulnerable sectors where short-term engagement is viable and/or for workers in precarious situations. In Denmark, private service labour, the strategic choice of the developers, is a comparatively underorganized sector with both a higher prevalence of marginal part-timers, students and labour migrants, and more regulation gaps reflecting more undeclared and informal employment (Andersen & Felbo-Kolding, 2013; Rasmussen et al., 2016; Ilsøe et al., 2017; cf. Weber, 2017, p. 22). To realize their envisioned market for standardizable tasks among interchangeable parties, the platform developers must choose a sector of labour where workers are willing to engage.

The containment to vulnerable sectors of work reflects the structural features of the Nordic labour markets. Although data are sparse, the use of platforms appears to be slightly less prevalent in the Nordic countries than in comparable Western labour markets. The most extensive quantitative studies of the Nordic countries indicate that only 1–2% of the population regularly use digital platforms to find labour, and that many of these work on the platforms as a supplement to other activities (Jesnes et al., 2016, pp. 22, 27; Ilsøe & Madsen, 2017, pp. 40–42). This cannot *only* be understood in terms of the low job quality of the platforms. For many workers, the low unemployment, high organizational level, opportunities for education and relatively generous social benefits of the Nordic welfare regimes provide the structural and institutional power resources to disengage with the platforms. The lack of public and institutional recognition of work on the platforms also means that organized workers perceive the loss of employment benefits as insecure (Redder, 2016). It is thus questionable whether the platforms will unilaterally create a large-scale shift towards precarious work without an employment relationship in the Nordic labour markets.

This also poses a dilemma for unions and regulators in the Nordic countries as to whether to recognize the platforms' business models. Whereas a qualitative improvement of the depicted problems would depend on some form of recognition of the new platforms and probably increase their prevalence, continued exclusion is likely to delimit the platforms but risks retaining the relatively precarious working conditions.

Initially, in Denmark, the unions succeeded in utilizing communicative power and the ideal of 'the Danish model' to delegitimize and thus exclude the new business models which did not participate in organized negotiations as employers. This strategy led to the rejection and exclusion of the Uber platform, where the unions highlighted its incommensurability with the laws for taxi fares and undermined public acceptability of the platform. Further, the rejection of Uber is not limited to Nordic countries. It was also a result of the developers' lack of will or ability to comply with national legislation. This strategy of delegitimization has been effective but might be specific to the Uber platform and dependent on a remobilization with regard to each new platform for state regulation and/or political consumption to become more generally effective. Most importantly, it did not rely on a mobilization nor improve the situation of the workers engaged on the platform. Furthermore, although other platforms have also suffered from the polemics, they are still in business.

Another strategy increasingly used by labour market parties is to begin organizing and cooperating with the platforms. This is in line with the institutionalized class compromises of the Nordic countries and could potentially lead to qualitatively different platforms that take on responsibilities as employers. As recognized by the director of the case platform presented earlier, 'you can make some setbacks, some limitations, you can make it illegal, but it WILL emerge, either in a new form or a limited or regulated form'. The case presented here seems to exemplify a broader trend where the Nordic platforms take on more responsibilities as employers to improve their brand by taking out insurance schemes, setting minimum wages, setting standards for the work, establishing long-term relationships with workers and mediating between customers and workers (cf. also Dølvik & Jesnes, 2017, p. 30).

Within the sectors involved, the 'capital arms race' in the development of technological infrastructure with effective management of labour will lead to the selection of relatively few and well-known companies and position them as 'gatekeepers' for both workers and customers (Srnicek, 2017, p. 98). To illustrate this, two out of eight of the Danish platforms for task labour identified as background research for this case study in 2016 have already closed (cf. also Rasmussen et al., 2017, pp. 8–9). The selection of the few most competitive platforms bodes for a politicization, where not only consumers and regulators but also the labour market parties can influence their development by cooperating with them as employers. The competitive advantage of capital concentration and the rationality of systematization in the development of the digital infrastructure illustrated in the case study could pave the way for transparency and homogenization of the working conditions for workers engaged on the platforms.

Under much public attention, the Danish unions have recently made a collective agreement with the Hilfr platform. This provides a voluntary option to join the agreement for workers active on the platform. In this way, Hilfr is attempting to create a good brand for their platform to attract consumers. Furthermore, unions not only point consumers towards the platforms with relatively better working conditions but also attempt to demonstrate the continued ability of the labour market parties to regulate work through negotiated cooperation. This could suggest an integration and an improvement of working conditions on the platforms. The agreement with Hilfr could be the first of many to come.

However, if the unions do not in fact organize the workers engaged on the platforms, it is a fragile agreement. The question is whether workers have a long-term orientation towards work on the platforms which makes them willing to enter into these agreements. The shift in orientation of the platforms towards creating fairer working conditions reflects the change in public opinion of the platforms. But the unions here depend on public understanding of the need for 'political consumption' to pressurize platforms into creating the brand value of fair working conditions. The public is fraught with a deep-seated ambiguity between respect for proper working conditions and orientation towards the flexibility and acceleration of the platforms. This is not just about wage competition. Even if wages are decent, the platforms must be pressurized to prevent workers competing on flexibility to take on tasks, as depicted in the case study. The workers are vulnerable to shifts in public opinion to pressure the platforms to set high standards.

The core issue is whether workers have opportunities to develop the work or whether they are continuously subject to management-controlled, marketized production systems. The Danish union HK reports increasing willingness to organize among translators, who experience many of the same problems of immediate engagement with tasks on the platforms that were presented in the case study. This points towards the most radical reaction to the emerging platforms, as unions could then build both structural and associational power by developing their own platform. But this too poses dilemmas considering the institutionalized mode of cooperation with employers; it is unclear who will then have to take on the responsibility as employers. And although the unions can then negotiate their degree of profit more directly, they risk depending on platform developers' ability to make a profit from the development in any case. Furthermore, the development of a platform gives legitimacy to the models, and it is thus latently in conflict with the strategy to delegitimize existing, transnational platforms making their way into the Nordic countries, which has been so successful in rejecting the bad working conditions of Uber.

Another illustrative case is how a Danish–Swedish platform has taken even more initiatives than the case platform to legitimize their business model, attempt cooperation with unions and yet failed to establish a collective agreement. It illustrates the tension between existing institutionalized regulation in the form of collective agreements and the flexibility of platforms. The platform has tried to let workers procure creative, non-standardized and specialized tasks, lowering the profit per transaction and most importantly having a limit on the income and automatic tax registration to demonstrate that the work is *supposed* to be supplementary to other activities. But, most importantly, the flexibility of the type, time and organization of the work has hindered a collective agreement. Furthermore, the limited hours and non-standardized tasks make it difficult to scale up activity on the platform in the standardized manner of the case platform. This is due to the structural economic conditions in the form of the existing societal division of labour. Firstly, the structural differentiation constrains the development of platforms as technological acceleration is a continuous challenge to let workers shape the digital infrastructure at a rate of development that matches the financialized technical innovation of the competitors, which might better meet customers' demands for efficiency and accountability within a certain sector of work. Secondly, the different sectors form a basis for the institutionalized modes of agreement between unions and employers in the labour market, and this is a challenge for platforms that do not want to adhere to this division of labour in their definition of the tasks.

There are thus several structural features which might provide for a divergent development of Nordic labour platforms. The low unemployment rate, the extensive social security system and the political mobilization of unions, both in the public domain and through organization of workers, might exclude platforms as legitimate actors and limit their expansion. The pressure to create fair working conditions might pave the way for an incorporation of platforms into existing modes of negotiated cooperation between the parties in the labour market. On the other hand, the structural conditions for the development of platforms in the form of dependence on finance capital, the existing mode of institutionalization in the labour market and the dominance of the cultural norms of efficiency, flexibility and spatio-temporal acceleration illustrated in the case challenge the development of alternative models in a form consistent with the existing regulation on the labour market. Future developments will depend on the labour market parties' handling of these dilemmas, public attention to issues surrounding work on the platforms, the platform developers' strategies and the continued social benefits for the workers ensured through political development of the welfare regimes.

Conclusion

I have here engaged with the development of Nordic labour platforms. The rationale has been twofold. Firstly, it is pertinent to explore the development and working life consequences of the labour platforms in a Nordic context. Secondly, problems related to labour platforms in the relatively well-functioning Nordic labour markets can highlight global problems with such platforms and potential institutional mechanisms to address them.

What makes the discussion of labour platforms difficult is both that the phenomena are dynamic and politicized and that empirical knowledge is vulnerable to conceptual inconsistencies. In political discourse, the platforms are often considered an opportunity to ensure taxation of undeclared labour and national competitiveness through employment, better resource utilization and economic growth (Danish Ministry of Taxation, 2016; Danish Ministry of Industry, Business and Financial Affairs, 2017). To amplify the sensitivity towards both risks and potentials of the technologies, I have drawn on international literature to separate the profit-oriented development of patented labour platforms from the ideals and values advanced with open technologies developed for sharing. An emerging literature highlights how the strategy of platform capitalism is to accumulate capital in a technically superior solution, attract demand and establish a monopoly for managing the conditions for agreements on tasks in the relevant sectors. The risk is that this shifts the balance of power in the labour market.

Although empirically limited, the case study presented here illustrates the emergence of platform capitalism in the Nordic labour markets. With an interest in the characteristics of working life in Nordic platform capitalism, we can interpret the case study as an illustration of the presence of the working life problems depicted in the international literature. Even in Denmark, we can find platforms where: 'The rules of product and service development, as well as marketplace interactions, are set by the platform owner' (Srnicek, 2017, p. 29). Taken together with the existing literature on platforms in the Nordic countries, the findings indicate that workers on the Nordic platforms rely neither on the structural power of indispensable qualifications nor on the institutionalized cooperation of the labour market parties. Further, not only do the platforms disregard their responsibilities as employers, they potentially compartmentalize work into 'gigs' organized 'just-in-time' to meet customer demands. This can have profound implications for the quality of working life, as it robs the workers of control and undermines sustainable rhythms in their working lives. The platforms' utilization of a 'well-known judicial grey-zone' (Rasmussen & Kongshøj Madsen, 2017, p. 56) with respect to the conditions of employment are also a substantive problem of the extreme flexibility in their everyday organization of labour.

It is, however, important to emphasize that the low overall unemployment and the relatively extensive welfare benefits seem to limit workers' engagement with the platforms in a Nordic context. They are thus unlikely to create a large shift towards precarious working conditions in the Nordic labour markets. Rather, the platforms seem to *reinforce* invisible working life problems of workers who are already in precarious positions. These groups are supplemented by a group that use it out of convenience and are not engaged in the development of the platforms. The most likely result of the interplay between the platforms and the welfare regimes thus seems to be a polarization. At this point, the stronger position of workers in Nordic countries suggests a disengagement with the platforms, rather than a completely different mode of organization of labour on the platforms. But the extent of the platforms is likely to depend on overall developments in the welfare regimes.

Therefore, the problems of working life in platform capitalism demand continuous innovation in the regulation of the labour market to ensure that the rationalization of the organization of work with the technologies not only leads to business models that are viable but also are sustainable for the workers. The uncertainties of unions, politicians and employers reflect what Rosa (2013, pp. 251ff) calls the 'steering problems' introduced by the accelerated rate of social change. As the history of the Nordic labour markets shows, sustainability can be created not only by changing the organization of work but also by improving the complex interrelation of cooperation in the labour market and state-provided social security.

The enduring specificities of Nordic platforms have yet to appear clearly, and given the limited data, they are difficult to foresee. In any case, it is imperative to engage with the working life experience of the platforms, as this is key to understanding and developing the broader institutional mediation of technological changes in work. With an interest in the *international* development of platform capitalism, we can perhaps understand the case studied here as a critical case of the working life issues of the flexible organization of labour on the platforms (Flyvbjerg, 2006, p. 230). Although the institutionalized regulation of the Nordic welfare regimes provides comparatively more power resources to the workers, the problems of unsustainable working life rhythms remain on a Danish platform. If these problems prove to persist in this context, we can hypothesize that they are a globally prevalent consequence for workers in precarious positions engaging with the customer-oriented flexibility in the organization of labour on the 'just-in-time' platforms. Depending on perspective and future developments, we might come to emphasize the 'threat' of transnational business models backed by financialized technological development or how their limited scope and differing character illustrate the continued development in the provision of institutional power resources to workers in the Nordic welfare regimes. In principle, the Nordic countries' high wages, low unemployment and extensive social security could further the development of the sharing economy, which remains a potential for work on the platforms.

References

Andersen, S. K. & Felbo-Kolding, J. (2013) *Danske virksomheders brug af østeuropæisk arbejdskraft [Danish Companies' Use of Eastern European Labour]*, Copenhagen: FAOS.

Antonio, R. J. (2015) Is Prosumer Capitalism on the Rise?, *The Sociological Quarterly*, 56(3): 472–483.

Barta, K. & Neff, G. (2016) Technologies for Sharing: Lessons from Quantified Self About the Political Economy of Platforms, *Information, Communication & Society*, 19(4): 518–531.

Belk, R. (2013) You Are What You Can Access: Sharing and Collaborative Consumption Online, *Journal of Business Research*, 67(8): 1595–1600.

Berg, J. (2016) *Income Security in the On-Demand Economy: Findings and Policy Lessons from a Survey of Crowdworkers*, Geneva. www.ilo.org/wcmsp5/groups/public/---ed_protect/---protrav/---travail/documents/publication/wcms_479693.pdf.

Botsman, R. and Rogers, R. (2010) *What's Mine Is Yours: The Rise of Collaborative Consumption*, 1, New York: Harper Collins.

Cheng, M. (2016) Sharing Economy: A Review and Agenda for Future Research, *International Journal of Hospitality Management*, 57: 60–70.

Danish Ministry of Industry, Business and Financial Affairs (2017) *Strategi for vækst gennem deleøkonomi [Strategy for Growth through Sharing Economy]*.

Danish Ministry of Taxation (2016) Aktuelle skattetal: Sort arbejde på vej ned [Current Numbers: Undeclared Labour on the Downturn]. www.skm.dk/media/1339607/aktuelle-skattetal_sort-arbejde-falder_marts-2016.pdf.

Demary, V. (2014) *Competition in the Sharing Economy, Cologne Institute for Economic Research*, Cologne, Germany. www.iwkoeln.de/fileadmin/publikationen/2015/235445/Sharing_Economy_Policy_Paper.pdf.

De Stefano, V. (2016) *The Rise of the 'Just-In-Time Workforce': On-Demand Work, Crowdwork and Labour Protection in the 'Gig Economy'*, Geneva. www.ilo.org/wcmsp5/groups/public/---ed_protect/---protrav/---travail/documents/publication/wcms_443267.pdf.

Dølvik, J. E. and Jesnes, K. (2017) *Nordic Labour Markets and the Sharing Economy: Report from a Pilot Project*, Copenhagen: Nordic Council of Ministers.

Dredge, D. & Gyimóthy, S. (2015) The Collaborative Economy and Tourism: Critical Perspectives, Questionable Claims and Silenced Voices, *Tourism Recreation Research*, 40(3): 286–302. www.tandfonline.com/doi/full/10.1080/02508281.2015.1086076.

Dredge, D. & Gyimóthy, S. (2017) Collaborative Economy and Tourism, In: *Tourism and Collaborative Economy: Perspectives, Politics, Policies and Prospects*, Cham, Switzerland: Springer, 1–12. doi: 10.1007/978-3-319-51799-5.

Flyvbjerg, B. (2006) Five Misunderstandings About Case-Study Research, *Qualitative Inquiry*, 12(2): 219–245.

Gyimóthy, S. (2017) Business Models of the Collaborative Economy, In: *Tourism and Collaborative Economy: Perspectives, Politics, Policies and Prospects*, Cham, Switzerland: Springer, 31–39. doi: 10.1007/978-3-319-51799-5_3.

Hill, S. (2015) *Raw Deal: How the 'Uber Economy' and Runaway Capitalism Are Screwing American Workers*, New York: St. Martin's Press.

Holt, H., Hvid, H., Lund, H. L. & Kamp, A. (2013) *Et arbejdsliv i acceleration: tiden og det grænseløse arbejde [A Working Life in Acceleration: Time and the Boundaryless Work]*, Frederiksberg, Denmark: Roskilde Universitetsforlag.

Huws, U., Spencer, N. H. & Joyce, S. (2016) Crowd Work in Europe: Preliminary Results from a Survey in the UK, Sweden, Germany, Austria and the Netherlands. www.feps-europe.eu/assets/39aad271-85ff-457c-8b23-b30d82bb808f/crowd-work-in-europe-draft-report-last-versionpdf.pdf.

Hvid, H. (2006) *Arbejde og bæredygtighed [Work and Sustainability]*, Frederiksberg, Denmark: Frydenlund.

Ilsøe, A. (2017) Digitalizing Service Work: Social Partner Responses in Denmark, Sweden and Germany, *Transfer – European Review of Labour and Research*, 23(3): 333–348.

Ilsøe, A., Larsen, T. P. & Felbo-Kolding, J. (2017) Living Hours under Pressure: Flexibility Loopholes in the Danish IR-Model, *Employee Relations*, 39(6): 888–902.

Ilsøe, A. & Madsen, L. W. (2017) *Digitalisering af arbejdsmarkedet. Danskernes erfaring med digital automatisering og digitale platforme [Digitization of the Labour Market. Danes' Experiences with Digital Automatization and Digital Platforms]*, Copenhagen: FAOS.

Jesnes, K., Sletvold Øistad, B., Alsos, K. & Nesheim, T. (2016) *Aktører og arbeid i delingsøkonomien [Actors and Work in the Sharing Economy]*, Oslo: FAFO.

Kamp, A., Lund, H. L. & Hvid, H. S. (2011) Negotiating Time, Meaning and Identity in Boundaryless Work, *Journal of Workplace Learning*, 23(4): 229–242.

Mailand, M. & Larsen, T. P. (2011) *Trade Unions and Precarious Work: Danish Country Report to the BARSORI-Project*, Copenhagen: FAOS.

Meged, J. W. & Christensen, M. D. (2017) Working Within the Collaborative Tourist Economy: The Complex Crafting of Work and Meaning, In: Dredge, D. & Gyimóthy, S. (eds) *Tourism and Collaborative Economy: Perspectives, Politics, Policies and Prospects*, Cham, Switzerland: Springer, 203–220.

Molz, G. (2013) Social Networking Technologies and the Moral Economy of Alternative Tourism: The Case of Couchsurfing.Org, *Annals of Tourism Research*, 43: 210–230.

Rasmussen, S. & Kongshøj Madsen, P. (2017) Platformsøkonomien og prekariatet [The Platform Economy and the Precariat], *Tidsskrift for Arbejdsliv*, 1: 46–62.

Rasmussen, S., Madsen, P. K., Saloniemi, A., Ólafsdóttir, K., Dølvik, J. E., Jesnes, K., . . . & Berglund, T. (2017) *Nordic Labour Markets and the Sharing Economy*. doi: 10.6027/NA2017-904.

Rasmussen, S., Refslund, B., Sørensen, O. H., Larsen, T., Sørensen, O. H. & Larsen, T. P. (2016) *Reducing Precarious Work in Europe through Social Dialogue: The Case of Denmark (Final National Report)*. www.research.mbs.ac.uk/ewerc/Our-research/Current.

Ravenelle, A. J. (2017) Sharing Economy Workers: Selling, Not Sharing, *Cambridge Journal of Regions, Economy and Society*, 10(2): 281–295.

Redder, G. (2016) *Danskerne utrygge ved at tage job på nye digitale platforme [Danes Insecure about Work on New Digital Platforms], Ugebrevet A4*. www.ugebreveta4.dk/danskerne-utrygge-ved-at-tage-job-paa-nye-digitale-pl_20632.aspx.

Richardson, L. (2015) Performing the Sharing Economy, *Geoforum*, 67: 121–129.

Rifkin, J. (2015) *The Zero Marginal Cost Society: The Internet of Things, the Collaborative Commons, and the Eclipse of Capitalism*, Reprint ed., New York: St. Martin's Griffin.

Ritzer, G. (2015) Prosumer Capitalism, *Sociological Quarterly*, 56(3): 413–445.

Rogers, B. (2016) Employment Rights in the Platform Economy: Getting Back to Basics, *Harvard Law & Policy Review*, 10(2): 480–519.

Rosa, H. (2013) *Social Acceleration: A New Theory of Modernity*, translated by J. Trejo-Mathys, New York: Columbia University Press.

Rosa, H. (2015) Capital as a Spiral of Dynamisation: Sociology as Social Critique, In: Dörre, K., Lessenich, S. & Rosa, H. (eds) *Sociology, Capitalism, Critique*, London and Brooklyn, NY: Verso.

Rosa, H., Dörre, K. & Lessenich, S. (2017) Appropriation, Activation and Acceleration: The Escalatory Logics of Capitalist Modernity and the Crises of Dynamic Stabilization, *Theory, Culture & Society*, 34(1): 53–73.

Rosa, H. & Scheuerman, W. E. (2009) *High-Speed Society Social Acceleration, Power, and Modernity*, University Park, PA: Pennsylvania State University Press.

Scholz, T. (2016) *Uberworked and Underpaid: How Workers are Disrupting the Digital Economy*, Cambridge, UK and Malden, MA: Polity Press.

Scholz, T. & Schneider, N. (2016) *Ours to Hack and to Own: Platform Cooperativism. A New Vision for the Future of Work and a Fairer Internet*, New York and London: OR Books.

Schor, J. B., Attwood-Charles, W., Cansoy, M., Ladegaard, I. & Wengronowitz, R. (2017) Dependence and Precarity in the Platform Economy, Unpublished paper, Boston College, MA. www.bc.edu/content/dam/files/schools/cas_sites/sociology/pdf/Dependence and Precarity Feb 2017.pdf.

Srnicek, N. (2017) *Platform Capitalism, Theory Redux*, Cambridge, UK and Malden, MA: Polity Press.

Standing, G. (2014) *The Precariat: The New Dangerous Class*, London and New York: Bloomsbury Academic.

Standing, G. (2016) *Corruption of Capitalism*, London: Biteback Publishing.

Sundararajan, A. (2016) *The Sharing Economy: The End of Employment and the Rise of Crowd-Based Capitalism*, Cambridge, MA: The MIT Press.

Weber, S. S. (2017) *Arbejdslivet I Platformsøkonomien: et case-studie af udviklingen af en platform til organisering af rengøringsarbejde [The Working Life in the Platform Economy: A Case Study of the Development of a Platform for Organization of Cleaning Labour]*, Roskilde, Denmark: Roskilde University.

Yin, R. K. (2003) *Case Study Research: Design and Methods*, London: SAGE.

Closure

The end of the story?

Helge Hvid and Eivind Falkum

Nothing lasts forever. One day, each and every one of us will agree: the Nordic model, or the Nordic approach, as we prefer to call it, is not with us anymore. Will it be ten years before it passes away? 50 years? 100 years? Or longer? Will we at that time still find enduring remnants from the Nordic approach, or will it have all died out? Will the Nordic experience be relevant to work and production in the future?

Will collective organization around common interests still be perceived as relevant?

Will working life in the Nordics still be characterized by relatively high levels of:

- equality
- employee influence on management
- autonomy
- learning
- employment security.

Or are European and global trends so comprehensive, irresistible and invincible that everything we see today as typically Nordic will have disappeared?

There are certainly many issues that can undermine the Nordic approach and delete all traces of it. Here we will highlight some of them.

From interest-based management to expert-based management

Well-educated, humanistic-oriented HR experts, production engineers and IT developers can undermine the essence of the Nordic approach: the safeguarding of collective interests.

A study (Dyreborg, 2011) on working environment activities in the construction sector concluded that the working environment had become too important to involve employees and their representatives. To obtain contracts, companies were dependent on their ability to demonstrate a high level of security. Therefore, they recruited security experts. The experts managed the security work through extensive bureaucratic procedures and by imposing a wide range of managerial requirements on the workers. It is now no longer the workers who co-create their working environment; instead, the workers have become objects of security management. Similar trends are found in a variety of other areas:

- The psychological working environment is handled by psychologists employed in HR departments and not through negotiations of workload, work organization and influence of the employees.
- Management has become very explicit in many jobs regarding expectations for the individual employee, e.g. by setting Key Performance Indicators (KPIs). There may be a dialogue between the individual employee and his or her leader about the KPIs, but in most jobs, the KPIs are not the object of collective bargaining.
- IT developments in many cases shape the workplace in completely new ways. Employees may be consulted in the creative processes of IT developers. However, often they have very little influence on the final result of the design process.

It is a huge challenge for collective organizations to make the new trends in working life a collective matter and not just an issue for experts. This issue is already being addressed in organizations.

Falling union density

The level of employers' organization is relatively constant, but for the unions, the level of organization has been declining since the mid-1990s. If this development continues, it will at some stage be an obstacle to the collective approach to working life issues.

Perhaps the difficulty in getting young people to organize themselves is diminishing. There are signs of this in both Denmark and Norway (Caraker et al., 2015; Steen et al., 2017). Young people are more positively oriented towards the unions and collective solutions than they were in previous decades. The move towards individualization may have stopped.

However, new approaches to organizing employees and employers need to be developed. One of the challenges is to make unions relevant to temporary employees in low-paid and insecure service jobs. Another challenge is that the conditions for organizational work have changed. Membership of an organization is now less perceived as a lifelong commitment and more as a means for solving acute issues.

Sustainable development

Humanity and the planet as a whole face enormous challenges. NGOs, business organizations, politicians and companies are oriented towards sustainability. Where do the collective labour organizations stand in that game?

Are organizations built on specific collective interests an obstacle to developments towards sustainability? Interest organizations pursue the interests of their members and may therefore not be in a position to take responsibility for our common future. Interest organizations can be united in a common agenda on growth and progress in employment and income. However, does that harmonize with the sustainability agenda? Do we need a moral economy, beyond interest-based organizations, where growth and employment are not ends in themselves, but means of achieving sustainability?

Conversely, it can be argued that the collective organizations in the labour market have already gained experience in pursuing common interests beyond those of individual employees and individual companies. Collective organizations have contributed significantly to the development of the welfare societies. Perhaps these experiences can be productive in creating a sustainable society? Perhaps employers' organizations can contribute to the development of sustainability by creating links between companies, environmental organizations and humanitarian organizations? Perhaps employer and labour associations can help employees to take an active part in the development towards sustainability by allowing them to apply their knowledge and experience in everyday innovations to make production and work more sustainable? Perhaps the labour organizations can actively support a green business policy? There have been a number of initiatives over the years in this direction (Hvid, 2006). However, the sustainability agenda has not yet created major changes in the expression of collective interest in the labour market.

Beyond wage work

The robots are coming. Social scientists believe that a very large part of the work we know today will disappear over the next 20 to 30 years (Greve, 2017). In their assessment, employment will fall sharply.

We do not know whether the predictions of the decline in wage work are correct, but it seems not entirely unlikely that wage labour will shrink in scale due to technology and a global division of labour and perhaps also because we will witness changes in people's wishes and expectations for their lives. However, an eventual decrease in the amount of wage work does not necessarily mean that work as a whole will decrease. There is already almost as much work done outside wage labour as within it, such as work in families and voluntary work. Incidentally, levels of volunteering are very high in the Nordic countries (EUROFOUND, 2011).

Perhaps this is a new and important role for the collective organizations? Perhaps it is possible to continue the experience from the Nordic approach to the labour market by including unpaid workers in organizations. In the voluntary field, there are problems of unfair use of free labour. Bad leadership. Difficulty in finding 'the right job'. A collective organization of voluntary work could help create an attractive alternative to wage work, and perhaps productive competition between paid work and voluntary work could be established?

Is the Nordic approach an obstacle to the 'necessary changes'?

There are public debates on the liberal right, who believe that the Nordic approach stands in the way of the necessary transformation to the relentless global competition. There are not so many of these voices because, as we have pointed out in several places in this book, the Nordic countries are performing relatively well in global competition. Furthermore, in many areas, the Nordic countries are already liberal ideals.

Although there may be few liberalists who are sceptical to collective organization, the basic liberal understanding of what is necessary may become a serious threat to collective organization. Public discourses have already been penetrated by ideas of economic and market necessities. It is common not to understand the 'good life' as an end in itself. However, the 'good life' can be a useful means for creating growth and employment. Influence and involvement in work contribute to a good life. However, today, the decisive argument for involvement is that it contributes to innovation and growth. Previously, influence, involvement and democracy at work were values in themselves. Education and learning are good because they contribute to growth. Enlightenment is not an end in itself. Wellbeing is good because it also contributes to growth.

If the unions are to remain legitimized, they have to orient themselves to perspectives that are beyond growth

On the traditional left, there is also tough criticism of the Nordic approach. Acceptance of employers' rights to direct and distribute work, an acceptance of the market and an acceptance of employers' needs to generate profit are all obstructions in the necessary confrontation with wage work and capitalism. However, this is not a point of view that has a particular appeal at present. Most of the left is now prepared for a long future with wage work and capitalism. Aspirations are now more about regulating wage work and capitalism. Here, in some areas, the Nordic countries are ahead of most other countries.

Finally, we have the greens, who are likely to think that collective organizations belong to the era of the industrial society. Collective organizations tend to maintain the outdated institutions of industrial society. Instead of the collective organization of interests, we all need to take an independent responsibility for the future. Organizations help to maintain people in paid work and traditional jobs, although there is a need for greater diversity in forms of life, working methods and organizational forms.

However, we do not doubt that in the green society there will also be a need for organizing collective interests, while access to power and resources will still not be equally distributed in the green society. However, as we have already mentioned, it is also necessary for the collective organizations in the labour market to orient themselves towards the green agenda.

How will the Nordic approach end its life?

Nothing lasts forever. Neither will the Nordic approach. At one point or another, it will die, but how?

In an ethnocentric perspective, the ideal death of the approach will be caused by its success. If the Nordic approach should spread to the whole world, there would be no specific Nordic approach. The former Nordic approach would simply be the approach.

In the best possible world of the liberals, labour unions have been taken over by organizational psychologists and graduates from business schools specialized in Human Resources Management. They are in charge of hiring, employee assessment, wage formation, competence development and development of the work organization – all of this with smart productivity development in mind.

In the green ideal world, trade unions and employers' organizations have been absorbed into a much larger project than the project of the old welfare society. Trade unions have returned to the guild system, where the guild sets the norms for quality and accountability in a sustainable perspective. Employers' associations have been infiltrated by a myriad of stakeholder organizations that help to run the business in a green and socially responsible direction.

The future of the Nordic approach is unclear. We all hope for a beautiful end to the story, but we probably do not fully agree on what that means.

References

Caraker, E., Høgedahl, L., Jørgensen, H. & Møberg, R. J. (2015) *Fællesskab før forskellighed, Hovedrapport fra APL III – projektet [Community before diversity, main report from the APL III project]*, Copenhagen: LO&FTF.

Dyreborg, J. (2011) 'Safety Matters Have Become Too Important for Management to Leave it Up to the Workers': The Nordic OSH Model Between Implicit and Explicit Frameworks, *Journal of Working Life Studies*, 2011-01-01. https://doi.org/10.19154/njwls.v1i1.2339.

EUROFOUND (2011) *Second European Quality of Life Survey Participation in Volunteering and Unpaid Work*, Luxembourg.

Greve, B. (2017) *Technology and the Future of Work: The Impact on Labour Markets and Welfare States*, Cheltenham, UK: Edward Elgar.

Hvid, H. (2006) *Arbejde og Bæredygtighed [Work and Sustainability]*, Copenhagen: Frydenlund.

Steen, A., Ellingsen, D. & Nygaard, M. O. (2017) *Norsk arbeidsliv 2017 [Norwegian Working Life 2017]*, Oslo: YS Arbeidslivsbarometer.

Index

For Product Safety Concerns and Information please contact our
EU representative GPSR@taylorandfrancis.com Taylor & Francis
Verlag GmbH, Kaufingerstraße 24, 80331 München, Germany